Africa's Radicalisms and Conservatisms

Annals of the International Institute of Sociology

President
Craig Calhoun (*Berggruen Institute, Los Angeles, CA*)

Past President
Björn Wittrock (*Swedish Collegium for Advanced Study, Uppsala*)

Bureau Members
Rajeev Bhargava (*Centre for the Study of Developing Societies (CSDS), Delhi*)
Roberto Cipriani (*Roma Tre University*)
Lyudmila Harutyunyan (*Yerevan State University*)
Huang Ping (*Chinese Academy for Social Sciences, Beijing*)
Shalini Randeria (*The Graduate Institute, Geneva*)
Grazyna Skapska (*Jagiellonian University, Krakow*)

VOLUME 14

The titles published in this series are listed at *brill.com/aiis*

Africa's Radicalisms and Conservatisms

Volume I: Politics, Poverty, Marginalization and Education

Edited by

Edwin Etieyibo, Obvious Katsaura and
Muchaparara Musemwa

BRILL

LEIDEN | BOSTON

Cover illustration: Design by Christopher Ngalu, 2020

Library of Congress Cataloging-in-Publication Data

Names: Etieyibo, Edwin E., editor. | Katsaura, Obvious, editor. | Musemwa, Muchaparara, editor.
Title: Africa's radicalisms and conservatisms. Volume I, Politics, poverty, marginalization and education / edited by Edwin Etieyibo, Obvious Katsaura, Muchaparara Musemwa.
Other titles: Politics, poverty, marginalization and education
Description: Leiden ; Boston : Brill, [2021] | Series: Annals of the international institute of sociology, 1568-1548 ; volume 14 | Includes bibliographical references and index. |
Identifiers: LCCN 2020047696 (print) | LCCN 2020047697 (ebook) | ISBN 9789004444690 (hardback) | ISBN 9789004445079 (ebook)
Subjects: LCSH: Radicalism–Africa. | Conservatism–Africa. | Africa–Politics and government. | Africa–Social conditions.
Classification: LCC HN780.Z9 R324 2021 (print) | LCC HN780.Z9 (ebook) | DDC 303.48/4–dc23
LC record available at https://lccn.loc.gov/2020047696
LC ebook record available at https://lccn.loc.gov/2020047697

Typeface for the Latin, Greek, and Cyrillic scripts: "Brill". See and download: brill.com/brill-typeface.

ISSN 1568-1548
ISBN 978-90-04-44469-0 (hardback)
ISBN 978-90-04-44507-9 (e-book)

Copyright 2021 by Koninklijke Brill NV, Leiden, The Netherlands.
Koninklijke Brill NV incorporates the imprints Brill, Brill Hes & De Graaf, Brill Nijhoff, Brill Rodopi, Brill Sense, Hotei Publishing, mentis Verlag, Verlag Ferdinand Schöningh and Wilhelm Fink Verlag.
All rights reserved. No part of this publication may be reproduced, translated, stored in a retrieval system, or transmitted in any form or by any means, electronic, mechanical, photocopying, recording or otherwise, without prior written permission from the publisher. Requests for re-use and/or translations must be addressed to Koninklijke Brill NV via brill.com or copyright.com.

This book is printed on acid-free paper and produced in a sustainable manner.

Contents

Preface IX
List of Figures, Maps and Tables XI
Notes on Contributors XIII

Introduction 1
    Muchaparara Musemwa, Obvious Katsaura and Edwin Etieyibo

PART 1
Conservatism, Radicalism and Politics

1   Beyond Conservatism and Radicalism? A Decolonial Glimpse into the Post-truth World   11
    Madina Tlostanova

2   Moderating Conservatism and Radicalism in Post-colonial Sub-Saharan Africa: Some Objections and Clarifications through Conversational Thinking   31
    Maduka Enyimba

3   Politics of the Countryside after Zimbabwe's Land Reform Programme: Expectations and Demands of the Youth   45
    Clement Chipenda

4   'Not Too Young to Run' Law and Political Participation among Youths in Nigeria   70
    Ebenezer Babajide Ishola

5   'Dirty-Relevance' of Youths Culture in Nigeria's Fourth Republic Politics: A Study of Delta and Lagos States   88
    Jonah Uyieh

6   Political Opportunism: Populism as a New Political Tactic in South Africa   117
    Bright Nkrumah

PART 2
Social Justice and Poverty

7 Social Justice and Persons with Disabilities in Nigeria   143
    Edwin Etieyibo

8 Poverty and Persons Living with Disabilities in Nigeria   164
    Odirin Omiegbe

9 Poverty and Illicit Drug Use among Youths in Lagos Metropolis, Nigeria   186
    Adekunle Victor Owoyomi

10 The Politics of Poverty in Sub-Saharan Africa   201
    Jonathan O. Chimakonam

11 Informality, Marginality and the State: A Case Study of Low-Income Households in Budiriro, Harare, Zimbabwe   217
    Tafadzwa Chevo

PART 3
Marginalization, Terrorism and Intolerance

12 Intolerance: The Activities of Ethnic Militias in Nigeria   237
    Adeshina Francis Akindutire

13 A Complementarity Reflection on Human Interest and Common Good in Africa: Examples of Nigeria's Ghana-Must-Go and South Africa's Xenophobia   262
    Phillip A. Edema and Adewale O. Owoseni

14 Boko Haram Terrorism and Out-of-School Children in North East Nigeria   280
    Temitope J. Owolabi

PART 4
Minorities and Education

15 Academic Abuse and Violence against Students in Delta State, Nigeria and Its Impact on Their Learning Behavior   297
    Israel Oberedjemurho Ugoma

16 Effects of Lessons on Empathic Response and Perception on Conflict Reduction among Secondary School Adolescents   308
    Peter Kwaja

17 Ethical Dimensions in Research: Informed Consent and Female Gender in Nigeria   321
    Olufunke Olufunsho Adegoke

    Index   341

Preface

The idea for this volume emerged during the 42nd World Congress of the International Institute of Sociology (IIS) held jointly with the School of Social Sciences, Faculty of Humanities at the University of the Witwatersrand, Johannesburg, South Africa, 5-7 September, 2018. Discussions about hosting and organizing the conference at the University of the Witwatersrand began in 2014 between Professor Adam Habib, Vice Chancellor and Principal of the University of the Witwatersrand and Professor Craig Jackson Calhoun, the President of the IIS, and Professor of Social Sciences at Arizona State University, USA. Following the discussions, the School of Social Sciences started putting in place the infrastructure to host the conference in 2018 after Professor Calhoun had secured a grant from MasterCard Foundation to meet the conference costs.

With the assistance of Professor Ruksana Osman, the former Dean of the Faculty of Humanities and now Deputy Vice-Chancellor (Academic), Professors Muchaparara Musemwa (Head of the School of Social Sciences), Edwin Etieyibo (Head of the Department of Philosophy) and Dr. Obvious Katsaura (Senior Lecturer in the Department of Sociology) constituted the local organizing committee. The committee formulated a conference call for papers with the theme *The Social Sciences, New Conservatisms and New Radicalisms* – a theme that we imagined would have an interdisciplinary appeal beyond just Sociology and enable us to have a critical multidisciplinary, and inter-locutional re-thinking of the constitution of life – of emerging political, social, cultural and economic forms – in contexts characterized by new and rising conservatisms as well as radicalisms.

The conference attracted many young, upcoming and established scholars and academics who presented papers that touched on diverse themes and represented disciplines such as education, sociology, history, anthropology, business, politics, philosophy, media studies, and geography. Most of these conference delegates came from Zimbabwe, Botswana, Nigeria, Ghana, USA, Uganda, Angola and South Africa. A number of the presentations (including some of the keynote addresses) covered topics related to youth identities and politics; youth radicalism; youth struggle narratives; politics and the youth; education and the youth; youth and marginalization; neoliberalism/capitalism and globalization; globalization and inequalities; globalization and poverty; capitalism and inequalities; capitalism and poverty; the politics of poverty; nature of poverty; politics, governance and social justice; poverty and culture; causes of poverty; poverty and distribution of resources; poverty and social inclusiveness; poverty and justice, disabilities and poverty.

Over the course of the three-day conference the editors of this volume decided that it was important to mobilize and capture the diverse range of concrete examples that helped to explicate what are very often highly abstract concepts, namely, radicalisms and conservatisms as the book title reflects. We believe that it is critically important to have a volume that encapsulates and portrays the diversity of multiple meanings and understandings of these concepts from the African stand-point especially as they intersected with ordinary people's resilient lived experiences and how they have grappled with politics, poverty, marginalization and access to education. This explains the origin of this volume entitled, *Africa's Radicalisms and Conservatisms I: Politics, Poverty, Marginalisation and Education*.

Figures, Maps and Tables

Figures

3.1　Land access by the youth. Source: Own fieldwork　61
8.1　Relationship between poverty and disability in society. Source: YEO, R. 2005. *Disability, Poverty and the New Development Agenda. Disability, Knowledge and Research Programme*　167
11.1　The trend of Budiriro people leaving employment from 1970–2015　223
12.1　Biafra flag. Source: https://commons.wikimedia.org/wiki/File:Flag_of_Biafra.svgMysid / CC BY-SA (http://creativecommons.org/licenses/by-sa/3.0/)　251
12.2　Nigeria flag. Source: Jon Harald Søby, https://commons.wikimedia.org/wiki/File:Flag_of_Nigeria.svg, Public domain　252

Maps

5.1　Map of Delta State showing all the location of local government areas Source: "Delta at 26: State govt says it won't roll out drums", Reformer Online, Friday, 25 August 2017, http://reformeronline.com/delta-at-26-state-govt-says-it-wont-roll-out-drums/. Accessed 16 August, 2019　94
5.2　Map of Lagos State showing all the location of local government areas. Source: J. Afolabi & Olalekan, Adedamola & Oluwaji, & Fashola, Olawunmi. (2017). "Socio-Economic Impact of Road Traffic congestion on Urban Mobility: A Case Study of Ikeja Local Government Area of Lagos State, Nigeria". *Pacific Journal of Science and Technology*. 18. 246–255　95

Tables

3.1　Interest in land ownership by the youth　60
3.2　Political participation　63
9.1　Socio-demographic status of the respondents　193
9.2　Respondents' involvement in illicit drug use　194
9.3　Distribution of respondents by youth unemployment and involvement in illicit drug use　195
9.4　Distribution of respondents by low family income and youth involvement in illicit drug use　197

13.1 Asouzu's complementarity approach: human interest in view of common good in contemporary Africa   276
15.1 Mean and standard deviation scores of students in English language, mathematics and basic science   302
15.2 T-test statistics on differences in mean scores of students who entered school at the earlier and those who entered at normal age in English language, mathematics and basic science   303
16.1 Mean of post test (conflict mean scores) of adolescents exposed to LERP and control group   315
16.2 Mean of post test (empathic mean scores) of adolescents exposed to LERP and control group   315
16.3 Mean of post test (conflict mean scores) of male and female adolescents exposed to LERP and control group   316

Notes on Contributors

Olufunke Olufunsho Adegoke
is a Medical Sociologist and a trained Health Social Worker, whose area of interests are Maternal and Child Health, Sexual and Reproductive Health and Gerontology. She lectures at the University of Ibadan, Nigeria in the Department of Sociology. She is a member of the International Sociological Association (ISA), Nigerian Anthropology and Sociology Association (NASA) and Nigerian Association of Social Workers (NASOW). An awardee of Teaching and Research Assistantship at the Postgraduate College, University of Ibadan and recipient of travel grants for international conferences. She has published both in local and international journals.

Adeshina Francis Akindutire
is a Lecturer in the Department of Sociology, Ambrose Alli University, Ekpoma, Edo state, Nigeria. His areas of research are: Criminology and Penology. He has many publications both in local and international journals. Also, he has co-authored four textbooks: *Crime and Delinquency*; *Anthropology: An Introductory Text*; *Society and Health Illness* and *The Military in Developing Nations: A Sociological Approach*. He is a member of many professional organization such as, the Forensic Sciences and Criminality Research, International Sociological Association, Australian and New Zealand Society of Criminology, International Research and Capacity Building Foundation, Institute of Security.

Tafadzwa Chevo
is a Senior Lecturer at the University of Zimbabwe and a Research Associate at Rhodes University's Institute of Zimbabwean Studies. He obtained his PhD from Rhodes University's Sociology Department and holds two Masters Degrees in Urban Social Development from Erasmus University and Sociology & Social Anthropology from the University of Zimbabwe. For his doctoral research, Tafadzwa conducted a diachronic and synchronic study of livelihood practices in low-income urban areas to obtain insights on agency, marginality and territorial stigmatisation. His research interests revolve around urban sociology, climate change, social policy, livelihoods and resilience building in rural and urban localities.

Jonathan O. Chimakonam
(PhD) is a Senior Lecturer in the Department of Philosophy, University of Pretoria. He taught at the University of Calabar, Nigeria for several years before moving to Pretoria. His teaching and research interests include African

philosophy, logic, environmental ethics, philosophy of mind and various topics in postmodern/postcolonial/decolonial thought, poverty, digital identity and ethics. He aims to break new grounds in African philosophy by formulating a system that unveils new concepts and opens new vistas for thought (conversational philosophy); a method that can drive most theories in African philosophy and beyond (conversational thinking); and a system of logic that grounds them both (Ezumezu). His articles, chapters and books have appeared in several refereed journals and international presses.

Clement Chipenda
(PhD) is a Research Associate with the SARChI Chair in Social Policy at the University of South Africa. His research interests are in agrarian political economy, land reform, social policy, youth development, rural development, citizenship, food security and child rights. He is a holder of a DPhil in Sociology (University of South Africa), MSc in Development Studies (National University of Science and Technology, Zimbabwe) and BSc Sociology (Hons) from the University of Zimbabwe). He has recently published articles in *Africa Review*, *Canadian Journal of African Studies* and *African Journal of Economic and Management Studies*.

Philip Akporduado Edema
(PhD) is a Senior Lecturer at Department of Philosophy and Religious Studies, Augustine University, IIara-Epe, Lagos, Nigeria. His teaching, competence and research interest cover applied ethics, metaphysics, Karol Wojtyla's personalism, philosophical anthropology, socio-political philosophy, African philosophy, Logic and philosophy of peace studies. He has published a number of papers both in journals and anthologies.

Maduka Enyimba
(PhD) is a Senior Lecturer in the Department of Philosophy, University of Calabar. He holds a Post-graduate Diploma in Education from Usman Danfodio University, Sokoto and a Master's degree in Socio-Political Thought. His teaching and research interests include, epistemology, African philosophy, environmental ethics, philosophy of education, development studies, philosophy of literature and philosophical anthropology. He has authored papers in a number of journals and presented papers at national and international conferences in some of these areas. He is a member of Conversational Society of Philosophy (CSP) and a Fellow of the Society for Research and Academic Excellence (FSR).

Edwin Etieyibo
(PhD) is Professor of Philosophy at the University of the Witwatersrand (Wits). His areas of expertise are in ethics, political philosophy, African philosophy,

social contract theories/and history of, history of philosophy, epistemology, early modern philosophy, Descartes, philosophy of law, applied ethics, African socio-political economy, philosophy of education and with children. He is co-author, editor and co-editor of several books including, *Disabilities in Nigeria: Attitudes, Reactions, and Remediation, Perspectives in Social Contract Theory*; *Decolonisation, Africanisation and the Philosophy Curriculum*; *Method, Substance and the Future of African Philosophy*; *Ka Osi Sọ Onye: African Philosophy in the Postmodern Era*; *Deciding in Unison: Themes in Consensual Democracy in Africa, African Philosophy in an Intercultural Perspective*. He is presently the Editor-in-Chief of the *South African Journal of Philosophy*, Chair of the Wits Philosophy Department and Secretary of the African Philosophy Society.

Ebenezer Babajide Ishola
is a Doctoral Student as well as an Academic Staff in the Department of Political Science, University of Lagos, Nigeria. His research interests include thematic areas such as comparative politics and political economy, notably development studies. He is currently researching on regional cooperation for development as a development strategy for countries in the Global South.

Obvious Katsaura
(PhD) is a Senior Lecturer in the Department of Sociology at the University of the Witwatersrand. He is an urban sociologist whose current research interests are in, and at the intersections of, the fields of transnational urbanism, transnational religiosity, religious urbanism, urban politics and urban violence. Some of his works have been published in the following journals: *International Journal of Urban and Regional Research, Urban Forum, Social Dynamics, Culture and Religion, African Identities*, and *Religion*.

Peter Kwaja
(PhD) is a young and self-motivated academic in the Department of Educational Psychology of the College of Education, Agbor, Delta State, Nigeria. Still in the process of becoming, he holds a Nigeria Certificate in Education (NCE) 1996 from KSCOE Ankpa Kogi State, Bachelor of Education (First Class Honours), Master of Education and Doctor of Philosophy Degrees in Guidance and Counselling from the University of Nigeria in 2004, 2007 and 2014 respectively. He is certified by the Teachers Registration Council of Nigeria and a member of Texas Counselling Association (TCA) Austin, Texas, U.S.A. and Counselling Association of Nigeria (CASSON).

Muchaparara Musemwa
(PhD) is an Associate Professor of History and Head of the School of Social Sciences in the Faculty of Humanities at the University of the Witwatersrand.

He is a past President of the Southern African Historical Society; former editor of the *South African Historical Journal*; serves on the executive boards of directors of the International Consortium of Environmental History Organisations; European Society for Environmental History; and International Water History Association. He serves on the editorial boards of the *Water History Journal* and the *Environment and History* journal. He has published widely on environmental history and on water history and politics in Zimbabwe.

Bright Nkrumah

is a Postdoctoral Research Fellow in the School of Social Sciences, University of KwaZulu Natal, South Africa. He received his Dphil from the Center for Human Rights, University of Pretoria, where he assessed the conditions under which citizens could mobilisation and trigger food reform. His research interest focuses on political contestation, climate change, food (in)security, youth dissent and democratisation.

Odirin Omiegbe

(PhD) lectures at the College of Education, Agbor, Nigeria and Delta State University Abraka, Nigeria. He holds a degree in Special Education from the University of Ibadan, Nigeria, and got his Doctoral degree from the University of Benin, Nigeria. He is a member of several professional associations and has presented papers in local and international conferences. He has published over 22 articles in journals and 5 books in special education, psychology, guidance and counselling, curriculum and other related disciplines. One of his most recent work is a coauthored book on disabilities, *Disabilities in Nigeria: Attitudes, Reactions, and Remediation*.

Temitope J. Owolabi

is an academic member and Doctoral Student in the Department of Sociology, University of Lagos, Nigeria. He holds a Bachelor's and Master's degrees in Sociology. His research interests cover Industrial Sociology, Demography, Development and Youth Studies. He has publish in local and international journals in these areas. He holds membership in several academic and professional bodies such as the Chartered Institute of Personnel Management (CIPM); Member, Institute of Strategic Management of Nigeria; Member, International Union for Scientific Study of Population (IUSSP); and Alumnus, Lagos Business School (Pan Atlantic University).

Adewale O. Owoseni

is a Doctoral Student and Assistant Lecturer in the Department of Philosophy, University of Ibadan, Nigeria. His research interests include African philosophy,

NOTES ON CONTRIBUTORS   XVII

philosophy of culture, and animal ethics. He is a recipient of short study research and conference grants such as CHCI Andrew Mellon Foundation, Arab Council of the Social Sciences, and China in Africa Africa in China Research Network (CAAC) among others. He has published a number of articles in various outlets such as *Intersectionality of Critical Animal Studies* (2019), *Springer Encyclopedia of Psychology and Religion* (2018), *Africology – JPAS* (2016) *and Caribbean Journal of Philosophy* (2016).

Victor Adekunle Owoyomi

(MSc) is a Postgraduate Student in the Department of Sociology at the University of Lagos in Nigeria. He is a Visiting Lecturer in Sociology and Psychology at Trinity University, City College, Lagos State in Nigeria. He is the chief consultant/project director of Princecrown Impact Management Consult, Lagos, Nigeria. He is a research fellow at Brown International Advanced Research Institute (BIARI), Brown University, Providence City, USA.

Madina Tlostanova

(PhD) is Professor of Postcolonial Feminisms at Linköping University, Sweden. She focuses on decoloniality, feminisms of the Global South, indigenous cosmologies, postsocialist sensibility. She has authored 10 monographs, over 280 articles, published in several languages. Her most recent books are *Postcolonialism and Postsocialism in Fiction and Art: Resistance and Re-existence* (Palgrave, 2017) and *What Does it Mean to be Post-Soviet? Decolonial Art from the Ruins of the Soviet Empire* (Duke UP, 2018). She recently coauthored a book with Tony Fry, *A New Political Imagination. Making the Case* (Routledge, November, 2020).

Israel Oberedjemurho Ugoma

(PhD) teaches psychology at Delta State University, Agbor affiliated campus, and biology to high School students in Asaba, Delta State, Nigeria. He holds a Bachelor's degree in Biological Sciences, a Master's and Doctoral degrees in Educational Psychology. He is a member of the Nigeria Council of Educational Psychology (NCEP). His research focuses on learning and development of children towards the 21st century technologies where parents tend to be neurotic in hurrying their tender children to grow up quickly not minding nature's clock on development and life skills acquisitions. He has several publications in local educational journals.

Jonah Uyieh

is a Doctoral Candidate at the Department of History and Strategic Studies, Faculty of Arts, University of Lagos, Nigeria – with specialisation in Comparative

Development Studies. He also holds a Master of Science degree in Political Science from the Faculty of Social Sciences, University of Ibadan, Nigeria; and a Bachelor of Arts degree from the Department of History and Strategic Studies, University of Lagos.

Introduction

Muchaparara Musemwa, Obvious Katsaura and Edwin Etieyibo

The two concepts of *radicalisms* and *conservatisms* can be viewed as mere binaries around which to organize knowledge. This volume distances itself from this view and practice. Instead, the chapters and case-studies in the collection aim to demonstrate that these concepts have multiple and diverse meanings as perceived and understood from different disciplinary vantage points; hence, the deliberate pluralization of the terms. In addition, the localized studies also show what happens when you juxtapose them and how they are easily intertwined when different peoples' lived experiences of poverty, political and social alienation, youth activism, social (in) justice, violence, etc. across the length and breadth of Africa are brought to bear in our understandings of these two particularisms. These concepts have attained a certain hegemonic dominance precisely because they are part and parcel of global Western discourses, and quite often examples used to explain them are picked from Western local sites.

Yet, Africa has its own radical-conservatives and conservative-radicals to use Madina Tlostanovas terms in chapter one (in this volume), "Beyond Conservatism and Radicalism? A Decolonial Glimpse into the Post-truth World." Indeed, we remain the poorer in our knowledge when we fail to engage or bring the two concepts or camps into a dialogue, in what Maduka Enyimba calls 'conversational thinking in chapter two (in this volume), "Moderating Conservatism and Radicalism in Post-colonial Sub-Saharan Africa: Some Objections and Clarifications through Conversational Thinking." Clive Gabay (2017) effectively underscored this point when he observed how Hastings Kamuzu Banda, the late former President of Malawi, was "often side-lined and maligned in considerations of post-colonial African leaders for being an authoritarian comprador in service to western interests". Instead, Gabay would argue against such a sweeping generalization and recognize that "Banda's life and practice illustrates a complex interplay between two types of conservatism: a more radical anti-colonial conservatism and a more reactionary post-colonial conservatism."

These conversations should also extend to analyses of the rise of a perilous brand of *populism* on the African continent and other parts of the globe (Roth, 2017). Its greatest proponents are the African political elite who include some presidents who, in the pursuit of power and fearing popular defeat at the polls, have trampled the rights of people arguing that it is these so-called rights that leave states exposed to Western machinations of regime-change. Alienation, marginalization, poverty, poor access to public health facilities (if available and functioning) have led to despair among the poor people. Instead of owning up to having played a role in causing these crises and impoverishing their states, populist leaders have, however, habitually impugned Western governments for causing their problems and for threatening their hard-won sovereignty and independence. Armed with this self-satisfying justification they have gone on to constantly remind the populace about the evils of Western imperialism and have treated civil society campaigns for the restoration of human rights as mere proxies of the West bent on facilitating 'regime-change' – a term beholden to this type or clan of leaders. They have either ordered the proscription of these organizations or the arrest of their leaders often left to languish in jail without any clear charges being brought against them. By so doing, such states have seen not only the rise of populism but authoritarianism. This has been eminent and quite visible in Zimbabwe, Burundi, Malawi, Nigeria and many other African countries.

As Clement Chipenda demonstrates in Chapter 3 (in this volume), "Politics of the Countryside after Zimbabwe's Land Reform Programme: Expectations and Demands of the Youth," the late former president of Zimbabwe, Robert Gabriel Mugabe, repeatedly whipped up a mix of populist rhetoric and authoritarian repression as he instrumentalized the land question to keep his party in power. The fast track land reform programme he propagated resulted in the violent seizures of land from white commercial farmers from 2000 till he was overthrown in a bloodless coup in November 2017. In the process, he made the West, especially Britain and the USA, look like the enemies of his people when the two countries spearheaded the imposition of a raft of sanctions on Mugabe and his acolytes. Similarly, Ebenezer Babajide Ishola's case-study in chapter 4 (in this volume), "'Not Too Young to Run' Law and Political Participation among Youths in Nigeria," exemplifies another trait of African leadership, namely the tendency to marginalize certain social groups to weaken the threat they pose when they start agitating for employment. Instead of working with the youth to help them come up with projects and programmes of entrepreneurship and encourage them to go to school, they are treated as enemies of the state.

This brand of political leadership has often drawn on the same disgruntled youth to unleash them on opponents with such brute force that scars not just the targeted opponents but traumatizes the youth as well. Thus the youth are at one time discarded and, at another, retrieved from the rubbish dump of the unwanted and recycled to serve a particular selfish purpose. This sort of engagement and employment of the youth is what Jonah Uyieh in chapter 5 (in this volume), "'Dirty-Relevance' of Youths Culture in Nigeria's Fourth Republic Politics: A Study of Delta and Lagos States" aptly refers to as 'dirty-relevance', according to which they are dumped as soon as they have finished ministering to the vile desires of these 'gerontocratic conservatives' as Ishola calls them (in chapter 4). But this dangerous populism is not necessarily the simple preserve of the political elite in power for such tendencies have been observable in political parties that have emerged on a populist ticket that exploits the disgruntlement of the youth and the poor and ramps them up against the elite of the ruling party by using vicious expletives and mouthing all manner of obscenities. A typical case in point that encapsulates this trend is the Economic Freedom Front (EFF) of South Africa led by its demagogic youthful leader, Julius Sello Malema, the Commander-in-Chief; an appellation used by his political disciples as an expression of respect goes. Bright Nkrumah's chapter 6 (in this volume), "Political Opportunism: Populism as a New Political Tactic in South Africa," pertinently, untangles the fabric that went into the making of what he calls 'rightwing populism' thread by thread.

There are 17 essays in this book. And as part of untangling issues around radicalisms and conservatisms, the book is divided into four themes and parts relating to the manifestations of radicalism and conservatism at the intersections of politics, social justice, intolerance, and education. Part 1: Conservatism, Radicalism and Politics has 6 essays, Part 2: Social Justice and Poverty has 5 essays, Part 3 Marginalization, Terrorism and Intolerance has 3 essays, and Part 4 Minorities and Education has 3 essays.

1 Part 1: Conservatism, Radicalism and Politics

In chapter 1, Tlostanova offers decolonial thinking and conceptual tools that are useful for understanding entanglements of radicalism and conservatism. She argues against binary understandings of radicalism and conservatism; demonstrating that it is possible to be conservatively radical and radically conservative simultaneously. As such, Tlostanova suggests that fluid understandings of radicalism and conservatism are more appropriate for us, if we are to grasp our past, contemporary and future politics and society with more nuance. This reflective thread is taken up by Enyimba who, in Chapter 2, follows up with a mobilization of 'conversational thinking' to better understand new forms of conservatism and radicalism emerging in, and destabilizing, sub-Saharan Africa in the aftermath of the Cold War and the fall of the Soviet Union. Through conversational thinking, Enyimba proposes to arrive at a moderation and synthesis of the oppositions of radicalism and conservatism; taking a centric position as it were.

In Chapter 3, Chipenda takes us to Zimbabwe through an analytical exploration of how the 'authoritarian populism' of former president Robert Mugabe has reconfigured rural politics. He focuses on how the Fast Track Land Reform Program (FTLRP) has foisted the ruling party, the Zimbabwe National African Union – Patriotic Front (ZANU-PF) on the rural population; becoming one of the main social structures of rural Zimbabwe, in ways that reproduce power for the ruling party.

Ishola, in Chapter 4, takes us to the problem of gerontocratic conservatism in Nigerian electoral politics. He explains how the domination of politics by an elderly male elite in the Nigerian body politic has marginalised the youth. As such, there is a new drive through legal instruments, to encourage youth participation in electoral and leadership politics in Nigeria. Relatedly, in Chapter 5, Uyieh discusses how the marginalised youth in Nigeria become embroiled in 'negative cultures' of hooliganism, violence, militancy and other social vices. In this case, these youths or young people become instruments in the hands of an aggressive political elite and victims or participants in the violent political contests of elite politicians. Uyieh mobilises the notion of 'dirty-relevance' to understand the political usability and social vices of the youth in Nigeria.

Chapter 6 by Nkrumah analyses one of South Africa's opposition parties, the Economic Freedom Fighters (EFF), as epitomizing right-wing populism or what Imraam Baccus (2018) calls 'neo-fascist' demagoguery.' Nkrumah qualifies this by exploring the anti-establishment and anti-elite postures of the EFF.

2   Part 2: Social Justice and Poverty

Edwin Etieyibo, in Chapter 7 ("Social Justice and Persons with Disabilities in Nigeria"), critically analyses the marginalisation of persons with disabilities in Nigeria. He offers a critique of discriminatory practices that entrench the unfair, unjust and unequal treatment of people with disabilities. His analysis recounts the Nigerian government's failures to protect people living with disabilities.

In Chapter 8 ("Poverty and Persons Living with Disabilities in Nigeria"), Odrin Omiegbe joins the debate with a discussion of the social and physical death of people with disabilities, as a result of extreme poverty and societal neglect. He uses the example of Nigeria to explore the 'vicious cycle' of disability and poverty.

Adekunle Victor Owoyomi, in Chapter 9 ("Poverty and Illicit Drug Use among Youths in Lagos Metropolis, Nigeria"), employs the concept of 'relative deprivation' to draw connections between poverty and illicit drug use by the youth in the Lagos megacity. The chapter highlights the need for government's structural economic intervention to facilitate youth employment as well as localized and extensive social work interventions, to address the twin problems of youth poverty and illicit drug use.

In Chapter 10 ("The Politics of Poverty in Sub-Saharan Africa"), Jonathan Chimakonam problematises the politics of poverty through a critique of three common hypothetical interpretations given to explain poverty in sub-Saharan Africa. These are the neocolonial hypothesis, the dictatorship hypothesis and the ineptitude hypothesis; all of which respectively attribute poverty to neo-imperial interests of the West, corrupt and dictatorial forms of African statecraft, and sheer incapabilities to foster positive socioeconomic progress by the African ruling classes.

Tafadzwa Chevo, in Chapter 11 ("Informality, Marginality and the State: A Case Study of Low-Income Households in Budiriro Harare Zimbabwe"), returns us to Zimbabwe where he uses the case of Harare to examine the urbanisation of poverty. He deploys the Wacquantan concept of 'urban marginality' to demonstrate how Zimbabwe's multiple and long-drawn economic and political crises have reproduced marginality, informality and poverty in the high-density townships of Harare.

3 Part 3: Marginalisation, Terrorism and Intolerance

In Chapter 12 ("Intolerance: The Activities of Ethnic Militias in Nigeria"), Adeshina Francis Akindutire examines the disruptions wrought by ethnic militias and insurgents on Nigeria's 'democracy', security and development. He relies on the example of the separatist movement of the Indigenous People of Biafra (IPOB) to demonstrate how militia and insurgent groups undermine Nigeria's 'nationhood'.

Phillip A. Edema and Adewale O. Owoseni, in Chapter 13 ("A Complementarity Reflection on Human Interest and Common Good in Africa: Examples of Nigeria's Ghana-Must-Go and South Africa's Xenophobia"), use the idea of 'human interest' to discuss the motivations of xenophobic sentiments and actions in Nigeria and South Africa. The chapter references the 'Ghana-Must-Go' campaign in Nigeria and the several successive episodes of xenophobic attacks against foreigners in South Africa.

In chapter 14 ("Boko Haram Terrorism and Out-of-School Children in North East Nigeria"), Temitope Owolabi examines the halting of formal schooling caused by Boko Haram insurgencies in Nigeria. The chapter highlights the seriousness of the problem by demonstrating that there are 20 million children that are out of school in Nigeria, 13.2 million of which were driven out of school because of Boko Haram insurgencies. This has posed a serious problem on the education system in Nigeria, with potentially serious ramifications for the future.

4   Part 4: Minorities and Education

Israel Ugoma Oberedjemurho, in Chapter 15 ("Academic Abuse and Violence against Students in Delta State, Nigeria and its Impact on Their Learning Behavior"), offers a critique of the education system in Nigeria for taking in pupils or students who are premature in terms of age. He reads this situation as amounting to intellectual abuse of, and violence on, the children. This is happening with the complicity of parents, who are sending children as young as 3 or 4 years into primary school, 8-9 years into secondary school and 12-13 years into tertiary education. Oberedjemurho recommends a reversal of this premature entry of children into the various stages of the formal schooling system to undo this educational injustice on children.

In Chapter 16 ("Effects of Lessons on Empathic Response and Perception on Conflict Reduction among Secondary School Adolescents"), Peter Kwaja discusses the utility of the learning tool 'Lessons on Empathic Responding and Perception' (LERP), for contexts of adolescent learning. This learning tool, Kwaja argues, could help reduce (future) conflict by inculcating an ethics of empathy in the learners.

Olufunke Olufunsho Adegoke, in Chapter 17 ("Ethical Dimensions in Research - Informed Consent Process on Female Gender in Nigeria"), explores the importance of informed consent for research that involves women. This is against a backdrop of women's vulnerabilities to exploitation in scientific research, especially that which focuses on experimentations on the female body. In this case, Adegoke refers to the necessity of informed consent in biomedical research involving female participants in Nigeria.

The untangling, manifesting and discussions of the two concepts of radicalisms and conservatisms and their connection to other socio-political and economic issues do indeed shed light on how and why we should think of radicalisms and conservatisms not as mere binaries around which to organize knowledge and to disseminate them. And by focusing on Africa, it is clear that there are issues around radicalisms and conservatisms that merit more interrogation. We hope that this volume provides a glimpse of such interrogation.

References

Buccus, Imraan. 2019. "What Does Change in Presidency Mean for Opposition?" Auwal Socio-Economic Research Institute, February 19. Available at https://www.notes-fromthehouse.co.za/opinion/item/187-what-does-change-in-presidency-mean-for-the-opposition.

Gabay, Clive. 2017. "The Radical Reactionary Politics of Malawi's Hastings Banda: Roots, Fruits and Legacy." *Journal of Southern African Studies*, 43(6): 1119–1135.

Roth, Kenneth. 2017). "The Dangerous Rise of Populism: Global Attacks on Human Rights Values," *Human Rights Watch, World Report*, 2017. https://www.hrw.org/sites/default/files/populism_0.pdf Accessed 30 May 2020.

PART 1

Conservatism, Radicalism and Politics

CHAPTER 1

Beyond Conservatism and Radicalism? A Decolonial Glimpse into the Post-truth World

Madina Tlostanova

1   Introduction

The theme of 'Conservatism' and 'radicalism' has appeared in a number of recent conferences.[1] Toplin (2006), Klein (2017), Mering (2013), and Berlet (2019) seem to indicate a present rather paradoxical moment in the evolvement of the global coloniality, a moment in which the former political antipodes such as 'democracy' and 'authoritarianism', 'left' and 'right', 'nationalism' and 'cosmopolitanism' and also 'conservatism' and 'radicalism' are clearly undone and become increasingly meaningless and at times interchangeable. Global coloniality is a term that was introduced by decolonial thinkers around the end of the Cold War. It is the indispensable constitutive darker side of modernity which in its turn is understood in decolonial thought not in a conventional Eurocentric way associated with the Enlightenment, the French and industrial revolutions and other familiar markers, but rather with the two hundred years earlier colonization of the Americas, the genocide of the indigenous population, the gigantic slave trade and the emergence of the modern/colonial racially grounded human taxonomy classifying people according to their proximity to the imperial sameness (Dussel 1996). This understanding of modernity which always comes with its darker irrational colonial underside - that of coloniality, is different from and should not be confused with (neo)colonialism (Quijano 1992).Colonialism and neocolonialism are historical and descriptive terms which do not attempt a deconstruction of epistemic and affective grounds of the modern/colonial project.

---

1   These conferences include the International Conference on Conservatism, Radicalism and Fundamentalism, held in May 2012 at the University of Debrecen; the 42nd World Congress of the International Institute of Sociology, "The Social sciences: New Conservatisms and New Radicalisms" that took place 5–7 September, 2018 at the University of the Witwatersrand in Johannesburg, South Africa; the Nordic Conference on Violent Extremism organized in the fall of 2019 in Aarhus University; Radicalism and Violence conference organized by the Council for European Studies in 2020 in Reykjavik.

Global coloniality or in other words, the colonial matrix of power, is a specific kind of imperial/colonial relations that emerged in the Atlantic world in the sixteenth century, and brought imperialism and capitalism together thus launching modernity as an overarching global project, with the help of racial taxonomizing, management of knowledge production and distribution, shaping of subjectivities and sexual and gender identities (Tlostanova and Mignolo 2012). Global coloniality therefore is a human condition we all share in different roles and capacities. The 'post-dependence' condition connects in a transversal way such diverse dimensions of modernity/coloniality as post-Fordism, post-colonialism and post-imperialism, post-apartheid, post-dictatorship, post-socialism, secondary Europeanism, etc. It is crucial not to withdraw into any local standpoint experience of oppression, but create instead conditions for an *other* vision and coalitions against all modern/colonial forms of dependence.

Global coloniality refers to existential, epistemic, affective and other traces of colonialism, or, in other words, a design of the modern/colonial world (Fry 2017; Tlostanova 2017). These traces continue to exist long after colonialism is over and flourish in subjectivities, human taxonomies, disciplines and academic divisions, in the production and distribution of knowledge, in gender and sexual norms and identities, in aesthetic canons and practically all other spheres of life made subservient to the totality of modernity and its darker colonial side. Consequently decoloniality concerns itself, in Walsh's and Mignolo's recent formulation, with

> a critique and delinking from the habits modernity/coloniality implanted in all of us", with how it has worked and continues to work to negate, disavow, distort and deny knowledges, subjectivities, world senses and life vision. (Walsh and Mignolo 2018, 4)

Modernity is indeed a global ontological design defining the fundamental relations between people, the world and objects. This modern/colonial ontological design has normalized vectorial time and progressivist teleology, rigid and absurdly rationalized managerial strategies applied to the spheres of knowledge and subjectivity production, the preference of urbanism over rurality, the sanctification of technological development and applied forms of ecology aiming at the nature's preservation for its more successful exploitation in the future, the cult of the future and the dismissal of the negatively marked traditional past, particularly if this is a spatially alien past, with regular lapses into exoticism and antiquarianism one of which we witness today.

Retaining its major characteristics linked originally with a particular combination of Christianity, capitalism and racism (Quijano 2000), and therefore with coloniality of power, of being, of knowledge, of gender, of sensing, in more than five centuries of its reign, global coloniality has gone through several major shifts. Its present form is linked with the crisis of the idealized model of globalization which was associated with the decline of the nation-state and the emergence of the "post-territorial coloniality in contemporary global society" (Çaliskan and Preston 2017, 199).

The populist take over on a global scale that has marked the 2010s generally indicates the failure of the previous positive image of globalization which now seems to be finally buried by the Covid-19 pandemic and crisis. At the same time it makes the yesterday's populist agenda vulnerable as well for it is becoming clear now that nationalists and populists have the "point but do not have a solution" (Krastev 2020). The pandemic in this sense has only accelerated the already obvious array of contradictions in the way governments, transnational unions and people try to reconcile the increasingly empty signifiers of democracy and authoritarianism, free trade and economic protectionism, conservatism and radicalism, the equality of enslaved and the freedom of unequal increasingly competing for mere survival. As Ivan Krastev points out in his *After Europe*, "the outcome is unworkable: you end up with democracy without choices, sovereignty without meaning and globalization without legitimacy" (Krastev 2017, 70). Yet from a decolonial view point the shift from neoliberal globalism to right-wing nationalism is not that important as it essentially leaves the colonial matrix of power intact.

Additionally there is a discrepancy between populist nationalism and cultural protectionism that are used to keep the population at bay and often hijack the postcolonial and decolonial rhetoric top down for advancing the state interests, and the remaining real global flows. The latter are still controlled by the neoliberal logic, although may change the original vectors in the frame of dewesternizing tendencies (Mignolo 2013) and shifting and multiplying the centers of influence. Claiming that the colonial matrix of power is no longer controlled and managed by the West, dewesternizers (such as BRICS countries) accept some of the economic and technological aspects of the present order yet question its unipolarity and try to divide the economic and axiological aspects.

Yet dewesternizing remains limited as it does not question the colonial matrix of power as such merely claiming a better place in today's repartition and redrawing of the world. Polycentric capitalism merely releases the steam and creates an illusion of the possible win-win situation but does not save from easily sliding into yet another misanthropic (Maldonado-Torres 2007, 245) model of dispensable lives – human and other. Indeed live remains equally precarious in any of the existing scenarios—under the unipolar hegemony of the North or under the local repression by various nationalist, quasi-neocolonial and authoritarian regimes.

2 The Socialist Modernity as an Elephant in the Room

Here it might be useful to recollect how and at whose expense the happy globalization chant first came into being. The elephant in the room is the state socialist modernity which no one wants to remember today including its own participants – willing and forced. The almost overnight dismantling of the socialist world after 1989 has led to a Western understanding of postsocialism exclusively in temporal (a period after socialism) and not in spatial terms, thus ignoring the millions of people who shared the experience of being branded for several decades as 'the (communist) East' and are still inhabiting this symbolic East which is breaking now under the pressure of the new geopolitical divisions and North/South axes (Tlostanova 2017a). We woke up to find ourselves displaced from Francis Fukuyama's 'end of history' discourse (Fukuyama 1992). Today's intolerant populists and right-wing fundamentalists taking over in many parts of the world are a logical result of the fall of the state socialist system and the short-lived neoliberal claims of owning the world. If the Cold war logic allowed the state socialist system to act as a counterbalance for the capitalist world and thus gave some opportunities to the people to fight for their rights, today this function is performed by different institutions – nationalist, religious, populist, protectionist, and other such local forms which act as a steam release creating an illusion of change.

When Fukuyama was celebrating the defeat of the sate socialist modernity and the coming of neoliberal globalization with no borders, decolonial thinker Anibal Quijano introduced the concept of coloniality "as a response from the underside to the enforced homogeneity of neoliberal modernity and to the realization that the state cannot be democratized or decolonized" (Walsh and Mignolo 2018, 106). At that moment the Cold War term decolonization started to shift to decoloniality. The state Socialist modernity (now turned into the non-region (Suchland 2015, 87) thus has acted as an invisible and silent trigger and at times mediator of the lighter (end of history) and darker (coloniality) interpretations of the present.

The optimistic neoliberal global chant of the shrunken world of happy consumers and erased borders has started to demonstrate its unsightly darker side. The movements of capital and goods and perhaps a few globe-trotters easily changing continents and jobs from one transnational corporation to another, was replaced with a threatening image of globalization in the center of which stands the figure of the refugee and the increasing flow of people who migrate to escape death, famine, war, and political repressions. The failure of the global promise has resulted in a next wave of particularisms grounded in a sober realization of the impossibility to provide a universal progress – even in a simplified neoliberal understanding. The neoliberal global model has soon manifested the same old darker colonial sides albeit at times in new wrappings, causing the revival of the stale geopolitics and the defensive strengthening of nation states with overt top-down nationalist or neo-imperial agendas.

The paradoxical nature of today's moment is linked with a negative reaction against the most devastating sides of neoliberal globalization increasingly infringing upon the interests of the people all over the world. The unresolved problems of modernity nearsightedly proclaimed outdated only a few years ago, have reemerged as ghosts of the pasts with full force confirming once again the discriminatory nature of most practices of the so called global culture, its unfair conditions of inclusion through erasing identities or through their exaggeration and commercialization. The disillusionment in the failed globalization promise is manipulated by the weakened nation-states and regrouping geopolitical unions and powers wishing to regain their control and divert the public attention from real problems to highly politicized and excessively emotional constructed issues so typical of the post-truth reality with completely disappeared objective shared standards for truth (Illing 2018) and an increased inability to "discern fact from fiction" (Arendt 1972). This reaction indicates a systemic crisis and possibly the beginning of the end of neoliberalism as the only remaining model of modernity, or perhaps, an ultimate discrediting of the project of modernity as such.

3   The Increasing Meaninglessness of "-ism"s

Conservatism and radicalism are political tags from the previous époque which increasingly fail to describe or explain the present reality and its difference from what was before. Conservative and radical political waves happened many times in history and these rather arbitrary phenomena could be ideologically filled with anything and at times turn into each other, feeding various open and closed social utopias and dystopias. The difference is perhaps in the radical change in polarities confusing and merging the stereotypical political identities associated with radicals and conservatives. Thus democracy in contemporary fortress Europe acts often as an instrument of exclusion rather than inclusion and the talk of the universal and abstract human rights is more and more often replaced with various security discourses.

Different radical groups calling for immediate changes often happen to be conservative and defensive rather than liberatory or leftist as it was previously the case. In this sense, it is a militant conservatism accusing the liberal majority of its status quo lack of principles. One of the stumbling points here is the question of diversity regarded as the major harm in today's populist discourses – both far right and increasingly, more mainstream. The tags of radicalism and conservatism therefore do not mean much and often become interchangeable.

This sickening metamorphosis of left and right or radical and conservative was detected by Lewis Gordon who claims in a recent interview that

> a shift in the geography of reason requires thinking anew and creatively how we understand concepts such as 'right' and 'left'. There are left-wing positions that can slide into the right when we understand their goals. After all, conservatism is a turn toward a past, a cherry-picked past, of supposed security, law and order, perfection. This often requires eliminating sources of dissent such as difference, creativity, and freedom…and if pushed to its extreme offers fascism. (Gordon 2018)

It is high time we stop hiding behind the past tags and indeed attempt a shifting not only in the geography of reason but also in our political and ethical responsibility to be able to see behind the thick fence of "–isms" what is more important for the contemporary moment and for the future of life as such and of the lives of those who remain not only anonymous to us but also perhaps, beyond our understanding. Following Frederick Douglass's, Simone Weil and Asma Abbas, Lewis Gordon calls this "not only a political responsibility but also a peculiarly political form of love" (Gordon 2018).

Yet the political form of love as an open potentiation is unfortunately balanced with the present increased accentuating of the negative emotional appeal within the economy of post-truth. It is grounded in heterosexism, misogyny and racism, and brings forward and justifies a politics of emotions aptly analyzed by Sara Ahmed reflecting on the defensive uses of hate within various fascist and other hate discourses that declare themselves as organizations of love:

> The ordinary white subject is a fantasy that comes into being through the mobilization of hate, as a passionate attachment tied closely to love. The emotion of hate works to animate the ordinary subject, to bring that fantasy to life, precisely by constituting the ordinary as in crisis, and the ordinary person as the real victim. (Ahmed 2004, 118)

It seems that today this sensibility is increasingly becoming mainstream thus revealing the negative potential of the global coloniality in its defensive stage.

A decolonial optics allows looking beyond the outdated but hastily revamped concepts of the West and the East, right and left, cosmopolitans and nativists, or a rather misleading contrast of conservatism and radicalism. All of these tags are indeed interchangeable in the face of the persistent modern/colonial mechanism of dehumanization implemented through coloniality of knowledge, of being and of perception, through racism, heterosexism, enforcement of modern/colonial aesthetic and ethical principles. In this sense the emotional anxiety of the post-truth politics simply camouflages the heightened pressure of neoliberal capitalist inequalities which need an energy of hatred for the collective others - necessary to continue deluding the same – the near future losers of modernity/coloniality.

Presenting conservatism and radicalism as extremes at the political and social scale seems misleading. What is considered to be a normative regime in this case? What is the hidden vantage point from which this opposition is formulated? Obviously it is a status quo centrist liberalism as a more or less normative modern mild reformist ideology. All of these concepts become especially problematic if we question the modern/colonial "translation of geography into chronology" (Mignolo 2000, 240) and the invention of tradition as a negative other of modernity – first the European own dark ages and later the colonial otherness. Radicalism today is an empty signifier as it can be leftist or rightist, and increasingly more rightist than leftist, wanting to bring society back to its presumable ideal previous state. An additional dimension of today's situation that helps better grasp the outdatedness of conservative and radical options, is the compressed reality and hence the imploded life. Regardless of our political persuasions we share the grim prospect of the shrinking resources, the dwindling options offered by late capitalism, and hence the emergence of more and more resentful groups marked by the sense of betrayal. These groups are the most quick to radicalize today. At the same time these are also the people who defend conservative values - be it a homogenous white heterosexual Europe, Christian fundamentalists in the USA or various nationalists in Eastern Europe. They all share a sense of resentment against the states or larger transnational unions that they had their trust in before.

Perhaps one of the most devastating consequences of the latest phase of modernity is the weakening and at times, a dying out of the political dimension, a complete dissociation of the people and their unwillingness and inability to create or maintain meaningful political coalitions and identities or much less to have a positive vision of the future that would be grounded in decolonial pluriversality as a universal principle linked with relationality or, in Amerindian terms, "*vincularidad* – an awareness of the integral relation and interdependence amongst all living organisms with territory or land and the cosmos" (Walsh and Mignolo 2018).

The former leftist utopia of the world revolution and a global brotherhood of the working classes are left behind and impossible to reanimate no matter what substitutes for proletarians are being offered (the masses, the multitude, etc.). Leftist discourses are also victims of the ubiquitous modern atomizing and the triumph of individualism which excludes any possibility of a meaningful collective agency, even if the Marxist commons remain one of the standard elements of leftist rhetoric. The left, in Gordon's words, become a "form of anarchy of the small, privatized sites of protection" (Gordon 2018) and this makes them indistinguishable from the right. Today's mass migrations in quest of better jobs, better lives or even mere survival, safety or future, which Krastev compares to a revolution - the exit driven revolution of individuals and families, remains a solitary revolution of the people who do not share a common ideology, leaders or manifests (Krastev 2017, 30). They vote with their feet and admit their defeat in changing anything in their own countries. This is perhaps one of the bitterest outcomes of the last decades.

The negative phase of globalization makes more and more lives dispensable and the post-truth rhetoric becomes the main sign of this phase, a form of perverse defense of exclusionary communities through a creation of fortress states and identities. Moreover, these negative coalitions *against* rather than *for* something or someone, coopt new members into their cohorts much easier than positive and inclusive initiatives. We can easily imagine a global negative community of racism, hatred, patriarchy, and nationalism.

4 The Old and New Others

The sensationalist traps of the post-truth reality and the misleading political tags of different "–isms" are unable to hide the persistent problem of modernity/coloniality which has only worsened in its contemporary moment. Within the logic of the global coloniality different groups of people are assigned different status in accordance with the human taxonomies invented in and by modernity. The production of the new others is grounded in the habitual modern/colonial operation of assigning whole groups of people living in the non-European or non-Western spaces to other times or rather, positioning them outside the only sanctioned course of time and the only appropriate way of life. This structure allows ontological, epistemic, and cultural existence of only those others who are for some reason profitable, commodifiable, whose difference is containable within the sameness and hence, rendered safe. The principles of this categorizing, subsequently naturalized and made universal are decided by those who have the means to authorize themselves to make the classification.

The modern/colonial division of people into humans and sub-humans (sexually and racially marked) and questioning the humanity of the *other*, are not ontological, but entirely epistemic and constructed. Previously the 'savage' was identified with nature and seen as incapable of thinking, feeling in terms of emotions rather than raw affects, or creating art objects in accordance with particular aesthetics as opposed to mere aesthesis. Today this logic is revamped in the treatment of migrants, refugees, and asylum seekers but also other, perhaps not so obvious undesirable groups. Therefore, it is important to uncover the role of particular 'situated knowledges' (Haraway 1998) or, in decolonial terms, the 'geopolitics and corpo-politics of knowledge' (Tlostanova and Mignolo 2012), in the construction of the modern/colonial ontology as a relationality of human and non-human being, existence, becoming, and reality as well as their epistemic representations.

The present configuration of sameness and otherness is not really a new challenge. Or, perhaps, it is new only in the sense that it thrashes onto the forestage of history provisionally new groups who are then subject to the modern/colonial dehumanizing. The ontological erasing of the anthropos (Nishitani 2006) is a universal mechanism of modernity/coloniality which we witness in the way indigenous people, refugees, migrants, missing citizens (les citoyens manquants", in Rada Iveković's apt formulation (Iveković 2015) and many other undesirable groups are treated today. This dehumanizing has acquired more advanced technological forms but has retained its main *raison d'etre* – to classify the humankind in such a way as to legitimate the exclusive rights of a rather small group and the decreasing scale of rights of all others, with a growing numbers of those whose human status is fundamentally in question. The methods of discrimination are often also recycled from previous epochs and fully correspond to the logic of modernity/coloniality.

Alluding to W. B. Dubois's well-known idea Jane Anna and Lewis Gordon point out that racism and colonialism generated people "marked as the continued sign of ill fate and ruin. Problem people" (Gordon and Gordon 2010, 19). More and more population groups, countries and whole regions are marked by this post-Duboisean collective sense of subjects with delayed or questionable humanity and no place in the new architecture of the world. This sensibility has also served as a hotbed of populist right-wing sentiment and induced quite scary historical analogies.

A critique of epistemic coloniality leading to a peculiar ontologization of difference, that is a view that essentialises differences as innate, given once and for all and often biologically determined and 'objective', has been central for decolonial thinking from the start. S. Castro-Gomez calls it the "hubris of the zero point" - a specific Eurocentric positionality of the sensing and thinking subject, occupying a delocalized and disembodied vantage point which eliminates any other possible ways to produce, transmit and represent knowledge, allowing for a world view to be built on a rigid essentialist progressivist model (Castro-Gomez 2007).

The modern/colonial human taxonomy continues to use agonistics and victimhood rivalry as its most efficient tools of keeping populations at bay. It is assumed that everyone has to accept the existing hierarchy where we are all assigned a precise and never questioned place. Being unhappy with this status, everyone is afraid of losing their precarious position and being associated with those who stand even lower.

For instance, the former state socialist subjects are one group that felt forgotten with the emergence of other media agendas such as the refugee crisis in Europe. This triggered an outbreak of victimhood rivalry that has always prevented the others of modernity/coloniality from building horizontal coalitions and alliances. Victimhood rivalry including the one among the postcolonial and post-socialist groups does not let break free from the universally accepted agonistic paradigm 'compete or perish'. Decoloniality among other things means delinking from this logic and refusing to compete for a higher place in modernity, or for a tag of a victim, which would allow gaining access to charity and affirmative action.

In the situation of increasing normalization of the permanent state of exception even outside the actual zones of war and conflict, and especially with the ongoing Covid-19 pandemic and crisis, more and more people are turned into the new '*anthropos*' whose human rights are systematically revoked, restricted and inverted. The majority of people are regulated, threatened and monitored through disciplinary regimes and different forms of immobilization such as racial, ethnic and religious profiling, identity controls, draconian immigration laws as forms of excluding individuals from the ontological reality and effectively denying their existence as humans. The maximal dehumanizing and turning people into emblems of suffering and at times of aggression and threat symbolizes the deep internal contradictions and unresolved dilemmas of modernity/coloniality in the conditions of declining global capitalism. Allowing the other to speak and to look, to have a name, a face, a life story is dangerous as it turns the other from an abstract victim in need of salvation into a living complex human being who is equal and therefore has the right to be different and who must be treated ethically. Hence the inadequacy of both charity and 'civilizing mission' models that are still being widely applied.

Condescending tags of development, transit, emerging democracies and the like are introduced and reintroduced to keep the modern/colonial human taxonomy intact, while the initial rhetorical promises of inclusion on the condition of model behavior are never fulfilled. Transition marked by a permanent time lag has become a chronic condition for many countries and whole regions.

5 A Futureless Ontology

One of the omnipresent signs of the late phase of the losing neoliberal globalization is the lost future dimension. I analyzed this issue in relation to Russia and its former and present colonies under the name of the "futureless ontology" (Tlostanova 2018, 16), that is a being and existence in which no one is promised happiness even in the distant future, to say nothing of the possibility of any future per se. At the core of the state Socialist utopianism stood the idea of universal happiness and consequently a happy future for everyone. Way too soon utopia became sealed and exclusionary. But the social contract of the Soviet people was linked to this imagined future happiness that they were offered to exchange for the hardships and difficulties of the present. Today the belt-tightening rhetoric is no longer compensated with any promise of the universal happiness in near or distant future.

However, futurelessness is not only a post-Soviet story. The neoliberal modernity/coloniality at large is closing any future options for larger and larger groups of population. The underside of this problem is that the global consumers nurtured in the last decades as the main inhabitants of the global world long for a populist politician who will not ask them to change the future and even speak of that future at all. On the contrary, the consumers need an eternal status quo of the endless present in which they do not need to change, are good the way they are. Such was president Vladimir Putin's rhetoric up to the point when it became impossible to maintain the desired economic level for the happy consumers and it became necessary to rescue the moth-eaten ideologies of besieged camp, enemies of the people and foreign agents - anything to keep the consumer for a little while longer at bay. This strange kind of populism though militant on the surface, is not really offering any common project to defend or much less fight for, simply wanting to prolong obedience for a little while longer.

The closing of utopias has taken place not only at the level of rival ideologies most of which seem to be outdated, but also at a more global level of life as such marked by defuturing. The latter term was offered by Australian design theorist Tony Fry. The human species, in spite of our mutual dehumanizing tactics and growing economic and social asymmetries, still share some elements of ontological condition and some pluriversal challenges. Unfortunately, most of these elements and challenges today are negative, as opposed to the lighter side of modernity's original universalist formulations that nevertheless always excluded some groups. They are negative in the sense that they describe the conditions of lack, loss, and void or, in Fry's terms, the 'defuturing' tendencies. Fry defines defuturing as a condition of mind and action that materially erodes (un-measurably) planetary finite time, thus gathering and designating the negation of 'the being of time,' which is equally the taking away of our future', as much as it can serve as a tool of resurgence. (Fry 2011, 21)

More and more people become subjected to the futureless ontology which allows for different degrees and forms of inequality and vulnerability, yet forces more and more groups into the permanent state of exception, war ethics, or a naturalized competition for the pittance from those who have the power to decide.

6 On Re-existence and Decoloniality

And yet a multiple decolonial answer to these grim challenges is becoming louder and more diverse in different parts of the world and in different forms – from decolonizing museums to decolonizing universities and social movements. In a rather dark picture of today's world a decolonial shift from resistance to re-existence seems to be one of the few promising steps. The concept of re-existence was offered by Adolfo Albán (Albán 2009). As summarized by Catherine Walsh, re-existence is a "redefining and re-signification of life in conditions of dignity. It is a praxis of the otherwise" (Walsh and Mignolo 2018, 18).

Walsh also stresses the importance of the positive 'for' element of decoloniality. "It is the *for* that takes us beyond the anti-stance. It is the *for* that signifies, sows and grows the otherwise of decoloniality" (Walsh and Mignolo 2018, 18) as an insurgency. The present examples of such positive re-existent ontologies include the well-known *Sumac Kawsay*, Vandana Shiva's earth democracy and many other social movements and intellectual insurgencies. A re-existent stance allows delinking from the dominant politics of knowledge, being, and perception grounded in suppression of geo-historical dimensions of affects and corporalities. Re-existence is far from a primordialist call to return to some essentialised and constructed authenticity. On the contrary, it is a way to relive the main elements of erased and distorted value systems while necessarily taking into account the temporal lag and experiences of struggle and opposition, compromises and losses that have taken place. Re-existence is not mere repetition; it is also variation in which there is not only always a stable core but also a necessary creative element of difference, and hence of dynamics and change, a development of the native tradition in dialogue and in argument with modernity. It is an enrichment of our perspective, a constant balancing on the verge—neither here nor there or simultaneously here, there, and elsewhere.

7   Deep Coalitions

To make re-existence and decoloniality *for* a working model it is necessary to take a more proactive stance on building coalitions and alliances for an alternative world of the future. What is needed is a shifting away from the dominance of the unnamed but presupposed US and Western European discourses that only allow for adding the new factual material to be analyzed still using the Western-centric optics. Truly transnational inclusive methodology should take into account the close interrelation between being, existence and agency, the principle of relational-experiential rationality and building knowledge not outside the human experience and not by presenting the problem outside the context, but through a never ending process of learning, unlearning, and relearning (Tlostanova and Mignolo 2012), humbly listening to others and entering their worlds with a loving (Lugones 2003, 96) rather than agonistic perception. Such an approach is grounded in complexity and relationality, complementarity and reciprocity and the shift from the subject-object division to subject-subject type of learning and understanding.

Relationality as a methodological principle and as a philosophy of radical contingentism (Sharma 2015) that is an ontology without subject, objects and processes that are intrinsically existent by themselves (Escobar 2018, 212) stresses the weaving patterns connecting differences rather than focusing on the 'nature of the components' as such (Glissant 1997, 190). It means *processes* across cultures, nations, regions, imperial and colonial histories, and geopolitical configurations. Successful coalitions across racial, ethnic, religious, linguistic, ideological and other borders, based on relationality and communality, are always in the making. They are the opposite of essentialist standpoint positions trapped in limitations of victimhood rivalry and unwilling to build alliances because they follow the modern/colonial agonistic logic.

Coloniality of knowledge precludes the possibilities of horizontal connections, alliances and coalitions among different others who are collectively seen as the object of analysis. Maria Lugones's idea of 'deep coalitions' can be potentially seen as a ground for truly transnational and transmodern agendas. These agendas can be maximally inclusive to an infinite multiplicity of ideas and voices. They would help structuring research, collaboration and activism bypassing the uncontested mediation of Western theory. According to Lugones,

> deep coalitions never reduce multiplicity, they span across differences. Aware of particular configurations of oppression, they are not fixed on them, but strive beyond into the world, towards a shared struggle of interrelated others (Lugones 2003, 98).

Such coalitions require maintaining complexity and heterogeneity rather than taking them to homogenous sameness on both universalized global and/or particularized local grounds.

The continuing power asymmetries can be shaken, if the direct south to south and south to semi-periphery coalitions are developed without the Western/Northern mediation and the West/North stops prescribing the rules of discourse and the categories of analysis, classifying others according to their proximity to the Western/Northern norm. This means a refusal to start any analysis from the Western/Northern blueprint and building any position or idea into the pre-existing template. Designing alternative trajectories and drawing re-emerging genealogies is a difficult but necessary task before we can hope to start dismantling the hidden binaries and persistent hang-ups of presumably universal theories of culture, politics, and society.

8 An Afterword: Covid-19 Crisis as a Magnifying Glass and a Catalyst of the Global Crisis

A powerful example of the tendencies traced above has forcefully arrived on a global scale two years after the first draft of this essay was presented at the 42nd World Congress of the International Institute of Sociology at the University of the Witwatersrand in Johannesburg, South Africa. I mean the Covid-19 pandemic, which can be regarded as a fast and in-your-face crisis as opposed to the slower climate change which is also invisible and therefore easily deniable and prone to post-truth style misinformation and distortion. Covid-19 accurately reflects the complex junctures and messy entanglements of contemporaneity. This crisis has further discredited and cancelled the remaining tiny illusion of the possibility to continue forever the neoliberal global sprint. The persistent downplaying of the growing inequality and the slow but steady normalization of the state of exception and taking away citizens' rights, to say nothing of those who cannot even become citizens, while simultaneously pedaling the open borders for the selected few - all came to the fore and clashed in a matter of days under the Covid-19 crisis, devilishly turning the yesterday's advantage into today's public threat. This freedom of movement for the advantaged is precisely what has led through the air travel to a rapid spread of the virus and generated yet another dimension of social hatred and discontent of those with no money to buy plane tickets and entry visas and often no passports into which these visas could be stamped. Today the majority of these people struggle for mere survival unable to solve the dilemma of losing their jobs and staying safe at home.

The normalization of the state of exception has been undoubtedly taken to a new level, as a result of the Covid-19 crisis. It is already leading to what N. Klein has named a 'pandemic shock doctrine' (Klein 2020) which might, exploit the public's disorientation to push through radical free market policies under the cover of 'saving rhetoric'.

Only recently the total neural implantation of all people and other extreme elements of the coloniality of technology and the old/new division into the valuable and dispensable lives, based on technologies, seemed to be the grim posthuman cyberpunk fantasy of not so near future. Today these scenarios are very close to be realized in several countries under the excuse of the Covid-19 crisis. This shift threatens to normalize not just the state of exception but the state of the constant and total surveillance including in the so-called democratic countries.

Covid-19 crisis has accelerated the social, economic, political and semiotic disasters that have started previously and have often been left unexamined and analytically unconnected (due to derelational nature of contemporary knowledge and disciplines). Piled up and entangled in complex ways they legitimize the absence of future for us all, the bankruptcy and swift phasing out of international institutes and organizations, of democratic nation-state model which in its neoliberal version is too easily prone to sacrifice the vulnerable for the salvation of the unsustainable economy that is expected to return to the 'normal' pre-crisis numbers and rates.

This one more time indicates the nearsightedness of the current leadership unable to connect the total economization and commercialization of life and the crisis - not just the short term Covid-19 crisis (though indirectly this one as well) but the global crisis of modernity's legitimacy. It is the crisis of the ruling liberal and especially neoliberal conceptions of politics and the political, of the long normalized relations of the free autonomous individuals and societies, whose freedom today mainly comes to freedom to consume without taking anyone or anything else into consideration. It is a crisis of citizens and states, of humans and the material world in which we live and which we constantly redesign. The closing of the remains of the social sphere in the global north, the restriction of movement, and increasingly militarized means of social control, as a result of the Covid-19 crisis, to say nothing of the global south and the semi-periphery where precarious lives were simply dismissed, have only increased the already severe problems of psychological alienation, chronophobia (the fear of time and rejection of change), global unsettlement, the lack of foresight and imagination with at least mid-term planning in mind. As a result, once again, we arrive at the reinstatement of futurelessness.

It is significant that although 'virus does not discriminate' based on nationality, race or religion (Stiglitz 2020), the very crisis itself has not resulted (with an exception of a number of local initiatives), in a will to create a new global (comm)unity as a negative solidarity against the virus. Making sense of the 'communovirus', Jean Luc Nancy states that we are yet unable to reflect on such a community:

> The problem is that the virus is still its main representative; that between the surveillance model and the welfare model, only the virus remains as the common property. (Nancy 2020)

Nancy is right offering us yet another glimpse into the lacking political imagination, and a sad awareness of the human inability not just to solve but even to adequately realize the scale and main elements of the crisis which we largely created ourselves.

The Covid-19 crisis has also allowed flourishing of the post-truth politics, previously rehearsed during the US elections. It is clear in the problems with dissemination of public information in an environment where misinformation was and is rife, especially that negative information is usually taken in contemporary media and social media as true, valuable, serious and reliable while positive content is often seen as a 'fake' (Pocheptsov 2020). The latter seriously unsettles even the relatively privileged 'working from home' and socially distancing ex-consumers as it de-legitimates for them the remaining scarce bastions of trust and confidence. At the darker side of modernity where this reliance and responsibility were always missing, the shift from the lighter to the darker closing phase of neoliberal globalization has only intensified the already powerful dispensability of lives.

However, this situation of increased abandonment could potentially lead to a faster emergence of the informal communities not just as disadvantaged spaces, but also as loci of empowerment, delinking and (re)building life outside the skidding modernity. The Covid-19 crisis that has exposed the extreme unsustainability of the global economy can open a window for a shift that was considered too radical before. It is connected with the rise of the local economic autonomy and refusal to (re)join the failed globalization in the capacity of service states and precarious lives. This window can soon close if a substantial effort from the local communities themselves, from the social movements and grass root initiatives is not going to change the situation. Politically these communities could potentially turn to alternative group-rule principles more adequate in the imminent conditions of de-growth, de-urbanization, diversification of decentered and rhyzomatic economic and social models. One of such principles is the systematically applied self-governance principle (supported by non-etatist federalism as a principle of bottom-up horizontal decision-making under which no decision is ever made against the will of the group whose interests it effects and without their direct participation in decision making).

How is the Covid-19 short term crisis linked to the decolonial optics? On the one hand, the main decolonial premises and arguments stay intact in this unprecedented situation as it only demonstrates once again the contra-life core of coloniality which is continued in new forms. On the other hand, crises such as Covid-19, in my view, are potentially capable of accelerating meaningful shifts in decolonial thought itself, of preventing it from becoming tamed, normalized or even hijacked by the ultra-right and conservative agendas in their desperate reanimation of the nation-state, ethnic-cultural, religious, Eurocentric and other mythologies normalizing rootedness and othering the non-belonging.

More concretely, triggered by the Covid-19 crisis decolonial thought could finally open up more towards the contemporary. Most acute in its critical interpretations of the past and its effects on the present, decolonial critique so far has not only avoided focusing on the present, but has also been reluctant to leave its positionality of 'exteriority' unintentionally excluding all other forms of critical thinking from possible coalitions and dialogues. In the face of the complex crisis such stand-pointism becomes counter-productive and defutures us all even more, because today the struggle for representation is being rapidly subsumed by the struggle for survival. At the dark moment of Covid-19 crisis the decolonial attention to the resurrection and reclaiming of the past should perhaps shift to efforts to imagine the future in the context of the tectonic shifts the world is rapidly going through. Extending the decolonial critique to the present and especially the future could bring forward decolonial agency and bottom-up activism (political, social, artistic) rather than merely academic thinking.

There are no ready recipes for giving the world back its future dimension. It can stem only from a radical delinking from the modern/colonial logic and overcoming modernity from decolonial and other cracks and fissures and advancing a different pluriversal idea of the world, of knowledge, of being and of sensing. This is a long and painstaking process requiring a collective effort to foster alternative forms of life. But it is already at work in different parts of the world-from the political society, from social movements, from grass roots struggles for autonomy and various decolonial thinking, doing and creativity initiatives. It would be naïve to assume that these decolonial tendencies will soon prevail. Yet they are able to somewhat counter-balance the cheerlessness of today's reality with a humble promise of a possibility of a different world and a different future. In Arundhati Roy's words: "Another world is not only possible, she is on her way. On a quiet day I can hear her breathing" (Macy 2007, 17).

References

Ahmed, Sara. 2004. "Affective economies". *Social Text* 79. 22.2: 117–139.
Albán, Adolfo. 2009. "Artistas Indígenas y Afrocolombianos: Entre las Memorias y las Cosmovisiones. Estéticas de la Re-Existencia." In *Arte y Estética en la Encrucijada Descolonial*, edited by Zulma Palermo, 83–112. Buenos Aires: Del Siglo.
Arendt, Hanna. 1972. *Crises of the Republic; lying in politics, civil disobedience on violence, thoughts on politics, and revolution*. San Diego: Harcourt Brace Jovanovich.
Berlet, Chip, ed. 2019. *Trumping Democracy: from Reagan to the Alt-Right*. London: Routledge.
Castro-Gómez, Santiago. 2007. "The Missing Chapter of Empire: Postmodern Reorganization of Coloniality and Post-Fordist Capitalism". *Cultural Studies*. 21. 2–3: 428–448.
Dussel, Enrique. 1996. *The Underside of Modernity: Apel, Ricoeur, Rorty, Taylor, and the Philosophy of Liberation*. New York: Humanity.
Çalışkan, Gül and Preston, Kayla. 2017. "Tropes of fear and the crisis of the west: Trumpism as a discourse of post-territorial coloniality". *Postcolonial Studies* 20. 2: 199–216.
Escobar, Arturo. 2018. *Design for the Pluriverse*. Durham and London: Duke University Press.
Fry, Tony. 2011. *Design as Politics*. Oxford, New York: Berg.
Fry, Tony. 2017. "Design for/by 'the Global South'." *Design Philosophy Papers* 15.1: 3–37.
Fukuyama, Francis. 1992. *The End of History and the Last Man*. New York: Free Press.
Glissant, Edouard. 1997. *Poetics of Relation*. Ann Arbor: University of Michigan Press.
Gordon, Jane Anne, and Lewis R. Gordon. 2010. *Of Divine Warning. Reading Disaster in the Modern Age*. Boulder: Paradigm Publishers.
Gordon, Lewis and Madina Tlostanova. 2018. "Interview." *Colta.ru*. November 22. https://www.colta.ru/articles/society/19794-luis-gordon-vysokomernoe-zabluzhdenie-vseh-imperiy-v-tom-chto-oni-otkryvayut-dveri-v-odnu-storonu
Haraway, Donna. 1998. "Situated Knowledges: The Science Question in Feminism and the Privilege of Partial Perspectives". *Feminist Studies* 14.3: 575–599.
Hawley, George. 2017. *Making Sense of the Alt-Right*. New York: Columbia University Press.
Illing, Sean. 2018. "A philosopher explains America's "post-truth" problem". *Vox*, 14 August. https://www.vox.com/2018/8/14/17661430/trump-post-truth-politics-philosophy-simon-blackburn
Iveković, Rada. 2015. *Les Citoyens Manquants*. Paris: Al Dante.

Klein, Naomi. 2017. *No is not Enough*. London: Penguin Books.
Klein, Naomi. 2020. "Coronavirus Capitalism": Naomi Klein's Case for Transformative Change amid Coronavirus Pandemic." *Democracy Now. Independent Global News*. https://www.democracynow.org/2020/3/19/naomi_klein_coronavirus_capitalism
Krastev, Ivan. 2017. *After Europe*. Philadelphia PA: University of Pennsylvania Press.
Krastev, Ivan. 2020. "Seven early lessons from the coronavirus." March 18. *European Council of Foreign Relations*. https://www.ecfr.eu/article/commentary_seven_early_lessons_from_the_coronavirus
Lugones, María. 2003. *Pilgrimages/Peregrinajes. Theorizing Coalition against Multiple Oppression*. New York and Oxford: Rowman and Littlefield Publishers.
Macy, Joanna. 2007. *World as Lover, World as Self. Courage for Global Justice and Ecological Renewal*. Berkeley: Paralax.
Mering, Sabine von and Timothy W. McCarty, eds. 2013. Right-Wing Radicalism Today: Perspectives from Europe and the US. London: Routledge.
Mignolo, Walter. 2000. "Coloniality at Large: Time and the Colonial Difference." In *Time in the Making and Possible Futures,* edited by Enrique R. Laretta, 237–272. Rio de Janeiro: Unesco-ISSC-Educam.
Mignolo, Walter. 2013."Geopolitics of sensing and knowing: On (de)coloniality, border thinking, and epistemic disobedience." *Confero,* 1.1: 129–150
Nancy, Jean-Luc. 2020. "Communovirus." 27 March. *Verso*. https://www.versobooks.com/blogs/4626-communovirus
Nishitani, Osamu. 2006. "Anthropos and Humanitas: Two Western Concepts of Human Being", *Translation, Biopolitics, Colonial Difference*, edited by Naoki Sakai and John Solomon, 259–273. Hong Kong: Hong Kong University Press.
Pocheptsov, Georgy. 2020. "Strakhi kak dvizhuschaja sila nashego mira, osobeeno v period koronavirusa" (Fear as an impetus of our world, particularly in the time of coronavirus). *Rezonans*. 19 March. https://rezonans.kz/strahi-kak-dvizhushyaya-sila-nashego-mira/
Quijano, Anibal. 1992. "Colonialidad y modernidad/racionalidad". *Peru Indigena* 13.29: 11–20.
Quijano, Anibal. 2000. "Coloniality of Power, Eurocentrism, and Latin America". *Nepantla: Views from South* 1.3: 553–580.
Sharma, Kriti. 2015. *Interdependence. Biology and Beyond*. New York: Fordham University Press.
Stiglitz, Joseph. 2020. "Combat the Coronavirus Pandemic with Progressive Capitalism." *Democracy Now. Independent Global News*. https://www.democracynow.org/2020/3/19/joseph_stiglitz_says_trump_s_response
Suchland, Jennifer. 2015. *Economies of Violence: Transnational Feminism, Postsocialism, and the Politics of sex Trafficking*. Durham and London: Duke University Press.

Tlostanova, Madina. 2017. "On decolonizing design." *Design Philosophy Papers*, 15.1: 51–61.

Tlostanova, Madina. 2017a. *Postcolonialism and Postsocialism in Fiction and Art: Resistance and Re-Existence*. Cham: Palgrave Macmillan.

Tlostanova, Madina. 2018. *What Does It Mean to Be Post-Soviet? Decolonial Art from the Ruins of the Soviet Empire*. Durham and London: Duke University Press.

Tlostanova, Madina, and Walter Mignolo. 2012. *Learning to Unlearn. Decolonial Reflections from Eurasia and the Americas*. Columbus: Ohio State University Press.

Toplin, Robert Brent. 2006. *Radical Conservatism. The Right's Political Religion*. Lawrence: University Press of Kansas.

CHAPTER 2

Moderating Conservatism and Radicalism in Post-colonial Sub-Saharan Africa: Some Objections and Clarifications through Conversational Thinking

Maduka Enyimba

1   Introduction

My aim in this chapter is to show that political landscape of post-colonial (contemporary) Africa is marked with numerous cases of instability as a result of the negative polarizing effects of conservatism and radicalism. My argument is that a close scrutiny of these two opposed ideologies reveals, that they are not inherently flawed and they share a common ground upon which they can harmoniously interact. I contend that through the application of the method of conversationalism towards moderation, the positive elements of both political ideologies can be harnessed for the improvement of the present state of African politics. The method of conversationalism entails a formal, willful, critical, creative and procedural engagement between two epistemic agents with the purpose of creating room for further engagement towards the development of new ideas.

Conservatism as a political and social philosophy promotes the maintenance of existing traditional order and institutions. It is a political attitude that opposes any move towards changing the status quo. This is opposed to radicalism which is a political theory and attitude that advocates change and altering of existing social and political structures and values in a revolutionary manner.[1] In recent times, Sub-Saharan Africa has seen numerous social crises, political upheavals and economic instability among other challenges, due to the polarizing effects of conservatism and radicalism. Most countries in Sub-Saharan Africa, for instance, tend to move from one form of conservatism or radicalism to another. This appears very unhealthy if there must be some form of stability in the socio-political and economic conditions of Sub-Saharan Africa.

I begin by clarifying the nature of conservatism and radicalism in order to make clear the sense in which they are used. Secondly, I make an exposition of

---

1   Utley (1989, 87), Clark (1989, 17), Gadamar (1989), Alexander (2015, 989), Baradat (1994).

the nature of the socio-political conditions of Sub-Saharan Africa. Following this, I articulate the dynamics of conversational thinking with which I attempt to moderate between radicalism and conservatism for a peaceful socio-political system.

2 Conceptualizing the Debate on Conservatism and Radicalism

According to Michael Oakeshott, conservatism is a political disposition which prefers the familiar to the unknown, the actual to the possible, the limited to the unbounded, the near to the distant, the convenient to the perfect.[2] Oakeshott's conception of conservatism is another way of saying that it is an attitude that takes delight in the maintenance of existing status quo in a manner that does not create room for change of beliefs or traditional institutions. Stove puts it this way: 'Conservatism argues that there is no obligation to change the world because human imperfection, on the one hand and unforeseen circumstances on the other, make it impossible to know that any change will be for the better.[3]

In other words, man's imperfection and inability to foresee the future cannot guarantee that any envisaged change will be better than the present state, hence, if anything must change, it should be in terms of the considered judgments of the past, for the reason that we cannot depend on our experience. Thus conservatism is backward looking, in that it looks towards the very traditions and structures which radicalism puts into question. This is so because conservatism does not seek liberation from tradition, rather it has a criterion which is an extension of the original criteria, but which is extended so far that it appears to require the restoration of a traditional order.

Karen Stenner[4] identifies three kinds of conservatism, namely "status quo conservatism", "Laissez-faire conservatism" and "authoritarianism". According to her, status quo conservatism consists of an enduring inclination to favour stability and preservation of the status quo over social change. Authoritarianism constitutes an enduring predisposition in all matters political and social to favour obedience and conformity over freedom and difference. Laissez-faire conservatism constitutes a persistent preference for a free market and limited government intervention in the economy. Despite the distinctions Karen Stenner attempts to establish among these forms of conservatism, I think that they

---

2 Oakeshott (1991, 87).
3 Stove (2003, 171).
4 Stenner (2009, 142).

are underlined by one basic principle, namely resistance to change, and this is what makes it possible to describe them as forms of conservatism, irrespective of their minor differences as shown by Karen Stenner.[5]

Similarly, J. W. Miller argues against the view that conservatism cannot be analyzed as a coherent political ideology. He proposes a multi-dimensional approach to understanding conservatism, in which case he distinguishes sociological, methodological, dispositional and philosophical conservatism. He adds that only if two of these four dimensions are present in a particular variety of political thought, then could it be justified to speak of political conservatism. Again, it must be noted that there is no significant difference between and among these shades of conservatism. They are, in my thinking, reflections of the numerous features of conservatism. The point I am making is that no matter the dimension of conservatism in focus, conservatism generally is an attitude, a disposition or an orientation that does not favour fundamental changes of existing structures, statutes or values even though there may be differences in the degree of disfavour.

One must recognize the fact that conservatism whether it is conceived as a political or intellectual attitude, orientation, disposition or an ideology, exercises caution in decision making and therefore places emphasis on order, obedience and tradition.[6] Thus, conservatives are supporters of the status quo not because they do not desire a better state of affairs, but rather because they believe it is the best that can be achieved at the moment. Hence, by conservatism in this work, I refer to a socio-political or intellectual orientation that prefers to defend the system from those who threaten to destroy it.[7] Conservatism is most times described as the "right-wing" political ideology.

Giddens describes radical politics as the breaking away from the holds of the past while simultaneously bringing and controlling such change. Giddens' definition points to a key notion central to the idea of radicalism, and that is the notion of change. Radical movements of any shade often demands for progressive change of the status quo, which is what I believe Giddens implies with the clause "breaking away from the holds of the past".[8] In a similar sense Monica B. Gabriela[9] defines radicalism as an advocacy of and commitment to bringing about a sweeping social, political or religious change and a total,

---

5   Ibid, 144.
6   Hoa (2001), Hirsh,Walberg and Peterson (2013, 14–20), Robinson, Cassidy, Boyd and Fetterman (2015, 391).
7   Giddens (1994, 1).
8   Giddens (1994, 1)
9   Gabriela (2015, 34).

political and social transformation. The implication of Monica's conception of radicalism is the suggestion that, radicalism can be a legitimate challenge of the established norms or policies of a society.

What is evident here is the understanding that radicalism, radical movement, radical politics or whatever name by which it is represented by scholars is determinative in its demand for change of existing social, political, economic, religious, status quo and the transformation of traditional values, institutions and structures. This fact is evident in the works of scholars like Justyna and Anna, Boucher and Carter.[10] In general, one can describe radicalism or a radical as a person who is extremely dissatisfied with the society as it is and therefore is impatient with less than extreme proposals for changing it. As Baradat observes, all radicals would favour an immediate and fundamental change in the society. In fact, all radicals and therefore radicalism favour revolutionary change.[11] Hence, it must be noted that the criteria that distinguish one form of radical or radicalism from another are mainly the methods they would use to bring about a particular change.

3   The Nature of Sub-Saharan African Political Landscape

Sub-Saharan African represents countries of predominantly black indigenous population that are not often considered within the geographical ambit of North Africa which is considered a part of Arab world. Post colonial African politics has been characterized by numerous crises such as civil strife, civil wars, ethnic sentiments, socio-economic instability, and unreliable electoral processes.[12] These problems are further aggravated by poor political culture emanating from the polarizing effects of conservatism and radicalism. This is so because adherents of conservatism and radicalism as forms of political culture seem to be unduly opposed to each other in such a manner that seems to fuel some of the crises mentioned above.

Hassan Mudane giving an account of African political thought, states that African political theories and ideologies enumerated in the speeches, autobiographies, writings and policy statements of African statesmen and scholars vary according to historical circumstances and constantly changing African and world political environments.[13] According to him, African nationalism

---

10   Justyna and Anna (2014, 14), Boucher (2016, 26), Carter (2018,14).
11   Baradat (1994, 16–17).
12   Nnoli (1986, 129), Ake (1995, 26), Okereke (1998, 217–222).
13   Mudane (2018,5).

advocates African development through African personality, history and culture. This is closely related to Pan Africanism which is a political and cultural movement. It is aimed at regrouping and mobilizing Africans in Africa and in Diaspora against foreign dominion and oppression. Both political ideologies (African nationalism and Pan Africanism) are forms of conservatism, proponents of which include E. W. Blyden, J. E. C. Hayford, W. E. B. Dubois, Marcus Garvey, L. S. Senghor and a host of others.

A radical form of African nationalism is African socialism, which is a rejection of capitalism as alien to African culture and traditions. It is based on the African tradition of communalism, according to which the group takes precedence over the individual. The socialist model of development includes a state-led development strategy based on planning, land reform, industrialization and the nationalization of the economy.[14] African countries who adopted socialist ideologies include Algeria, led by Ahmed Ben Bella, Ghana led by Kwame Nkrumah, Guinea led by Ahmed Sekou Toure, Mali led by Modibo Keita and Tanzania led by Julius Nyerere. This took place between 1960 and 1970.[15]

Following Hassan's analyses, one can observe that, a more radical movement based on African theory of revolution emerged later on this period. According to Frantz Fanon[16] one of the proponents of the theory of an African revolution, the peasantry is a revolutionary force in Africa under the guidance of revolutionary intellectuals. He argues that it is only through violence that the colonized people can achieve their freedom. Decolonization was thus, seen as a violent revolution that destroys the social and political structures of the colonial regime, liberates consciously and creates a new man. Adherents of the radical ideology were so violent in the pursuit of political or economic emancipation. Amilcar Cabral[17] believes that foreign domination must be totally eliminated, but he suggests that culture serves as a better weapon in the hands of the people to eliminate oppression. This period also witnessed a lot of violent military interventions in most African counties in Sub-Saharan African.

In the early 1980's African populism – a political approach that strives to appeal to ordinary people, who feel that their concerns are disregarded by established elite groups, appeared borrowing elements of both African socialism and Marxism-Leninism. African populism places the people at the centre of democracy and development in Africa. Its main policy is to satisfy the basic needs of the peasantry. African populist regimes advocate popular democracy

---

14 Ibid, 6.
15 Ibid.
16 Fanon (1968).
17 Cabral (1972).

and people-centered development. Such regimes include Thomas Sankara's Burkina Faso, Jerry Rawling's Ghana, Muammer Gaddafi's, Libya and Robert Mugabe's Zimbabwe, some of which eventually became tyrannical. These historical events suggest the idea that there might be different theories of democracy, some of which are conservative in orientation and some of which are radical.[18]

Mudane has identified three African scholars, namely, Claude Ake, Daniel Tetteh Osabu-kle and Mueni Wa Muiu, who have recently developed people-centered theories of democracy and development.[19] He notes that Ake advocates popular development in which people are the end, agent and means of development and popular democracy which emphasizes political, social and economic right. According to Hassan, David Osabu-ke argues from the assumption that indigenous African political culture was essentially democratic and consensual, based on the accountability of the rulers to the people, such that only a democracy compatible with the African cultural environment is capable of achieving the political conditions for successful development in Africa.

It is my submission that these movements from one political ideology to another in the socio-economic history of sub-Saharan African states reflect one form of conservatism and radicalism or the other. These movements further reflect attempts by adherents of these ideologies to engender one form of progress and development or the other in the society. The only seeming problem is their different approaches and orientations. It is therefore, their inability to moderate these differences on the platform of their similarity or common goal that continually elicit crisis and instability. I shall attempt in subsequent sections to show that the application of conversational thinking to these varied ideological orientations is what is needed to moderate between conservatives and radicals in a manner that will broker harmony, peace and socio-political stability in sub-Saharan Africa.

4   Conversational Thinking

Conservational thinking is the reasoning pattern that underlines conversational philosophy. Conversational philosophy articulated by Jonathan Chimakonam thrives on rigorous and rational questioning or inquiry that gives room for continuous development of ideas or knowledge. It is thus distinguishable from mere exchange of ideas or mere dialogue. The method of conversational

---

18 Mudane (2018, 6).
19 Ibid, 7.

philosophizing is conversationalism which as construed by Chimakonam presupposes a critical, creative and complimentary relationship existing between two or more epistemic agents.[20] Conversational thinking is thus, a formal, willful, critical, creative and procedural engagement between two epistemic agents known as *Nwansa (proponent)* and *Nwanju (opponent)* with the purpose of creating room for further and continuous engagement towards the development of new ideas and knowledge.

According to Chimakonam[21] Conversational thinking is very distinguishable from Socratic dialectics in that while Socratic dialectics can be said to be dogmatic as it absolutizes a given position over its negation for a period of time and when new evidences are available, dethrones the original position and absolutizes the opposite over another period of time pending the availability of new evidences; conversational thinking applies more caution. Both proponent (*Nwansa*) and opponent (*Nwanju*) are more discreet in their interaction with each other, such that their awareness of the possibility of new evidence or alternatives presenting themselves, makes them to be concerned more with sustenance of their relationship by the suspension of judgment on each other. That is by refusing to absolutize or dogmatize their different positions. In other words, while the aim of the Socratic Method is to debunk a view and present an alternative, the conversational method seeks to reconstruct both positions via intellectual struggle and contestation. This suggests that conservational relationship is a continuous relationship that may not seek a synthesis or an end, but thrives on rigorous questioning and answering.

Conversationalist scholars like Mesembe Edet,[22] Nweke Victor[23] and Diana-Abasi Ibanga[24] have in their different works shown how conversational thinking through its method of conversationalism enhances continuous and progressive contestations and protestations and therefore better relationship between and among epistemic agents and variables known as *Nwansa (proponent) and Nwanju (opponent)*. Chimakonam argues that the result of such contestations and protestations on the veracity of thoughts and ideas these epistemic or philosophical variables opens a new vista into the Global Expansion of Thought (GET). The essence of GET as articulated by Chimakonam is to sustain conversation among world philosophies, to demonstrate that two different philosophical visions on the same issue could be tenable and possible, to demonstrate the possibility of a new synthesis from two or more rival

---

20 Chimakonam (2017ª, 15, 2017ᵇ, 116, 2015ª, 15).
21 Chimakonam (2017b, 16)
22 Edet (2017).
23 Nweke (2015).
24 Ibanga (2017, 79).

visions, to demonstrate that no synthesis is sacrosanct and that every synthesis is a new vista from which new questions can emerge to sustain the conversation, and above all, to demonstrate that a synthesis is not even the main target of dialectical conversations, but the unveiling of new thoughts and concepts from old ones.[25]

It is important to note at this point, that, there are two major pillars of conversational philosophizing without which the edifice of conservational philosophizing may neither thrive nor be sustained. These two pillars for me are the two epistemic agents designated as *Nwansa* (proponent) or *Nwanju* (opponent). Their willful creative, critical and continuous interactive engagement is very fundamental to any conservational thought pattern. Thus, there is no conversational thinking or philosophizing devoid of *Nwansa* and *Nwanju* relationship. For instance, *Nwansa* and *Nwanju* are very fundamental operational variables in the attainment of the goals of Global Expansion of Thought (GET). The idea of Global expansion of thought as articulated by Chimakonam embodies the intellectual drive towards a point where all philosophical traditions move from their particular philosophical places to a universal philosophical space where they continue their interactions in a conversational, continuous and sustainable manner.

Nwansa and *Nwanju* are mutually dependent on each other in any conversational proceedings. Conversational thinking presents *Nwansa* and *Nwanju* as very significant one to the other, such that without *Nwansa*, there is no *Nwanju* and, without *Nwansa* and *Nwanju* there is no conversational thinking, and no Global Expansion of Thought.[26] Thus, conversational philosophizing thrives on a mutually complementary relationship, which is itself constitutive of two or more agents or an interactive engagement of exchange of ideas or views through re-examination of each other's positions in a manner that is sustained for a long time. In what follows, I shall show that this fact about conversational philosophy through the *Nwansa* and *Nwanju* engagement is what can bridge the gap between radicalism and conservatism and hence douse their polarizing effects on sub-Saharan political landscape.

5   Conservatism, Radicalism and Conservational Thinking

My task in this section is to show the characteristics, aims and approaches of both conservatives and radicals in any political set up, based on which I shall

---

25 Chimakonam (2015[b], 413).
26 Enyimba (2019, 18).

argue that both of these groups aim at the development of the society though from different perspectives. I contend that their differences can be moderated through the instrumentality of conversational thinking, since both strive towards some form of change. Furthermore, following the fact that no particular position is sacrosanct nor absolute, neither conservatism nor radicalism on its own can present sub-Saharan Africa with the right political set up that will ensure peace and stability, but a harnessing of the positive aspects of both ideologies.

Conservatism is inclined to hold onto what it has rather than seek what it does not have because of the belief that it owes a debt to both the living and the dead.[27] Conservatives resist change and argue that if we must change anything, it should be in terms of the considered judgments of the past, for the reason that we cannot depend on our own experience. What should be noted here is that, conservatives' resistance to change is not rigid rather; it is concessionary in the sense that it accepts the necessity of change provided only that such change is also a continuity of the past and tradition.[28] Simply put, conservatives advocate for a restoration of traditional order because of their scepticism over the possibility of a change that will be better than the status quo and not worse. Thus, instead of total transformation, conservatives call for total restoration.

Conservatism is also said to be characterized by cautiousness or what, Hao, Li describes as "over cautiousness". According to Hao, conservative attitude reflects concern for the adverse effects of implementing new ideas with unknown future consequences, hence the need for caution. Hao, thus, equates caution with conservatism.[29] What is again evident in Hao's proposition is that while conservatism resists change of traditional order, it does so as a matter of caution in order not to create future problems through the desired change. It is this line of thought that probably informs the view that religious individuals tend to be more conservative as they place more emphasis on order, obedience and tradition. Conservatives are said to favour certainty and to value tradition by focusing on the past unlike the radicals who favour change despite its uncertainty by focusing on the future. L. P. Baradat also lends emphasis on this character of conservatives.[30]

Generally opposed to conservatism, radicalism is characterized with extreme dissatisfaction with the way society is and as such makes extreme proposals for its change. In other words, unlike conservatives, radicals demand immediate,

---

27 Burke (1999, 193).
28 Utley (1989, 87), Scruton (1984, 11,) Clark (1989, 17), Gadamer (1989), Stove (2003).
29 Hao (2001, 618).
30 Baradat (1994, 21).

fundamental and revolutionary change in the society. Radicalism and of course radicals make the establishment, uncomfortable, they challenge the most cherished values and assumption of society. They reject the institutions of the establishment, calling for a more humane, egalitarian and idealistic social and political system. Radicals' contempt for society's values is so complete, their remedies so unorthodox that they are feared with intensity far beyond what is necessary to deal adequately with the challenges they pose.[31]

This is one of the major reasons why radicalism and radicals are branded extremists and violent and hence condemned entirely by most political analysts. The truth however is that radicalism does not necessarily imply extremism and violence. It is only a demonstration of frustration with the state of things in the polity and a demand for immediate social transformation and progressive change. Radicals settle for nothing less than their desired goals. This is the basic differences I think, exist between conservatism and radicalism. Conservatives may not be comfortable with the state of things in the polity and may desire change but are not ready for immediate, transforrmatory and progressive change for the fear that it may give birth to a worse situation. Hence, they advocate for a cautious change through gradual restructuring, amendment and maintenance or preservation of the existing order.

It is these differences that create conflicts and crisis between and among groups and individuals who are adherents to any of these political orientations, and further create social upheavals, and political instability in post-colonial Sub-Saharan African states. However, a cursory look will show that both radicals and conservatives have good intentions for the society. Both are uncomfortable with the state of affairs. Both desire a better condition and state of affairs and are therefore willing or open to some of change. The only difference is the degree of their willingness or openness to the much desired change. While conservatives are retrospective in their pursuit after change, radicals are progressive and revolutionary.

It is at this point that conversational thinking through the interactive relationship between *Nwansa* and *Nwanju* can create a symbiotic and convivial atmosphere that can moderate the conflict between radicals and conservatives and as such create room for social and political stability in Sub-Saharan African politics. Following conversational proceedings, *Nwansa* and *Nwanj*u as the two basic epistemic variables do not aim at synthesis or confluence whereby both would dissolve into each other in order to achieve an end. Rather, *Nwansa* and *Nwanju* maintain their respective peculiarity while interacting progressively with each other. The purpose is not to come to an agreement or a synthesis,

---

31 Ibid, 18.

rather to create a convivial atmosphere that will warrant peaceful, harmonious interaction or relationship that will lead continually to new ideas, knowledge and further development in the society.

On the basis of the above, conservatives can take up the place of *Nwansa* whereas radicals can take up the position of *Nwanju* as they proceed in a conversational exchange that will create room for continuous co-existence and for peace. It must be borne in mind from the onset that as variables, *Nwanju* and *Nwansa* does not each maintain permanent position; hence, they are not static. As a result, conservatives as *Nwansa* and radicals as *Nwanju* are not static but are open to adjustments of their positions and convictions so as to give room for mutual co-existence. What I am saying here is that the relationship between conservatives and radicals should be a form of *Nwansa* and *Nwanju* relationship. As variables *Nwansa* (conservatives) and *Nwanju* (radicals) can interchange their positions depending on the context and progression of their relationship. Thus, conservatives can become *Nwanju* and radicals can be *Nwansa* as they progress in their conversational interaction. This is very possible through a genuine attempt by each party to wear the other's lenses and to see things from the other's perspective. My contention is that, the nature of the interaction between *Nwansa* and *Nwanju* is what is needed for the moderation between conservatives and radicals and to further bridge their polarizing effects on sub-Saharan African political set up.

Thus, just as in conversational order, *Nwansa* and *Nwanju* do not disregard or exclude each other as unimportant in the development process, so also should the political variables initiated as conservatives (*Nwansa*) and radicals (*Nwanju*), not exclude or disregard each other in the strive towards socio-political growth. This is what will lead to a moderation of the differences between conservatives and radicals in order to create room for political stability. Again, just as *Nwansa* makes *Nwanju* significant and *Nwanju* makes *Nwansa* significant in the conversational processes so should conservatives and radicals as *Nwansa* and *Nwanju* respectively and as political variables make each other significant in the process towards political stability. The point here is that, opposites make each other relevant. For instance, an appreciation of the meaning and significance of the good, is in juxtaposition with the meaning and significance of the bad. White and black make each other significant, so it is with male and female, matter and spirit, cause and effect etc.

It is in this sense that conversational thinking through its *Nwansa-Nwanju* inter-relationship enables each other's significant roles to be seen. This makes it possible for the virtues of both radicalism and conservatism to be harnessed for the benefit of the society. Without conservatives and their opposing posture, the relevance or otherwise of the radicals will not be unveiled. The same is applicable to radicals in relation to conservatives. Neither conservatives nor radicals on its own can present sub-Saharan African states with a stable, economy and socio-political state. This is based on the fact that in conversational thinking, there is no *Nwansa* without *Nwanju* and there is no *Nwanju* without *Nwansa*. Without *Nwansa* and *Nwanju* there is no conversational philosophizing, no conversationalism and no Global expansion of thought. Thus, without conversational interaction between conservatives and radicals, there will be no moderation and without moderation between conservative and radicals through *Nwansa-Nwanju* interaction in a conversational order, there will be no stability where there has been the polarizing effects of these two ideologies.

6 Conclusion

I have argued that conservatism and radicalism are not too completely opposed political ideologies that are irreconcilable. There is a common ground upon which both ideologies and their adherents can co-operate peacefully and harmoniously for a stable society. I claimed that sub-Saharan Africa experiences political crises and numerous conflicts as a result of the practice of different forms of conservatism and radicalism. My submission is that, given the background of the political crises and the historical circumstances of Sub-Saharan Africa, conservatives and radicals of different shades can be moderated on the platform of their similarities through conservational thinking.

References

Ake, C. 1995. "Democracy and Leadership in Africa." *Cooperate,* October.
Anita, Powell. 2016. "The World According to Julius: South Africa's Most Radical Politician Speaks". *Voice of Africa (v.o.a) News.*
Baradat, Leon P. 1994. *Political Ideologies: Their Origins and Impact.* London: Prentice Hall International.
Burke, E. 1999. *Reflections on the Revolution in France.* Indianapolis, IN: Liberty Fund.
Cabral, Amilcar. 1972. *Revolution in Guinea.* New York: Monthly Review Press.
Chimakonam, Jonathan O. 2015a. "Conversational Philosophy as a New School of Thought in African Philosophy: A Conversation with Bruce Janz on the Conceptof Philosophical
Space". *Confluence: Online Journal of World Philosophies.* 3.9–40.
Chimakonam, Jonathan O. 2015b "Transforming the African Philosophical Place through Conversations: An Inquiry into the Global Expansion of Thought (GET)". *South African Journal of Philosophy.* 34. 4. 41–479.

Chimakonam, Jonathan O. 2017a. "Conversationalism as an Emerging Method of Thinking in and Beyond African Philosophy". *Acta Academica*. 49. 2. 11–33.

Chimakonam, Jonathan O. 2017b. "What is Conversational Philosophy?: A Prescription of a New Theory and Method of philosophizing in and Beyond African Philosophy". *Phronimon*. 18. 115–130.

Clark, S. R. L. 1989. "Reason, Value, Tradition" *Civil Peace and Sacred Order: Limits and Renewals*. Ed. Clark SRL. Oxford: Clarinda Press. 1–26.

Boucher, David. 2016. "Radical Ideologies and the Sociology of Knowledge: A Model for Comparative Analysis" from the *SAGE Social Science Collection*.

Ibanga, Diana-Abasi. 2007. "Philosophical Sagacity as Conversational Philosophy and its Significance for the Question of Method in African Philosophy". *Fiosofia Theoretica: Journal of African Philosophy, Culture and Religions*. 6.1. 69–89.

Edet, Mesembe. 2007. Afroxiology, Conceptual Mandelanizaton and the Conversational Order in the New Era of Africa\n Philosophy with Conversations from Members of CSP, Calabar: 3rd African Publishing.

Carter, Elizabeth. 2018. "Right-Wing Extremism/Radicalism: Reconstructing the Concept". *Journal of Political Ideologies*. 1–26.

Enyimba, Maduka. 2019. "Sustainable Inclusive Development through Conservational Thinking: The Case for Africa-China Relations". *Filosofia Theoretica: Journal of African Philosophy, Religion and Culture*. 8.1.1–20.

Fanon, Frantz. 1968. *The Wretched of the Earth*. New York: Grove.

Gabriela B. Monika, 2013. "50 Shades of Radicalism: An Analysis of Contemporary Radical Parties in Europe". *Interdisciplinary Political and Cultural Journal*. 17. 1. 27–41.

Gadamer, H. G. 1989. *Truth and Method*. New York: Continuum.

Giddens, A. 1994. *Beyond Left and Right: The Future of Radical Politics*. Cambridge Oxford: Polity Press.

Hao, Li 2001. "A Theory of Conservatism". *Journal of Political Economy*. 109. 3., 617 – 636.

Mudane, Hassan. 2018. "African Political Thought in a Nutshell". *Encyclopedia of Political Science*. Ed. George Thomas K. www. Researchgate.net/publication/323388382, 25th February.

Hirsh, Jacob B, Walberg, Megan, D. and Peterson, J. B. 2013. "Spiritual Liberals and Religious Conservatives". *Social Psychological and Personality Science*. 4.1.14 20.

James, Alexander. 2015. "The Major Ideologies of Liberalism, Socialism and Conservatism". *Political Studies*. 63. 980–994.

Justyna, M. and Anna, T. 2014. "The Radicalism of the Enlightenment: An Introduction to the Special Edition". *Diametros* 40. 1–4.

Michael, Oakeshott. 1991. "On Being Conservative". *Rationalism in Politics and other Essays*. Ed. Michael O. Indianapolis: IN Liberty Fund. 407–437.

Michael, Robinson D. Cassidy Deurdre M, Boyd, Ryan, L. and Fetterman, Adam K. 2015. "The Politics of Time: Conservatives Differentially Reference the past and Liberals Differentially Reference the Future". *Journal of Applied Social Psychology*. 45.391–399.

Muller, Jan-Werner. 2006. "Comprehending Conservatism: A New Framework for Analysis. *Journal of Political Ideologies*. 11, (3), 339 – 365.

Nnoli, O. 1986. *Introduction to Politics*. England: Longman.

Nweke, Victor C. A. 2005. "Postmodernism and the Objectivity of the Social Science: An Interrogative Conversation with Augustine Atagbor". *Filosofia Theoretica: Journal of African Philosophy, Culture and Religions*. 7.1. 71–81.

Okereke, O. O. 1998. "Succession to Power in Africa". *African Politics*. Eds. Emezi, C. E. and Ndoh, C. A. Owerri: Achugo Publications. 217–222.

Scruton, R. 1984. "The Meaning of Conservatism" *On Enlightenment*. Ed. Stove D. London: Transaction. 171–178.

Stenner, Karen. 2009. "Three Kinds of Conservatism". *Psychological Injury: An International Journal for the Advancement of Psychological Theory*. 20. 2–3. 142 – 159.

Stove, D. 2003. "Why Should I be Conservative?" Stove, D. *On Enlightenment*. London: Transaction. 171–8.

Utley, T. E. 1989. *A Tory Seer: The Selected Journalism* of T. E. Utley. London: Hamish Hamilton.

CHAPTER 3

Politics of the Countryside after Zimbabwe's Land Reform Programme: Expectations and Demands of the Youth

Clement Chipenda

1 Introduction

In 2000, Zimbabwe officially undertook a state sanctioned land reform programme, which has now become known as the fast track land reform programme (FTLRP). The FTLRP was radical and unprecedented and was a third attempt at land reform, after two previous attempts had not been successful, only managing to resettle 70 000 households on 3.4 million hectares of land in almost two decades against a target of 182 000 set in 1982 (Moyo 1995, 2013; Bhatasara and Hellicker 2018). In over a decade, the FTLRP saw 180 000 families being resettled on 13 million hectares of land (Moyo 2013). The reforms were necessitated by the need to reverse a racially skewed land tenure system which the country had inherited in 1980, which was titled against the black majority. Due to the magnitude of the FTLRP, for years it attracted much academic interest and scrutiny. Consequently, there emerged a divisive and polemical debate which polarised academia for over a decade. The programme was criticised for being captured by the political and business elite, exercised through nepotism and corruption. It was also accused of causing food insecurity, industrial decline, environmental degradation and economic collapse. Human rights abuses and the undermining of property rights as enshrined in the constitution were also seen as being caused by the 'chaotic' FTLRP (see Alexander 2006; Richardson 2005). The polemical debates on the FTLRP saw theories of neo-patrimonialism being used to conceptually understand how the programme had been carried out and its immediate impact. The overall impression which came from this analysis was that the claim that the FTLRP had mainly benefitted the clients of the ruling party ZANU (PF), but these have been contested (Moyo and Chambati 2013; Scoones et al 2015). Over the past few years there has been witnessed a change in focus on the scholarship of the FTLRP. Academics have gradually moved from this polemical debate to focus on the outcomes of the programme. The change in direction was necessitated by pleas from Cliff et al (2011) and Scoones et al (2011) for scholars to move beyond this debate and focus on land reform outcomes.

From the FTLRP, there are a lot of important insights that can be gained on agrarian transformations and land reform in post-settler colonies. Despite the contestations that surrounded the programme, what remains clear which scholars concur is that the FTLRP was unprecedented and redistributive (Moyo and Chambati 2013, Scoones et al 2011). It entailed a dramatic transformation in the country's agrarian structure and a reconfiguration of the country's rural landscape especially in the former large-scale commercial farming areas (LSCFS). The reconfiguration is well documented as shown by a number of empirical studies undertaken in different parts of the country. The studies have shown that the creation of a new and diversified rural landscape has seen the fusion of people of various socio-economic, political and cultural backgrounds. This has had an interesting and diverse impact on the 'newly' created rural communities ranging from enhanced accumulation and livelihood trajectories as well as peasant differentiation among other dynamics (see Murisa 2009; Chibwana 2016; Shonhe 2017; Mkodzongi 2018; Chiweshe and Chabata 2019; Muchetu 2019).

Given the unprecedented and radical nature of the FTLRP, it is of interest in this chapter to explore the current situation of young people[1] in the farming areas and the nearby communal areas with specific focus on their expectations and demands. This is in a context where the FTLRP bequeathed prime agricultural land, farm equipment, infrastructure, natural resources and other material and non-material benefits to the previously marginalised indigenous group of people who now make up the older generation in the resettlement areas. Despite its fast track nature, the FTLRP can be seen as having provided for opportunities for 'accumulation from below' for this generation. The reconfiguration of the rural landscape was not only confined to productive activities and the social landscape, but it also extended to political reconfiguration with the politics of these farming areas playing a role in determining the livelihood trajectories of the youth.

This chapter thus interrogates three cross cutting and interrelated issues. It takes a look at the local political dynamics, the opportunities and challenges of the youth and how they are carving out diverse livelihoods in rural Zimbabwe. The chapter contends that in order to understand the situation of the rural youth in relation to how they are carving out diverse livelihoods, it is important to understand their interrelationships with local authority structures existing in the farming areas. This however needs to be understood as part of a

---

1 These are those aged between 15–35 years who according to Zimbabwean law are the youth.

historical case analysis in which the state used authoritarianism and populism as it reconfigured the rural landscape so as to maintain political control. In this study it is worth noting that firstly, the findings are relevant to the study area and cannot be generalised for the whole country, secondly the youth are a demographic that is always transitioning, but the study focused on those who were currently the youth in the study area during the study.

2   Study Area and Methodological Notes

The study was undertaken in Goromonzi District, Mashonaland East Province. The district lies in close proximity to the capital city of Harare and other urban centers like Marondera and Chitungwiza. This proximity has to some extent shaped the agricultural production activities undertaken in the district which are geared towards agricultural production for urban markets and export. The district lies in Natural Region II which is suitable intensive crop and livestock production and it accounts for 75- 80% crops produced in the country (FAO 2006). Due to the FTLRP, the district now has a tri-modal agrarian structure. An important outcome of the FTLRP was that the land tenure system transitioned from the colonially inspired bi-modal to a tri-modal agrarian structure (Moyo 2011). This tri-modal agrarian structure is characterized by a restructured social organization of labour which has three modes. There is the differentiated peasantry comprising of the communal and A1 farmers, then there are the small to medium scale farmers comprising of the A2 farmers and lastly there are the few remaining large-scale farmers, agro-estates and conservancies. These make up the tri-modal agrarian structure and they are discernible in the study area as noted by Chambati (2017) and Chipenda (2018). They point out that in Goromonzi, there can now be found 2 822 A1 farmers on 32 628 hectares of land. This land was previously owned by just 71 former LSCF. There are 846 farms in the A2 sector occupying 84 455.75 hectares of land previously owned by 51 LSCF's. Lastly, there are 16 LSCF and agro-estates which still remain.

Empirically grounded field-based evidence is critical in any academic discussion on the FTLRP, given its history and contestations. To this end the study purposively targeted 13 former large-scale commercial farms (LSCF) which have since been subdivided into smaller A1 farms to inform the study. These farms were Dunstan, Chibvuti, Warrendale, Rudolphia, Belmont, Kambeu Trust Farms, Brunton, Bains Hope, Manor Estate, Glen Avon, Xanadu, Bellevue and Mashonganyika farms. To get alternative insights and lived experiences of the youth for comparative purposes, the study targeted the three communal areas of Seke, Chinyika and Rusike.

Pragmatism was used in the study as well as the mixed methods research approach. Given the nature and complexity of the subject under investigation, a pragmatic approach was seen as suitable. Dewey (1931) notes that pragmatism is based on realist and idealist metaphysics which accepts events and things as occurring independent of any observers, but emphasis is on reason and thought as originators of elements of the external world. For Morgan (2007), pragmatism is an approach whose purpose is to determine the practical solutions and meanings which are useful for programmatic or intervention-based studies. It takes a middle position between positivist and interpretivist ontologies; hence it is labeled as constructive realism or symbolic realism (Goles and Hirschheim 2000). Due to its ability to strengthen data by combining qualitative and quantitative approaches and breaking the traditional distinction between them (see Modell 2009 and Morgan 2007), this paradigm was considered ideal. It was seen as having the advantage of allowing the researchers to have more flexibility in choosing the research instruments used and there was choice in selecting what was meaningful from either the qualitative or quantitative approaches (Shannon-Baker 2016; Tran 2016). The mixed methods approach was chosen as it allows for data to be collected in a complimentary and integrative manner (Onweugbuzie and Johnson 2006).

The study employed a multi-stage sampling method combining purposive, random and snowballing sampling techniques. A variety of data gathering tools were employed including the structured survey questionnaire, in-depth interviews, focus group discussions and observations. This was complemented by secondary data. In the farming areas, the study targeted 50 young farmers on A1 farms as well as 30 young people who are not necessarily into farming but engage in diversified land-based livelihood activities. In addition, there were 40 young people from the communal areas and of these 30 engaged in full time and part-time farming activities. Twelve respondents drawn from government departments, local government authorities, traditional leadership and local institutions participated in the study as key informants.

3 Conceptual Framework

How does one interrogate three crosscutting but interrelated issues which involve different actors with an investigation involving historical case analysis with insights from contemporary developments? This was a question in my mind as I undertook the study. An answer to this complexity was figurational sociology after Elias (1978), which I saw as an appropriate conceptual and heuristic tool to understand and analyse the political dimensions, post land reform. But what is figurational sociology? Elias (1978), notes that figurations are simply patterns of interaction between interdependent human beings who exist either as individuals or groups. In societies, there is a political environment in which individuals compete for status, power and capital. Figurations become important in understanding salient social (and oftentimes politicised) social dynamics (Munch and Veit 2018, Rocha 2003). The interdependent ties which exist in society are key in understanding figurations. The term figurations is derived from these ties which "…exist as long as actors orient their actions towards each other…(and do so) due to interdependencies that exist between them…the sum of interdependency between a pair of actors constitutes their power balance and are a major part of explaining actor behavior and the outcome of their interactions." (Munch and Veit 2018:271). Dolan (2014) notes that central to figuration sociology is the character of social relationships and the mutual dependency of individuals within the network of ties. The concept of figurational sociology was thus seen as key in understanding social and political relationships in post land reform Zimbabwe.

4   Zimbabwe's Reconfigured Rural Areas and Youth Realities Post-1999

In order to understand the emergent political dynamics which are at play in rural Zimbabwe, this chapter contends that it is important to take into perspective events and processes which occurred during the FTLRP process which influenced the emergence of institutional formations. These institutional formations are now playing important roles in the farming communities. Moyo (2000:3) argued that the FTLRP was a 'bottom up' initiative which marked the climax of a longer, less public and dispersed struggle over land shortages and land demand in the post-independence period. It is seen as having come as a result of grievances over the slow pace of land reform. This is however disputed, with Mugabe and ZANU (PF) being accused of taking advantage of the grievances of the landless and hijacking the movement of the landless people, this has been however subject to debate. While there is still this contestation, it can be argued that Mugabe being a seasoned politician saw it as an opportunity to increase his political clout which was at an all-time low. Literature is abound with different scholars arguing that Mugabe and ZANU (PF) saw the demands for land reform as an opportunity to revive their waning political fortunes. They are accused of having highjacked genuine grievances for land. In the process they managed to consolidate their grip to power which was severely under threat for the first time in two decades (see Sachikonye 2003, Rutherford 2007, Mujere, Sagiya and Fontein 2017).

In doing this Mugabe instituted a state sponsored campaign in which the media, state institutions and local authority structures were mandated with the responsibility of pushing forward the FTLRP process. At the centre of it all was the push of an ideology of pan-Africanism, anti-imperialism, anti-colonialism, nationalism and the *chimurenga* rhetoric aimed at stirring up national feeling and endearing the people to the FTLRP (Mujere *et al* 2017; Nyawo 2012). Populism became the central driving force behind the FTLRP with the farming areas becoming fiercely contested political arenas which in some instances culminated in physical violence that resulted to loss of property and lives. In some instances, productive activities on some farms were disrupted. The state media became a platform for churning out propaganda in which the state was presented ats being at war to defend the country from 'neo-colonialists'. This saw the popularization of jingles like *rambai makashinga* and others which encouraged citizens to remain resolute during the FTLRP process, amidst an onslaught from the enemies of Zimbabwe (from the West) (see Chikowero 2011). Selective citizenship, race and ethnic identities were conveniently used to label some sections of the population as outsiders (whites) while others were labelled as insiders (the indigenous people).

Whenever Mugabe and his top government officials had the opportunity, they insisted that their actions were justifiable. The FTLRP was touted as being the final stage in liberating the country, and there was need to dislodge the 'outsiders' (the white farmers) from the land as they were a symbol of colonialism (see Hammar and Raftopolous 2003). During this period, Ranger (2004) and Primorac (2005) argue that there was the emergence of a new and narrow nationalist historiography labeled 'patriotic history'. Through this historiography and 'master fiction', ZANU (PF) was seen reviving the anti-colonialist ideology in which the party used its liberation war credentials and identified itself with the masses through the use of the 'languages of the suffering' (Mujere *ibid*). For Ndlovu-Gatsheni (2009), there was the unfolding of a particular form of nationalism with those embraced as citizens in 1980 being ostracized, labeled as aliens and required to renounce dual citizenship. Nativism and the concept of sacred space were also deployed as tools to further the ideological aspect of the FTLRP process. It was highlighted on many occasions that it was the sacred duty of the indigenous people to protect their land rights and whites were supposed to be domiciled to Europe (Mlambo and Chitando 2015). War veterans, the youth and peasants, were mobilized to push forward the FTLRP agenda. In all this Mugabe's charismatic personality stood out and played a pivotal role. Government departments and state security institutions were instructed to provide all the necessary support for the FTLRP. He crushed dissent (using violence) and created a powerful alliance between traditional leaders, war veterans and the state machinery which was used to forcefully push forward an unplanned land acquisition programme despite national and international outcry (see Hammar *et al* 2003; Raftopolous and Phimster 2004).

It was against this background that there was seen to be the need for political control of the farming areas hence the adoption of local authority structures in the resettlement areas. Local forms of control through authority structures have not been new to Zimbabwe but had existed for decades. They have their origins in the colonial period where the government put in place local government structures to ensure localised and absolute control of areas where the indigenous people resided (Alexander 2006, Murisa 2018). These local forms of control continued in the post-independence period and were buttressed by several legal enactments, government policies and reforms at different historical junctures over two decades. It was due to this that there could be found a plethora of local institutional formations operating at different levels in rural Zimbabwe and examples were the rural district councils, the district administrators office, ward and village development committees, the district development committee among others (see Bratton 1986, Rahmato 1991 and Tshuma 1997).

With the FTLRP, Murisa (2009, 2018) argues that there can be found many interrelated associational formations of co-operation which exist in the new farming areas. This view is supported by Moyo *et al* (2009) and Chiweshe (2011) who see these associational formations existing on the farms. Some of them have seen A1 households co-operating in the sharing of productive and social infrastructure, they share in advice, information, farming operations and in the marketing of agricultural produce. They also co-operate in labour pooling and access to critical inputs. These associational formations operate in a context where there has been limited rolling out of social services. Some of these associational formations and local authority structures stand accused of at times playing a partisan role.

5 The Youth in Zimbabwe: A Brief Synopsis of Their Context

Like many countries in sub-saharan Africa, Zimbabwe has a young and growing youthful population. In the last national census held in 2012, it was noted that young people account for 77 percent of the population and the youth who are aged between 18–35 years are at 36 percent (ZimStat 2012). The youth in the country have not been immune to the turbulent socio-economic environment which has been witnessed in the country in the past few years. These challenges have included economic challenges (with an unprecedented hyper-inflationary environment, limited financial support and credit lines from international financial institutions), smart or targeted sanctions against the ruling elite (this has been disputed with the argument that they were targeted against the country), serious political disputes, human rights violations among other challenges (see Grebe 2010 and Makochekanwa 2009). These challenges have in different ways shaped the world view of the young people in the country. High unemployment levels in the country (whose figures are highly contested) and poverty have compounded the challenges faced by the youth.

With the socio-economic challenges facing the country, focus is being turned on agriculture as providing alternative livelihood pathways for young people. The agrarian economy is seen offering opportunities for the youth in the face of economic constraints. The statistics from the ZimStat Inter Censal Demographic Survey (2017) presents an interesting dimension that 52 percent of the economically active population is involved in agricultural activities (upstream and downstream with the task of scholars now being to locate and understand the role being played by the youth).

As the youth make up a reasonable proportion of the economically active group, it can be assumed that they represent a significant population of the economically active group of 15 years and above which makes up 69.5 percent of the population (ZimStat 2017). Important policy documents which underpin Zimbabwe's development trajectory until 2030 where it envisages it will reach middle income country status also underpin the importance of youth involvement in agriculture and it related value chains. These documents are the Transitional Stabilisation Programme and the Draft Policy on Agriculture (Ministry of Finance and Economic Development 2018b, GoZ 2018). In addition, in the 2019 Budget speech, the Zimbabwean Minister of Finance underlined the importance of the youth in agriculture, with the Ministry of Agriculture receiving the second highest budget allocation, underlining its growing importance (Ministry of Finance and Economic Development 2018a).

In the face of a challenging socio-economic environment, agriculture appears to present an alternative pathway for livelihoods but the question which remains is the extent to which young people are prepared to embrace it. It is in this context that several emerging studies aimed at understanding the impact of the FTLRP on their lived experiences and their perceptions. Some of the studies have been undertaken by Tom (2019), Chigumira (2019), Scoones (2019) and Chipenda (2019) among others. They present interesting dimensions on the rural youth post FTLRP. These studies indicate that the FTLRP has had different impact on the youth in different areas.

6 The Youth and Interactions with Local Authority Structures

> Our interactions with the Committee of 7 (Co7) and the *sabhukus* (traditional leaders) in this area are low. They interact more with those who were allocated farms and these are the people whom they mostly deal with not us. I also think that for most youth, our interactions may not be with them in their official capacities as this is a small community but we may meet at the stores, at the beerhall or dip-tanks as we are doing our different activities. In some instances, we may interact with them as they provide part time work that is when we interact.

The statement above by Koroni[2] of Chibvuti farm provided insight on the interactions between the young people in the farming areas and local institutional structures particularly the Co7[3] and the *sabhukus*.[4] It provides a view that found resonance on most of the A1 farms, that interactions between young people and members of the Co7 and *sabhukus* in their official capacities are in most instances minimal. This was the case mostly for those youth who are not landowners who indicated that there are few areas of common interest between them and the officials hence the contact is minimal. Participants in focus group discussions (FGD's) felt that this was disadvantaging them as it limited the chances of their grievances and expectations becoming known by persons of influence. In the study it was noted however that the youth who own land, have a higher rate of contact with the Co7 members and the *sabhukus* in their official capacities. The interactions which they have with these authorities were said to differ but the common ones revolved around meeting to discuss agricultural production issues and activities, land access issues, farm infrastructure maintenance, farm use among other issues. The youth who have minimal interactions with the Co7 could be seen labelling it as being an institution that was not interested in the welfare of young people who are not landowners. The youth were said not to be much of a priority to the institution.

At a focus group discussion held at Dunstan farm, one participant raised an issue which was also raised in other areas but which some participants were reluctant to discuss further given its sensitive nature. She indicated that while the Co7 purported to represent landowners and their interests, it was in fact

---

2 All names in this chapter are not the respondent's real names so as to protect their identity.
3 This is an elected committee which comprises of landowners and it has oversight over the farms.
4 On A1 farms, the model of local governance found in the communal areas was adapted to the farms and it entailed the appointment of *sabhuku's* who oversee the farms by Chiefs in areas under their jurisdiction.

more of a political organisation or part of the local political structures which usually pursued a political agenda. It was accused of being an extension of the ruling party in the farming areas and examples were given of how it canvassed for support during elections, vetted and provided lists of beneficiaries for state supported input schemes, food relief and public works programmes. If one was not 'politically correct', they said one would not benefit. The situation was not helped by the fact that most of its members on A1 farms were mostly ZANU (PF) members with some holding party positions at cell, district and provincial levels. Mateu of Rudolphia farm had supported this viewpoint adding that there was a blurred line between party activities and those of the Co7 and the *sabhuku* hence in most instances they were seized with pushing the political agenda of the party and rarely had time to look at the concerns of the younger generation. This viewpoint was also confirmed in other areas particularly in Goromonzi North where respondents in FDG's said the Co7 was an unofficial extension of ZANU PF hence it could be seen playing different roles for the party including mobilisation, selection of beneficiaries for party and government input programmes and donations.

This view by the youth was disputed by members of the Co7 in different areas who participated in in-depth interviews. They pointed that the Co7's role was not political as claimed but it focuses on administrative and developmental initiatives which involve interactions with political, civil and state institutions hence it is easy think that it is political. The main responsibilities of the Co7 was said to safeguard the interests of the farmers, ensuring that their productive capacities were enhanced, maintenance of common infrastructure and resources and their equitable use as well as ensuring social cohesion. It was also highlighted that being a member of the Co7 was a voluntary and unpaid position in which the farm volunteered their time with a long term goal of improving their wellbeing on the farms. In such a context, it did not make sense for them to depart from their core activities. The other issue which was raised was that farming communities are small, people know each other well and in most instances they are members of different voluntary associations. It is therefore not surprising to see people having multiple institutional or organisational affiliations. In addition, the farming areas by the nature of their creation are highly sensitive areas politically hence political parties and state security agencies were said to be interested in these areas for different reasons and as the Co7 and the *sabhukus* are the highest authorities at a local level from time to time they interact with these agencies. It was said to be difficult for outsiders to understand this relationship which has existed for years.

Co7 members also revealed that there was no reason for young people to complain about being ignored or excluded from the Co7 as in all committees it was mandatory for there to be a youth representative. A Secretary of one of the Co7 indicated that there is a slot which is set aside for the youth. He said that:

> Yes, we have a representative of the youth who articulates their issues and concerns. Let me point out that we know their issues and concerns in this area things like jobs, some want land for housing and some for agriculture they want skills training centres we know those things their youth representative informs us. Their role of the committee member responsible for youth is to report on any issues they may raise and to provide feedback on what we would have decided to the youth and any other issues of concern. The problem which we have is that the young people are not interested in these things, they are busy chasing after money and other things. They ignore us and communication is poor, only for them to cry foul and claim that they are being neglected but that is not the case.

The youth who participated in the focus group discussions were dismissive of their representative in the Co7's, indicating that having one was just cosmetic as they are not effective and do not represent their interests. At Dunstan farm, an example was given of one of the youth representatives who was said to be about 43 years of age. They complained that such an older person who was not a youth could not be expected to understand or articulate their desires and concerns. The other complaints were that the youth representatives were either invisible, visible but inactive or were virtually unknown even by the constituency which they were expected to represent. Having an older person as a youth representative was confirmed as happening in most Co7's and it was defended by Co7 members who were interviewed who indicated that such a position needed an older and mature person who could articulate issues without difficulty, and someone whom the Co7's would respect and listen to. Having a youth representative did not necessarily mean that the representative had to be a young person.

7 The Sabhuku's and the Youth

The study also sought from a figurational sociological perspective to understand the interdependencies and connections between actors. To this effect it looked at the interactions between the youth and the *sabhuku's* in both the farming and communal areas. The *sabhukus* indicated that there is a lot of interaction between them and the youth in their jurisdiction and beyond. The *sabhuku's* in the farming area indicated that their interactions with the youth are for both developmental and personal reasons with their role as the custodians of traditions and culture being at the centre of their relationships. A *sabhuku* at Mashonganyika farm indicated that the office which he occupies makes him interact with young people who reside in his village and beyond. In a context where the country has been witnessing economic challenges, he said in his role of having oversight over natural resources, he assists the young people to legally access and sustainably use natural resources by giving them permission to undertake some activities. This was confirmed by another *sabhuku* at Dunstan farm who said land has become scarce in the district as all the plots had been taken up. With a lot of young people looking for land to undertake agricultural activities he indicated that he allocates two acre plots to them along the Manyame and Muswiti river[5] where they usually cultivate horticultural crops as a means of livelihood. At the time of the fieldwork, there were eight young people who were cultivating on these small plots. The other *sabhukus* pointed out that in a challenging socio-economic environment they were assisting the youth to access part time employment, they assist those with tenure documents to access inputs, extension services and markets. The other important interaction is where there is violation of cultural norms and values and in cases of petty criminality or deviance. Such cases are tried at the *sabhukus* traditional courts and it is here that the *sabhuku* indicated that they meet many of the young people.

The youth had a different perspective on their interactions with the *sabhuku's*, but there were many areas of convergence. What was noted during the study was that the relationships and interactions are not homogeneous and they differ from place to place. From FGD's held, it was noted that the youth felt that the *sabhukus* interact more with their peers, the resettled farmers and not with the youth with whom they have few things in common. One participant indicated that *sabhuku's* just like the Co7's were political functionaries. They were accused of being interested in the youth when they were required to mobilise them, when there were meetings or gatherings called for by political parties, or when they wanted them to provide menial labour which was usually lowly or not paid. This observation found resonance in the communal areas particularly at Seke and Rusike where the youth accused the traditional leaders of being interested in them during times of political mobilisation or when they required their (free) labour.

---

5 This was criticized by the Lands and Agricultural Extension Officers who indicated that it was illegal for the *sabhuku* to allocate land as they do not have those powers and streambank cultivation is illegal.

8   The State, Local Authority Structures and Natural Resources

While for the youth the institutions of traditional leadership and C07 were not seen as being of importance, for the state they were said to be critical for the purposes of local governance and administration on the farms. Insights on the importance of these institutions were provided by the Lands Officer and the Agricultural Extension Officer. They indicated that one of the important outcomes of the FTLRP was that it broadened access to flora and fauna which was in abundance on the previously enclosed LSCF. This was not unique to Goromonzi but had been observed in other areas as well (see Mkodzongi 2016). Wild animals and natural, untouched woodlands were in abundance on most farms. The FTLRP had seen farming areas being opened up and wild animals being exploited for sale and for household consumption. The same had happened to the woodlands with trees being cut and exploited. A consequence of this was that there had been an unprecedented and unsustainable exploitation of natural resources. Informants said the C07 and the *sabhuku*'s were now integral local authorities in the fight against the unsustainable exploitation of common resources. The exploitation of flora and fauna in the district according to respondents was heavily politicised with the elite said to be using their influence and resources in order to access them. It was only when there was unity of local institutional structures and government agencies and departments like the Environmental Management Agency, the Departments of Natural Resources and Lands, and law enforcement agencies (mainly Neighbourhood Watch Committees) that progress was being made in the fight against unsustainable use of natural resources. The C07 and *sabhuku*'s were seen as being very active in fighting against unsustainable natural resource exploitation but there is a lot of politicisation in this area.

The *sabhukus* on farms in the southern part of Goromonzi, blamed young people from neighbouring communal areas of Seke and Chinyika for coming into the farming areas and illegally exploiting natural resources. They said that this trend was not new and had occurred over a number of years. They said that they acted in connivance with their counterparts from urban areas to come into the farming area under the cover of darkness to illegally cut woodlands or poach river and pit sand which was sold in the nearby urban areas (mainly Epworth and Ruwa). Load shedding of electricity which had become common in the past years, lack of electrification in peri-urban locations and the exorbitant prices of alternative fuels was said to have created a market for firewood hence high demand. It was this market which illegal firewood traders were said to target. There was consensus from respondents that the young people who are into farming rarely engage in unsustainable natural resource exploitation as some of them are reliant on the natural resources for their livelihoods. Some have families that benefitted from the FTLRP, hence they would not do anything to jeopardise their inheritance. Other young people were said to be benefiting from some initiatives aimed at ensuring sustainable natural resources use. Some of the initiatives included being organised into groups and being allocated land to engage in income generating projects like bee keeping, fish rearing, horticulture, brick making and other activities.

In FGD's held in the communal areas, the youth who participated (who have not benefitted from the FTLRP) revealed that some of the youth do go into the communal areas were they illegally exploit the flora and fauna there. Some of the popular natural resources which they said are illegally obtained include firewood, sand, minerals and wild animals. They do this because the FTLRP had not benefitted them or anyone of their generation hence it is only right for them to access these resources, even if it means doing so illegally. The participants provided justification for their actions, saying everyone had a right to benefit from resources but there were elements in society as exemplified by the Co7s and political parties which were against community beneficiation from natural resources. It was due to this that they were engaging in illegal natural resource exploitation. The practice of illegal natural resource exploitation across different settlement models was confirmed by the Security Officer (Co7) at Glen Avon farm who said that the youth from the communal areas were the ones who usually came to cut trees and steal firewood, to poach sand and do illegal hunting at the farms. The firewood was sold in urban areas (where there is a ready market) and what worried them the most was that those who came to do these illegal activities were usually heavily armed and there had been incidents of violence. Farmers were said to be living in constant fear of being violently attacked if they confronted those who came to these areas to steal.

The contestations which occur in the farming areas over natural resources and over the interactions between the youth, the Co7 and the *sabhuku's* as well as the state and local authority structures raise some important dimensions on the latent and manifest political contestations which are now occurring in the farming areas. Access to natural resources in an increasingly challenging socio-economic environment where there are limited opportunities has seen the youth increasingly becoming vocal and demanding opportunities which would enhance their welfare and wellbeing. A worrying development is the tensions that are arising between communal and farming area dwellers over natural resource exploitation. These tensions are arising because there has not been any tangible plan to ensure resource distribution across generations and this is now raising tensions. The political tensions between those in authority and the youth in different social categories was visible during the study and it is something which is difficult to ignore.

9 Land Redistribution and Access Issues

As highlighted earlier, the primary objective of the FTLRP was to reverse a racially skewed agrarian structure. Moyo (2011, 2018) and Shivji (2019) go beyond this simplistic conceptualisation to argue that the FTLRP needs to be understood in a context where it was aimed at solving the country's agrarian question. This entailed the country solving its 'land question' as well as its 'peasant question'. These questions relate to the extent to which there was redistributive land reform with resolving labour, reproduction and accumulation issues which confront peasant households also being addressed. This is in a background where the world is seen as becoming increasingly neo-liberal and dominated by the political economy of the world capitalist system in which there are tensions between primitive accumulation and expanded reproduction (Shivji 2019). For Moyo (2018), in the case of Zimbabwe, although there were measures to address the agrarian question, it has still not been resolved. It was in this context that the study sought to understand the political nature of the generational issues which have emerged due to the FTLRP when it came to land redistribution, labour and accumulation.

While the study participants acknowledged that the FTLRP had been redistributive, there were concerns that it had only benefitted the generation of 2000 that had participated in the initial farm occupations. Communal area youths said that the FTLRP had its shortcomings which were now negatively impacting on their lives. Failure to derive any tangible benefits from the farming areas while others were benefitting appeared to frustrate the youth in the communal areas. This was in the background where they were critical of the FTLRP for causing rural unemployment and limiting economic opportunities for non-beneficiaries. Remigio of Kambeu Trust farms said:

> The land issue is a problem and it is not surprising if it explodes in the future. There are a lot of young people from the communal lands, some even have skills to do farming, but no land is available. The funny thing is that in some areas you see land which we all know belongs to the government being given to people whose origins we do not know. So, there is a lot of underhand dealings going on, there is no transparency in land allocations. In the communal areas, for example where I come from, the land is too poor and unproductive and we have had it for generations, families are too big and everyone wants some land so the pressure is too much.

Failure to have a plan in place which would accommodate the younger generation in terms of land ownership was considered to be a major challenge confronting the farming areas. The Lands Officer and the Livestock Extension

Officer (who was present during the farm occupations), acknowledged this challenge pointing out that the FTLRP process had been so dynamic and fast paced that there had been no prior preparations or proper land allocations during its initial stages. It was only later that settlements were regularised by government officials. Consequently, there had been no planning or foresight on land access by future generations. In the district, the situation had been worsened by high demand for land which had seen most of the plots being taken up in the early 2000's.

Interactions with youth in both the farming and communal areas revealed that one of the key demands and expectations is that they should at least be given the opportunity to own land either for housing or for agricultural purposes. This came out strongly in focus group discussions were it was reported that the youth face challenges in owning land and the situation is compounded by lack of regular income.

The Table 3.1 below summarises the number of young people surveyed from the farming and communal lands who indicated willingness to own land in the district. It showed that a large number were interested in owning land for both residential and agricultural purposes. In the farming areas 72.5 percent showed interest in owning land and it was at 70 percent in the communal areas. There were some young people who were not interested in owning land in both areas and it was 26.6 percent in the communal areas and 25 percent in the farming areas.

TABLE 3.1　Interest in land ownership by the youth

	Youth from farming areas (N = 40)			Youth from communal areas (N = 30)		
Interest in owning land	Yes		No		Not Sure		Yes		No		Not Sure	
	No.	%	No.	%	No.	%	No.	%	No.	%	No.	%
	29	72.5	10	25	1	2.5	21	70	8	26.6	1	3.3

SOURCE: GOROMONZI FIELDWORK, 2018

10　Land Access

Access to land and land redistribution was shown in the study as being contentious and having a lot of political dynamics with local authority structures and the political elite said to be exercising a lot of influence on its trajectories. In the study, it was noted that although some youths are bemoaning failure to access land, there are some who have managed to access land through different means. This demonstrates human agency which now exists in the farming areas linked to the use of ties and networks to access land. The breakdown of youth land access is shown in the Figure 3.1 below from 50 respondents. It shows that many of the youth 14 (28%) are co-sharing the land with their parents or relatives who were legally allocated land. This has become an important strategy of land access with the A1 farms being subdivided and given to family members. It is not a new phenomenon, but it is a practice adopted from the communal areas. The renting of land, legal allocations and inheritance also stand out as the major means through which young people are accessing land to undertake their agricultural production activities and it is summarised in Figure 3.1 below.

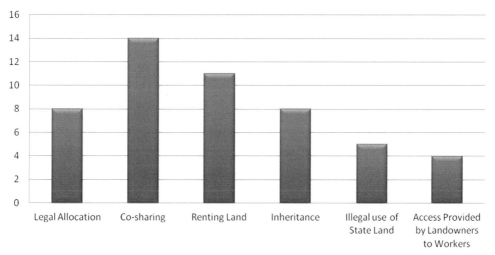

FIGURE 3.1   Land access by the youth
SOURCE: OWN FIELDWORK

Some of the youths who participated in the focus group discussions expressed concern over how some of their peers had accessed land, blaming corruption and nepotism for some of them being overlooked in the land redistribution processes. Those who have land refuted these accusations saying that they had applied for land and had been lucky enough to get it. Some indicated that they had followed due processes and had been allocated the land as deserving beneficiaries and no corrupt activities had ever occurred. A few believed that they had the added advantage of being active in developmental initiatives in the farming areas and having good relations with the local authorities hence their applications had been supported.

11   The Labour Dimension

Labour on the farms was another highly politicised and contentious issue which was raised by the respondents. Participants in FDG's accused the local political leaders, particularly those in the Co7s and the *sabhukus* of being selective and withholding information when vacancies arose in which the services of young people were sought, be it from the local district council, parastatals or individuals. They were said to have influence as who would be recruited and were said to be side-lining some of the youth in their areas. Examples were provided of some government parastatals which had sought the services of young people in the area, but those in authority had selected their relatives or members of their political parties and religious organisations. It was said that in the past local these authorities had not been involved in selections made for local vacancies but this had changed as they complained that outsiders were benefitting at the expense of locals. They therefore wanted to be included in the selection process. At a time where there was scarcity of employment given the low levels of production on the farms and their reliance on household labour, the youth felt that this was one of the serious issues requiring immediate attention.

The concerns of the youth raised important insights on the labour regime found on both the A1 and A2 farms and from a figurational sociological perspective the interdependencies connecting various actors in rural Zimbabwe. It was noted that there were few opportunities for full time employment with the part time employment being the most common. Remuneration on work done was said to be inadequate with the lowest paid for those lucky enough to be permanently employed ranging between US$50 and US$95 a month at the time of the fieldwork. Seasonal labour was the most common form of employment which some of the youth were able to access and it was remunerated according to the task at hand. At the time of the fieldwork it was US$5 for tedious tasks like digging, weeding and harvesting for an agreed portion and US$3 for tasks like planting and applying fertiliser. It was noted that most of the A1 farmers prefer family labour as it is cheaper for them and flexible. This has in turn contributed to the limiting of opportunities for young people to be employed and it touched on a key demand of the youth to be availed with more secure and well-paying employment opportunities in the farming areas.

12   Political Participation

Literature is abound with the importance of the youth to participate in politics as it allows them to be part of decision making processes, it allows for good governance, inclusiveness and democracy, participation in development processes, the fulfilment of rights etc (see Bincof 2018, Briggs 2017). As indicated earlier, the farming areas were created in a highly charged political context which has had a lasting impact on these areas as well as the country's agrarian sector. A perusal of literature will show that one of the criticisms of the FTLRP was that it was said to have benefitted supporters of ZANU PF as well as its political elite. In addition, it created institutional structures as has been indicated earlier which have been accused of being largely composed of ZANU (PF) members and pushing the political agenda of the party in the farming areas. These areas have for years seen opposition political parties and civil society organisations being labelled as regime change agents and denied access to populations residing in these areas (see Chipenda 2018).

Against this background that the study looked at the level of political participation by the rural youth and the different actors involved. It is important to note that when it comes to political issues in the farming areas, this is a very sensitive issue which is not easy to study. This stems from the polarisation that came about as a result of the land reforms in the country which at times culminated in violence and loss of life. The tensions and suspicions that emerged during the FTLRP especially against outsiders are still there and they make researching on politics in these areas challenging. Despite this limitation, the study looked at political participation by the youth, avoiding some thorny issues which would have made respondents uncomfortable or unwilling to participate in the study.

In line with this aim, the study sought to understand the level of political participation by the looking at their participation in the past election and its importance. Participation by the youth in the 2013 and 2018 harmonised elections[6] was looked at. This was seen as being indicative of their interest in selecting leaders of their choice, and their resolve to have leaders who would to some extent address their demands and expectations. Table 3.2 below shows the level of political participation by the youth in 2013 and in 2018.

TABLE 3.2   Political participation

	Yes	No	No comment	Yes	No	No comment
Farming areas	22	50	8	49	23	8
Communal areas	9	17	4	18	11	3

---

6 Harmonised elections are elections in which councillors, members of parliament and the President are elected in one election.

In 2013 in the farming areas, 22 young people participated in the elections and there was an increase to 49 in 2018. In the communal areas, in 2013 the number was nine while in 2018 it was 18. In the farming areas, the increase in 2018 was attributable to some of the youth who had reached the legal age allowed to vote (which is 18). Some indicated that they did not have the identity documents in 2013, but having them in 2018 had allowed them to vote. In addition, some had not registered in 2013 but managed to register in the 2018 elections. In 2018 in both the farming and communal areas, there were some cases of some youth who had voted in 2013 but had failed to vote in 2018 and they indicated that this was due to failure to register or check registration details, going to the wrong polling stations after restructuring of the voting system. In the communal areas there was a slight increase in voters in 2018 as well but it was just a marginal increase. The Table shows that there is an interest in participating in electoral processes by the youth in the study sample and this was acknowledged in the study where respondents indicated that for them it was important to participate in choosing their leaders and holding political office if called upon to do so. FGD's held just before the 2018 elections, had seen participants expressing willingness to participate in processes of selecting their leaders. At Dunstan farm for example, participants had expressed dissatisfaction with the conduct of their member of parliament who was also a government Minister. They accused her of not living up to her election promises, not conducting feedback meeting or providing opportunities for them to air their grievances to. They said that they had resolved not to have her re-elected because they felt she did not represent their interests and true to their word she did not make it despite representing ZANU (PF) in the elections. Overall, it was noted that in terms of political participation, the youth are very much aware of the need for them to participate in political processes and to choose local leaders of their choice.

13   Conclusion

The chapter has been important in exploring some of the emerging political dynamics in post land reform, Zimbabwe. From a figurational sociological perspective, the chapter has looked at interrelationships, connections and interdependencies that exist between the different actors. The chapter has shown that there are a number of political dynamics which are occurring in the rural areas which are having implications on the lives of young people. Some of the young people in the study showed that they have desires, plans and aspirations, but feel that structural and institutional constraints and the involvement of some social actors are an impediment to these aspirations. Despite the challenges which young people face, individual agency can be seen playing an important role in allowing young people to carve out diverse livelihoods and to be able to provide for themselves and their families. A new labour regime, diverse strategies to access land and political participation now characterise the lives of the young people. While this chapter has not been exhaustive of all emergent dynamics of rural Zimbabwe from a youth perspective, it has been important in flagging out new emergent issues which need further nuanced, empirical analysis.

References

Alexander, Jocelyn. *The Unsettled Land: State-making and the Politics of Land in Zimbabwe 1893–2003*. Harare: Weaver Press.

Bhatasara, S, and K Helliker. 2018. "The Party-State in the Land Occupations in Zimbabwe: The Case of Shamva District. 2018. *"Journal of Asian and African Studies* 53(1): 81–97.

Bincof, Mohamed O. 2018. "The Role of Youth in Political Participation in Somalia." *IOSR Journal of Humanities And Social Science* 23(10): 64–74.

Bratton, Michael. 1986. "Farmer Organisations and Food Production in Zimbabwe." *World Development* 14(3): 367–384.

Briggs, Jacqueline E. 2017. *Young People and Political Participation: Teen Players*. London: Springer Nature.

Chambati, Walter. 2017. "Changing Forms of Wage Labour in Zimbabwe's New Agrarian Structure." *Agrarian South: Journal of Political Economy* 6(1): 1–34.

Chibwana, Musavengana. 2016. *Social Policy Outcomes of Zimbabwe's Fast Track Land Reform Programme: A Case Study of Kwekwe District. PhD Thesis.* Pretoria: UNISA.

Chigumira, Esther. 2018. "Political Ecology of Agrarian Transformation: The Nexus of Mining and Agriculture in Sanyati District, Zimbabwe." *Journal of Rural Studies* 61: 265–276.

Chikowero, Moses. 2011. "The third chimurenga: Land and song in Zimbabwe's ultra-nationalist state ideology, 2000–2007." In *Redemptive or Grotesque nationalism? Rethinking Contemporary Politics in Zimbabwe*, by Sabelo J Ndlovu-Gatsheni and James Muzondidya, 291–313. Oxford: Peter Lang.

Chipenda, Clement. 2018. "After Land Reform in Zimbabwe: What About the Youth?" *A paper presented at the International Conference on 'Authoritarian Populism and the Rural World'. 15–19 March 2018. International Institute of Social Studies.* The Hague: Emancipatory Rural Politics Initiative (ERPI).

Chipenda, Clement. 2019a. "The Youth after Land Reform in Zimbabwe: Exploring the Redistributive and Social Protection Outcomes from a Transformative Social Policy Perspective." *Canadian Journal of African Studies*.

Chipenda, Clement, and Tom Tom. 2019b. "The Generational Questions after Land Reform in Zimbabwe: A Social Reproduction Perspective." *African Journal of Economic and Management Studies* 11(3):403–425.

Chiweshe, Manase K. 2011. *Farm Level Institutions In Emergent Communities In Post Fast Track Zimbabwe: Case of Mazowe District. Unpublished PhD Thesis.* Grahamstown: Rhodes University.

Chiweshe, Manase Kudzai, and Takunda Chabata. 2019. "The Complexity of Farmworkers' Livelihoods in Zimbabwe after the Fast Track Land Reform: Experiences from a farm in Chinhoyi, Zimbabwe." *Review of African Political Economy* 46(159): 55–70.

Dewey, John. 1931.*Context and Thought.* Berkely: University of California Press.

Dolan, Paddy. 2014. *Figurations.* Dordrecht: Springer.

Elias, Norbert. 1987. "The Retreat of Sociologists into the Present." *Theory Culture Society* 4(2): 223–47.

Elias, Norbert. 1978. *What is Sociology?* London: Hutchinson.

Food and Agriculture Organisation of the United Nations. 2006. *Fertiliser Use by Crop in Zimbabwe.* Rome: FAO.

Goles, Tim, and Ruby Hirschheim. 2000. "The Paradigm is Dead, The Paradigm is Dead...Long Live the Paradigm: The Legacy of Burell and Morgan." *Omega* 28(3): 249–268.

GoZ. 2018. *National Agricultural Policy Framework (2018–2030). First Draft June 20 2018.* Harare: Ministry of Lands, Agriculture and Rural Resettlement.

Grebe, Jan. 2010. "And they are still targeting: Assessing the effectiveness of targeted sanctions against Zimbabwe." *Africa Spectrum* 45(1): 3–29.

Hammar, Amanda, and Brian Raftopolous. 2003. "Introduction." In *Zimbabwe's Unfinished Business: Rethinking State and Nation in the Context of Crises*, by Hammar Amanda, Brian Raftopolous and Stig Jensen, edited by A Hammar, B Raftopolous and S Jensen, 1–47. Harare: Weaver Press.

Makochekanwa, Albert. 2009. *Clothed in Rags by Hyperinflation: The Case of Zimbabwe.* Munich: Personal RePEC Archive, Paper No 28863.

Ministry of Finance and Economic Development. 2018a. *2019 National Budget.* Harare: Ministry of Finance and Economic Development.

Ministry of Finance and Economic Development. 2018b. *Transitional Stabilisation Programme Reforms Agenda, October 2018 – December 2020: "Towards a Prosperous & Empowered Upper Middle Income Society by 2030".* Harare: Ministry of Finance and Economic Development, Zimbabwe.

Mkodzongi, Grascian. 2016. "'I am paramount chief, this land belongs to my ancestors': the reconfiguration of rural authority after Zimbabwe's land reforms." *Review of African Political Economy* 43(51): 99–114.

Mkodzongi, Grascian. 2018. "Peasant Agency in a Changing Agrarian Situation ijn Central Zimbabwe: The Case of Mhondoro Ngezi." *Agrarian South: Journal of Political Economy* 7(2): 188–280.

Mlambo, Obert B., and Ezra Chitando. 2015. "Blair, Keep Your England, and Let Me Keep My Zimbabwe: Examining the Relationship of Physical Space and Political Order in Zimbabwe's Land Redistribution Programme (2000–2008)." *The Journal of Pan African Studies* 8(8): 8–26.

Modell, Sven. 2009. "In Defence of Triangulation: A Critical Realist Approach to Mixed Methods Research in Management Accounting." *Management and Accounting Research* 21(2): 208–221.

Morgan, David. L. 2007. "Paradigms Lost and Pragmatism Regained: Methodological Implications of Combining Qualitative and Quantitative Methods." *Journal of Mixed Methods Research* 1(1)): 48–76.

Moyo, Sam. 2018. "Debating the Land Question with Archie Mafeje." *Agrarian South: Journal of Political Economy* 7(2): 211–233.

Moyo, Sam. 2011. "Land Concentration and Accumulation After Redistributive Reform in Post Settler Zimbabwe." *Review of African Political Economy* 38(128): 257–276.

Moyo, Sam. 2013. "Land Reform and Redistribution in Zimbabwe Since 1980." In *Land and Agrarian Reform in Zimbabwe: Beyond white-settler capitalism*, edited by S Moyo and W Chambati, 29–77. Dakar: CODESRIA.

Moyo Sam. 2000. *Land Reform Under Structural Adjustment in Zimbabwe: Land Use Change in the Mashonaland Provinces*. Uppsala: Nordiska Afrika Institute.

Moyo Sam. 1995. *The Land Question in Zimbabwe*. Harare: SAPES Books.

Moyo, Sam, and Paris Yeros. 2005. "Land occupations and land reform in Zimbabwe: Towards the national democratic revolution." In *Reclaiming the land: the resurgence of rural movements in Africa, Asia and Latin America*, edited by S Moyo and P Yeros, 165–208. London and Cape Town: Zed Books.

Moyo, Sam, et al. 2009. *Fast Track Land Reform Baseline Survey in Zimbabwe: Trends and Tendencies 2005/06*. Harare: African Institute for Agrarian Studies.

Muchetu, Rangarirai Gavin. 2019. "Family Farms and the Markets: Examining the Level of Market-Oriented Production 15 Years after the Zimbabwe Fast Track Land Reform Programme." *Review of African Political Economy* 46(159): 33–54.

Mujere, Joseph, Munyaradzi Elton Sagiya, and Joost Fontein. 2017. "'Those who are not known, should be known by the country': Patriotic history and the politics of recognition in southern Zimbabwe." *Journal of Eastern African Studies* 11(1): 86–114.

Munch, Phillip, and Alex Veit. 2018. "Intermediaries of Intervention: How Local Power Brokers Shape External Peace-State Building in Afghanistan and Congo." *International Peacekeeping* 25(2): 266–292.

Murisa, Tendai. 2009. *An Analysis of Emerging Forms of Social Organisation and Agency in the Aftermath of 'Fast Track' Land Reform in Zimbabwe*. Unpublished PhD Thesis. Grahamstown: Rhodes University.

Murisa, Tendai. 2018. "Land, Populism and Rural Politics in Zimbabwe a Paper Prepared for the ERPI 2018 International Conference - Authoritarian Populism and the Rural World." The Hague: Institute of Social Studies.

Ndlovu-Gatsheni, Sabelo J. 2009. "Making Sense of Mugabeism in Local and Global Politics: 'So Blair Keep Your England and Let Me Keep My Zimbabwe'". *Third World Quaterly* 30(6): 1139–1158.

Nyawo, Vongai Z. 2014. "Zimbabwe Post Fast Track Land Reform Programme: The Different Experiences Coming Through." *International Journal of African Renaisanse Studies – Multi-, Inter- and Transdisciplinarity* 9(1): 36–39.

Onwuegbuzie, Anthony J, and Burke R Johnson. 2006. "The Validity Issue in Mixed Research." *Research in the Schools* 13(1): 48–63.

Primorac, Ranca. 2006. *The Place of Tears: The Novel and Politics in Zimbabwe*. London and New York: Tauris Academic Studies.

Raftopolous, Brian, and Ian Phimister. 1997. *Keep on knocking: A history of of the labour movement in Zimbabwe*. Harare: Zimbabwe Congress of Trade Unions.

Ranger, Terrence O. 2004. "Nationalist historiography, patriotic history and the history of the nation: The struggle over the past in Zimbabwe." *Journal of Southern African Studies* 30(2): 215–234.

Richardson, Craig. 2005. "Loss of Property Rights and the Collapse of Zimbabwe." CATO *Journal* 25(3): 541–565.

Rocha, Robson S. 2003. *Towards a Theoretical Framework for Analysing Organisational Processes: Taking Norbert Elias and Pierre Bourdieu into Organisational Analysis*. Kobenhavn: Copenhagen Business School.

Rutherford, Blair. 2007. "Shifting grounds in Zimbabwe: citizenship and farm workers in the new politics of land." In *Making Nations Creating Strangers. States and Citizenship in Africa*, P Nugent, D Hammett and S Dorman (eds.), 105–122. Brill.

Sachikonye, Lloyd M. 2003. "From Growth With Equity to Fast Track Reform: Zimbabwe's Land Question." *Review of African Political Economy* 30(96): 227–240.

Scoones Ian. 2019. "Young people and land in Zimbabwe: Livelihood challenges after land reform." *Review of African Political Economy* 46(159): 117–134.

Scoones, Ian, Nelson Marongwe, Blasio Mavedzenge, Felix Murambarimba, Jacob Mahenehene, and Chris Sukume. 2011. "Zimbabwe's land reform: Myths and realities." *Africa Today* 57(4): 125–129.

Scoones, Ian, Nelson Marongwe, Blasio Mavedzenge, Jacob Mahenene, Felix Murimbarimba, and Chris Sukume. 2015. "Zimbabwe's Land Reform: New Political Dynamics in the Countryside." *Review of African Political Economy* 42(144): 190–205.

Shannon Baker, Peggy. 2016. "Making Paradigms Useful in Mixed Methods Research." *Journal of Mixed Methods Research* 10(4): 319–334.

Shivji, Issa G. 2019. "Sam Moyo and Samir Amin on the Peasant Question." *Agrarian South: Journal of Political Economy*, 1–16.

Shonhe, Toindepi. 2017. *Reconfigured Agrarian Relations in Zimbabwe*. Bamenda: Langaa RPCIG.

Tom, Tom. 2019. "A Youth Perspective to Participation and Local Governance in Zimbabwe's Post-Fast Track Land Reform Farms." In *Participation of Young People in Governance Processes in Africa*, edited by J Kurebwa and O Dodo, 220–246. Hershey, PA: IGI Global.

Tran, Thuyet Thi. 2016. "Pragmatism and constructivism in conducting research about university-enterprise collaboration in the Vietnamese context." *Ist International Symposium on Qualitatuve Reseach Volume* 55: 7–15.

Tshuma, Lawrence. 1997. *A Matter of (In)justice: Law, State and the Agrarian Question in Zimbabwe*. Harare: SAPES Books.

Zimbabwe National Statistical Agency (ZIMSTAT). 2012. *Zimbabwe National Census - 2012*. Harare: ZIMSTAT.

Zimbabwe Statistical Agency (ZimStat). 2017. *Inter-Censal Demographic Survey.* Harare: ZimStat.

CHAPTER 4

'Not Too Young to Run' Law and Political Participation among Youths in Nigeria

Ebenezer Babajide Ishola

1   Introduction

The eradication of exclusionary measures against the youth population which constitutes a significant proportion of Nigeria's population, is vital for consolidating the country's democratic experience. Popular participation constitutes the core ideal of the liberal strand of democracy adopted by Nigeria. However, democratic practices in Nigeria's political system are threatened by exclusionary strategies ranging from legal restrictions on the basis of age, cultural restrictions through the instrumentality of ethnicity and other primordial sentiments, the ritual of money politics, among others. The 'Not too Young to Run' Act assented by President Muhammadu Buhari on May 31st, 2018 touches on the problem of restriction from political participation via elections. The new law is a variant of the 'Not too Young to Run' bill initiated by a member of the lower parliament of Nigeria, the House of Representatives, Honourable Tony Nwulu, on July 27, 2017. The bill in its original form sought to reduce the legal age requirements for contestants for political offices. These offices include membership of the legislative and executive arms of government at the state and federal level. The bill also provides for the introduction of independent candidacy into Nigeria's electoral process.

The bill recommended that citizens of Nigeria aged twenty-five and above are permitted to contest for election into the House of Representative and House of Assembly. Furthermore, citizens of Nigeria aged thirty and above should be allowed to contest for the positions of governor, senator and president. The adverse effects of party politics (Joseph 1987; Onah and Nwali 2018) is also addressed by the bill with the introduction of independent candidacy to deemphasizes the role of political parties as the sole avenues for participation in electoral politics.

This chapter consequently interrogates the 'Not too Young to Run' law in relation to its impact on encouraging the active participation of youths in Nigeria's political process. In this regard, attention is paid to the potentials and pitfalls of the new law in boosting the participation of members of the younger generation in electoral contestation. The conceptual basis of the subject matter is provided in the next section where the central concepts of youths and political participation are examined from a variety of perspectives. The impact of political exclusion on democracy in Nigeria and the youth population at large are discussed in succession. Furthermore, the 'Not too Young to Run' law is examined as a solution to the challenge of political exclusion and its resultant apathy to politics among youths.

2 Conceptual Clarification

The concept of political participation has been subject to a variety of explanation. Conge (1988, 241–242) identified six dimensions to understanding what constitutes political participation. These include active or passive actions, aggressive versus nonaggressive forms, structural versus nonstructural focus, governmental or nongovernmental ends, mobilized or voluntary behaviour, intended versus unintended outcomes. Despite this miscellany of definitions of political participation, Conge (1998, 246) concluded that "political participation is any action (or inaction) of an individual or a collectivity of individuals which intentionally or unintentionally opposes or supports, changes or maintains some feature(s) of a government or community". In asserting that political participation is solely focused on governmental activities, Conge (1998, 247–248) noted that "politics involve the governments of states; hence political participation involves behavior within the realm of government… behavior outside the realm of government is best excluded from a definition of the concept".

The behavioural school of thought on politics extends the understanding of politics and political participation beyond the limits of government, its institutions and activities. The understanding of politics now includes all manifestations of contextual struggle for power in human society. Reflecting this development, Kasse and Marsh (1979, 42) argued that political participation involves all efforts by the people to contribute to political choices directly or otherwise at all levels in the political system. This understanding of political participation goes beyond government and its activities.

Beyond the definition of political participation, a pertinent question to ask is why people participate in politics. At the macro-level and in terms of governmental activities, an array of factors inform political participation. On the one hand, political participation is informed by the need to contribute to the governmental process such as selecting public officials and influencing policy; and on the other hand, it is driven by the obligation to perform civic duty

(Osumah 2016, 2). In contributing to the political system, political participation provides the opportunity for feedback which can inform new demands to be addressed by the machinery of government (Teorell, Torcal and Montero 2007, 334). Other factors that influence political participation include levels of income and education, occupation, gender, political institutions at the micro-level (constitution and electoral laws) and macro-level (political parties), ethnic group among others (Bratton 1999; Resnick and Casale 2011, 6).

Aristotle's assertion that man is by nature a political animal (Coleman 2000,197) underscores the ubiquity of politics in our society. Political participation is an indispensable activity by human beings, which has emerged in different forms. Melo and Stockemer (2014) distinguished between conventional political participation such as voting, campaigning and joining political parties; and forms of unconventional political such as protests, sit-ins and signing petitions. Claims of decline in political participation even in countries that stand as the epitome of liberal democracy made by Rosenstone and Hansen (1993) and Putnam (2000) are based on the level of conventional participation in politics such as voters' turnout, membership of political parties and electoral activities. Expanding the scope of political participation, Teorell, Torcal and Montero (2007), identify five forms of political participation namely voting, consumer participation, party activity, protest activity and contacting representatives.

In understanding political participation, the nature of the political system has to be considered. Chabal (2009) discussed three forms of interaction between citizens and the political system that have emerged in the aftermath of colonialism in Third World countries. The subject interaction is defined by the existence of an arbitrary state devoid of accountability. This is typical of the colonial era. Similarly, the client interaction mode is underscored by the existence of an unequal exchange between the rulers and the ruled. It is however not as arbitrary as the subject category. The citizen-based interaction is defined by the existence of mutual responsibility by the state to the people and vice versa (Chabal 2009, 85–105). The predominance of prebendalism where control of the state and the occupation of the institution of government are used primarily to protect and advance selfish interest, particularly economic interests (Joseph, 1987) is characteristic of the subject and client categories.

Delineating youth as a demographical category is dependent on the socio-cultural dynamics of the country or context under consideration (Federal Republic of Nigeria, 2009, 5; Oloruntoba 2008, 8). Nigeria's National Youth Policy defines the youth population as comprising citizens of the country ranging from the ages of 18–35 (Federal Republic of Nigeria 2009, 6). Beyond the age characteristic, the youth population is unique for some psychological features which include the quest for emotional independence, aggressiveness, anxiety and self-assertion (Ogundowole 2001, 5–7). This among other factors explains the explosiveness of youths' participation in politics, especially through unconventional forms such as protests and demonstrations as witnessed in the Arab spring. Nigeria's youth population (15–39 years) stands at 78 million, constituting 40 percent of Nigeria's estimated population of 193 million National Bureau of Statistics (National Bureau of Statistics, 2018a, 45). As at the third quarter of 2017, 21 million youths were unemployed and underemployed (National Bureau of Statistics 2017).

Abbink (2005) identifies three perspectives to academic discourse on the crisis of youth in Africa. The agency approach focuses on the role of youths in positively or adversely impacting on the society. The second perspective known as the interventionist dimension relates to the role of the state and civil societies in providing solutions to the crisis. The descriptive-analytic approach concerns a realistic discussion of the crisis of the youth population with "… particular interest in the interaction of structure, agency and normative or reflexive discourse" (Abbink 2005, 10). This paper aligns with the descriptive-analytic approach as it interrogates the attempt at the political inclusion of the Nigerian youth population through the instrumentality of the 'Not too Young to Run' law, and its implication for youths' political participation.

3   Political Exclusion and Liberal Democracy in Nigeria

The post-cold war era has ensured the predominance of liberal democracy in different forms across the world. The central tenets of this variant of democracy include the guarantee of fundamental human rights, independence of the press and judiciary, popular participation in government as an expression of popular sovereignty, free and fair regularly conducted elections, accountability of the government, rule of law, constitutionalism, multiparty system and an independent electoral commission (O'Neil 2010, 110–111; Tar 2009, 8). The adoption of these tenets by countries like Nigeria has however failed to yield the requisite developmental dividends in areas of education, health, infrastructure and economy. Nigeria's experience so far shows that liberal democracy has failed to engender popular empowerment, and has made a mockery of popular participation and accountability (Ashiru 2010, 47).

One of the challenges of liberal democracy in Nigeria is political exclusion. In measuring exclusion and inclusion in the political process, the concern is on the restriction of individuals and groups from participating in the political space. National Democratic Institute (2016, 1) defines the political space as "…

avenues, opportunities and entry points available for citizens to express their voice and influence political processes and outcomes". Instruments of exclusion from this political space include money, ideology and legal restrictions such as suffrage (Onah and Nwali 2018, 1) among others.

Depending on the instrument of exclusion, two broad categories of political exclusion can be identified namely official and unofficial exclusion. Official exclusion is distinguished by the existence of legal or constitutional guarantee to restrict access by individuals or groups to the political space. Example of official exclusion include the existence of limited suffrage, age barrier and financial conditions to limit popular participation in politics. Despite the introduction of the Elective Principle in 1922 in response to the demands by nationalists organized as the National Congress of British West Africa, a huge proportion of the population of colonial Nigeria were excluded from the political process as electoral activities were restricted to Lagos and Calabar, and to male adult citizens (21 years of age and above) who met the rigid criteria of having resided in the area for at least 12 months and earned a gross income of 100 pounds and 20 pounds for Lagos and Calabar respectively (Ogbogbo 2009, 43).

The extent of the exclusion is revealed in the total number of voters in the elections. Lagos with a population of 99,000 (Coleman 1971, 74) had only 4,000 registered voters, constituting 4 percent; Calabar had a voting population of 453, representing 0.2 percent of its total population of 15,438 (Tamuno 1966, 126). The minute population of Nigerian citizens earning 100 pounds and above in colonial times is largely explained by the exploitative and expropriating nature of colonial rule in Nigeria which ensured the immiseration of the population evident in the social relations between the peasant population and colonial authorities (Ake 1981, 60–65).

Another form of official exclusion is the existence of age limits for contesting in elections for political positions. While countries like Norway, Denmark and United Kingdom have a single age for citizens to exercise their suffrage (right to vote and be voted for), Nigeria's framework for elections prescribes 18 years as the minimum age for a citizen to exercise their franchise. The 1999 Constitution provides different criteria for contesting political positions at different tiers of government. Section 65 guarantees that only citizens of Nigeria aged 30 and 35 years are eligible to be members of the House of Representatives and Senate respectively, among other requirements. Section 106 stipulates that only adult citizens of 30 years and above can contest for membership of the House of Assembly. The same criterion applies for appointment as commissioners at the state level (Section 192).

The 1999 Constitution in Section 131 directs that candidates for the presidency must be at least 40 years of age; Section 177 requires that a governorship candidate should be, at least, 35-year-old at the point of contesting for the post. Membership of the Federal Executive Council like ministers must be 30 years and above (Section 147). These restrictions inform the demands by civil society groups organized as the 'Not too Young to Run' movement for the reduction of the age barrier to incorporate more youths in the political process (Africa Portal 2017).

Culture and its elements constitute the unofficial dimension of political exclusion. In Africa, elders are seen as repository of wisdom and experience which is indispensable for leadership (Dei 1994, 13). Youths are considered immature and lacking the needed clout to administer the affairs of the society. The predominantly elderly age of presidents in Africa lend credence to this position. Similar sentiments apply to the activities of the female folk in politics. Women are generally considered as the weaker sex, perpetually condemned to a subservient role in the society (Agbalajobi 2009, 77). Of the 469 members of Nigeria's 8th National Assembly (2015–2019), only 27 of them are female, representing 5.7 percent of the parliamentarians. National Bureau of Statistics (2018b, x) notes that only 5.76 percent of the members of the National Assembly between 1999 and 2015 were women, with 5.29 percent of the population of lawmakers at the state House of Assemblies women.

The prebendal nature of politics in Nigeria has ensured that money politics constitutes a major form of exclusion from political participation, albeit in an unofficial form. Money politics is when money plays an indispensable role in determining the limits of political participation, especially as regards elections. Money is useful for inducing voters, officials and other stakeholders before, during and after elections (Onah and Nwali 2018, 1). Important actors in money politics are prebendal lords that exercise "… the undying influence of big men who see themselves and are regarded as not only political party founders but as party financiers as well, never as joiners. They thereby wield tremendous influence as a result of their money" (Olurode 2017, 45).

The actions of these individuals represent a major threat to the democratic trajectory of Nigeria as their activities have continued to subvert popular will for personal and selfish interests. Intra-party crises in Nigeria, particularly among the major political parties, have been influenced by the activities of prebendal lords who ensure that a level playing field and internal democracy have remained a mirage (Olurode 2017, 45). Furthermore, the monetization of politics in Nigeria involves the need for funds to buy nomination forms, secure party's ticket, sort campaign logistics, incentivize voters on election day, remunerate party's agents and other officials at the polling booth on election day and hire legal services after elections (Onah and Nwali 2018). Money is also required for campaign logistics (entertainers, publicity, refreshment, security) and philanthropic gestures towards. In fact, "the line of expenditure is legion" (Olurode 2012, 4).

The provision of the Electoral Act (2010, as amended) has provided further impetus for money politics in Nigeria. The law prescribes the limits for campaign expenses as ₦1 billion (for presidential candidates), ₦200 million (for governorship candidates), ₦40 million (for senatorial candidates) and ₦20 million (for House of Representatives candidates). In the buildup to the 2019 general elections, the nomination fees for a major party in Nigeria, Peoples Democratic Party (PDP), were ₦500,000 (for House of Assembly candidates), ₦1 million (for House of Representatives contestants), ₦3.5 million (for senatorial candidates), ₦5 million (for governorship candidates) and ₦10 million (for presidential candidates), and candidates have to pay corresponding costs for expression of interest form (Ayitogo 2018)

The enormity of the role of money in Nigeria's politics is further evident in the total cost for the 2015 general elections which was put at $547 million (₦196 billion), with candidates spending as much as between $1.5 million and $2 million (Culture Custodian 2017). A fundraising dinner for the then incumbent president and 2015 presidential candidate of PDP, Goodluck Jonathan, raised ₦21 billion (TheCable 2014). The import of this is that a large fraction of the population will continue to suffer political exclusion due to lack of the requisite financial resources needed to prosecute political campaigns as the reality of Nigerian politics is that "those who cannot mobilize the necessary monies are thereby excluded from meaningful participation in politics" (Onah and Nwali 2018, 2).

Consolidating democracy in Nigeria requires demonetizing the political process. Section 91 of the Electoral (Amendment) Act, 2010 puts the limits of campaign expenses at ₦1 billion (president), ₦200 million (Governor), ₦40 million (senate), ₦20 million (House of Representatives), ₦10 million (house of assembly), ₦10 million (LG Chairman), ₦1 million (councillorship). In enforcing these limits and other financial regulations, the electoral commission is faced with challenges such as truculent attitudes by the political parties and its elites, wrong physical address, poor record keeping by the political parties and predominance of individual funds by candidates (INEC 2005). The establishment of an independent electoral offences commission similar to the Economic and Financial Crimes Commission as recommended by the 2008 electoral reform committee headed by Justice Mohammed Uwais, is necessary to give the needed life to the weak enforcement of legal restrictions on campaign spending as contained in the 2010 Electoral Act.

4 Youths and the Challenges of Political Exclusion

The enormity of the youth population generally makes it an important demography in the quest for societal peace, stability and development. For instance, the Igbo pre-colonial system accorded important responsibilities to the youth population organized in age-grade groups. These include the defence of the community from external aggression, maintenance of law and order, sanitation and construction of infrastructural facilities (Ezenagu 2017, 35). Furthermore, members of the younger generation around the world are playing more conspicuous roles in politics, notably actively occupying political positions. This includes Emmanuel Macron, (who became the President of France at 39 years of age), Kim Jong-un (who became the Supreme Leader of North Korea at 28-year-old), Justin Trudeau (who assumed the post of Canadian Prime Minister at 43 years of age), among others.

The African continent, particularly Nigeria, has not lacked youths as head of governments. The second military coup in the aftermath of Nigeria's independence produced a 31-year old, Gen. Yakubu Gowon who administered the affairs of Nigeria for nine years including the period of the 30-months civil war between the federal government and secessionist Biafra forces. Lieutenant General Olusegun Obasanjo (39 years) became Nigeria's Head of State in 1976 following the assassination of General Murtala Mohammed. Beyond Nigeria, Joseph Kabila at 29 years assumed the Presidency of war-torn Democratic Republic of Congo in 2001. At 34 years, Andry Nirina Rajoelina became President of Madagascar in 2009.

Federal Republic of Nigeria (2001, 1) recognized the indispensability of the youth population to the country's development. Youths are important for providing manpower, contributing to maintaining law and order, fostering national unity, mobilizing the populace for action and advancing nationalistic ideals (Ogundowole 2001, 20–25; Onuoha 2001, 29). In spite of their significance, the youth population in Africa, indeed Nigeria, is confronted with the ills of mass unemployment, health challenges, lack of family support, poor access to education, and marginalization (Abbink 2005, 1). Summarizing the conditions of youths, Abbink (2005, 7) asserted that "to be young in Africa came to mean being disadvantaged, vulnerable and marginal in the political and economic sense". This has ensured that the youth population is continuously susceptible to converting their youthfulness to violent activities such as insurgency or criminal activities such as the Boko Haram menace and Niger Delta militancy in Nigeria (Ogoloma 2013; Onuoha 2014).

Since the commencement of Nigeria's Fourth Republic in 1999, participation of youths in politics involve activities such as voting, participating in campaigns (offline and online), and pressure group activities. The characteristics of youths such as energy, vigour and vitality make their participation in politics unconventional and potentially explosive rather than conservative. Melo and Stockemer (2014, 49) asserted that youths are more likely to participate in politics via protests, demonstrations, signing petitions and other unconventional activities, rather than the conventional activity of voting as an index of political participation. The advent of the internet has offered a veritable medium for youths to express themselves on political issues. The attraction of the internet as an avenue for political participation is on the basis of its nature as a leveler devoid of command structures typical of formal institutions such as political parties, and its nature as a spontaneous medium (O'Toole 2015, 10).

Historicizing youth participation in politics in Nigeria, the period around independence and the First Republic witnessed youths occupying the centre stage in political activities. Notable among the youths in this era are Obafemi Awolowo who spearheaded the Western Nigeria branch of the Nigerian Youth Movement (NYM) at the age of 31, Nnamdi Azikiwe who provided leadership for Igbos and other non-indigenes in Lagos in 1935 at the age of 31, as well as Ernest Ikoli, Samuel Akinsanya, Dr. J. C. Vaughan and H.O. Davies who were founding members of the Union of Young Nigerians which metamorphosed to the Nigerian Youth Movement (NYM) in 1936 (Coleman 1971, 261). The NYM at inception sought to break the monopoly of Nigeria's first political party, Nigeria National Democratic Party (NNDP), particularly in Lagos.

The Zikist Movement was another youth-oriented organization that provided an active platform for political participation of youths during the independence struggle in Nigeria. Members of the Zikist movement were revolutionary as evident in their mien during the court hearing on the sedition charges leveled against them by the government in 1948. For instance, one of the members of the movement, Raji Abdullah, in his defence submits thus "I have not much to say than to request you to inflict upon me the maximum sentence if you are satisfied that it is a crime to fight for freedom of one's country" (Ogundowole 2001, 26).

Anthony Enahoro moved the motion for Nigeria's independence as a member of the House of Representatives in 1953 at the age of 30 (Coleman 1971). Ministers in Nigeria's First Republic such as Matthew Mbu, Mbazulike Amechi, Maitama Sule, and Shehu Shagari were youths. Instructively, the first military coup in Nigeria was perpetrated by young and idealistic officers such as Majors D. Okafor, E. Ifeajuna, A. Ademoyega, C. I. Anuforo, I.H. Chukwuka and T. Onwuateugwu; Captains E. N. Nwobosi, O. Oji and B. Gbulie; Lieutenants B. O. O. Oyweole, A. N. Azubuogu, O. Ojukwu and N. S. Wokocha (Osaghae 1998, 56).

This high level of participation of youths in politics changed following the intrusion of the military in 1966. Long years of military rule has adversely affected the consolidation of the role of youths in politics and the expansion of the political space to accommodate more marginalized groups. Through the instrumentality of cooptation and suppression during the years of the military midwifing transition to democracy, youths have been hindered from actively participating in politics (Oloruntoba 2008, 3–4). One of the ways the military achieved this was the banning of youth wings of political parties. Youth wings ideally are to mentor youths as an avenue for political socialization to sustain the party. The 1979 constitution prevented political parties from having youth wings on the excuse of their malevolent use in the first republic (Onuoha 2001, 33). The absence of youth wings in political parties has ensured the lack of seamless integration of youths into mainstream politics. The youths today therefore lack institutionalized opportunity for training and mentorship in active politics.

The role of youth leaders in Nigeria's major political parties today which should provide the needed avenue for training and mentoring youths has become fallacious. These youth leaders are not youths themselves, lacking the ground to advance and protect the interests of the demography they do not belong to. For instance, the youth Leader of the PDP, Udeh Okoye was 39-years-old on assumption of office in December 2017 (Tukur 2017). The lack of constructive avenues for youths to participate in politics make them willing tools to perpetrate violence and similar activities for political ends (Ashiru 2010, 57).

In the face of the exclusion of youths in politics, the National Youth Service Corps (NYSC) has continued to provide a major opportunity for youths' involvement in the electoral process. The NYSC scheme, 48 years after the civil war, has put youths at a vantage position as apostles of sociocultural inclusion in Nigeria (Olaiya 2014, 8–9). Under Attahiru Jega's leadership of the Independent National Electoral Commission which started in June 2010, youths became active part of the electoral process following INEC's decision to partner the NYSC and use corps members as electoral officials for general elections, giving them a sense of belonging and responsibility in the electoral process (Harris 2015).

The marginalization of youths in Nigeria's political process has been aggravated due to factors such as godfatherism, poverty, corruption, militarized political space and breakdown of social values (Oloruntoba 2008, 13). The cultural dimension where ability to hold and exercise power is equated with experience and old age is also a stumbling block. In most cultures in Nigeria, power is seen as undividable instrument exclusive for the elders' control (Abbink 2005, 13). Other factors such as the absence of nationalistic fervour, crisis of national identity and the oligarchical nature of party politics (Onuoha 2001, 35) contribute to the challenges of youth exclusion in politics.

The importance of correcting this status quo and engendering political inclusion of the youths is "…for more young people help shape their own future" (Juma 2011). Eliminating the barriers to increased youth participation in politics is vital for advancing and protecting the unique interest of this demographic category. Youth inclusion in politics is important as well for the sake of the country at large because "… the strength and weakness of a nation lies in the youth" (Omeruah 1998, viii). There is an urgent need to harness the potentials of the youth population for more inclusive development. Youths on their part have a major role to play in the fight for political inclusion through the press, students' union and civil society organizations (Onuoha 2001, 30).

5 Not Too Young to Run' Law: A Panacea for Political Exclusion

In the bid to achieve the consolidation of democracy, emphasis is being placed on the expansion of the political space to accommodate previously marginalized groups. One of the efforts in this regard in Nigeria is the 'Not too Young to Run' law which provides for a reduction in the age barrier for candidates contesting elections into political positions. The original bill sponsored by Hon. Tony Nwulu, a PDP member of the House of Representatives representing Oshodi-Isolo II Federal Constituency, provides for the reduction in the age for membership of the House of Assembly from 30 years to 25 years, House of Representatives from 30 to 25 years, Senate from 35 years to 30 years, as well as eligibility for election as Governor from 35 to 30 years and President from 40 to 30 years. The bill also prescribes the introduction of independent candidacy into Nigeria's electoral process.

The law which was assented by President Muhammadu Buhari on 31st May, 2018 retained the age conditionality for elections into the House of Assembly and House of Representatives as contained in the bill. It however increased the minimum age for President to 35 and failed to incorporate the independent candidacy provision. The law also did not amend the age requirements for the Senators and Governors as contained in the 1999 constitution.

The campaign for the reduction of age barrier in Nigeria influenced the global 'Not too Young to Run' campaign launched at the United Nations on 22nd November, 2016 (Krook and Nugent 2018, 60). This global campaign is aimed at obliterating barriers to active youth participation in politics all over the world as well as ensuring that youths become more active participants in civic and public affairs in their societies (United Nations 2016). This is a major goal considering that around 75 per cent of countries globally have age restrictions of above 18 years for candidates in elections (Krook and Nugent 2018, 61).

One of the immediate benefits of the 'Not too Young to Run' law is the increase in the number of younger Nigerians that contested in the 2019 general elections. Sanni (2019) identified 10 candidates below 40 years on the ballot paper for the post of president namely Nseobong Nsehe (33 years) of Restoration Party of Nigeria (RP), Chike Ukaegbu (35 years) of Advanced Allied Party (AAP), Ahmed Buhari (36 years) of Sustainable National Party (SNP), Babatunde Ademola (37 years) of Nigeria Community Movement Party (NCMP), Felix Nicholas (37 years) of Peoples Coalition Party (PCP), Emmanuel Etim (38 years) of Change Nigeria Party (CNP), Obinna Ikeagwuonu (38 years) of Action Peoples Party (APP), Ike Keke (39 years) of New Nigeria Peoples Party (NNPP), Robinson Akpua (39 years) of National Democratic Liberty Party (NDLP), and Shipi Godia (39 years) of All Blending Party (ABP).

Furthermore, a number of political parties such as Accord Party, Action Alliance, Allied Congress Party of Nigeria, Better Nigeria Progressive Party, Democratic People's Party and the National Democratic Congress Party, provided incentives including reduction of the cost of nomination forms, funding support for candidates, among others, for youths to participate in the elections (Premium Times, 2018). A total of 7,554 young Nigerians contested for elective positions across state and federal levels in the 2019 general elections, constituting 33.9 per cent of the total 22,306 candidates in the election (YIAGA Africa, 2019a, 2019b).

To further consolidate the gains of the new law, civil society groups demanded for the reduction of the cost of nomination forms, the conduct of direct and democratic primaries, and the implementation of quota with 298 out of 900 seats in the House of Assemblies nationwide, and 109 out of 360 seats in the House of Representatives reserved for the youths (YIAGA Africa 2018). Generally, the new law paved the way for the increase in the active participation in youths in the election in terms of contesting for positions from 21 per cent in 2015 to 33.9 per cent in 2019 (YIAGA Africa, 2019b).

The failure of the 'Not too Young to Run' law to incorporate independent candidacy represents a major defect of the law in encouraging political inclusion in Nigeria. The oligarchical nature of politics in Nigeria and the role of political parties in money politics justify the need for an alternative platform that independent candidacy offers, in order to provide equal opportunities for candidates contesting elections as well as increase the credibility of elections. This is particularly important for achieving youth inclusion in politics.

The increasing conscientization of the youth population to be not just a class in itself but also a class for itself is necessary. This is crucial for channeling the energy of the youth population for the positive end of development rather than for negative goals such as thuggery, violence, and partisanship. This will lead to the achievement of the objective of advancing and protecting the interests of the youth population through the actions of government, in terms of providing gainful employment, socioeconomic equality and adequate social welfare.

6 Conclusion and Recommendations

Political exclusion especially of a significant proportion of the citizenry can lead to a decline in popular participation (Bang 2005). This challenge is evident in societies like Britain and America where democracy defines the political system (Hay 2007). Furthermore, political exclusion has adverse impact on governance (Onah and Nwali 2018, 1) as governance is no longer in tandem with the principle of popular sovereignty. Consequently, it provides the elites with unrestricted access to the state which is an indispensable tool for accumulating economic benefits (Joseph 1987, 24).

The 'Not too Young to Run' law presently addresses only the systemic barrier of age to the participation of youths in politics. Other forms of exclusion of youths in politics that exist include money politics, gender, culture and party politics. Addressing these challenges is indispensable for boosting youths' political participation. Furthermore, the predominant culture of prebendalism where state officials are continuously prone to using their office for private gains in line with the prevailing norm (Odukoya 2007) needs to be reformed in order to encourage increased participation of youths in politics. The goal of assumption of public offices must be to hold power in trust for the people and impact positively on their lives, rather than using the state as an instrument of accumulation.

The adverse effect of money politics must also be curbed as it represents a major official and unofficial barrier to youths' inclusion in politics. A number of recommendations to achieve this include the cost of nomination forms should be in consonance with the prevailing national minimum wage, political parties should cater for delegates and avoid candidates incentivizing them, integrity of candidates rather than financial net worth should guide election of candidates at the intra-party and inter-party levels, enforcement of laws on financial limits (both giver and receiver should be guilty) with a separate agency saddled with the responsibility, and a survey of real election costs excluding inducements in order to arrive at a lesser and more realistic campaign spending limit (Onah and Nwali 2018, 18–19).

Furthermore, the loophole existing in Nigeria's electoral act where there is no limit to the total donations a candidate can get as well as limit on the total amount spent on elections by political parties, must be corrected (Adetula 2015, 12). This is necessary for reducing the impact of money in political contestation and encourage marginalized proportion of the population like the youths, to actively participate in the political space.

The average age of Presidents in Africa is currently 66 years, with the Presidents of Tunisia as the oldest at 92 years and Democratic Republic of Congo President youngest at 47 years. The reality on the continent informs the recommendation for the setting of upper age limits for contestants for public offices. The extant Nigerian civil service regulations provide that any civil servant who has attained sixty years of age or spent thirty years in service should be retired. In line with this provision, it is recommended that individuals who are more than sixty years of age should be barred from contesting for public offices in order to encourage younger candidates.

The agents of political socialization such as family, media, educational institutions, political parties and civil society organizations have a major role to play in eradicating the cultural barrier to youth participation in politics. In this regard, young Nigerians should be educated on eradicating the culture of subservience where public leadership is equated with age and experience. Beyond 'Not too Young to Run', the notion of 'Not too Young to Lead' must be incorporated into our political culture.

References

Abbink, Jon. 2005. "Being young in Africa: The politics of despair and renewal." In *Vanguard or vandals: Youth, politics and conflict in Africa*, edited by Abbink, Jon and van Kessel, Ineke, 1–36. Leiden: Koninklijke Brill NV.

Adetula, Victor. 2015. "Godfathers, money politics, and electoral violence in Nigeria: Focus on 2015 elections." Paper presented at the national conference on the 2015 general elections in Nigeria: The real issues organized by The Electoral Institute/INEC, Abuja, July 2015.

Africa Portal. 2017. "Q&A: All you need to know about Nigeria's Not Too Young To Run campaign." https://www.africaportal.org/features/q-nigerias-not-too-young-run-campaign/. Accessed May 29, 2018.

Agbalajobi, Damilola. 2009. "Women's participation and the political process in Nigeria: Problems and prospects." *African Journal of Political Science and International Relations,* 4(2): 75–82.

Ake, Claude. 1981. *A political economy of Africa*. New York: Longman Nigeria Plc.

Ashiru, 'Dele. 2010. "Youth, political participation and democratic consolidation in Nigeria." In *The Nigerian youth: Political participation and national development,* edited by Haruna Wakili, Habu Mohammed, Moses Aluaigba and Mustapha Ahmad, 46–61. Kano: Aminu Kano Centre for Democratic Research and Training.

Ayitogo, Nasir. 2018. "2019: PDP commences sale of nomination forms." *Premium Times*, August 28, 2018. https://www.premiumtimesng.com/news/top-news/281577-2019-pdp-commences-sale-of-nomination-forms.html. Accessed August 20, 2018.

Bang, Henrik. 2005. "Among everyday makers and expert citizens." In *Remaking governance: Peoples, politics and the public sphere,* edited by Newman, Janet, 159–179. Bristol: The Policy Press.

Bratton, Michael. 1999. "Political participation in a new democracy: Institutional considerations from Zambia." *Comparative Political Studies,* 32(5):549–588. Doi:10.1177/0010414099032005002.

Chabal, Patrick. 2009. *Africa: The politics of suffering and smiling.* London: Zed Books.

Coleman, Joseph. 1971. *Nigeria: Background to nationalism.* Berkeley & Los Angeles: University of California Press.

Coleman, Janet. 2000. *A history of political thought: From ancient Greece to early Christianity.* Oxford: Blackwell Publishers Ltd.

Conge, Patrick. 1988. "The concept of political participation: Toward a definition." *Comparative Politics,* 20(2):241–249. doi: 10.2307/421669.

Constitution of the Federal Republic of Nigeria [Nigeria], Act No. 24, 5 May 1999.

Culture Custodian. 2017. "2015 elections cost approximately 1 trillion Naira – INEC." http://culturecustodian.com/2015-elections-cost-approximately-1-trillion-naira-inec/. Accessed May 30, 2018.

Dei, George. 1994. "Afrocentricity: Cornerstone to pedagogy." *Anthropology and Education Quarterly*, 25: 3–28. doi:10.2478/s13374-011-0043-3.

Electoral (Amendment) Act. 2010. https://lawpadi.com/wp-content/uploads/2015/08/Electoral-Amendment-Act-2010.pdf.

Ezenagu, Ngozi. 2017. "Leadership styles in the management of Igbo cultural heritage in pre-European era." *Ogirisi*, 13: 22–45.

Federal Republic of Nigeria. 2001. *National youth policy and strategic plan of action.* Abuja.

Federal Republic of Nigeria. 2009. *Second national youth policy document.* Abuja.

Harris, Shehu. 2015. "Assessing the participation of youth corps members in the 2015 electoral processes." http://www.inecnigeria.org/wp-content/uploads/2015/07/Conference-Paper-by-ShehuBello-Idris.pdf. Accessed June 30, 2018.

Hay, Colin. 2007. *Why we hate politics.* Cambridge: Polity Press.

INEC. 2005. "Political party finance handbook." http://www.inecnigeria.org/wp-content/uploads/2013/01/Political_Party_Finance_Handbook.pdf. Accessed May 27, 2018.

Joseph, Richard. 1987. *Democracy and prebendal politics in Nigeria: The rise and fall of the second republic.* Cambridge: Cambridge University Press.

Juma, Calestous. 2011. "Why Africa needs to lower its voting age to 16." https://www.theguardian.com/global-development/poverty-matters/2011/feb/09/africa-youth-lower-voting-age-16. Accessed June 30, 2018.

Kaase, Max and Marsh, Allan. 1979. "Political action: A theoretical perspective." In *Political action: Mass participation in five western democracies*, edited by Barnes, Samuel, 27–56. Beverly Hills, CA: Sage Publication.

Krook, Mona and Nugent, Mary. 2018. "Not Too Young to Run? Age requirements and young people in elected office." *Intergenerational Justice Review*, 4(2):60–67. doi:10.24357/igjr.4.2.702.

Melo, Daniela and Stockemer, Daniel. 2014. "Age and political participation in Germany, France and the UK: A comparative analysis." *Comparative European Politics*. 12 (1): 33–53. doi: 10.1057/cep.2012.31.

National Bureau of Statistics. 2017. "Labor force statistics vol. 1: Unemployment and Underemployment Report (Q1-Q3 2017)." http://nigerianstat.gov.ng/download/694. Accessed June 1, 2018.

National Bureau of Statistics. 2018a. "2017 Statistical report on women and men in Nigeria." http://nigerianstat.gov.ng/download/775. Accessed June 1, 2018.

National Bureau of Statistics. 2018b. "2017 demographic statistics bulletin." http://nigerianstat.gov.ng/download/775. Accessed June 1, 2018.

National Democratic Institute. 2016. "A matter of political space." http://www.ndi.org/sites/default/files/issues%2050%/%20A%20Matter%20of%20PoliticaP%20Space.pdf. Accessed June 12, 2018.

O,Neil, Patrick. 2010. *Essentials of comparative politics*, 3rd edition. New York: W.W. Norton & Company, Inc.

O'Toole, Therese. 2015. "Beyond crisis narratives: Changing modes and repertoires of political participation among young people." In *Politics, Citizenship and Rights*, edited by Kirsi Pauliina Kallio, Sarah Mills and Tracey Skelton, 225–242. New York: Springer.

Odukoya, Adelaja. 2007. "Democracy, national question and legitimacy crisis in Nigeria: Agenda for national integration." In *Society and governance: The quest for legitimacy in Nigeria*, edited by Oyekanmi, Felicia and Soyombo, Omololu. Lagos: Department of Sociology, University of Lagos and Friedrich Ebert Stiftung, Lagos, Nigeria.

Ogbogbo, Christopher. 2009. "Historicizing the legal framework for elections in Nigeria." *Journal of the Historical Society of Nigeria*, 18 Special Edition: 42–60.

Ogoloma, Fineface. 2013. "Niger Delta militants and the Boko Haram: A comparative appraisal." *International Journal of Arts and Humanities* 2(1):114–131.

Ogundowole, Ezekiel. 2001. "The youth in theoretical perspectives." In *The youth, democratic and national development in Nigeria*, edited by Olugbemi, Stephen and Anifowose, Remi, 1–14. Lagos: Department of Political Science.

Olaiya, Taiwo. 2014. "Youth and ethnic movements and their impacts on party politics in the ECOWAS member states." *Sage Open* 2014:1–12. doi:10.1177/2158244014522072.

Oloruntoba, Solomon. 2008. "The role of youth in democratic consolidation in fragile states: The Nigerian experience." Paper presented at the International Conference on the Nigerian Youth, Political Participation and National Development, at Mambaya House, Bayero University, Kano, August 4–7, 2008.

Olurode, 'Lai. 2012. "Nigeria: The money culture and election campaign finance." *IFES Nigeria Political Finance Newsletter,* 3(9).

Olurode, 'Lai. 2017. "The slaughter's slab as a metaphor." An inaugural lecture delivered at the University of Lagos Main Auditorium on Wednesday, 22nd of March, 2017.

Omeruah, Samson. 1998. Opening address of the Honourable Minister of Youth and Sports at a two-day national conference on "The Youth, Democracy and National Development" at the University of Lagos, Akoka.

Onah, Emmanuel and Nwali, Uche. 2018. "Monetisation of electoral politics and the challenge of political exclusion in Nigeria." *Commonwealth & Comparative Politics,* 56(3): 318–339. doi: 10.1080/14662043.2017.1368157.

Onuoha, Browne. 2001. "The role of the youth in the democratization process in Nigeria." In *The youth, democratic and national development in Nigeria,* edited by Olugbemi, Stephen and Anifowose, Remi, 29–40. Lagos: Department of Political Science.

Onuoha, Freedom. 2014. "Why do youth join Boko Haram?" *Special Report* 348. Washington: US Institute of Peace.

Osaghae, Eghosa. 1998. *Crippled giant: Nigeria since independence.* London: C. Hurst & Co. Ltd.

Osumah, Oarhe. 2016. "Paradigm shift: Youth engagement in the conduct of the 2015 elections in Nigeria." *Journal of African Elections,* 15(1): 1–24.

Premium Times. 2018. "2019: Six political parties pledge incentives for young aspirants." https://www.premiumtimesng.com/news/more-news/279448-2019-six-political-parties-pledge-incentives-for-young-aspirants.html. Accessed August 31, 2018.

Putnam, Robert. 2000. *Bowling alone: The collapse and renewal of American community.* New York: Simon & Schuster.

Resnick, Danielle and Casale, Daniela. 2011. "The political participation of Africa's youth: Turnout, partisanship and protest." *Working Paper No. 2011/56.* UNN-WIDER.

Rosenstone, Steven and Hansen, John. 1993. *Mobilization, participation and democracy in America.* New York: Macmillan.

Sanni, Kunle. 2019. "FOR THE RECORD: Nigeria's 73 presidential candidates (FULL LIST)." *Premium Times,* February 15, 2019. https://www.premiumtimesng.com/news/313139-for-the-record-nigerias-73-presidential-candidates-full-list.html. Accessed August 20, 2018.

Tamuno, Tekena. 1966. *Nigeria and elective representation 1923–1947.* London: Heinemann.

Tar, Usman. 2009. The politics of neoliberal democracy in Africa: State and civil society in Nigeria. London: Tauris Academic Studies.

Teorell, Jan, Torcal, Mariano and Montero, José. 2007. "Political participation: mapping the terrain." In *Citizenship and involvement in European democracies: A comparative analysis*, edited by van Deth, Jan, Montero, José, and Westholm, Anders, 334–357. New York: Routledge.

TheCable. 2014. "PDP nets N21.27bn at fundraising for Jonathan." https://www.thecable.ng/pdp-makes-n21-27bn-fundraising-jonathan. Accessed August 15, 2018.

Tukur, Sani. 2017. "PROFILES: Meet newly-elected PDP exco members." *Premium Times*, December 16, 2017. https://www.premiumtimesng.com/news/top-news/252582-profiles-meet-newly-elected-pdp-exco-members.html. Accessed August 20, 2018.

United Nations. 2016. "Launching global campaign promoting right of young people to run for public office." https://www.un.org/youthenvoy/2016/11/launching-global-campaign-promoting-rights-young-people-run-public-office/. Accessed August 19, 2018.

YIAGA Africa. 2018. "Not Too Young to Run Movement Leads National Day of Action to demand Youth Candidacy, Democratic Party Primaries." http://yiaga.org/not-too-young-to-run-movement-leads-national-day-of-action-to-demand-youth-candidacy-democratic-party-primaries/. Accessed June 30, 2018.

YIAGA Africa. 2019a. "Youth candidacy in the 2019 general elections." https://www.yiaga.org/youth-candidacy-in-the-2019-general-elections/. Accessed June 30, 2018.

YIAGA Africa. 2019b. *How youth fared in the 2019 elections*. Abuja: YIAGA Africa.

CHAPTER 5

'Dirty-Relevance' of Youths Culture in Nigeria's Fourth Republic Politics: A Study of Delta and Lagos States

Jonah Uyieh

1   Introduction

In Nigeria, likewise many places across the world, youths are usually regarded as future leaders because of the gaps which they bridge between the children/younger ones and the matured persons in the society.[1] However, the extent to which youths fit into leadership roles depends on their individual's choices and personal life courses of the youths themselves. Such central positions too have reflected in the youths performing various functions which they either created for themselves or acculturated into within the ambit of the obtainable norms of their immediate and external environments. Evidently, in most areas in Nigeria, while some of the youths have been striving for a model lifestyle – irrespective of the conditions in which they found themselves – majority of them have also used the opportunity created by the widening gap of unemployment and other avenues of socio-economic and political ineffectiveness to fit into new forms of 'dirty-relevance' by adopting various vices as alternative patterns of living.[2] In this regard, this chapter examines these forms of youths' subculture as well as their immediate and extended impact on the environment from a political point of view through the analyses of the Fourth

---

[1]   The contextual age brackets of youths in this paper is relative. The United Nations categorisation of youths is that they are persons between the ages of 15 and 24 {for instance, see "Definition of Youth," *Secretary-General's Report to the General Assembly, A/36/215, 1981*; "United Nations: Youth," 1–3, accessed 13 August, 2019, http://undesadspd.org/Youth.aspx/pdf; and Alahira D. Nachana'a, "Democracy, Youth and Violent Conflicts in Nigeria's Fourth Republic: A Critical Analysis," *Research on Humanities and Social Sciences* 5, No. 2 (2015): 161–162}. However, during the course of the field research, it was observed that in both Delta and Lagos States, young persons as low as 13 years are being considered as youths, while some matured persons even up to the age of 45 years still refer to themselves as youths.

[2]   Cropped from the popular slogan among many Nigerians that *'politics is a dirty game,'* dirty-relevance is used contextually in this paper to relate to the justification of certain societal vices among the youths by some persons, especially because of the political and socio-economic forces and terrains that created them.

Republic's elections and post-elections periods in Delta and Lagos States of Nigeria.

Amongst others, in the literature, many authors have discussed the subject matters of general elections and politics in Nigeria before and during the Fourth Republic;[3] electoral violence and conflict in Nigeria;[4] and political dirtiness[5] – from various interesting perspectives. However, this paper is unique as it draws syntheses on how the associated political environments of the Fourth Republic have created lapses for many Nigerian youths to thrive in several vices, with attendant consequences for the society at large.

Specifically, since its inception, Nigeria's Fourth Republic has been a period for political and other associated developments in the country. Conceptually, the Fourth Republic depicts Nigeria's current democratic system of government that began on 29th May 1999 (after the 1999 general elections), which has also been characterised by series of successive changes and continuities of civilian administrations as in the cases of the 2003, 2007, 2011, 2015 and 2019 elections.[6] Politically, each of these four-year circle has created rooms for the citizens to exercise their civic rights – either in participating actively by vying under the various political parties for the respective elective offices at the federal, states and local governments levels, or as supporters for candidates and parties of their choice during elections and at the same time featuring as the subjects of any enthroned governments in power in post-election periods. Aside its main

---

3 Leke Oke, "Democracy and Governance in Nigeria's Fourth Republic," *African Research Review* 4, No. 3a (July 2010): 31–40; J. Shola Omotola, "Elections and Democratic Transition in Nigeria Under the Fourth Republic," *African Affairs* 109, No. 437 (Oct. 2010): 535–553; Dhikru A. Yagboyaju, "Nigeria's Fourth Republic and the Challenge of a Faltering Democratization," *African Studies Quarterly* 12, Issue 3 (Summer 2011): 93–106.

4 Omolere M. Ehinmore, and Odion S. Ehiabhi, "Electoral Violence and the Crisis of Democratic Experiment in Post-Colonial Nigeria," *Journal of Arts and Humanities* 2, No. 5 (June, 2013), 46–47; E. O. Abah and Paul M. Nwokwu, Political Violence and the Sustenance of Democracy in Nigeria," *IOSR Journal of Humanities and Social Science* 20, Issue 11, Ver. I (Nov. 2015): 33–44; Anthony Egobueze and Callistus Ojirika, "Electoral Violence in Nigeria's Fourth Republic: Implications for Political Stability," *Journal of Scientific Research & Reports* 13, No. 2 (2017), 1–11.

5 Haldun Evrenk, "Why A Clean Politician Supports Dirty Politics: A Game-Theoretical Explanation for the Persistence of Political Corruption," *Journal of Economic Behavior & Organization* 80 (2011): 498–510; Daniel S. Ajayi, "Towards the Enhancement of Morality in the Nigerian Politics," *Afro Asian Journal of Social Sciences* VII, No. IV (Quarter IV 2016): 1–20; Nigar Degirmenci, "Politics is a Dirty Game!: A Case Study of Political Cynicism in Turkey," International *Journal of Liberal Arts and Social Science* 4, No. 9 (December 2016): 114–132.

6 Oke, "Democracy and Governance," 31–40; Omotola, "Elections and Democratic Transition in Nigeria," 535–553; Alexander Thurston, *Background to Nigeria's 2015 Elections* (Washington, DC: Center for Strategic & International Studies, 2015), 10.

political features, the settings of the Fourth Republic have also served as avenues for many contemporaneous activities in the Nigeria's State, particularly in the socio-economic spheres. Hence, to many Nigerians, the rolling years of this republic could help in advancing their respective political, and socio-economic interests – thereby making them to key into several roles which they deemed fit.

The Fourth Republic too has created diverse options for the overall developments and activities of youths in Nigeria. It should be pointed out here that many youths in Nigeria are known for their virtuous living, in that, the privileged ones are excelling in their respective life's careers, while the others do struggle to make ends meet positively in order to satisfy their basic socio-economic desires. Such positive lifestyles are not limited to the varying backgrounds of the youths in areas which include the family, environmental, educational, and employment systems. Despite such variations, I will argue here that, although other internal and external factors count, the decision(s) of the youths to live a virtuous life or otherwise is a matter of personal choice. For instance, there are empirical cases of youths with enabling family and educational heritages that later turned out worse by engaging in vices and in the same vein, there are youths without any form of family, employment and other support systems who have chosen to live meaningfully by any means possible in the society. While such virtues are emulative, in most times, the opposite has been the case for many as a result of the manifestation of youths' negative traits in these political periods.

To a great degree, in recent times, there has been the increased vices among the Nigerian youths in multiple dimensions in their bid for survival in a complex national environment of limited opportunities and continuous drive for self-relevance by all means. Though it cannot be disputed that the negative lifestyles of youths have a history which go beyond 1999, nonetheless, the growing years of the Fourth Republic have been remarkable as they have witnessed unprecedented display of youths' vices – even at times in organised manners in many parts of the Nigeria. As such, the primary focus here is on the changing culture of the youths in seeking alternative forms of livelihood in their immediate and extended societies through 'dirty-relevance' in the Fourth Republic. Such forms of dirty-relevance include, but not limited to the individual's and group's activities of radicalism, hooliganism, violence, militancy, and other social vices of youths during elections and post-election political periods.

It is worrying to note that, while the negative activities of youths have had dramatic consequences on political activities in the nation, there seems to exist a form of unwritten code of partnership between the youths and most active politicians in Nigeria during the course of the Fourth Republic. This partnership has created recognition for some actions of the youths to be carried out in perpetuity, even when such are to the detriment of the masses, without meaningful reactions from the political class. It is within this context that the 'concept of dirty-relevance' is situated in its relative meanings to the youths themselves, the victims of their acts, and the political class. Thus, the emerging questions are: Why the rampant vices of youths in contemporary Nigeria? How has the Fourth Republic served as a catalyst for youths' culture of dirty-relevance? What have been some landmark impacts of such forms of dirty-relevance? To what possible ways out of the youths' culture of dirty-relevance? These and other critical issues are being examined here with a study of the Delta and Lagos States' cases owing to the rifeness of the culture of youths' dirty-relevance in them. For instance, Delta is among the States of the Niger-Delta where the trends of youths dirty-relevance have degenerated into militancy, particularly in its southern parts; while in Lagos State, youths' vices have reflected in the networking of the '*Agberos*' (Area-Boys) system and other obvious trademarks.[7]

2   Delta and Lagos States of Nigeria: An Overview

Delta and Lagos States are among the strategic locations of Nigeria in its present 36 states composition. Geographically, Delta State is located in the south-south region of Nigeria, and it was created out of the defunct Bendel State on 27 August 1991. According to official sources, the state has an overall 'size of about 18,050 km², of which more than 60% is land. It also lies approximately between Longitude 5°00 and 6°.45'E, and Latitude 5°00 and 6°.30'N. It is bounded in the north and west by Edo State; the east by Anambra, Imo, and Rivers States; southeast by Bayelsa State, and on the southern flank by the Bight of Benin which covers about 160 kilometres of the state's coastline.'[8] The state is moderately populated as captured by the National Population Census (NPC) figures of 2006 to be 4,112,445; and by the 2016 projections records of the National Bureau of Statistics (NBS), to have reached about 5,663,362 in its

---

[7] '*Agberos*' connote the various forms of Area Boys, motor-park touts, and street urchins who have become notable forces in the Lagos society. See for instance, Laurent Fourchard, "Lagos and the Invention of Juvenile Delinquency in Nigeria, 1920–60," *The Journal of African History* 47, No. 1 (2006): 15–137; Daniel A. Ikuomola, "Poverty, Road Culture and Deviance among Area-Boys in Lagos Central Neighbourhood," *International Journal of Prevention and Treatment* 1, No. 1 (2012): 1–10; Jonah Uyieh, "'Eko Gb'ole o Gbole': A Historical Study of Youth and Tout Culture in Shomolu Local Government Area, Lagos, 1976–2015," *Journal of African Cultural Studies* 30, No. 3 (2018): 323–328, DOI: 10.1080/13696815.2018.1463844.

[8] "Delta State Government: About Delta State," accessed 15th August 2019, https://www.deltastate.gov.ng/about-delta-state/html.

entire 25 Local Government Areas (LGAs).⁹ Delta State is economically notable among the oil-producing states (Niger-Delta States) of Nigeria.

On its part, Lagos State is located in the south-western region of the country, and was created on 27th May 1967 among the pioneering 12 states for the Nigeria's federation. Records of the Lagos State Government note that the geography of the area lies approximately on longitude 20 42'E and 32 2'E, and between latitude 60 22'N and 60 2'N respectively, in its overall 3,577 sq. km. size. The state is bounded in the north and east by Ogun State of Nigeria, in the west by Republic of Benin, and in the south by the Atlantic Ocean which stretches over 180 kilometers along the Guinea Coast of the Bight of Benin.'¹⁰ In terms of demography, Lagos is often rated as one of the most populated states in Nigeria (with controversial comparison only with Kano State in Northern Nigeria). In the overall 140,431,790 published figures for the country's population by the NPC in 2006, she was put at 9,113,605; and by the 2016 projections of the NBS, the population was said to have increased up to about 12,550,598 out of the overall national figures of 193,392,500.¹¹ However, the Lagos State Government has claimed that the projected overall population figure by January 2019 is 21 million, out of the national estimate of 200.96 million.¹² Economically, Lagos is understood in Nigeria as the commercial capital of the country.

Delta State is notable for its multiple indigenous ethnic configuration as there are diverse peoples with relative numerous languages being spoken in the different parts of the state. For example, Delta North comprises Asaba (Delta Ibo), Aniocha, Ika, Ukwuani and Ndoisimili regions;' while the 'Delta Central and Delta South is made up of Urhobo, Ijaw, Isoko, and Itsekiri people.'¹³ In addition to the entrenchment of indigenous cultural heritages and dialects among the various communities, the resulting ethnic diversity of the state has increased cultural diffusion among them. This has also made the Nigerian Pidgin to be highly developed as a major means of inter-tribal

---

9 "Delta State in Nigeria: Population," accessed 15th August 2019, https://www.citypopulation.de/php/nigeria-admin.php?adm1id=NGA010/html; National Bureau of Statistics, *Demographic Statistics Bulletin 2017*, (Abuja: NBS, May 2018), 7.

10 "Lagos State Government: About Lagos," accessed 15th August 2019, https://lagosstate.gov.ng/about-lagos/html.

11 "Lagos State in Nigeria: Population," accessed 15th August 2019, https://www.citypopulation.de/php/nigeria-admin.php?adm1id=NGA025/shtml; NBS, *Demographic Statistics Bulletin 2017*. 7.

12 "Lagos State Government: About Lagos;" "Lagos Population 2019," *World Population Review*, http://worldpopulationreview.com/world-cities/lagos-population/htlm; "Nigeria Population 2019," *World Population Review*, accessed 15th August 2019, http://worldpopulationreview.com/countries/nigeria-population/html.

13 "Delta State, Nigeria," accessed 16th August 2019, http://www.ngex.com/nigeria/places/states/delta.htm.

communication in many of its growing urban centres. In addition, Standard English is used in some formal quarters. Thus, in key cities like Warri, Ughelli, Sapele, Asaba, Agbor and a number of others, Nigerian Pidgin is the official language of communication.[14] In the case of Lagos State, the indigenous people are predominantly a Yoruba-speaking group. However, the rapid urbanisation of Lagos since the early 20th century as a result of many 'push and pull' factors has made the state to be occupied with various persons from almost all parts of the Nigerian society.[15] Overtime, this has created the environment for the multiple ethnic colouration of Lagos' population. In the same vein, the urban conurbation of Lagos State has further made English and Nigerian Pidgin to be popular languages of communication in most of its part, as well as a blend of other multiple indigenous languages depending on the cluster of native persons residing in each particular areas of the state. In spite of its multifaceted nature, the Yorubas are still recognised as the indigenous people of Lagos.

Politically, Delta and Lagos have played active roles in Nigeria's Fourth Republic since 1999. For Delta State, the government has been consistently under the control of the People's Democratic Party (PDP) since 1999. The Fourth Republic governors of the state have been Chief James Onanafe Ibori (1999–2007), Dr Emmanuel Eweta Uduaghan (2007–2015), and Sen. Ifeanyi Arthur Okowa (2015-incumbent). In Lagos State, the government has been dominated by series of political parties which ideals are diametrically opposed to that of the PDP since the inception of the Fourth Republic. Accordingly, from 1999 to 2003, the political parties in power in Lagos State have been the Alliance for Democracy (AD) (from 2003 to 2015), the Action Congress of Nigeria (ACN) and the All Progressives Congress (APC) (from 2015 to 2019). Also, the various governors that have been administering the state over the years are Sen. Bola Ahmed Tinubu (1999–2007), Mr Babatunde Raji Fashola (2007–2015), Mr Akinwunmi Ambode (2015–2019) and Mr Babajide Olusola Sanwo-Olu (May 2019-incumbent). Apart from these major administrative personalities in both Delta and Lagos States, there have numerous other politicians who have been elected on the umbrella of different political parties into the National Assembly, Houses of Assembly, and offices of the respective Local Governments Councils situated in them in the periodic elections of the Fourth Republic.

---

14   L. Marchese and A. Schnukal, "Nigerian Pidgin English of Warri," *Journal of Nigerian Languages* 1, (1982): 213–219; E. O. Mensah, "Grammaticalization in Nigerian Pidgin," *Íkala, Revista de Lenguaje y Cultura* 17, Issue 2 (May-August 2012): 167–179.
15   A. Adefuye, B. A. Agiri and A. Osuntokun, eds., *History of the Peoples of Lagos State* (Lagos: Lantern Books, 1987); L. C. Dioka, *Lagos and its Environs* (Lagos: First Academic Publisher, 2001); A. Olukoju, *Infrastructure Development and Urban Facilities in Lagos, 1861–2000* (Ibadan: IFRA, 2003).

Together with the prime offices of the President and Vice-President of the Federal Republic of Nigeria, the various political positions in Delta and Lagos States have helped in shaping their associated developments and other parts of the country in the course of the Fourth Republic.

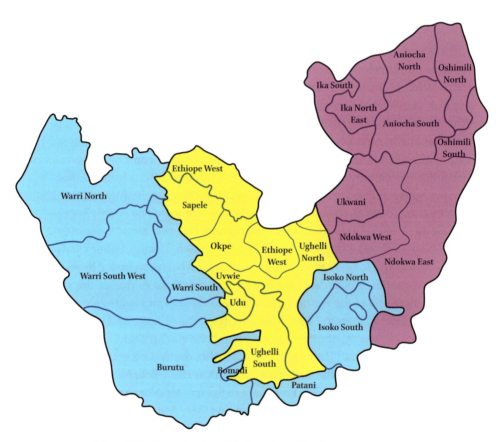

MAP 5.1   Map of Delta State showing all the locations of local government areas
SOURCE: "DELTA AT 26: STATE GOVT SAYS IT WON'T ROLL OUT DRUMS", REFORMER ONLINE, FRIDAY, 25 AUGUST 2017, HTTP://REFORMERONLINE.COM/DELTA-AT-26-STATE-GOVT-SAYS-IT-WONT-ROLL-OUT-DRUMS/. ACCESSED 16 AUGUST, 2019

3   Changing Culture of Youths' Dirty-Relevance in Delta and Lagos States: Theoretical Issues

This paper adopts some aspects of crime theories by exploring the perspectives of Rational Choice Theory and Broken Windows Theory. First, the Rational Choice Theory of crime, which is associated with the works of Becker, Clarke,

'DIRTY-RELEVANCE' OF YOUTHS CULTURE IN NIGERIA'S FOURTH REPUBLIC   95

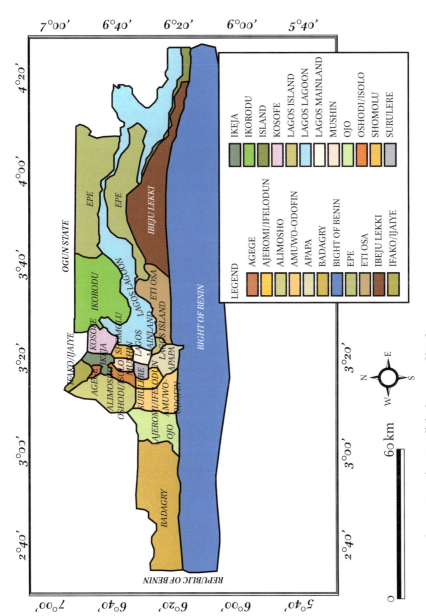

MAP 5.2   Map of Lagos State showing all the location of local government areas
SOURCE: J. AFOLABI & OLALEKAN, ADEDAMOLA & OLUWAJI, & FASHOLA, OLAWUNMI. (2017). "SOCIO-ECONOMIC IMPACT OF ROAD TRAFFIC CONGESTION ON URBAN MOBILITY: A CASE STUDY OF IKEJA LOCAL GOVERNMENT AREA OF LAGOS STATE, NIGERIA". *PACIFIC JOURNAL OF SCIENCE AND TECHNOLOGY*. 18. 246–255

and Cornish proposes that individuals usually arrive at their decisions after the consideration of various alternatives.[16] Hence, it is noted that individuals evaluate their choice of actions in accordance with each option's ability to produce advantage, pleasure and happiness. This theory emphasises responsibility on the part of the decision-maker since his actions are supposed to be the end product of choice after the rational weighing of the other options is carried out. Here, this theory is being drawn upon to explain the choices and attitude of some youths in taking up to the culture of vices in their societies instead of adopting a lifestyle of virtues under a political setting or other spheres of life.

Second, the Broken Windows Theory, is a criminological position introduced by Wilson and Kelling, which used broken windows as a metaphor for disorder within neighbourhoods.[17] Their theory links disorder and incivility within a community to subsequent occurrences of serious crimes, and posits that they usually evolve from minor infractions. Consequently, it sees serious crimes as the final result of a lengthier chain of events, theorising that such emanate from disorders; and that if disorders were eliminated, then serious crimes would not occur.[18] In this study, the theory provides explanations for why the lack of effective early response to youths' vices in Delta and Lagos States by appropriate authorities, can open the way for the entrenchment of the culture of dirty-relevance among the youths which is mainly manifested through violence and criminal activities in their respective environments.

4 Causes of Youths' Culture of 'Dirty-Relevance' in Nigeria's Fourth Republic

Several causes have been identified as being responsible for the changing culture of dirty-relevance among the youths in Nigeria's Fourth Republic which are also applicable to the peculiar cases of Delta and Lagos States. First, the pre-1999 political foundations have been among the contributory factors to the entrenchment of youths' vices in many parts of Nigeria. Historically, at independence, Nigeria was considered to be a 'Manifest Destiny' for the African continent as a result of the combination of her resource endowments and massive population

---

16 Gary S. Becker, "Crime and Punishment: An Economic Approach," *Journal of Political Economy* 76, No. 2 (Mar. - Apr., 1968): 169–217; Derek B. Cornish and Ronald V. Clarke, eds., *The Reasoning Criminal: Rational Choice Perspectives on Offending* (New York: Springer-Verlag, 1986).

17 J. Q. Wilson and G. E. Kelling. "Broken Windows: The Police and Neighborhood Safety," *Atlantic Monthly* (March 1982), accessed 17th August 2019, https://www.manhattan-institute.org/pdf/atlantic-monthly-broken-windows.pdf.

18 Adam J. McKee, "Broken Windows Theory: Academic Theory," accessed 17th August 2019, https://www.britannica.com/topic/broken-windows-theory/html.

strengths.[19] Rather than fulfilling this wish, the post-independence period have manifested in the country's inability to provide adequate solutions to the course of its nation-building and development. In the political setting, the various elections during the First Republic (1960–1966), Second Republic (1979–1983), and Third Republic (1988/89) were filled with recorded cases of irregularities, and at times, violence which acted as clogs in the wheel for the country as a whole.[20] Also, except those listed periods above, majority of the post-independence years, until 1999, were dominated by military rule. The country was subjected to forceful and autocratic regimes with extensive impacts for overall national development.[21] The inability of the contemporary Nigerian state to adequately cater for the overall welfare of all shades of the population has led to multifaceted consequences. For the youths, these years of ineffective political and socio-economic developments created elements of despair whereby majority of them had been left in a condition of self-help in several indices of livelihood. Therefore, these have resulted in many of the youths who had borne the burden or inherited the negative effects of the Nigerian state before 1999 to imbibe an ingrained culture of vices by continuously embarking on crime and violent acts even during the succeeding years of the Fourth Republic.

Second, the failure of the Nigerian state to provide democratic dividends since 1999 has created a fertile ground for the breeding of the vices among many youths. At the inception of the Fourth Republic, there was the popular term – 'new democratic dispensation' – which connotes the feeling that the return to civilian rule would address the hitherto challenges of the country in all ramifications.[22] However, as the years into the republic continue to increase, especially with the beginning and ending of the various tenures of government as signalled by the series of elections from 2003 to 2019, it has dawned on many Nigerians that even the Fourth Republic is a hopeless era since there has not been any tangible results from the leadership's efforts in addressing the dire socio-economic

---

19 A. Adedeji, "Charting the way forward," *Newswatch*, 13 November 2000, 46; Daniel C. Bach, "Nigeria's 'Manifest Destiny' in West Africa: Dominance without Power," *Africa Spectrum* 42, No. 2 (2007): 301–321.

20 Ikyase Tersoo J. and Anthony E. Egberi, "Political Violence and Democratic Stability in Nigeria: Reflecting on the Past and Chatting the Way Forward," *Review of Public Administration and Management* 4, No. 8 (December 2015): 35–36; Egobueze and Ojirika, "Electoral Violence in Nigeria's Fourth Republic," 3–4.

21 Ehinmore and Ehiabhi, "Electoral Violence," 46–47; O. V. Ojo, "Turbulent Election History: An Appraisal of Precipitating Factors in Nigeria," *International Journal of Politics and Good Governance* 5, No. 52, Quarter II (2014): 1–18.

22 Eghosa E. Osaghae, "Democratization in Sub-Saharan Africa: Faltering Prospects, New Hopes," *Journal of Contemporary African Studies* 17, No. 1 (1999): 4–25; Yagboyaju, "Nigeria's Fourth Republic," 93.

and political challenges of the country. For instance, some of the fundamental problems such as corruption, leadership failure, unemployment, lack of welfare packages, increasing rate of poverty, infrastructure decay, ethnicity, violent conflicts, and overall national development have turned for the worse in the Fourth Republic; instead of their improvement from the previous eras.[23] As such, the failing governance structure, in relations to the yearnings of the masses, have created the pathetic condition whereby majority of the population, particularly the youths are not incorporated into the active and productive sectors of the economic and political systems of their respective societies. In this regard, while some of the youths are managing along in positive terms by fitting themselves into any situation possible, majority of them have taken advantage of the hopelessness associated with this republic to reinvent themselves into negative forces of self-help by engaging in several vices and the display of restiveness which have had extended consequences for the country at large.

Third, increasing unemployment rate in Nigeria is among the propelling factors for the youths' culture of dirty-relevance. There is a popular adage that 'an idle mind is a devil's workshop.'[24] Many young persons in Nigeria are ready to be engaged in any employment capacities – whether they are graduates or not. Unfortunately, the degenerating nature of the country's economy before and during the Fourth Republic has resulted in increasing unemployment which has also directly been affecting the youth population. The shocking revelation is that, instead of improving, the unemployment rates have been worsening year by year in the course of the Fourth Republic. For instance, official records by the NBS have it that the country's unemployment rates have increased from an average of 9.07% in 1998 to an unprecedented tune of 23.1% in the last quarter of 2108.[25] Even, according to the recent release by the NBS:

> The economically active or working age population (15 – 64 years of age) increased from 111.1 million in Q3 2017 to 115.5million in Q3 2018. … (while) the total number of people classified as unemployed increased from 17.6 million in Q4 2017 to 20.9 million in Q3 2018.[26]

---

23 G. Omotoso, "Cock-Crow for Civil Service," *The Comet*, Wednesday, 30 June 2004, 17; Oke, "Democracy and Governance," 34.
24 Oral Interview with Mr. Jimoh I. Dawodu (52), Trader, Sabo Market, No. 16 Queen's Street, Sabo-Yaba, Lagos State, 5th June 2019.
25 National Bureau of Statistics, "Unemployment," accessed 19th August 2019, https://www.nigerianstat.gov.ng/html; "Nigeria: Youth Unemployment Rate from 1998 to 2018," accessed 19th August 2019, https://www.statista.com/statistics/812300/youth-unemployment-rate-in-nigeria/; Oladeinde Olawoyin, "Nigeria's Unemployment Rate Rises to 23.1% – NBS," *Premium Times*, 19 December 2018, accessed 19th August 2019, https://www.premiumtimesng.com/news/headlines/301896-nigerias-unemployment-rate-rises-to-23-1-nbs.html.

This is the discouraging situation in which the Nigerian youths find themselves. Therefore, in a bid to satisfy their economic desires, many of the youths who have been deprived of gainful employment have taken up different negative lifestyles for the sake of survival.' For example, in some parts of Delta State, particularly the urban settlements, many unemployed youths have resorted to criminal acts such as stealing, armed robbery, kidnapping and militancy as veritable options for economic survival in an environment of no valuable job opportunities for them. Also, in Lagos State, majority of the youths who engaged in crimes and even the popular *Agbero* sets are part of the unemployed sections of the State's teeming population.

Certain unhealthy practices among Nigeria politicians have also encouraged the culture of youths' 'dirty-relevance' in different environments. A notable feature in this regard is the ingrained system of godfatherism in the Fourth Republic's political activities which has extended to establishing a hierarchical code of perpetual loyalty in the lifestyles of some politicians and their supporters.[27] For the active politicians, some of them are hand-picked and sponsored during elections by certain individuals who are perceived as lords/godfathers, so that if elected, they are expected to also serve the interests of the latter along their prior official duties in government. Concerning the youths, many of them who are political supporters/followers, are thus incorporated as foot soldiers of the politicians in carrying out the desires of their respective candidates and godfathers – if need be – with the hope of being rewarded at the end of the day. Another political motivation here, is the influence of the political environment in promoting the notion of 'stomach infrastructure' during electioneering periods. This concept which was popularised by the former Governor of Ekiti State – Mr. Ayodele Fayose – in 2014, involves inducing potential voters to support a particular candidate in an election by first supplying the masses with food and other necessities that can meet their immediate survival means at a given point in time before considering other detailed issues of development in the society.[28] Hence, many youths have been part of the targeted recipients of such

---

26 National Bureau of Statistics (NBS), *Labor Force Statistics - Volume I: Unemployment and Underemployment Report – Q4 2017-Q3 2018* (Abuja: NBS, December 2018), 1.

27 O. A. Adeoye, Godfatherism and the Future of Nigerian Democracy," *African Journal of Political Science and International Relation* 3, No. 6 (2009): 268–272; M. Aderonke and F. O. Awosika, "Godfatherism and Political Conflicts in Nigeria: The Fourth Republic in Perspective," *International Journal of Management and Social Sciences Research* 2, No. 7 (July 2013): 70–75.

28 Popoola Babalola, "Fayose Explains Concept of 'Stomach Infrastructure," *The Eagle Online*, 17 October 2014, accessed 20th August 2019, https://theeagleonline.com.ng/fayose-explains-concept-of-stomach-infrastructure/html; Emmanuel O. Stober, "Stomach Infrastructure: Lessons for Democracy and Good Governance," *Management Dynamics in the Knowledge Economy* 4, No. 3 (2016): 449–460.

temporary survival provisions. The direct and indirect impact of the stomach infrastructure system has made some youths to be relying on any temporary support systems they can be getting from politicians during elections and post-elections periods rather than opting for other long-term beneficial courses of life.

Lastly, the rationality of an individual in making personal life choices is among the causative factors of youths' culture of dirty-relevance in Delta and Lagos States. Every young person is responsible for making ultimate decision(s) about the definitive lifestyle to live.[29] The end-product of such may either be to live an ethical life devoid of vices or to take up to street life which is marked by recklessness and violence. Hence, this study found out that while the other above causative factors are appropriate, yet, the reasonableness of each youth in settling for an alternative life of virtue or that of vices in the society is very important in his life's course – irrespective of the background, parenthood or present youthful predicaments.

5 Characteristics of Youths' Dirty-Relevance in the Fourth Republic Politics of Delta and Lagos States

The changing culture of youths' dirty-relevance in Delta and Lagos States has exhibited several characteristics. These characteristics are examined here under two main subjects, namely categories and activities of youths' dirty-relevance.

Categories of Youths in the Culture of Dirty-Relevance: Findings from both Delta and Lagos States show that the youths who are prominent in the culture of dirty-relevance could be grouped.[30] The first group is the level of the organised setting of the Arrow-Heads and Top-Lords among the youths' hierarchies. These topmost youths' officials are persons who have attained certain levels of ruggedness and are recognised as nucleus or overall leaders over a set of youth gangs within particular communities and zones. They attain such leadership positions within the gangs through the elimination of rivals, relocation to new areas where there are no apparent arrow-heads and establishment of their reigns over

---

[29] Uyieh, "Eko Gb'ole o Gbole," 324.
[30] Youths that fall under the main categories and activities of this study relate more to the male folk. During the course of the field work, it was observed that the males are the most prominent in displaying the culture of youths' dirty-relevance in Delta and Lagos States. Although, the females are not exempted from such culture, their roles are featured mainly in such activities like prostitution, stealing, wives/girl-friends to notorious youths' members, political supporters, or other subtle roles as facilitators in the schemes of the 'guys' network of events.

there, offering loyal services to existing overlords who may grant authority to any of them after the latter might have risen up to a higher level of life's satisfaction, or, in some cases, elections as youth representatives in a domain.[31] In Delta State, for instance, youths' lords/arrow-heads apply to top militant leaders in identified zones, youth leaders of secluded communities, and top loyal boys of recognised political godfathers in a given area. While in Lagos State, such prime heads relate to the overall chairman and sectional heads of the National Union of Road Transport Workers (NURTW), acclaimed area-boys' leaders of popular streets or broader areas known as the '*Alayes*', and top loyal boys of recognised political godfathers in the state or in other notable quarters.[32] The uniqueness of these top youths' leaders is that, although they operate under certain unwritten codes their authorities are well recognised within certain well-defined areas, localities, communities, or zones as the case may be. Also, such authorities trickle down in descending order to other sub-loyal boys until they get to the base of the hierarchical structure of the youths' leadership.

A second category are the members of secret cult groups in Delta and Lagos States (and by extension, the neighbouring states). Right from their inception from the pioneering activities of Pyrates Confraternity (the earliest one in 1953) and other emerging ones, the initiates and fraternities of the secret cult societies were initially limited to the tertiary institutions' levels in Nigeria.[33] Moreover, in the growing years of the Fourth Republic, the expansive political climates have made cultism to be a common phenomenon among many Nigeria's communities. As such, today, it is not uncommon to see rugged students and graduates, artisans, ordinary persons and even loafers who are boastful members of one cult group or the other in the various communities of Delta and Lagos States.[34] Although their lists are numerous, in Delta State, the dominant ones include the Supreme Vikings Confraternity (SVC) and the Black Axe Confraternity (*Ayes Men*); while in Lagos State, the prominent ones are the Eiye Confraternity (Bird) and the Black Axe Confraternity. Functioning at the broader national level, designated states systems and clustered local

---

31 Oral Interview with Mr. Fidelis O. Utomudo – aka *Akamaka I* (32), President Isoko National Youth Council, at his residence at Igwreovie Community, Ughelli, Delta State, 15th June 2019.
32 Oral Interview with Mr. Olalekan Adeleke – aka *Ballo* (38), Youth Leader, Empire Zone, Jibowu-Yaba, Lagos State, 7th June 2019.
33 Adewale Rotimi, "Violence in the Citadel: The Menace of Secret Cults in the Nigerian Universities," *Nordic Journal of African Studies* 14, No. 1 (2005): 79–98; N. P. Ololube, Nwachukwu, C. N. Agbor, and O. A. Uriah, "Vicious Hazard to Peace Culture in Tertiary Education: The Activities of the Secret Cults," *British Journal of Education, Society & Behavioural Science* 3, No. 1 (2013.): 65–75.
34 B. A. Akinpelu, "Trends and Patterns of Fatalities Resulting from Cult Societies and Belief in Witchcraft in Nigeria, 2006–2014," *IFRA-Nigeria Working Papers Series* 40, No. 1 (2015): 1–24; Uyieh, "Eko Gb'ole o Gbole," 332.

governments/communities' operation units, these secret cults' groups have over the years in the course of the Fourth Republic, incorporated many youths in Delta and Lagos States into their networks and activities. Even, in elections times, some politicians usually patronise cult groups for snatching of ballot boxes and other forms of malpractices.[35] Hence, whether during election periods or not, the regimented activities of these cults (which have in most times manifested in several vices) have shaped the life patterns of youths who are parts of the memberships.

Another major set of youths in dirty-relevance in Delta and Lagos States are those that can be collectively referred to as members of motor parks unions. In the commercial road transportation schemes in Nigeria, some organisations have emerged to protect the interests of their members (the drivers/operators) and provide linkages with the government on concerned issues affecting the transport sectors. However, in practical terms, these motor park unions, through their surrogates, collect tolls from operators of taxis and commercial buses, motorcycles (okada) and tricycles (keke Marwa) and they are most times generically called 'agberos' (motor park touts in Nigerian parlance). Prominent among these motor park unions are the NURTW, Road Transport Employers Association of Nigeria (RTEAN), Motorcycle Operators Association of Nigeria (MOAN) and the Tricycle Operators Association of Nigeria (TOAN).[36] In Delta and Lagos States, these bodies, particularly, the NURTW, which from its formal registration 1978, has now peaked to be the most recognised transport union in Nigeria and has developed extensive networks which incorporate the youths as dominant population of the field workers as they are visibly seen in the various motor parks and bus terminuses collecting tolls from commercial transporters. Here, remarkable differences exist between the operations of the Delta and Lagos States motor park unions. For example, in Delta State, the *Agberos* function only in recognised motor parks for the loading and dropping-off of passengers or some notable junctions of large communities where there are no constructed motor parks/bus-stops; patrolling with vehicles by watching out for erring drivers that might contravene the state/locality's operational motor-parks guiding rules; and their operations are permissible only between the hours of 7am and 5pm (except in rare cases when there is an agreeable extra time between the transport operators and the *Agberos* for

---

35 "Niger Delta Watch 2019: A Citizen-Led Election Observation Project Report," *Niger Delta Watch 2019 #3*, 17 December 2018, 8, accessed 23rd August 2019, http://www.stakeholderdemocracy.org/wp/content/uploads/2018/12/Niger-Delta-watch/pdf.
36 Olukoju, *Infrastructure Development*, 135; Oladipo O. Olubomehin, "The Nigerian Motor Transporters since the 1920s," *International Journal of Humanities and Social Science* 2, No. 12 (June 2012): 230–237.

rates' collections).[37] While in Lagos State, the *Agberos* networks of the NURTW and other faceless bodies dotted all parts of the cities as their activities are visible at motor parks, along major high ways, and at almost every desired bus stop by the linking expressways and internal road networks of the state. They stop and chase moving commercial mini-buses (*Danfo*), medium-bodies' buses (*LT*) and luxurious buses (*Molue*) for the collection of varying fixed and unfixed charges as regular tolls. Also, the operational periods in Lagos is not fixed as *Agberos* can be seen collecting tolls and rates as early as 4:30am up to 11:30pm (or anytime deemed fit when the commercial transportation vehicles are seen to be working).[38]

Organised community-based youth groups are another category of youths who participate in the activities of dirty-relevance in politics. These groups of youth are more prominent in the different communities of Delta State, and in minor cases, some adjoining rural settlements in Lagos State. For the classical Delta State's arrangements, the youths are usually recognised as among the units of the overall coordinating (administrative) authorities in most communities. They are meant to efficiently provide certain internal and external services. Internally, many Delta youths feature actively in communal services such as providing security and creating policing architectures. Externally, the youths, especially in the oil-producing areas of Delta States, are meant to serve as the active channels to demand that the oil companies in their communities provide the statutory corporate social responsibilities and other forms of assistance to the community and to react to unfavourable government policies and actions of general interests in ensuring that they and their communities at large benefit regularly from the perceived resources being generated from their areas.[39] It should be noted that communities' youths embrace a very broad outlook which incorporates all desired indigenous members of the secluded communities – whether they are active or passive participants, and cultists or non-cultists' members, as well as any foreigners who have stayed for a long time in the host communities and have been absolved without discrimination into the known systems.

Activities of Youths in Dirty-Relevance: In the political environments of Delta and Lagos States, the youth culture of dirty-relevance in the Fourth Republic is manifested in various activities which spread across the pre-election, election

---

37 Oral Interview with Mr. Emmanuel Ossai (35), Inter-City Taxi Driver, Koka Park, Asaba, Delta State, 18th June 2019.
38 Oral Interview with Mr. Kazim Olawolu (45), Danfo Driver (Mini-Bus Operator), at Oshodi Under-Bridge Bus Stop, Oshodi, Lagos State, 7th June 2019.
39 P. Oromareghake, R. O. Arisi, and O. M. Igho, "Youth Restiveness and Insecurity in Niger Delta: A Focus on Delta State," *Global Journal of Human Social Science* 13, Issue 3 Version 1.0 (2013): 47–53; Oral Interview with Mr. Fidelis O. Utomudo, 15th June 2019.

and post-election periods. During the pre-election periods, the political activities of youths feature prominently and that usually attract much official and unofficial attention to them. Such pre-election activities include engagement in political campaigns and rallies and acting as spies for election candidates. Also, some of the hardened and notorious youths act as hired assassins to kill the political opponents of their clients.[40] Though such acts distract from democratic consolidation and reflect negatively on the electoral processes, youths engage in them for economic and political gains. Such activities also boost the electoral chances of their patrons.

In periods of elections, the youths play vital roles which make them stand out among the population. Positively, many of the youths in Delta and Lagos States have been performing their civic responsibilities in the series of elections of the Fourth Republic by casting their votes for candidates and political parties of their choice; while some enabled ones have even contested for political positions under the umbrella of any suitable political parties of their constituencies. Nonetheless, the youths' culture of dirty-relevance have been brought to bear too during these elections. This is because, they are the major persons that are used by reckless politicians for the rigging of elections, snatching of ballot box, and the creation of violent scenes which have led to damaging impact in their areas of operations.[41]

Also, in post-election political periods of the Fourth Republic, the youths' activities have been visible in both Delta and Lagos States. Their activities here could be subsumed into the two main parts of active and passive political services. For the active political services rendered, the youths that support successful politicians are rewarded with political appointments, jobs in the public service, jobs in private organisations, money and cars. Some are retained as political thugs.[42] On the other hand, those youths that were not so lucky enough to be captured in the active political and economic services, would seek for alternatives avenues to be part of their societal systems through any means possible. Thus, the inactive political services of many youths in the display of the culture of dirty-relevant include opting for the hardened life of becoming among the Niger Delta militants in the case of Delta State and touting/area boys

---

[40] Oral Interview with Mr. Olufemi Temidayo – aka *Olubembem* (38), NURTW Member, Mile 2 Bus Stop, Amuwo-Odofin, Lagos State, 6th June 2019; Oral Interview with Mr. Ekemena Akpofure – aka *Scorpio* (35), Secretary Otor-Ogor Youth Association, Otor-Ogor Community, Ughelli-North, Delta State, 15th June 2019.

[41] N. O. Obakhedo, "Curbing Electoral Violence in Nigeria: The Imperative of Political Education," *International Multidisciplinary Journal* 5, No. 5, Series 2, (October, 2011), 103–104.

[42] Oral Interview with Mr. Olalekan Adeleke, 7th June 2019; Oral Interview with Mr. Ekemena Akpofure, 15th June 2019

lifestyles in the case of Lagos State, involving in other forms of social menace in their associated communities, and loafing around in search of any means that would suffice for survival pending when they will be engaged along again.

6   Impact of Youths' Culture of Dirty-Relevance in Delta and Lagos States

The culture of youths' dirty-relevance in their society, especially in the context of the political climate of the Fourth Republic in Delta and Lagos States has resulted in wide-ranging impacts for the youths themselves, their environments/communities, and the broad state and national developmental issues.

As regards the youths themselves, first, the culture of dirty-relevance has led to the entrenchment of individual and group's survival strategies that do not regard governmental or institutional arrangements. Second, it has promoted rivalry and antagonistic relationships among youth groups. Third, it has created the avenues for crimes and violent dispositions such as stealing, armed robbery, street gangsterism, hooliganism and social violence. Fourth, it has led to increasing drug abuse among many youths. Fifth, it has encouraged perpetual servitude of youths to politicians in order to gain inordinate benefits from the latter. Also, it has contributed to the negative attitudes of many youths to education. Some of them prefer quicker routes to getting rich rather than engaging in the rigours of academic and other professional trainings.[43] In addition, it has led to the untimely deaths of many unfortunate youths who engaged in various negative activities.

With particular reference to their respective environments and communities, youths' culture of dirty-relevance in the Fourth Republic have had dramatic impacts on the political culture of Delta and Lagos States. Among others, this has led to social disorderliness as some of the communities are thrown into full rampage and conflict owing to the violent activities of the youths. For instance, the series of clashes that have emerged from the rivalry between youths' arrow-heads in establishing their exclusive domain over an area or in declaring independence from former lords, as well as other forms of violent conflicts that have occurred among factions of youths have resulted in a high scale of insecurity in their respective communities with attendant consequences for all stakeholders therein.[44] Second, such culture has led to

---

[43] Oral Interview with Mr. Monday Ayomide (25), Street-Hussler, Tejuosho Area, Surulere, Lagos State, 8th June 2019; Oral Interview with Mr. Kinsley Uvoh (30), Okada-Man (Motorcycle Rider), Oleh, Delta State, 17th June 2019.

[44] Uyieh, "Eko Gb'ole o Gbole," 334.

the entrenchment of cultism in many communities of Delta and Lagos State. Before the era of excessive political activities of the Fourth Republic, many communities of these States were places of socio-cultural integration and the promotion of communalism among the youths. However, with the growing years of the Republic, the opposite has been the case as majority of the youths' associations have been infiltrated by memberships and practices of secret cults – depending on the dominant ones in any locality. Another major impact of youths' dirty-relevance has been the increasing availability of arms and weapons. Overtime, many youths have used their connections with violent inclined politicians and other secret networks to acquire deadly arms and weapons such as dangerous daggers and swords, pistols, double barrel guns, AK47 and other ranges of riffles for themselves. The possession of such arms and ammunitions have shaped the expanding context and impact of youths' negative activities in their communities and beyond.[45] Furthermore, youth's negative culture has led to political extremism in different communities of both states. Instead of promoting the attitude of peaceful engagements, many youths have turned to political extremists which have resulted in extensive consequences for various persons in their environments.

Concerning the broad issues of national development, youths' culture of dirty-relevance has had much impacts in Delta and Lagos States. First, in both states, youths' negative activities have led to recorded cases of high insecurity – especially from the political angle. At times the heated political landscape of campaigns and voting periods have resulted in violent clashes among rival camps of the youths. To cite some recent examples, in Ughelli South LGA of Delta State, during the gubernatorial and House of Assembly Election of 9th March 2019, youths who are political thugs opened fire on voters which led to the death of one person and the injury of many other persons.[46] Also, it was reported that a 28-year-old man was shot dead at Uvwie Local Government Area of Warri by unknown gun men on 16th February 2019, and post-election clashes among rival cult groups were rampant in the area in the months of February and March 2019.[47] Earlier, on 8th January 2019, during one of the APC gubernatorial elections campaigns at Ikeja, Lagos State, some rival groups of youths of NURTW invaded a rally where the then sitting, Governor Akinwumi Ambode,

---

45 Oromareghake et al, "Youth Restiveness and Insecurity;" NPDI, "Organized Crime in the Niger Delta: Implications for the 2019 Elections," Niger Delta Partnership Initiatives and Partnership Initiatives in the Niger Delta, Conflict Briefing, (Abuja, April 2018), 1–4.
46 Timothy Onimisi and Omolegbe L. Tinuola, "Appraisal of the 2019 Post-Electoral Violence in Nigeria," *Malaysian Journal of Social Sciences and Humanities* 4, Issue 3 (2019):107–113.
47 "Niger Delta Watch 2019," 18.

and the aspiring one, Babajide O. Sanwo-Olu, were present and started shooting sporadically. This led to the death of three persons and caused serious injuries to the youth leader – MC Oluomo – and other persons.[48] In Lagos too, during the 23rd February, 2019 presidential elections, some youths who were political thugs visibly invaded the parts of Okota dominated by the Igbo ethnic group, disrupted elections and forced the accredited voters to stay away from the polling booths.[49] The above and other similar reports about youths' disruptive actions during the 2019 elections and in previous elections are really disturbing.

Second, each of these states have been associated with certain dominant tendencies among the youths as a result of their culture of dirty-relevance. For Delta State, majority of her youths, particularly those that originated from the oil-producing communities of southern part, have degenerated into the wider scope of the Niger Delta militants. Though some Lagos communities have youths that possess deadly weapons, the case of Delta State (likewise many other Niger Delta States) is exceptional – as most of the urban and rural settlements are dominated by available modern guns/riffles and other weapons at the ready disposal of the youths. These communities are volatile since there are ingrained underlying issues.[50] Therefore, many Delta youths have justified their militant activities with reference to the Niger Delta struggle against the federal government for resource control. In the case of Lagos, the youths' negative activities have resulted in the formal manifestation and escalation of the *Agberos* or Area-Boys culture. They prey on the operators of commercial transportation everywhere and anytime, straddle the streets at will, and at times, are even parts of the political system.

Aside the above, other impacts of the youths' culture of dirty-relevance at the states and national levels include the enthroning of the attitude of 'do or die politics' among the youths as foot soldiers at the service of politicians – whether at elections or not; increasing and trickling down of corruption as a national bane to all shades of the population; and the expression of hopelessness among many youths' leadership ability at all levels of government as a result of the contemporary and future lifestyles which many of them are adopting.

---

48 "NURTW Official MC Oluomo, Eight Others Stabbed at APC Lagos Rally," *Punch*, 8 January 2019, accessed 28 August 2019, https://punchng.com/nurtw-official-mc-oluomo-eight-others-allegedly-stabbed-at-apc-lagos-rally/html.
49 "2019 Elections: Watered by Blood of Nigerians," *Punch*, 26 February 2019, accessed 28 August 2019, https://punchng.com/2019-elections-watered-by-blood-of-nigerians/html.
50 Foundation for Partnership Initiatives in the Niger Delta (PIND), *A Report on Niger Delta Region Youth Assessment, June 2011* (Abuja: PIND, AA-YA-01-October 2011), 9–13

7 Curbing Youths' Culture of Dirty-Relevance in Delta and Lagos States

The negative influences of youths' vices on the society and the emerging forms of their dirty-relevance is not a welcomed development. As such, over the years, different bodies have responded and reacted practically to either stop these vices, or at least reduce them to manageable levels. These bodies include the governmental and non-governmental organisations.

Government has reacted to negative activities by youths through forceful and conciliatory means. On the first approach, the Nigerian Federal Government and the authorities of Delta and Lagos States have relied on the Nigerian Police for the purpose of protecting the security of the society. The government has ensured that police stations staffed with numerous policemen are established in various areas of these states so as to fight against all forms of crime and to facilitate police-community relations.[51] The policemen often patrol or parade the major areas and streets of Delta and Lagos States in order to monitor any forms of social disorder – whether such disorders are from the youths or not. Consequently, some of the suspected dangerous youths who are aimlessly roaming the streets or who gather in designated positions are regularly arrested and detained. Those that are caught with evidence of criminality are further prosecuted and punished so as to serve as a deterrent to other persons in embarking on criminal activities.[52] Also, during violent clashes of the youths, the police usually take it upon themselves to respond to such situations by shooting tear gasses, and in critical conditions, armed bullets, in order to curb violence and reduce the number of casualties at such deadly moments. Moreover, in the peculiar case of Delta State, the Federal Government had at times dispatched military men and Joint Task Forces to communities where the youths' violent actions are directly against the oil-producing resources of the Niger Delta region so as to quell such attacks.

Another dimension of government response to the menace of youths' culture of dirty-relevance is through peaceful methods. Since the inception of the Fourth Republic, the authorities of Delta and Lagos State Governments – at both states and local governments levels – have made some concerted efforts in the rehabilitation and reformation of many youths through different schemes. In line with this, from 1999 till date, some vocational training and poverty alleviation centres have been established for the less privileged people – including the youths – to learn any trade of their choice and earn an income for their survival.

---

51 *Police Act*, Sections 23–30, accessed 28 August 2019, www.placng.org/new/laws/P19.pdf.
52 Oral Interview with Sgt. Joe Oladumokun (53), Police Officer, Bariga Police Station, Bariga, Lagos, 29th July 2019.

Accordingly, some of these youths have been taught catering, carpentry, gardening, tailoring, shoe-making, craft-weaving, bricklaying and other useful works in these centres through these gestures.[53] In the example of Delta State, some of its militant youths in the oil-producing areas have been benefitting from the Niger Delta Amnesty Programme which was launched by the Federal government since 2009.[54] Thus, these attempts, no matter the degrees of success, have transformed some former negatively-inclined youths into good citizens with a high level of economic responsibility and morality in their respective communities.

On the other hand, non-governmental bodies have contributed their quotas in helping to check the negative activities of youths in Delta and Lagos States. Notable among these are the indigenous communities' vigilante systems in Delta State and the Oodua Peoples' Congress (OPC) in Lagos State. The positive sides of these indigenous architectures are evidently reflected through the control of crimes and effective complementation of police efforts in ensuring community security in their respective environments. They have been so effective through the performance of vigilante activities, cleansing operations and guard duties. In both states, cleansing operations consist of actions carried out by members of these indigenous security forces at regular intervals to dislodge criminals from their strongholds, restore order to temporary chaotic situations and track down elusive criminals who are handed over to the police for further governmental actions.[55] One thing to note here is that, in most times, these indigenous security forces bye-pass the police, by passing instant judgement and direct punishment on their culprits. This is usually done by applying the 'jungle justice' which entails beating up perceived criminals and, at times, setting the alleged criminals ablaze with vehicle-tyres and petrol fire. In addition, to complement the roles of professional security bodies, members of these indigenous vigilantes usually form the large section of the civil security personnel – either as watchmen or night guards – that are employed by several community-based associations and personal organisations for the security of their environment in Delta and Lagos States.

---

53 Oral Interview with Mr. Niyi Ogundele (42), Secretary, Information Department, Shomolu Local Government Council, 2 Durosimi Street, Off Oguntolu Street, Shomolu, Lagos State, 25th July 2019.
54 Chijioke E. Ekumaoko, The Amnesty Question in Post Conflict Niger Delta and Peace-Building," *Arabian Journal of Business and Management Review* 2, No.10 (May 2013): 4–11; Lucy Jegede and Olufayo Olu-Olu, "Amnesty Policy: Temporal Salvation in the Niger-Delta," *British Journal of Education, Society & Behavioural Science* 7, No. 4 (2015): 273–280.
55 Oral Interview with Mr. William Ejegbe (48), Chairman, Isoko-North Vigilante Associations, at Ellu Community, Delta State, 22nd June 2019; Oral Interview with Mr. Gbedebo Akin (42), OPC Member, 21 Olabiran Street, Shomolu, Lagos State, 26th July 2019.

Furthermore, the courts of traditional rulers in the various communities of Delta and Lagos States also have measures for checking the social menace that are associated with youths' vices. The traditional courts ensure that the inhabitants in their domains live peacefully wherever they are. As such, if any person (youth) is reported or noticed to constitute a threat in their communities, the Elders-in-Council will summon the person – either to advise him or apply liberal discipline – with the objective of making him to change for the good at his own pace. But if such a person persisted in the negative deeds, the traditional rulers will proceed to apply strict punishment in accordance with the customary practices of such communities. If the matter is higher than what the indigenous courts can handle, the criminal would be handed over to the police for prosecution.

Significantly, in terms of overall assessment, the attempts by the different aforementioned bodies have not been entirely useless and at the same time not entirely successful as far as the solving of youths' culture of dirty-relevance is concerned in Delta and Lagos States. While the above efforts have produced positive results at certain levels, some of them have turned out to be counter-productive as well. On the positive angle, the multiple steps taken by the several bodies against the menace of youths' vices have at time worked productively for the two States. In this sense, the actions of the police and other related security bodies have had serious impact on these youths. Many of them have served punishments ranging from imprisonment to death. Consequently, some of the former negatively inclined youths are now increasingly seeking lawful means of livelihood, in order to avoid the wrath of the law. Also, some of the established rehabilitation and vocational centres have catered for the welfare of many youths. Owing to these, many of the youths are now utilising their acquired skills in various business ventures. Even, the more favoured ones are now entrepreneurs and employers of labour.

Nevertheless, the several attempts at controlling the youths' negative culture have not been far reaching enough to eradicate their associated vices or reduce their impact to a manageable degree. This is mainly because the treatment is superficial, as some of the fundamental issues are yet to be addressed. As earlier indicated, the youths' culture of dirty-relevance are the direct products of prevailing socio-economic and political conditions in the society. Prime among these, is the propelling factor of unemployment. As of now, the thrust of government policy is geared more towards the taking up of arms against violent youths without providing employment opportunities through which these groups of people can satisfy their basic necessities of life. Also, the vocational centres founded so far have targeted only a few persons and some of the trained persons from these centres end up without the needed start-up capital that would have facilitated the all-around reintegration into their communities as productive beings. Even, the Niger Delta Amnesty Programme has been heavily criticised as it has been beneficial to mainly few militant youths of the Ijaw ethnic group who were absolved from the camps of some selected warlords in the Niger Delta struggle, without continuous expansion to effectively accommodate the youths from the other oil-producing ethnic groups in the Niger Delta.[56] Therefore, on a balanced scale, the efforts made so far in this regard are so inadequate; when compared to the swamp of youths perpetuating the culture of dirty-relevance in many parts of Delta and Lagos States.

In the same vein, in both states, there are no specific legal frameworks to effectively curtail youths' culture of dirty-relevance. Despite the rampage of militants and touts in different parts Delta and Lagos States over the years, up till date, the authorities of these states have not made any official policy against them, neither have they enacted any direct law(s) whose implementation could help in the dislodgement of militants, *Agberos* or Areas Boys from their popular operational bases. Also, some of the security agents are paying lip-services to their official duties. Many communities in Delta and Lagos States are still being dominated by 'bad boys,' irrespective of the many police propaganda about the elimination of criminals. The Lagos example is worrying at times too, when in some cases, police officers and *Agberos* are seen standing side-by-side collecting bribes from drivers/conductors; without any attempt by the police to curb the criminal activities of the *Agberos*. In the environment of these inefficiencies, the youths' cultures of dirty relevance are still on the reign in different areas of Delta and Lagos States in their versatile escapades during the Fourth Republic.

8 Recommendations and Conclusion

This study reveals that over the years in the Fourth Republic, the youths' changing culture of dirty-relevance has really constituted important components of the political and socio-economic structures of Delta and Lagos States with dramatic consequences on these societies from multiple dimensions. Therefore, in order to find a lasting solution to the youths' menace in the political sphere, the following suggestions will be useful too.

First, practical and continuous efforts in understanding the deep roots of youths' culture of dirty-relevant in the society should be carried out. These should be done in both states with the sure steps of reaching the roots with groundwork solutions. For example, the adoption of the key aspects of the models of 'positive peace' by Johan Galtung; 'management of protracted social

---

56 Oral Interview with Mr. Fidelis O. Utomudo, 15 June, 2019.

conflict' by Edward Azar; and the 'moral and dignity training systems' of the indigenous African communities could helped greatly in this regard.[57]

Second, comprehensive employment opportunities should be created by the government, corporate bodies and private individuals through which the youth readily partake in for prospective living; rather than seeking alternatives in vices in the absence of none. In this regard, there should be equal opportunity for all persons to participate fully in the economic, political and social sectors of their societies.

Third, thorough arms limitation and disarmament control should be carried out by both federal and states governments' relevant authorities. Also, politicians should desist from the umbilical patronage of radical youths during elections and other political activities so as to avoid giving a leeway to negatively inclined youths from establishing their dirty-relevance in the overall political system.

The Legislative arm of government should enact laws that are meant for the well beings of citizen at all times; and stringent measures should be taken by the Delta and Lagos State Governments to check the increasing radicalism among youths in their respective domains.

Lastly, youths should channel their lifestyles toward positive and useful activities (no matter the condition they found themselves); rather than the notorious lifestyles of 'dirty relevance' during elections and post-elections periods – which majority of them are still known for till date in both Delta and Lagos States. In this sense, the paper is of the strong opinion that the youths should be guided by their individual life's choices in focusing on prospective courses as responsible agents of change in their societies with reference to their entire activities and life circle.

On the whole, the practical implementation of these recommendations will go a long way in combating the youths' culture of dirty relevance in Delta and Lagos States, and by extension to other parts of Nigeria. They will also help in influencing and changing the lives of youth from negativity to positivity; and the entire society more directed towards viable development.

References

Abah, E. O. and Paul M. Nwokwu. 2015. "Political Violence and the Sustenance of Democracy in Nigeria." *IOSR Journal of Humanities and Social Science* 20, Issue 11(1): 33–44.

---

[57] Johan Galtung, *Theories of Peace: A Synthetic Approach to Peace Thinking* (Oslo: International Peace Research Institute, 1967); Edward Azar, *The Management of Protracted Social Conflict: Theory and Cases* (Aldershot: Dartmouth Publishing Company, 1990); Oral Interview with Chief Ayinde Adetomi, 26th July 2019.

Adedeji, A. 2000. "Charting the way forward." *Newswatch*, 13 November 2000.

Adefuye, A., B. A. Agiri and A. Osuntokun, eds. 1987. *History of the Peoples of Lagos State*. Lagos: Lantern Books.

Adeoye, O. A. 2009. "Godfatherism and the Future of Nigerian Democracy." *African Journal of Political Science and International Relation* 3(6): 268–272.

Aderonke, M. and F. O. Awosika. 2013. "Godfatherism and Political Conflicts in Nigeria: The Fourth Republic in Perspective." *International Journal of Management and Social Sciences Research* 2(7): 70–75.

Ajayi, Daniel S. 2016. "Towards the Enhancement of Morality in the Nigerian Politics." *Afro Asian Journal of Social Sciences* VII, No. IV: 1–20.

Akinpelu, B. A. 2015. "Trends and Patterns of Fatalities Resulting from Cult Societies and Belief in Witchcraft in Nigeria, 2006–2014." *IFRA-Nigeria Working Papers Series* 40(1): 1–24.

Azar, Edward. 1990. *The Management of Protracted Social Conflict: Theory and Cases*. Aldershot: Dartmouth Publishing Company.

Babalola, Popoola. 2014. "Fayose Explains Concept of 'Stomach Infrastructure." *The Eagle Online*, 17 October 2014. Accessed 20 August, 2019. https://theeagleonline.com.ng/fayose-explains-concept-of-stomach-infrastructure/html.

Bach, Daniel C. 2007. "Nigeria's 'Manifest Destiny' in West Africa: Dominance without Power." *Africa Spectrum* 42(2): 301–321.

Becker, Gary S. 1968. "Crime and Punishment: An Economic Approach." *Journal of Political Economy* 76(2): 169–217.

Cornish, Derek B. and Ronald V. Clarke, eds. 1986. *The Reasoning Criminal: Rational Choice Perspectives on Offending*. New York: Springer-Verlag.

"Definition of Youth. 1981." *Secretary-General's Report to the General Assembly, A/36/215, 1981*.

Degirmenci, Nigar. 2016. "Politics is a Dirty Game!: A Case Study of Political Cynicism in Turkey." International *Journal of Liberal Arts and Social Science* 4(9): 114–132.

"Delta State Government: About Delta State." Accessed 15 August, 2019. https://www.deltastate.gov.ng/about-delta-state/html.

"Delta State in Nigeria: Population." Accessed 15 August, 2019. https://www.citypopulation.de/php/nigeria-admin.php?adm1id=NGA010/html;

"Delta State, Nigeria." Accessed 16 August, 2019. http://www.ngex.com/nigeria/places/states/delta.htm.

Dioka, L. C. 2001. *Lagos and its Environs*. Lagos: First Academic Publisher.

Egobueze, Anthony and Callistus Ojirika. 2017. "Electoral Violence in Nigeria's Fourth Republic: Implications for Political Stability," *Journal of Scientific Research & Reports* 13(2): 1–11.

Ehinmore, Omolere M. and Odion S. Ehiabhi. 2013. "Electoral Violence and the Crisis of Democratic Experiment in Post-Colonial Nigeria." *Journal of Arts and Humanities* 2(5): 46–47.

Ekumaoko, Chijioke E. 2013. "The Amnesty Question in Post Conflict Niger Delta and Peace-Building." *Arabian Journal of Business and Management Review* 2(10): 4–11.

Evrenk, Haldun. 2011. "Why A Clean Politician Supports Dirty Politics: A Game-Theoretical Explanation for the Persistence of Political Corruption." *Journal of Economic Behavior & Organization* 80: 498–510.

Foundation for Partnership Initiatives in the Niger Delta. 2011. *A Report on Niger Delta Region Youth Assessment, June 2011*. Abuja: PIND, AA-YA-01-October.

Fourchard, Laurent. 2006. "Lagos and the Invention of Juvenile Delinquency in Nigeria, 1920–60." *The Journal of African History* 47(1): 15–137.

Galtung, Johan. 1967. *Theories of Peace: A Synthetic Approach to Peace Thinking*. Oslo: International Peace Research Institute.

Ikuomola, Daniel A. 2012. "Poverty, Road Culture and Deviance among Area-Boys in Lagos Central Neighbourhood." *International Journal of Prevention and Treatment* 1(1): 1–10.

Jegede, Lucy and Olufayo Olu-Olu. 2015. "Amnesty Policy: Temporal Salvation in the Niger-Delta." *British Journal of Education, Society & Behavioural Science* 7(4): 273–280.

"Lagos Population 2019." Accessed 15 August, 2019. *World Population Review*, http://worldpopulationreview.com/world-cities/lagos-population/htlm.

"Lagos State Government: About Lagos." Accessed 15 August, 2019. https://lagosstate.gov.ng/about-lagos/html.

"Lagos State in Nigeria: Population." Accessed 15 August, 2019. https://www.citypopulation.de/php/nigeria-admin.php?adm1id=NGA025/shtml.

"Map of Lagos State Showing all the location Local Government Areas." Accessed 16 August, 2019. https://www.google.com/search?q=map+of+lagos+state+showing+all+the+local+government&sxsrf=ACYBGNRnwZnbhYlHuOcNwLFIYL1lhbUIsg:1569686377528&tbm.jpg.

Marchese, L. and A. Schnukal. 1982. "Nigerian Pidgin English of Warri." *Journal of Nigerian Languages* 1: 213–219.

McKee, Adam J. "Broken Windows Theory: Academic Theory." Accessed 17 August, 2019. https://www.britannica.com/topic/broken-windows-theory/html.

Mensah, E. O. "Grammaticalization in Nigerian Pidgin." 2012. *Íkala, Revista de Lenguaje y Cultura* 17(2): 167–179.

Nachana'a, Alahira D. 2015. "Democracy, Youth and Violent Conflicts in Nigeria's Fourth Republic: A Critical Analysis." *Research on Humanities and Social Sciences* 5(2): 161–162.

National Bureau of Statistics (NBS). 2018. *Labor Force Statistics - Volume I: Unemployment and Underemployment Report – Q4 2017-Q3 2018*. Abuja: NBS, December.

National Bureau of Statistics (NBS). 2018. *Demographic Statistics Bulletin 2017*. Abuja: NBS, May 2018.

National Bureau of Statistics. "Unemployment." Accessed August, 2019. https://www.nigerianstat.gov.ng/html.

Niger Delta Watch 2019. 2018. "Niger Delta Watch 2019: A Citizen-Led Election Observation Project Report." #3, 17, December 2018. Accessed 23 August, 2019, http://www.stakeholderdemocracy.org/wp/content/uploads/2018/12/Niger-Delta-watch/pdf.

"Nigeria: Youth Unemployment Rate from 1998 to 2018." Accessed 19th August 2019. https://www.statista.com/statistics/812300/youth-unemployment-rate-in-nigeria/.

NPDI. 2018. "Organized Crime in the Niger Delta: Implications for the 2019 Elections." Niger Delta Partnership Initiatives and Partnership Initiatives in the Niger Delta, Conflict Briefing. Abuja, April 2018.

Obakhedo, N. O. 2011. "Curbing Electoral Violence in Nigeria: The Imperative of Political Education." *International Multidisciplinary Journal* 5, No. 5, Series 2, 103–104.

Ojo, O. V. 2014. "Turbulent Election History: An Appraisal of Precipitating Factors in Nigeria." *International Journal of Politics and Good Governance* 5, No. 52, Quarter II: 1–18.

Oke, Leke. 2010. "Democracy and Governance in Nigeria's Fourth Republic." *African Research Review* 4(3a): 31–40.

Olawoyin, Oladeinde. 2018. "Nigeria's Unemployment Rate Rises to 23.1% – NBS." *Premium Times*, 19 December 2018. Accessed 19 August, 2019, https://www.premiumtimesng.com/news/headlines/301896-nigerias-unemployment-rate-rises-to-23-1-nbs.html.

Ololube, N. P., Nwachukwu, C. N. Agbor, and O. A. Uriah. 2013. "Vicious Hazard to Peace Culture in Tertiary Education: The Activities of the Secret Cults." *British Journal of Education, Society & Behavioural Science* 3(1): 65–75.

Olubomehin, Oladipo O. 2012. "The Nigerian Motor Transporters since the 1920s." *International Journal of Humanities and Social Science* 2(12): 230–237.

Olukoju, A. 2003. *Infrastructure Development and Urban Facilities in Lagos, 1861–2000.* Ibadan: IFRA.

Omotola, J. Shola. 2010. "Elections and Democratic Transition in Nigeria Under the Fourth Republic." *African Affairs* 109(437): 535–553.

Omotoso, G. 2004. "Cock-Crow for Civil Service." *The Comet*, Wednesday, 30 June 2004.

Onimisi, Timothy and Omolegbe L. Tinuola. "Appraisal of the 2019 Post-Electoral Violence in Nigeria." *Malaysian Journal of Social Sciences and Humanities* 4, Issue 3 (2019):107–113.

Oromareghake, P., R. O. Arisi, and O. M. Igho. 2013. "Youth Restiveness and Insecurity in Niger Delta: A Focus on Delta State." *Global Journal of Human Social Science* 13, Issue 3, Version 1.0: 47–53.

Osaghae, Eghosa E. 1999. "Democratization in Sub-Saharan Africa: Faltering Prospects, New Hopes." *Journal of Contemporary African Studies* 17(1): 4–25.

Police Act, Sections 23–30. Accessed 28 August, 2019. www.placng.org/new/laws/P19.pdf.

"Political Map of Delta State." Accessed 16 August, 2019. http://reformeronline.com/wp-content/uploads/2017/08/Delta-State-Political-Map.jpg.

Punch. 2019a. "NURTW Official MC Oluomo, Eight Others Stabbed at APC Lagos Rally." 8 January 2019. Accessed 28 August, 2019. https://punchng.com/nurtw-official-mc-oluomo-eight-others-allegedly-stabbed-at-apc-lagos-rally/html.

Punch. 2019. "2019 Elections: Watered by Blood of Nigerians." 26 February 2019. Accessed 28 August 2019. https://punchng.com/2019-elections-watered-by-blood-of-igerians/html.

Rotimi, Adewale. 2005. "Violence in the Citadel: The Menace of Secret Cults in the Nigerian Universities." *Nordic Journal of African Studies* 14(1): 79–9.

Stober, Emmanuel O. 2016. "Stomach Infrastructure: Lessons for Democracy and Good Governance." *Management Dynamics in the Knowledge Economy* 4(3): 449–460.

Tersoo, J. Ikyase and Anthony E. Egberi. 2015. "Political Violence and Democratic Stability in Nigeria: Reflecting on the Past and Chatting the Way Forward." *Review of Public Administration and Management* 4(8): 35–36.

Thurston, Alexander. 2015. *Background to Nigeria's 2015 Elections*. Washington, DC: Center for Strategic & International Studies.

"United Nations: Youth." Accessed 13 August, 2019. http://undesadspd.org/Youth.aspx/pdf.

Uyieh, Jonah. 2018. "'Eko Gb'ole o Gbole': A Historical Study of Youth and Tout Culture in Shomolu Local Government Area, Lagos, 1976–2015." *Journal of African Cultural Studies* 30(3): 323–328. DOI: 10.1080/13696815.2018.1463844.

World Population Review. "Nigeria Population 2019." Accessed 15 August, 2019. http://worldpopulationreview.com/countries/nigeria-population/html.

Wilson, J. Q. and G. E. Kelling. 1982. "Broken Windows: The Police and Neighborhood Safety." *Atlantic Monthly*. Accessed 17th August 2019. https://www.manhattan-institute.org/pdf/atlantic-monthly-broken-windows.pdf.

Yagboyaju, Dhikru A. 2011. "Nigeria's Fourth Republic and the Challenge of a Faltering Democratization." *African Studies Quarterly* 12(3): 93–106.

CHAPTER 6

Political Opportunism: Populism as a New Political Tactic in South Africa

Bright Nkrumah

1   Introduction

The last two decades have witnessed a rebirth of populist movements across the globe. Spanning from the resurgence of charismatic leaders proclaiming populist policies, to the increasing shares or political or electoral votes won by populist parties in (Latin) America and Europe, modern democracies appear to be shifting towards a more populist approach. The proliferation of political movements of "the people" versus "the elite" across the globe are common in several quarters – from the Red Shirt in Thailand to the Tea Party in the United States. The Global South, and to be more exact, South Africa has not been spared from this global phenomenon, especially with one of such movements, the Economic Freedom Fighters (EFF), gaining ground in its polity. The EFF, popularly termed "the red berets" (due to their distinctive headgear) made huge impressions at the 2019 polls and increased their share of the national votes. From its 6.35% share of the votes in 2014, this grew to 10.77 in 2019, which gives it 44 seats in parliament compared to its previous 25 seats (Head, 2019).

To some observers, populism as a political style does not entirely deviate from the key tenets of democracy (Canovan 1999; Canovan 2004; Lee 2006). Even though it is often branded as a perversion of democracy, it is perceived by others as an attractive and alternative political project in response to the perceived shrinkage of democracy under state's pro-capitalist agenda. This is why the paper finds Laclau's (2005) thesis on *Populist Reason* exceptionally refreshing. One of his observations is particularly striking. To him, beside the incipient noises and claims for universal participation of the ordinary people, populism does not fall short of collapsing the class system in pursuit of equality, and protection of the have-nots against the exploitative elites. Mouffe (2018: 5) echoes this sentiment when she asserts that "populism, understood as a discursive strategy of construction of the political frontier between 'the people' and 'the oligarchy', constitutes, in the present conjuncture, the type of politics needed to recover and deepen democracy."

The objective of this chapter is straightforward, to assess two related issues which have an impact on the socio-political discourse of contemporary South Africa, that is, the evolution of populism and the conditions under which populist movements and leaders thrive. Against this backdrop, although the term populism tends to preclude balanced debate due to its inflammatory tone and the emotions it evokes, this paper will, nonetheless, assess the 'political style' of the EFF (as a classic example of populist party) in order to understand how it intends to influence the country's politics through this approach (Moffitt and Tormey, 2014: 387). To this end, I now shift my attention to provide a comprehensive definition of populism through which ordinary citizens, activists, freedom fighters, politicians and scholars could draw from, and apply to specific phenomenon. But first, an analysis of some of the conceptual confusions surrounding the term suffices.

2   Theorizing Populism

Populism has evolved to become a common political theme, and debates around its definition is relatively rich – actually, so rich that is has been labelled a "many-headed monster" (Canovan, 2004). My starting point is to define populism as a political opportunism or a political ideology which seeks to obtain the support of the ordinary people by creating enmity between the common people and the elite.[1] Although this definition is closely aligned with the one offered by Mudde (2004), where he defines populism as a concept which divide society into two antagonistic groups, the corrupt elite and the good people, many scholars will still context its universality.

Three main impediments hinder a universal definition of this term. First, the concept is often used to demonise and marginalise rather than simply assess a phenomenon. This can be traced to the fact that over the years, the term has become so loaded with derogatory or pejorative meaning that they should only be used with great care if one hopes for a constructive dialogue. For instance, as a term of abuse, "populist" has come to be used by major global financial institutions to imply fiscal recklessness of underdeveloped countries. Also some disdainful liberals tend to associate populist with racial intolerance and dangerous manipulation of the poor (Canovan 1999; Nanda 2001; Roth 2017).

Second, populism is rarely claimed by organisations or people themselves. Most often, it is rather ascribed to others as a distinctly unfavourable connotation. Even the rather few obvious cases of populist leaders such as the

---

[1]   Political opportunism can be defined as unethical political strategy, which is adopted to increase political influence or maintain political support.

murdered Dutch politician Pim Fortuyn or the former Argentine president Juan Peron did not self-identify as populist. Third, the conceptual confusion in this field is further illustrated by Ionescu and Gellner's (1969) edited volume in which various commentators defined populism as a syndrome, a movement, and an ideology.

To further hinder an overarching definition, commentators working on different continents and regions are inclined to define populism based on their particular local circumstance, and occasionally equate populism with somewhat different phenomena. For example, in the Latin American context, populism is employed to refer to economic mismanagement and clientelism, whereas in the European debate it is often used to make reference to xenophobia and anti-immigration. As a result, while some consider populism to be merely a conceptual term, and that is deserving to be confined to politics and the media, others argue that its normative vagueness is too big for it to be a relevant notion in the political sciences. Some critics, in addition, argue that the concept has been (ab)used and (over)used to the point that it has become meaningless and lost its analytical value (Moffitt and Tormey, 2014). Although I share in their frustration, the concept is too dominant in South African polity to simply do away with.

While many authors may reject any specific definition, many do agree that it has evolved in waves. The first wave can be traced to the end of the 19th Century when the American People's Party (APP) and the Russian *Narodniki* were formed and gained support, particularly among the agrarian populations (Pedler 1927). Both political movements represented the interest of poor farmers and mobilised them to challenge the control of the economy by industrialists and bankers (Lee 2006). Specifically, the APP was a left-wing agrarian party which emerged in the early 1890s in the Western and Southern US. It eventually collapsed in 1896 after nominating Democrat William Bryan in the US presidential election (Mooney and Hunt 1996). The *Narodniki*, on the other hand, were fairly a small group of (city middle class) academics who believed that the liberalisation of the tsarist regime could be attained through political propaganda among the peasantry which would subsequently lead to the awakening of the masses to revolt against the tzar. Since Russia was mainly an agricultural economy, the peasants represented a greater percentage of the people (*narod*), thus, the labelling of the social movement, *narodnichestvo*, or "populism", and *narodniki*, or "populist" (Pedler 1927). The narodnikis migrated to the villages in the 1870s to educate the peasantry on their important contribution towards a revolution (Tanaka 1970). Even though they did not achieve their intended purpose of mobilising farm labourers, they inspired Russian socialists during the first decades of the 20th century (Balabkins 2005). Besides being forged in the same era, the three movements shared two major similarities worth citing:

1. Economic ideology: the APP and the Narodniki's had a firm belief that capitalism had no future in the American northern plains or Russia (Elliott 1965; Smith 1989). They advocated for re(shaping) of the economic structures to ensure government (or peasants) interventionism in the key sectors of the economy (Argersinger 1974; Balabkins 2005). Their claim was that government-led financial system or state-owned enterprises will enhance competition in the market and ensure fair price for peasants. Akin to these movements, one of the key policy objectives of the EFF has been government control of strategic sectors of the economy, such as banks, mines and expropriating of land without compensation. Like its 19th century forebears, the party argues that this is the panacea to alleviate millions of South Africans from poverty.
2. Target group: the American and Russian populist movements targeted a particular section of the population whom were considered as true holders of sovereignty yet rendered powerless by the elite. These, in the 19th century were the peasants who were placed in opposition to an exploitative political regime or monarchy (Pedler 1927; Hicks 1931). The EFF, similarly advocates similar notion when it avows to be a party for the majority, yet poor black South Africans who are objects of exploitation by corrupt and exploitative elite, to be exact, white capitalists and ANC party officials.
3. Appearance: while the dress code of the APP was not much distinct from those of their contemporaries, the *Narodniks* (while being intellectuals) and arguably aristocrats, thought that all peasants dressed poorly, hence in order to fit in, they also addressed as poorly as was possible (DiTella 1969; Goldschmidt 1972). Even though this strategy had an adverse effect as the peasants were suspicious of them (since poorly dressed individual was perceived as powerless and without credibility), the EFF has adopted similar strategy of identifying itself with the poor and working class through clothing.

The second wave of populism can be traced to the post-World War II Latin American populism or the 20th Century Latin American authoritarian and state-led populist movements. A classic example of this era was Peronism in Argentina. The third wave, often termed as the "new" populism emerged during the 1970s. It is usually associated with the evolution of European far right and populist radical right parties like the Swiss People's Party, Vlaams Belang in Belgium and National Rally in France. Like the first two waves, subsequent populist movements claim to represent "the people" against the corrupt "elites". However, like the previous wave, populism once again visited Latin America. For instance, besides populist like Juan Perón of Argentina, a new form of populism in the shape of Evo Morales of Bolivia, Jose Mujica of Uruguay,

Hugo Chavéz of Venezuela and others have emerged in Latin America. What has been of interest to scholars of comparative politics is that, contrary to the first wave, the second and third wave have witnessed the rise of populist movements(such as the EFF) with progressive electoral success (Kriesi. 2014; Immerzeel & Pickup 2015). And for many commentators, the rise of Donald Trump is an indication that populists are not entirely riding on the waves of Latin America and Europe (Kazin 2016).

I must admit that although there is no important concept which is beyond contestation, debates on populism relate not only to what it *is*, but whether it *exists* at all. Observers who have attempted to define populism often base their definitions on three different kinds of categories: (a) the type of discourse used by populists (Panizza 2005); (b) structure of their movement (Weyland 2001); and (c) their ideologies (Mudde 2004). Generally, most of these scholars perceive populism in a negative light, often as indicating an emotive politics that incites people to supress their sense of reason. The concept, therefore, appears to be a convenient term sometimes invoked to simply dismiss actors whose politics we disagree with. Yet, considering the wide spectrum of populist movements that do not fall under any of the three caveats listed above, the explanatory utility of the term is constantly in doubt. In order to transcend such rather unhelpful pitfalls, Canovan (1999:5) introduces the concept of "[t]he populist style of politics". According to her, one of the key indicators of populists is their ability to communicate in simple, direct language. This style of speaking involves simple expressions, and since ordinary people usually concern themselves with ordinary things, they prefer simple explanations to their daily problems. For instance, when touching on the state of education in the country, the land question and revelation at the state capture commission of inquiry, Malema plainly mooted that "data is expensive in South Africa. You buy MTN data now and when you wake up tomorrow it has grown legs" (Lekabe 2019). Accordingly, any attempt to make things appear subtle becomes a target for populist ridicule. In addition to disliking technicalities, populists proffer political solutions which are mostly direct and simple. While it is considered as a questionable tactic since it helps sow public discord and inflame expectations, it has been routinely used by opposition parties to strengthen their power base.

Moreover, populists seek to protect "the people" who they classify as decent, good and wise from the elite who are seen as corrupt and incompetent. In some left-wing formulations, 'the people' signify something akin to the ordinary working class as opposed to the outspoken politicians. In the right-wing context, the term connotes something like "our people" and refers to those who belong versus those who do not (foreigners, affluent, members of the ruling government). On the basis that they speak for the people, populist tend to apply this term in three different instances, although these instances may sometimes overlap. The first instance is in reference to the country, nation or the *united people*, in contrast to the opposition parties which oppose them. This aspect of populism is considered harmless by liberals since it often adopts slogans such as "Divided we Fall", which has an integrative appeal. The second relates to *our people*, which mostly implies to our race, ethnic, or kith and kin as opposed to those who do not belong, such as whites, the rich, elite or foreigners. This inference makes liberal commentators wary due to its divisive nature. The third concerns mobilisation of the silent majority of what used to be called "the common people", but now are better known as the "ordinary people". The aim of the next section is to test whether this conceptualisation is in practice or prevalent in post-apartheid South Africa.

3   Populism: The Case of South Africa

While the use of populist appeal is by no means a new phenomenon in modern South Africa, the conditions for its expression are relatively new. In fact, as a political tactic, populism has been a running theme within the liberation party, the African National Congress (ANC). However, besides allowing its Youth League to occasionally make wild statements, the ANC largely avoided cheap political populism since it was elected into office in 1994. But then, the ANC's 2009 electoral campaign is considered as one of the defining moments of populism in the country for two reasons, namely, it provided an opportunity for voters to get a taste of the *populist* style of former president Jacob Zuma, and it marked the arrival of Julius Malema (Commander-in-Chief (CIC) of the EFF) on the political scene.

The ANC's 2009 election campaign took on a populist flavour as a response to the perception that it had abandoned its pro-poor aspirations. It travelled across the country preaching an anti-elitist message in ordinary language to ordinary people. Also in seeking to distance himself from his predecessor (Thabo Mbeki, whose speeches were full of arcane phraseology and classical references), Jacob Zuma was seen as being plain-spoken. Moreover, rather than shying away from attention, the partying, dancing and avuncular Zuma seemed to thrive on the public eye, whereas his predecessor was often estranged from his electoral base, with his disposition often distant and snappish. Further, in sharp contrast to his Mbeki's reputation as a pipe-smoking intellectual, Zuma's proudly unschooled background coupled with his sexual frailties lent him a mantle of ordinariness.

An important event which lent credence to accusations of elitism against Mbeki's administration was his refusal to provide simple leadership on the then HIV/AIDS problem. While an estimated 7.5 million people suffered from the pandemic, Mbeki (rather than speaking plainly on the issue), pontificated and intellectualised by rejecting antiretroviral drugs as the panacea for the virus. Zuma, on the other hand, took advantage of the situation to propel his ambition, particularly through his rape case While many people were intrigued by the case, their focus was not so much about the (mis)conduct of the accused, his presidential hopes. To be specific, South Africans' chanting and singing during the proceedings provide the following account: "Zuma for president", "Why are you crucifying Zuma" and "100% Zulu boy" (Evans and Wolmarans, 2006).

Clearly, the ANC's turn to populism or the manner it has elected to position itself seem to have a more deeply embedded populist trajectory. Any individual who does not conform to their line of reasoning is not only ignored but are labelled as enemies of the people or insane. For instance, in 2009, as chairman of the Sedibeng branch of the ANC Youth League, Jason Mkhwane labelled former ANC chairman, Mosiuoa Lekota and his Congress of the People (COPE) breakaway group as "cockroaches" who ought to be crashed, Angie Motshekga (then president of the ANC Women's League) mooted that "the dogs are leaving", while Malema added that they must be "suffering from a serious illness" (Forde, 2008). This name calling is worrying since similar propaganda triggered the mass murder of millions of Tutsis who were branded as "cockroaches" that deserve to be annihilated. Before taking a closer look at the policy and practice of a typical populist party, it is worth returning to the second objective of this paper, which is, analysing the factors which have served as fertile grounds for populism in contemporary South Africa.

4   Conditions Hospitable to Populism

In grappling to understand why so many politicians and people are subscribing to populism in present-day South Africa, one of the obvious avenues, and yet, usually ignored is "whether the outbursts of populists have merits?" Are populist like the EFF perhaps gaining ground because their claims are true? There are five elements to emphasise:

1. *Perceptions of rising corruption*: Is the ANC and the white elite in contemporary South Africa more corrupt than they were during the Nelson Mandela-Mbeki regime? Certainly, there is no straightforward answer to this question,

especially as corruption (like populism) is a contentious notion. It is also cumbersome to obtain comparative, reliable data considering that by definition corruption is a shady affair. Although Statistics South Africa has, since 1994, conducted numerous surveys, it has not yet produced an overarching report on the state of corruption within a particular era. We cannot, therefore, emphatically conclude that one administration is more corrupt given that prevalence of corruption within ruling parties is not new. What may be new, according to Heywood and others (2002: 196–7), "is the likelihood that a scandal will be produced once the evidence of corruption has been exposed". So in this context, the State of Capture report by Thuli Madonsela which implicated former president Zuma and some government officials could be of some assistance (PPSA 2016). Nonetheless, although the scope of this report is limited to only the Zuma administration, similar scandals rocked the previous administrations, with key illustrations being Sarafina II, the Arms Deal, Travelgate (Crawford-Browne 2004; Fourie 2005). To this end, allegations of corruption could not necessarily be the trigger of the recent resurgence of populism in contemporary South Africa.

2. *Increasing unemployment and inequality*: Can the rise of populism be tied to the widening gap between groups, their representatives and the people's formal political representatives? As von Beyme (1996: 84) notes "[t]here are many tendencies in modern democracies which strengthen the separation of a political class from its basis". In the case of South Africa, it could be poverty, rising unemployment, widening inequality, or co-operation of government and opposition. Although it is globally acclaimed that the Truth and Reconciliation Commission and the 1996 Constitution ushered in liberation for all South Africans, the inequality between "the people" and the elite remains as entrenched as ever. Clearly, the ANC's emphasis on reconciliation did not take into consideration the full extent of the lingering legacy of apartheid during the country's transition to democracy (Hamilton, 2015). The liberation party's ineffective effort to combat poverty in the first few years after apartheid and the socioeconomic crisis in recent years have created fertile grounds for the emergence of populist politics (Heese and Allan 2018).

Also, the increasing amount of support for a populist party like the EFF demonstrates that the liberal constitutionalism which was forged as an important aspect of the country's transition to democracy has not been fully integrated into the country's political culture. As shown by the widespread discontent, South Africa is increasingly facing acute socioeconomic crisis grounded on the inter-related challenges of poverty, rising inequality and high unemployment (Alexander 2010). Consequently, South Africa has, since the start of the new century, been witnessing an increasing rebellion of the poor in the form of rising service delivery protests which reflects disappointment with the fruits of democracy. To Hamilton (2014), the crony capital which existed before 1994 has not only been maintained, but reinforced. In reality, South Africa is still controlled by a two classes of economic and political elite: the first group composed of those from the old economic elite who have direct access to the highest seats of political power for reasons which can be traced back to the country's negotiated transition, and the second, thanks to the policy of Broad-Based Black Economic Empowerment (BBBEE), the new entrants to the economic elite is composed of influential ANC members (Hamilton 2014; Faull, 2016). This widening gap was once again proven in the Marikana massacre. It was against this backdrop that Hamilton (2015), for instance, advised the ruling government to improve the lives of the disposed by amending its macro-economic policies, distributive mechanismd and property ownership. In re-echoing Hamilton's recommendation, Adam Habib (2018), drew the attention of president Cyril Ramaphosa's ANC to frame a feasible socioeconomic polices to reverse the exclusionary nature of the country's existing political economy. Thus, the high unemployment rate which has left hundreds of people, who, having been unable to seek placement in any (in)formal structures of employment often provide foundation for populist agitation. Put differently, the enduring legacy of inequality coupled with high unemployed youth provides a breeding ground for populist parties like the EFF.

3. *Media quality*: Certainly, the increase of populism is inseparably tied to the transformation of the print and electronic media. Under apartheid, the ruling National Party (NP) used censorship to dictate what the media published, especially in terms of constitutional accountability and the country's politics (Neisser 1994). To reinforce its grip on journalists, the state adopted the Publications Act of 1974 which sought to forestall any entertainment programmes, books, plays or movies which criticizes the government (Wasserman 2010). In 1985, the state appointed a minister of Home Affairs with the mandate of requiring all reporters to register with the government (Strelitz and Steenveld 2010). According to Harber (2004), the essence of this registration was to shift focus from penalising newspaper corporations to giving jail sentences to individual reporters who fail to conform to the provisions of the Act.

After 1994, the media begun to operate in an environment where freedom of expression is constitutionally guaranteed (Liebenberg 2000). Also with the advent of cyberspace and social media (blogs, YouTube, websites, text messages, e-mails, Facebook, Twitter and WhatsApp), information could easily be disseminated and accessed with a click of a button. Hence, the mass media has evolved to be an important source for dissemination of information to marginalised communities, especially in disadvantaged rural areas.

The media has not only undergone significant transformation in terms of the range, role and importance, but has witnessed a growing competition for viewers and readers. More important than the real proliferation in corruption and sleaze in politics is the different context which the media reports on politics. For instance, in recent times both public and private media have been known to place emphasis on the sensationalist and negative aspect of news. Two reasons account for this shift, namely, commercialisation and independence. First, as the country transitioned to democracy, so did the media gain its independence to report on broad range of issues. Second, for purposes of commercialisation and a quest for dominance, most electronic and print media have shifted their focus to more scandalous and extreme aspects of politics, since it seems this is what appeals to many viewers and listeners. In addition to serving as a highly receptive medium for populist to appeal to highly receptive audience, this form of broadcast strengthens the anti-elite sentiments within the masses. In sum, although "populist rhetoric and ideology" may have been pervasive in, and contributed to the split of the NP in March 1982, an improved access to media has enhanced the flow of information to not just bourgeoisie, but even marginalised section of the population (Charney 1984: 272).

4. *The clever black*: Somewhat paradoxically, and more positively, an important reason why some South Africans have become seduced by populism is because they have become better educated and more liberated. Due to the progressive increase in adult literacy rate, especially in urban centres, South Africans today feel more competent to judge their political representatives and expect more from them (Knoema 2019). This cognitive mobilisation has led the people to no longer blindly swallow what the elites tell them. They have, also stopped accepting that politicians actually do think for them. In recent times, a growing number of South Africans seem to convince themselves that they are more capable of framing and implementing better policies than mainstream politicians. This implies that over the last decade, the relationship between the people and the elite has significantly changed, and possibly irrevocably (Fakir 2014). This development, however, does not imply that all of them want to actually hold political office in order to trigger socioeconomic transformation. This factor also provides a basis why modern populist actors benefit from their role as fighters against political correctness and taboo breakers. Although taboos or the elephant in the room, most notably exploitation by the ruling elite and capitalists are barely new phenomenon in post-apartheid South Africa, one might argue that in recent years, they have been more rigidly enforced. Not

surprisingly, it is here that populist found their niche as taboo breakers by calling for the demystification of the public realm and found the most receptive audience.

5. *Ideological polarisation*: The fifth flourishing condition for populism is the lack of a dominant political ideology in South Africa. The first potential candidate for dominance in post-apartheid South Africa was socialism. However, this concept is presently in doctrinal disarray as it has retreated globally. Perhaps, the second candidate could have been some form of black-nationalism. Yet, although South Africa battled with racial segregation, and still confronted with material deprivation, literal forms of African nationalism and formal doctrines of black solidarity have still not proved popular in contemporary times. Both socialism and black nationalisms have been undercut from below by the specific tribal identities and superseded from above by the non-racial character of the dominant ANC alliance. The liberation party's doctrinal resources have been swept away by the need for compromise in embracing the unconquered Afrikaner power and very greatly redefined the national economic and political landscape. The ruling party under these conditions has been condensed to a carefully modulated citizen nationalism and greatly circumscribed commitment to redistribution which, even though commendable for its rationality, civility and inclusivity, is somewhat bland. There is, then some sort of doctrinal void in the country's politics in which conservatism, liberal democracy, nationalism and socialism are all insipid, either in force of expression or numbers. One might argue that a significantly de-idealogised politics is exactly what is needed in present-day South Africa (Kriesi 2014; Immerzeel & Pickup 2015).

Although the factors listed above are hospitable to populism, the credentials of newly elected President, Cyril Ramaphosa has the potential of limiting the spread of populism (Du Preez 2018; Umraw 2018). Since assuming leadership role of the ruling party, he has taking upon himself the mission of forging a "new dawn" by combining financial probity with popular enthusiasm, organisational accountability and bureaucratic efficiency (Shubin 2019: 44). Second, Ramaphosa has popular authority and enormous credibility, and deploys these qualities with considerable deep organisational loyalty, discipline and intellectual agility (Beckmann 2019). Irrespective of his discernible taste for the exercise of personal authority and commanding personal popularity, he makes promises on behalf of the party instead of his own (Alence & Pitcher 2019). These assets, which are the arch rivals of populism, make him key in appealing to the rank and file of the ANC. Yet, the president's personal problems omissions sins have not gone undetected. At the time of writing in April 2020, the EFF has filed an application in the Supreme Court alleging supporting the findings of the Public Protector Busisiwe Mkhwebane that the president "wilfully misled Parliament" on his campaign donations (Thamm 2020). The PP's report followed an admission by the president that R500, 000 received from the controversial Bosasa Company was a donation to his election to the ANC's presidency (Nako 2018). This incident has enabled the PP and EFF to accuse the president for breaching the executive code and constitution when he made a mistake in his response to opposition leader, Mmusi Maimane that the money was initially meant for his son, Andile Ramaphosa for services rendered to the company (Ashman 2019). Thus, to rule r out Ramaphosa as a destination for populist agitations, he must correct his past errors by taking a firm stand to forestall corruption in the public and private sectors.

Having established the conditions fostering populist agenda, the paper now takes a closer look at the EFF as an exemplar of populist party. Since populism, as defined above encompasses policies with the aim of pleasing the electorates, the next section takes a closer look at the EFF's policies, strategies and how it has exploited the above conditions to become the third largest political party after the ruling ANC and Democratic Alliance (the main opposition party).

5 The Economic Freedom Fighters

In May 2014, the ruling African National Congress (ANC) once again won post-apartheid South Africa's fifth general election. Although past elections had witnessed the party slowly increase its number of voters, there was a sufficient reason to believe that while the 2014 election might return the party to power, its victory margin would be somewhat compromised (Nieftagodien 2015). This anticipation was borne out of signs of decline in support due to allegations of corruption and poor service delivery (Mbete 2015). Subsequently, the party's support base was reduced from 65.9% to 62.1% between 2009 and 2014 respectively (Sapa 2014). To some commentators, this development could somewhat be attributed to the new kid on the block, the EFF (Alexander 2016; Houser 2016).

I must indicate here that the historical legacies of the ANC continue to define the contours of contemporary political debate, even though we are witnessing the surge of political movements which appear to be independent from the liberation movement. The 1955 Freedom Charter, in particular, continues to remain the Bible or Quran in political debates. Besides the liberation movement, an opposition party which continues to draw inspiration from it is the EFF. An important tactic of the EFF has been to develop a rhetoric which aims at reclaiming this tradition as its own. A caveat must, however, be added that while the EFF is grounded on the ideals of the Freedom Charter, its policies and practices have largely been inspired by Malema's personal hero, Peter Mokaba. To be exact, even though the Preamble of the Charter avows that "South Africa belongs to all who live in it, black and white", Mokaba, in the early 1990s became known for his use of the slogan "Kill the farmer, kill the Boer", which could roughly be interpreted as inciting racial violence against whites (Grootes 2011). Inspired, Malema in 2010 raised fears of increasing racial polarisation when he re-echoed Mokaba's song, claiming that black South Africans have not sufficiently benefitted from 16 years of democracy (Grootes 2011). As discussed above, the EFF has (unlike other breakaway parties like COPE and the United Democratic Movement), abandoned any pretence of support for non-racialism. The result has been an exponential use of the "us" against "them" rhetoric by claiming to give back to poor black communities the voice which has been confiscated by white elites (Mouffe 2019).

The EFF sprung out of the ANC Youth League (ANCYL) in 2013, which merged with other (like-minded radical political) movements like the September National Imbizo (SNI). The party was born out of crisis after its head of policy, Floyd Shivambu, and its leader, Malema, were expelled from the ANCYL in 2012. Since then, it has received its motivation from several other crises, such as the hullabaloo over the development of former president Zuma's Nkandla residence, anti-government protests in several communities and the Marikana massacre. Yet, in stark contrast to other break-away parties, the EFF, being formed only a year before the 2014 general election, was quick to organise and mount an effective campaign. The party gained a rather disproportionate level of media coverage due to the personality of its charismatic leader, Malema (Mbete 2015). The paper now turns its attention to assess whether the policies and political style of the EFF merits the brand of a full fledge right-wing populist party.

5.1 *EFF Populist Rhetoric*

Historically, nationalisation has been on the ANC's economic agenda. The Freedom Charter indicates that "the national wealth of our country, the heritage of South Africans, shall be restored to the people". Yet, although the party kept this long-lasting commitment to nationalisation in their policy plans, it was soon dropped in the course of the negotiated transition to democracy. As Rantete and Giliomee (1992) notes, the bilateral talks between the NP and ANC which commenced in the latter part of the 1980s were ineffective platforms in shaping economic policies, as Afrikaner elites continue to define the contours of economic reforms and ownership of production. Thus, to some factions within the ANC, there is a need to rectify the resultant pact which kept "nationalization and agrarian reform off the agenda" (Rantete & Giliomee 1992: 516). This policy objective has, however, remained an aspiration for Malema, both now as CIC of the EFF and during his days as the ANCYL president (Buccus 2019).

It was evident that in the period leading up to the 2014 election, the EFF was struggling to contain the mixture of competing ideological tendencies within its fold (Sosibo 2014). This tension can be linked to the fact that three different parties with three distinct ideological bents agreed to campaign with, and allow their candidates to be formally part of the EFF (Sosibo 2014). These were the Black Consciousness Party, the Socialist Party of Azania and the troubled Pan Africanist Congress of Azania. One important recruit during the formation of the EFF was Andile Mngxitama and his SNI (Sosibo 2014). Inspired by the ideologies of black consciousness, Mngxitama was instrumental in the framing of the EFF's manifesto for the 2014 election (Sosibo 2014). The strength of the document lies in the party's simple and clear critique of the failures of the ANC regime to address socioeconomic crisis. In doing so, the EFF draws on a common populist tactic which provides simple solutions to the complex economic grievances of the ordinary people (Sosibo 2014). In its entirety, the document contains a combination of three "isms": Marxism, Fanonism and Pan-Africanism (Sosibo 2014). The overarching vision of the EFF revolves around its seven cardinal pillars of economic freedom, which according to the party, represent an overarching statist approach to addressing South Africa's poverty and inequality crises. The two dominant areas of this strategy are nationalisation of strategic sectors of the economy and land redistribution without compensation (Sosibo 2014).

The first of the EFF's seven pillars highlighted in the 2014 election manifesto and with clear connection to the legacies of the apartheid era is "expropriation of South Africa's land without compensation for equal redistribution" (EFF 2014). This theme speaks directly to the black African majority especially considering its emotive nature. As mentioned above, since 1994, there has been very limited progress on land reform mainly as a result of the ANC's government policy of "willing seller, willing buyer".

As Smith (2010) convincingly suggests, following his visit to Zimbabwe in 2010, Malema, then leading the ANCYL was inspired by Mugabe's controversial land reform. Nonetheless, in few months leading up to the 2014 election, Shivambu stated that if the party is elected into power, it will not be one of its objectives to replicate the Zanu-PF's land reform in South Africa. Against this backdrop, the position of the EFF on land reform has become less radical as the party's leadership, including Malema, has recently put forward a new proposal. In this proposal, it has added a caveat which calls for the expropriation of land by the state and the people having to obtain a license from the government in order to use them. It is important to note that this approach may not necessarily address the needs of the poor, especially as the wishes of the *state* may replace those of the private landowner. It was in this light that Greenberg (2015) argues that "[p]erhaps it is true that the state will act more favourably towards the dispossessed, but this is in no way guaranteed".

This revised position on land was, however, not supported by all members of the party. To be exact, Mngxitama decried that the party has shifted from its initial position of "expropriation of all land" to "unoccupied", then "non-productive land [that] has had the effect of protecting white farmers" (Mngxitama 2015). With underlying ideological contestations, mundane issues of corruption and power struggles culminated in the expulsion of Mngxitama and two members of parliament (MP)in 2015 (Poplak 2015).

It is common knowledge that many of the top-ranking members in the EFF developed their political careers within the ANCYL and the ANC in general. In seeking to situate his politics as part of the ANC's long Charterist tradition, Malema, in particular, draws inspiration from the founders of the ANCYL in the 1940s. As a consequence, it is not surprising that when framing their economic policies, the party relies heavily on the Freedom Charter, a symbolic text in the ANC's liberation struggle against apartheid. Nonetheless, whereas Malema has revitalized long-standing battles between nationalist and communist factions, according to Forde (2014), his use of political links to obtain business concessions and his neo-nationalist politics make this a very selective reading of history.

Nevertheless, in line with the party's populist underpinnings, Malema in his introduction to the party's 2014 election manifesto, stated that the EFF is a movement for all South Africans (Fogel 2014). However, rather than representing everyone (irrespective of race), the party has depicted itself as the vanguard of black South Africans. For instance, Malema has on numerous occasions invoked the word black. As noted by one commentator, the EFF's populist rhetoric is aimed at appealing to the people who are placed in opposition to the evolving advantaged ANC elite and historically advantaged white capitalists (Mbete 2015).

In sum, this section assessed the EFF's call for "economic freedom", which I argue underscores the party's populist appeal to its mainly black African support base. This is centred on a return to cardinal principles of the ANC's Freedom Charter. In its determination to appeal to its mainly black youth constituency, the party has been engaging in the politics of spectacle, to which I now turn to.

5.2   EFF's Political Style

The argument as to why the EFF warrants the label "populist party" is centred both on their ideologies or polices as discussed above and their approach to politics. In terms of their political style, I consider three important features of its strategies: first, the outfit of its members of parliament (MPs); second, the use of disruptive strategy in formal political spaces; and third, its association to various protests.

EFF MPs, right from their first appearance in the provincial legislatures and National Assembly in May 2014, have attempted to portray themselves as representatives of black labourers by wearing hard hats, maid uniforms or bright red overalls. In line with their populist strategy, this approach has enabled them to distance themselves from other parties and politicians who they describe as the (corrupt political) elite. This fashion, according to its chief whip, Shivambu, is an indication to the poor and working class that "now [..] they've got representatives in parliament" (BBC 2014). It, however, appears a touch ironic for Malema to claim he represents the poor, especially in light of his reputation for lavish lifestyle during his tenure as the ANCYL president (Posel 2014).

It must be noted that the party's choice of outfit is not only a challenge to the compromises made during the country's negotiated settlement that led to democracy, but an opposition to the Western conventions upheld in the country's legislature. This clearly fits in with populism's thin ideology: building politics firmly on an "us" versus "them" setting or building an image of a society split into a pure people and an untouchable corrupt or Westernised elite. For this reason, officials of both the Eastern Cape and Gauteng provincial legislatures removed EFF representatives from parliament for dressing inappropriately. Their inappropriate outfit in parliament says: guess what me, the maid, and me, the miner, as real citizen, with equal political significance to any MP. Since the outfits speak directly to the party's anti-establishment rhetoric, the party made a political capital out of parliaments attempt to ban it. Criticising the parliamentary dress code of the EFF as inappropriate reinforces the major divide characterising post-apartheid South Africa. On the one hand, are the majority for whom the right to vote has yet to give them proper rights of citizenship and access to all the democratic benefits, and on the other, are the few for whom democracy has brought or further entrenched full citizenship. The red beret, consequently, seems to make those people who have been actually excluded from full citizenship audible and visible.

To cut a long conceptual elaboration short, Malema mobilised the party's followers and staged a sit in protest at the Gauteng legislature building in July 2014 (Goldhammer 2014). This protest affirms: How dare anyone, and the ANC in particular, to say that the majority black labourers on whose backs this country was built are *inappropriate* in the National Assembly and other parliamentary chambers? After the EFF successfully challenged the provincial legislatures' decision in the South Gauteng High Court, disgruntled ANC MPs threatened they were going to ensure the banning of the red workers' uniform by using their numbers to amend the rules of parliament. Eventually, EFF members disrupted numerous committee meetings held to deliberate on possible amendment on rules governing dress code in the provincial and national legislatures. At the time of submitting this paper for review, EFF MPs continue to dress in their distinctive outfit. Whereas this serves to highlight the sense of victimisation that populist movements typically rely on, it also gives them significant media coverage.

Their fashion strategy has been fortified by their use of disruptive tactic in the provincial and national legislatures, which has generated publicity for the party. They have, since their election in 2014, decided to stage a walkout of the chamber in protest on numerous occasions. In one particular incident, which occurred on 12 February 2015, fights broke out in the chamber as EFF MPs were forcibly removed by parliamentary protection officials (PPOs) for disrupting the president's State of the Nation (SONA) address. It is reported that at least one police officer was armed (SP, 2015). In a speech few days afterwards, it was alleged that Baleka Mbete, speaker of the house, labelled Malema a "cockroach" and later tendered her apology. In condemning the disruptive approach of the EFF, a leading member of the South African Communist Party (SACP), Jeremy Cronin, touted that his counterparts were merely "disrupting the procedures of Parliament for their own theatrical purposes" (SP 2015). In view of that, on 30 July 2015, the National Assembly passed a proposal to amend the rule on how to address disruptive conduct in the chamber. The only MPs who voted against the motion were EFF representatives (Mbanjwa 2009). To be exact, in instances where an MP refuses a request to leave, these new rules give the PPOs power to remove such a member. Since October 2015, the EFF has become regular beneficiaries of these new rules where they are frequently forced out of the chamber. Malema was also suspended in October 2015 for refusing a request to retract a statement which labelled Ramaphosa, then deputy president, a murderer for his alleged orchestration of the Marikana massacre (SP 2015).

EFF MPs, have on many occasions demonstrated constant disruptive behaviour leading to their constant removal from the floor of parliament. A case in point was their forced removal out of the chamber during the 2017 State of the Nation Address. On their exit, they chanted "Zupta must fall", implying the unhealthy links between the influential Gupta family and then president Zuma. There is, however, a tension between the EFF's ability to become a key player in parliament in the longer-term and its strategy of disruption within parliament. For the party to contribute effectively in the National Assembly, particularly in terms of scrutinising the policies of the executive, it has to learn to adhere to the formal processes of parliamentary committees while developing its research capacity (Mbete 2015).

Beyond formal politics, the EFF has associated itself with several protests, with the 2015 "#Feemustfall" campaign being one of the most notable. The frequent deployment of riot police in response to the revival of student activism against the proposed increases to university fees and triggering many media reports evoked memories of the 1976 Soweto student unrest. By using the power of the media, the protest which started at the University of the Witwatersrand quickly spread to other universities. In an attempt to appease the protesters, the government initially decided on a 6% cap on student fees. However, a nationwide march to the Union Buildings on 23 October 2015 led to a U-turn in state policy, where then president Zuma announced that the decision to increase fees for 2016 has been rescinded. Nonetheless, some observers have argued that the reason for the student protest went beyond the simple issue of student fees (Heese and Allan 2018). For example, as the campaign swept across the provinces, it became evident that it was a response to the post-apartheid political system which still favours privilege white to the detriment of the majority black population who are burdened with poverty and unemployment. Besides the fees, the campaign agitated for an end to the universities' outsourcing of low-paid administrative jobs.

With the ANCYL's inactivity, the EFF saw a political capital to cash in. And, unlike the DA whose leader Mmusi Maimane was chased away from an attempt to participate in the student protest in Cape Town, the EFF was notably more effective as an opposition during this unrest. On that account, the party did not miss an opportunity to chastise the SACP's General Secretary, Blade Nzimande, then Minister for Higher Education and Training. The EFF, further offered solidarity to the students by issuing several official statements in support of the uprising. It specifically, declared that not only is "South African politics changing to reflect the militant, radical, fearless and direct character of the EFF" but since the formation of the party "student activism in South Africa is gaining prominence and ascendance" (EFF 2015). To demonstrate that the party does not separate its disruptive strategy to formal politics within the National Assembly and its engagement with protest politics, the party's MPs on 21 October 2015, disrupted the medium-term budget of Nhlanhla Nene, then Finance Minister, by chanting "Fees Must Fall". Like previous incidents, scuffles broke out as the speaker instructed PPOs to yet again remove these MPs from the chamber.

This section, in sum, has highlighted the link between the EFF's key doctrines of a populist approach and its politics of spectacle. A key feature of the emergence of the EFF as a political party has been their flagship economic policies and concerted attempts to distance themselves from elite politics in general and the ANC-led government in particular. The section further demonstrates how its MPs have relied on disruptive tactic and distinct clothing to formal politics as a means of achieving this end.

6   Conclusion

In order to explicate the dynamics of populism as a way of contributing to recent political debates in South Africa, I begun this chapter with the aim of responding only to the question of whether populism is new in contemporary South Africa. The essay argues that although populism is not a new phenomenon, the conditions which underpin it are new. Yet, in the process of reflecting on the oratorical and presentational style of a thriving populist party - the EFF -, I became increasingly convinced that I had to take a step back and develop a historical and theoretical framework for my analysis before focusing on the current state of populist politics. The chapter contends that the polices and political style of the EFF are not distinct or removed from the strategies of populist movements of the past. The party's radical tactics, opposition to rules of parliament, style of dressing, penchant for state-ownership of major sectors of the economy, and claiming to represent the poor, clearly place the party within the global pattern of populism. Once I accepted this proposition, an issue that kept coming up as being a logical transition point in my analysis was: *Why is populism (gradually) gaining ground*? The essay found four main reasons which serve as the fertile ground for populism: ideological polarization, new black middle class, the advent of social media and press freedom, and increasing unemployment and inequality. Through its populist strategy, the EFF (in the just ended national elections) increased its number of votes and seats in parliament, it remains to be seen whether its combative tone and procedural contestation will undermine or enhance the constitutional mandate of parliament.

References

Alence, Rod & Pitcher, Anne. 2019. "Resisting State Capture in South Africa." *Journal of Democracy* 30: 5–19.

Alexander, Peter. 2016. "Marikana Commission of Inquiry: from narratives towards history." *Journal of Southern African Studies* 42: 815–839.

ANC. 1955. The Freedom Charter.

Argersinger, Peter. 1974. *Populism and Politics: William Alfred Peffer and the People's Party*. Kentucky: The University Press of Kentucky.

Ashman, Sam. 2019. "Financialised accumulation and the political economy of state capture: state capture." *New Agenda* 75: 6–11.

Balabkins, Nicholas. 2005. "Russian Economic thought and its Debilitating Legacy", *Journal of the History of Economic Thought* 27: 207–217.

BBC (British Broadcasting Corporation). 2014. "South Africa's EFF MPs dress as maids and miners", 21 May, 2014, https://www.bbc.com/news/world-africa-27504666

Beckmann, Johan. 2019. "Thuma mina and education: Volunteerism, possibilities and challenges." *South African Journal of Education* 39: s1-s8.

Boone, Catherine. 2009. "Electoral Populism Where Property Rights Are Weak: Land Politics in Contemporary Sub-Saharan Africa", *Comparative Politics*, 41: 183–201.

Buccus, Imraan. 2019. "What chance does the 'left' have in the 2019 elections?", *DailyMaverick*, 18 November, 2018, https://www.dailymaverick.co.za/opinionista/2018-11-18-what-chance-does-the-left-have-in-the-2019-elections/

Canovan, Margaret. 2004. "Populism for political theorists?" *Journal of Political Ideologies* 9: 241–252.

Canovan, Margaret. 1999. "Trust the People! Populism and the Two Faces of Democracy." *Political Studies*, 47: 2–16.

Charney, Craig. 1984. "Class conflict and the National Party split." *Journal of Southern African Studies*, 10: 269–282.

Chauke, A. 2011. "'Zuma's not my friend': Malema", *Timeslive*, 30 August, 2011, https://www.timeslive.co.za/politics/2011-08-30-zumas-not-my-friend-malema

Crawford-Browne, Terry. 2004. "The arms deal scandal." *Review of African Political Economy* 31: 329–342.

Di Tella, Torcuato. 1969. "Explorations in Populism" *Government and Opposition*, 4:526–533.

Du Preez, Max. 2018. "Cyril's choice: Populism or the South African economy" *News 24*, 9 January, 2018, https://www.news24.com/Columnists/MaxduPreez/cyrils-choice-populism-or-the-south-african-economy-20180109

EFF (Economic Freedom Fighters). 2014. *Founding manifesto of the Economic Freedom Fighters. PoliticsWeb*, 25 July, 2013, https://www.politicsweb.co.za/news-and-analysis/founding-manifesto-of-the-economic-freedom-fighter

EFF (Economic Freedom Fighters). 2015. "EFF statement on students' protest to Parliament", *EFF Online*, 22 October, 2015 https://www.polity.org.za/article/eff-eff-statement-on-students-protest-to-parliament

Elliott, Charles. 1965. "The Populists and the Legal Marxists: Another View." *Australian Journal of Politics & History*, 11: 163–169

Evans, J & Wolmarans, R. 2006. "Timeline of the Jacob Zuma rape trial" *Mail&Guardian*, March 21, 2006, https://mg.co.za/article/2006-03-21-timeline-of-the-jacob-zuma-rape-trial

Fakir, E. 2014. "Fragmentation and Fracture –The loss of trust and confidence in political parties." EISA.

Faull, Andrew. 2016. "Politics, democracy and the machinery of the state." *SA Crime Quarterly*, 1–5.

Fogel, B. 2014. "Remaking the South African Left." *Jacobin*, December 16, 2014 https://www.jacobinmag.com/2014/12/south-africa-numsa-cosatu

Forde, F. 2008. "Youth League blames 'poor English.'", *IOL News*, November 26, 2008 https://www.iol.co.za/news/politics/youth-league-blames-poor-english-426885

Forde, Fiona. 2014."Still an Inconvenient Youth: Julius Malema Carries on" Picador: Africa.

Fourie, Pieter. 2005. "Government's management of the South African aids epidemic: lessons for public administrators." *Journal of Public Administration* 2: 392–403. *future prospects*. Auckland Park: Jacana.

Goldhammer, Zack. 2014. "The Coded Clothes of South Africa's Economic Freedom Fighters." *The Atlantic*, 1 August, 2014, https://www.theatlantic.com/international/archive

Goldschmidt, Eli. 1972. "Labor and populism: New York City, 1891-1896." *Labor History*, 13: 520–532.

Götz, Graeme., Khanyile, Samkelisiwe., and Katumba, Samy. 2016. "Voting patterns in the 2016 local government elections", GCRO, https://www.gcro.ac.za/outputs/map-of-the-month/detail/voting-patterns-in-the-2016-local-government-elections

Greenberg, Stephen., 2015. "Making Sense of the EFF's Land Policy. The South African Civil Society Information Service." The South African Civil Society Information Service, https://sacsis.org.za/site/article/2271

Grootes, Stephen. 2011. 'Kill the Boer' ruling: Malema's loss is also SA freedom's loss. DailyMaverick, September 13, 2011, https://www.dailymaverick.co.za/article/2011-09-13-kill-the-boer-judgement-malemas-loss-is-also-sa-freedoms-loss

Habib, Adam. 2018. "Op-Ed: Is Ramaphosa's ANC managing the challenge from the EFF?" *Daily Maverick*, March 12, 2018, https://www.dailymaverick.co.za/article/2018-03-12-op-ed-is-ramaphosas-anc-managing-the-challenge-from-the-eff/

Hamilton, Lawrence. 2014. *Freedom is power: Liberty through Political Representation*. Cambridge University Press.

Harber, Anton. 2004. "Reflection on Journalism in the Transition to Democracy" *Ethics & International Affairs* 18: 79–87.

Head, T. 2019. "Election results: How the EFF have grown in every province." *The South African*, 11 May, 2019, https://www.thesouthafrican.com/news/2019-election-results-eff-every-province/

Heese, Karen and Allan, Kevin. 2018. "ANC has every reason for alarm over losing control in 2019 election'". *Businesslive*, April 04, 2017, https://www.businesslive.co.za/bd/opinion/2017-04-04-anc-has-every-reason-for-alarm-over-losing-control-in-2019-election/

Heywood, Paul, Jones, Erik and Rhodes, Martin. 2002. *Developments in West European Politics 2*. London: Palgrave Macmillan.

Hicks, J.D. 1931. *The Populist Revolt: A History of the Farmers' Alliance and the People's Party*.
Minneapolis: The University of Minnesota Press.

Houser, Myra Ann. 2016. "Liberation Movements in Power: Party and State in Southern Africa", *South African Historical Journal*, 68: 139–142.

Immerzeel, Tim, and Pickup, Mark. 2015. "Populist radical right parties mobilizing 'the people'? The role of populist radical right success in voter turnout." *Electoral Studies* 40: 347–360.

Ionescu, Ghita and Gellner, Ernest. 1969. *Populism: Its Meanings and National Characteristics*. London: Palgrave Macmillan.

Kazin, Michael. 2016. "Trump and American populism: Old whine, new bottles." *Foreign Affairs* 95: 17–24.

Knoema. 2019 "South Africa - Adult (15+) literacy rate" https://knoema.com/atlas/South-Africa/topics/Education/Literacy/Adult-literacy-rate

Kriesi, Hanspeter. 2005. "The populist challenge." *West European Politics* 37(2014): 361–378.

Laclau, Ernesto. 2017. *On Populist Reason*. London: Verso.

Lee, Michael. 2006. "The Populist Chameleon: The People's Party, Huey Long, George Wallace, and the Populist Argumentative Frame." *Quarterly Journal of Speech* 92(2006): 355–378.

Lekabe, Thapelo. 2019. "13 best quotes from Julius Malema's fiery manifesto speech." *EyeWitnessNews*, February 02, 2019, https://ewn.co.za/2019/02/02/13-best-quotes-from-julius-malema-s-fiery-manifesto-speech

Liebenberg, Sandra. 2000. "Human development and human rights: South African country study." Human Development Report: Background Paper.

Malema, Julius. 2015. *South Africa's Changing Opposition*. London: Chatham House.

Mbanjwa, Xolani. 2009. "Malema is rude and disgusting - Zille" *IOL News*, 25 February, 2009, https://www.iol.co.za/news/politics/malema-is-rude-and-disgusting-zille-435672

Mbete, Sithembile. 2015. "The Economic Freedom Fighters: South Africa's Turn Towards Populism?" *Journal of African Elections*, 14: 35–59.

Mngxitama, Andile. 2015. "How Malema sold out on land reform." *Sunday Independent*, 10 May, 2015, https://www.iol.co.za/sundayindependent/how-malema-sold-out-on-land-reform-1856288

Moffitt, Benjamin, and Tormey, Simon. 2014. "Rethinking Populism: Politics, Mediatisation and Political Style." *Political Studies*, 62: 381–397.

Mooney, Patrick, and Hunt, Scott. 1996. "A repertoire of interpretations: Master frames and ideological community in US Agrarian mobilisation." *Sociological Quarterly* 37: 77–197.

Mouffe, C. 2019. "Demonising populism won't work-Europe needs a progressive populist alternative." *European Politics and Policy*: 1–2.

Mouffe, Chantal. 2018. *For a Left Populism*. London: Verso.

Mudde, Cas. 2004. "The Populist Zeitgeist." *Government and Opposition*, 39(4): 541–563.

Nako, Nontsasa. 2018. "Decolonising the South African prison." *SA Crime Quarterly* 66: 1–4.

Nanda, Meera. 2001. "We are all hybrids now: The dangerous epistemology of post-colonial populism." 28(2) *The Journal of Peasant Studies*: 162–186.

Neisser, Eric. 1994. "Hate Speech in the New South Africa: Constitutional Considerations for a Land Recovering from Decades of Racial Repression and Violence." *Journal of International Law and Practice* 3: 336–356.

Nieftagodien, Noor. 2015. "The Economic Freedom Fighters and the Politics of Memory and Forgeting", *South Atlantic Quarterly* 144: 446–456.

Panizza, Francisco. 2005. *Populism and the Mirror of Democracy*. London: Verso.

Pedler, Anne. 1927. "Going to the people. The Russian Norodniki in 1874–5." *The Slavonic Review*: 130–147.

Poplak, Richard. "Full Trotsky: EFF deals with Andile Mngxitama." *DailyMaverick*, 6 Febraury, 2015, < https://www.dailymaverick.co.za/article/.

Posel, Deborah. 2014. "Julius Malema and the post-apartheid public sphere." *Acta Academica* 47: 32–54.

PPSA (Public Protector South Africa). 2016. *State of Capture*. http://www.saflii.org/images/329756472-State-of-Capture.pdf

Rantete, Johannes, & Giliomee, Hermann. 1992. "Transition to Democracy through Transaction? Bilateral Negotiations between the ANC and NP in South Africa." *African Affairs* 91: 515–542.

Roth, Kenneth. 2017. "The dangerous rise of populism: Global attacks on human rights values." *Journal of International Affairs*: 79–84.

Sapa. 2014. "It's official: 2014 election results announced." *Mail&Guardian*, 10 May, 2014, https://mg.co.za/article/2014-05-10-07-its-official-2014-election-results-announced/

Shubin, Vladimir.2019. "South Africa: a new dawn?" *Brazilian Journal of African Studies* 4: 33–50.

Smith, David. 2010. "ANC's Julius Malema lashes out at 'misbehaving' BBC journalist", *The Guardian*, 8 April, 2010 https://www.theguardian.com/world/2010/apr/08/anc-julius-malema-bbc-journalist

Smith, Gordon. 1989. "Core persistence: Change and the 'people's party", *West European Politics* 12(4): 157–168.

Sosibo, Kwanele. 2014. "EFF launches its election manifesto." *Mail&Guardian*, 22 February 22, https://mg.co.za/article/eff-launches-its-party-manifesto/

SP (Staff Reporter). 2015. "Nzimande: Defeat EFF's anarchy and neo-fascist behaviour." *Mail&Guardian*, 8 March, 2015, <https://mg.co.za/article/2015-03-08-blade-nzimande-defeat-the-effs-anarchy-and-neo-fascist-behaviour/

Strelitz, Larry & Steenveld, Lynette. 2010. "The fifth estate: Media theory, watchdog of journalism." *Ecquid Novi* 19: 100–110.

Tanaka, Masaharu. 1970. "The Narodniki and Marx on Russian Capitalism in the 1870's-1880's." *The Kyoto University Economic Review* 39: 1–25.

Thamm, Marianne. 2020. "EFF in court bid to support Public Protector's challenge of flawed CR17 campaign report." *Daily Maverick*, 4 April, 2020, https://www.dailymaverick.co.za/article/

Umraw, Amil. 2018. "'I Answered Honestly' on Bosasa: Rampahosa." *TimesLive*, 14 December, 2018, https://www.timeslive.co.za/politics/2018-12-14-i-answered-honestly-on-bosasa-ramaphosa/

Von Beyme, Klaus. 1996. "The Concept of Political Class: A New Dimension of Research on Elites?" *West European Politics*, 19: 68–87.

Wasserman, Herman. 2010. "Political Journalism in South Africa as a developing democracy-understanding media freedom and responsibility." *Communicatio* 36: 240–251.

Weyland, Kurt. 2001. "Clarifying a Contested Concept: Populism in the Study of Latin American Politics." *Comparative Politics* 34: 1–22.

PART 2

Social Justice and Poverty

CHAPTER 7

Social Justice and Persons with Disabilities in Nigeria

Edwin Etieyibo

1   Introduction

Disability is a global issue and people with disabilities constitute one of the world's largest minorities. Throughout history and in different societies, people with disabilities hve suffered all forms of discrimination (See Coleridge, 1993; Pfeiffer, 1993; World Health Organisation, 2011, 5; Munyi, 2012; Livneh, 1982; Pritchard, 15–30; Teaching for Diversity and Social Justice, 2007). In Nigeria, where it is estimated that there are about 19 million people with disabilities, the story is the same.[1] However, in the last several decades greater importance has been placed on ensuring fair and equal treatment of people with disabilities. Embodying this importance is the recognition of the rights of persons with disabilities in the Convention on the Rights of Persons with Disabilities (CRPD), which enjoins state parties to "take appropriate measures, including legislation to modify or abolish existing laws, regulations, customs and practices that constitute discrimination against" persons with disabilities (United Nations. 2006a, CRPD, Article 4). The CRPD and its Optional Protocol (Optional Protocol to the Convention on the Right of Persons with Disabilities) were adopted on 13 December 2006 at the United Nations (UN) Headquarters in New York and entered into force on 3 May 2008. The CPRD as a key international instrument on the rights of persons with disabilities is the first comprehensive treaty on the rights of persons with disabilities of the 21st century (United Nations, 2006a; United Nations, 2006b).

Being the only UN human rights Convention and instrument with an explicit social development dimension, it marks a 'paradigm shift' in attitudes towards

---

1   This figure is provided in 2009 and attributed to David Anyaele, the executive director of the Centre for Citizens with Disabilities (See *Next.com* Editorial, 2009b). However, if we use the related statistics of the World Health Organisation that about 15% of the world population has some form of disability, then given that the estimated 2020 population of Nigeria has increased from that of 2009 to about 214 million (see Central Intelligence Agency, n.d.; WHO, 2018), one may suppose that the figure should be around 30/32 million people with disabilities in Nigeria.

people with disabilities. It has provided a major impetus or drive for disabilities movements as well as a catalyst in the global movement from viewing people with disabilities as objects of charity, medical treatment and social protection towards viewing them as full and equal members of society. Because the CRPD is intended to promote and protect the rights and dignity of persons with disabilities it rightly and necessarily takes people with disabilities as individuals "with rights who are capable of claiming those rights and making decisions for their lives based on their free and informed consent as well as being active members of society." Given that the CRPD gives specific expression to the needs and situations of persons with disabilities it could be said to incorporate many of the provisions in other international instruments which recognize the rights of every human such as the Universal Declaration of Human Rights, the International Convention on Civil and Political Rights, and the International Covenant on Economic, Social and Cultural Rights—all of which form the International Bill of Human Rights (United Nations, 2006a; United Nations, 2006b; United Nations, 2011a; United Nations, 2011b; United Nations, 2011c).

Nigeria is a state party to both the CRPD and the International Bill of Human Rights. As part of its efforts at giving effect to the CRPD, several houses of the Nigerian upper legislative house (the Senate) has passed into law the Discrimination Against Persons with Disabilities (Prohibition) 2009/2011/2016 Act (which has not yet been signed by any of the last Presidents of Nigeria—Goodluck Jonathan and Muhammadu Buhari. The Discrimination Against Persons with Disabilities (Prohibition) Act (hereinafter, the Disabilities Act) has been passed three times (in 2009, 2011 and 2016. It was first passed on 10 March 10 2009. Six States of the Federation have also made moves to enact into legislation similar to the Disabilities Act. The Disabilities Act broadly recognises the social, economic, civil and political rights of persons with disabilities and advocates for equal opportunities for them as well as their full integration in society. Furthermore, it prohibits subjecting persons with disabilities to prejudices or harmful practices in any area of life.

This chapter is situated within these developments regarding the treatment and inclusivity of persons with disabilities in society and by so doing connects to broader issues of social justice social justice which can be construed not just about the distribution of wealth, opportunities, and privileges within a society but also about rights or human rights and equality and the treatment of people.[2] It particular, the chapter examines some practices in Nigeria that are discriminatory against people with disabilities and links these practices to some

---

2 For broader discussions relating to issues of disabilities in Nigeria in terms of attitudes, as well as reactions and remediations see Etieyibo and Omiegbe, 2017; and for the relationship between religion and culture in the context of discrimination against persons with disabilities in Nigeria see Etieyibo and Omiegbe, 2016.

of the rights of people with disabilities that are violated. The aim of doing this is twofold. Firstly, to show that notwithstanding Nigeria being a state party to the CRPD and the International Bill of Human Rights there is continued perpetuation of various discriminatory practices against people with disabilities in the country. Secondly, to make the case that Nigeria is not doing enough in ensuring fair and equal treatment of people with disabilities.[3]

2   Understanding Disability

Like many concepts, disability does not lend itself to an easy and straightforward definition. Disability covers a range of various levels of functioning at body, person and societal levels. The World Health Organization takes it as an "umbrella term, covering impairments, activity limitations, and participation restriction" (World Health Organisation, n.d; World Health Organisation, 2011a, 3–4) and it sees disability as "a human right issue" as well as a "development issue because of its bidirectional link to poverty" (World Health Organisation, 2011, 9, 10).

Furthermore, the World Health Organization understands disability as not just a health problem, but a complex phenomenon, reflecting the interaction between features of a person's body and features of the society or environment in which he or she lives. That is to say, disability does not simply refer to an individual's intrinsic feature but "a result of an interaction between a person (with a health condition) and that person's contextual factors (environmental factors and personal factors)" (World Health Organisation, n.d; World Health Organisation, 2011, 3–4).[4]

The World Health Organization's definition of disability provides a more comprehensive understanding of disability than that of the *medical* and *social models*. The former model sees disability as an attribute of an individual, that is "as a problem of the person, directly caused by disease, trauma or other health condition, which requires medical care provided in the form of individual treatment by professionals" (World Health Organisation, 2018a). The latter model views "disability mainly as a socially created problem, and basically as a matter of the full integration of individuals into society" (World Health Organisation, 2018a). Contrary to these models, the World Health Organization model and classification of disability neither sees disability as an attribute of the individual

---

3   For an in-depth discussion of human rights instruments, legal documents relating to the rights of people with disabilities and the idea of rights as a Western discourse or invention see Etieyibo 2020)
4   See also World Health Organisation, 2018a and see also World Health Organisation, 2018b.

nor as a socially created problem for which its management either requires some medical cure or an adjustment and behaviour change of the individual. Rather, disability on this model is a complex collection of conditions, many of which are created by the social environment and the management of which requires social action or the collective responsibility of society at large.

In other words, the World Health Organisation is cautioning against viewing disability and issues of disability narrowly, in particular, that it is wrong and problematic to present the medical model and the social model as contraries or dichotomous. Rather, for the World Health Organisation, "disability should be viewed neither as purely medical nor as purely social: persons with disabilities can often experience problems arising from their health condition (World Health Organisation, 2011, 4). It further adds that what we need is a balanced approach that gives "appropriate weight to the different aspects of disability..." (World Health Organisation, 2011, 4).

If we therefore follow this definition of disability and the World Health Organisation's approach to disability, then we will take disability to denote (a) impairments in body functions and structures, (b) limitations in activity, and (c) restriction in participation. And this will suggest that disability will require interventions to remove environmental and social barriers in order to overcome the difficulties faced by people with disabilities (United Nations, 2006a, CRPD, article 2). And as the World Health Organisation puts it, "The environment may be changed to improve health conditions, prevent impairments, and improve outcomes for persons with disabilities" (World Health Organisation, 2011, 4). Such changes will for example, involve legislation, policies, capacity building, or technological developments that target "accessible design of the built environment and transport, signage to benefit people with sensory impairments, more accessible health, rehabilitation, education, and support services, more opportunities for work and employment for persons with disabilities" in order for them to have a fulfilling and flourishing lives (World Health Organisation, 2011, 4).

3   Beliefs and Perceptions of Disability in Nigeria

Abosi and Ozoji (1985) hold that Nigerians in particular and Africans in general attribute causes of disabilities to different factors from witchcraft, juju,[5] sex, God and the supernatural. Desta (1995) notes that throughout Africa, people

---

5   Juju refers to objects, such as a charm, amulets, and spells used in parts of West Africa superstitiously as part of witchcraft or to affect others or events, negatively or positively.

with disabilities are seen as hopeless and helpless and disability as a curse. Others have also noted similar and different beliefs and perceptions of disability in Africa (See Munyi, 2012 and Omiegbe, 2001).

In Nigeria, as in many parts of Africa, disability is generally construed negatively. Disability is believed to be a curse and as such bad for the community. Many also believe that people with disabilities are inferior to people without disabilities, that those with disabilities are harbingers of evil although fruitful in procuring social and economic benefits (Abang, 1988, 71–77). In their observations of the attitudes of Nigerians towards people with disabilities, Kayode and Ekuase[6] claim that the beliefs that Nigerians hold about disability motivates discrimination against people with disabilities. Concerning beliefs about deafness, they describe the belief that the bodies of persons with auditory impairment are houses of evil spirits as false and a myth (See Madu and Ibrahim, 2004; *THISDAY*, 2010)

To understand beliefs about disability as false suggest that they are not scientifically or empirically demonstrable. If these beliefs are false, they are because of the status of the object or state of affairs that they designate, implying that visible features of persons with disabilities do not often and always supply the material on which beliefs about them are formed and developed. These beliefs fuel and inform the customary practices discussed below. That customs and practices are sensitive to various beliefs is seen from studies that show that culture has an influence on the behaviour of people and that belief about disability impact people's attitude towards persons with disabilities. Fishbien and Ajzen (1975) observe that beliefs about disability are the foundation of behaviour towards persons with disabilities. Similarly, Ozoji (1991) notes that the beliefs a person hold about disability are instrumental in determining the attitudes of that individual towards persons with disabilities. The effervescent link between beliefs and behaviour towards people with disabilities should not be surprising since it is generally the case that beliefs inform attitudes and actions.[7]

4   Persons with Disabilities and Customary Practices

The customary practices that constitute discrimination against persons with disabilities will be discussed under two categories. The first is community

---

6 D. Kayode and D. Ekuase, are respectively the chairpersons of the Lagos State and Edo State Associations of the Deaf.
7 See Triandis (1994) for discussion linking behaviour with culture broadly construed.

rituals. These are rituals that are community oriented in virtue of the fact that they are explicitly performed for the benefit of the community. The second category is personal rituals, which are performed to benefit the individual. Both sets of rituals are performed by people in rural and urban communities in Nigeria. The essential point about these rituals and their discussion here is to show that understood broadly as customary practices they are discriminatory against persons with disabilities, on the one hand, and are perpetuated by false beliefs about disability, on the other. Before proceeding to discussing this it will be helpful first to describe both categories of rituals.

Community rituals are done to cleanse the community and often have "religious" connotation although they may be motivated by personal utility. This may be for the purpose of appeasing the gods or ancestors, or warding off "evil spirits" from the community, or preparing the land for the planting and harvest seasons. These rituals are common in many communities in Southwest Nigeria and the Niger Delta region (Olupona, 1991). They are usually performed by herbalists, medicine men, or local priests on behalf of the communities under the guide of community elders who may be herbalists themselves. The rituals involve sacrifices, whereby all sorts of divinations are made and incantations invoked. When the sacrifices require blood, humans may be used in addition to animals (birds, goats, chickens, cows, etc.). That humans are often used for rituals can be seen from the following advert in a local newspaper, which reads: "stop these senseless killings of human beings and ritual murders. We will give you the same result with live cows and you will get 100% instant result and success. Come personally to: Dr. Jakes at NO 17 Losa Street, off Philomena Street, Santos Layout Dopemu – Agege, Lagos (*Punch*. 2001).

Like community rituals, personal rituals involve sacrifices, divinations, and incantations and may have a "religious" connotation. The difference however, is that the former is "publicly" driven whereas the latter is privately driven (individual prosperity, wellbeing etc.). An example of a practice that may have a religious connotation even though it is privately driven is the case of Tony Yengeni, a former whip of the African National Congress, who was sentenced to imprisonment for four years. After his early release from prison, Yengeni decided to celebrate by slaughtering a bull at his father's home in the Cape Town township of Gugulethu. Some interpreted this ritual practice as having a religious significance, i.e. the ritual was meant to appease Yengeni's family ancestors or gods. Others interpreted it as an expression of his "cultural liberty" and as a celebration of his cultural root. If one accepts the religious interpretation, then one could claim that the ritual has both religious and personal aspects. It has a religious aspect simply because of its religious significance and a personal aspect because it celebrates Yengeni's "cultural liberty". This reading is plausible if we take culture to subsume religion (Van der Vyver and Green, 2008, 337–356).

Parties to these rituals are an individual or group of persons (client) and an herbalist. The client meets an herbalist and requests assistance in enhancing certain aspects of the client's life. The herbalist then gives instructions on what needs to be done. The belief is that by following the instructions the client's individual's utility would be enhanced. The actions performed may include presenting the herbalist some objects (which may include animal or human parts) or doing certain things (walking naked at night, sleeping with a corpse or women with mental illness).

Ritual Killings and Rape of Persons with Disabilities: It is generally believed that many missing persons in various cities and communities in Nigeria are kidnapped and killed for rituals.[8] The killings of people with mental illness, albinism, angular kyphosis and the rape of women with mental illness either for community or personal rituals are more routine than may be assumed (Igwe, 2011). There are layers of people involved in these killings: the herbalist (who prepares portions from parts of persons with disabilities for use by clients), the client (either an individual or a group) that uses the portion; and others who lure, kidnap or kill persons with disabilities (generally for monetary rewards) and hand them or their body parts to the client or herbalist (Igwe, 2011).

Ritual Killings of Persons with Mental Illness, Albinism, and Angular Kyphosis: Like physical illnesses, mental illnesses can take many forms. Mental illness can be caused by physiological or psychosocial factors and is generally characterized by the impairment of cognitive, emotional, or behavioural functioning. According to the Public Health Agency of Canada, mental illness is "characterized by alterations in thinking, mood or behaviour (or a combination), and impaired functioning over an extended period of time." It further notes that the "symptoms vary from mild to severe depending on the type, the individual, the family and socio-economic environment" (Canadian Mental Health Association, 2011). People with mental illness may exhibit behavioural difficulties in numerous cases and in many communities in Nigeria they are believed to be suffering from super-natural causes such as witchcraft or under a spell by the gods (See Gureje, Lasebikan, Ephraim-Oluwanuga, Olley, and Kola, 2005, 436–441; Okhomina, 2004; Onyejekwe, 2003).

---

8 Emmanuel Ojukwu, the Public Relations Officer for the Nigeria Police Force told the News Agency of Nigeria in a 2009 interview that many kidnapping cases in Nigeria result in the dismemberment of bodies for ritual (*Next.com Nigeria*, 2009a). And for a report of how some that escaped from kidnappers recounted stories of Nigerians kidnapped for ritual purposes see Odejobi T. 2010).

People with mental illness are killed as part of community rituals and this can be motivated by either of three reasons: preventive, curative, or punitive. Preventive killing is when a person with mental illness and who may sometimes be branded a witch is killed in order to prevent any harm from befalling the community. Curative killing is when the person with mental illness is killed to promote the general wellbeing of the community. Punitive killing is when a person with mental illness is killed because of the belief that he or she has committed an abomination or is responsible for the ills of the community (see Okafor, 2003). Okafor notes that "some local ancient mythology has it that people with disabilities are social outcasts serving retribution for offences of their forefathers" (Okafor, 2003, 5).

People with mental illness are also killed as part of personal rituals. It is not always clear if there are preventive and punitive motivations in these sorts of killing or they are strictly motivated by individual utility as in the case with the recent burning to death of a middle aged woman with mental illness in Benin City, Edo State by a crowd because of the belief that she was a "witch" and was responsible for the various problems that some are dealing with in the community (See Oko, 2003; Houreld, 2009; McVeigh, 2007; Purefoy, 2010). This appears also to be the case with the number of reported instances of public lynching of people with mental illness in some communities in South-eastern Nigeria or the general stigmatisation of people with mental illness in Northern Nigeria (Audu, Idris, Olisah and Sheikh, 2013, 55–60).

People with oculocutaneous albinism are broadly discriminated against in Nigerian, from been isolated to being trafficked and killed.[9] According to Shehu Shagari, former President of Nigeria, discrimination against people with albinism in Nigeria is endemic. Speaking at the 4th National Conference on Albinism in Sokoto State (July 12, 2010) he noted that a good deal of the discrimination "suffered by people with albinism can be traced to ignorance on the part of the general public" (*Vanguard.* 2010). Because many people with albinism are targeted for ritual killings, most live in hiding (McVeigh, 2007; *Sky News*, 2008, 2; *The Sun News*, 2008; *Nigerian Tribune*, 2011).

Some are trafficked and killed as part of personal rituals, and others as part of community rituals. Those involved in personal rituals believe that the body

---

9 Oculocutaneous albinism (OCA) is a group of inherited disorders of melanin biosynthesis or a congenital disorder. This condition is characterized by a generalized reduction in pigmentation (called melanin) of the skin, hair and eyes. Individuals that are affected typically have very fair skin and white or light-coloured hair. Because of the lack of the eye pigment or the protective melanin, long-term sun exposure precipitates those with this condition to sun-induced skin disorders, including skin damage and skin cancers such as melanoma. See Grønskov, Ek and Brondum-Nielsen, 2007, 1–8; Okoro, 1975, 485–92; Christianson, Howson and Modell. 2006; Winship, 2003; Omiegbe, 1998).

parts of people with albinism could be used for portions which when used could make them wealthy or prolong their lives. Data regarding the exact number of people with albinism trafficked and killed in Nigeria are not available, however, there are reports suggesting that they are routinely targeted for rituals. There is the example of Chidima, a 17-month old with OCA who was decapitated by a group of albinism traffickers for rituals (Nwanze, 1999). There is also the case of two people with albinism that were killed in two communities not very far apart, both of whom were found days later with some parts of their bodies missing. One was in Ugbogui, a remote farm settlement in Edo State, who was beheaded while working on his farm, and the other was in Urhuoka Quarters, Abraka, Delta State who was killed in his home. The general belief is that they were used as sacrifice to boost the harvest season in both communities (*The Sun News*, 2010).

Like people with mental illness and people with albinism, people with angular kyphosis are mostly killed for rituals either for personal or public utility. Angular kyphosis is a common condition of a curvature of the upper spine and can either be the result of degenerative disease (such as arthritis) or developmental problems (Omiegbe, 2001, 26–28). There are reports in the local media that suggest that the trafficking of people with this condition is not uncommon.[10] Two notable cases happened in 2009. The first—a male herbalist—was killed in Benin City, Edo State and the second—Taibat Oseni, a 22-year-old female—in Osun State. Regarding the killing of the male herbalist it is alleged that ritualists baited him from his house under the pretext that they needed him to help administer treatment to a family member that was sick. His body was found days later in the outskirt of the town with his protrusion removed. As for the killing of Taibat Oseni, the Osun State Police Command claim that she was kidnapped from her home at about 10.30 p.m. on September 29 by some men and then taken to a 15-year-old abandoned building owned by a senator where she was killed and her protrusion removed (*THISDAY*, 2009; *The Sun News*, 2009).

Ritual Rape of Women with Mental Illness: Women with mental illness are also victims of rape in Nigeria. Many are homeless and are often seen on the streets in major cities in Nigeria. According to Dian Blair, the head of Amaudo Itumbauzo, an international NGO that caters for destitute that have mental illness in Nigeria, the sexual abuse of women with mental illness "is the greatest

---

10 In 2002, the Nigeria Police arrested a man in Ikot-Akpan Abia, Akwa-Ibom State, who traded mostly in parts of people with angular kyphosis and who had been in the business for over a decade. In his confession, he claimed that he sells the parts to herbalists for rituals and that kidnapping of people with angular kyphosis is very widespread. According to him, a person with angular kyphosis attracts the sum of N400, 000 (US$2,650). See *THISDAY*, 2002. May 2002.

assault on the rights of female psychiatric patients" (THISDAY, 2005). In her keynote address at the UN Human Rights Day in Abakaliki, Ebonyi State, Blair notes that there are ritual dimensions to the sexual abuse of many women with mental illness and that many of them are raped because of the belief that having intimacy with them could bring wealth or prolong an individual's life. She notes that this is unfortunate since the results "are the legion of born abandoned children on the streets, who turn out to utterly depend on passers-by for food."

5   Other Discriminatory Practices against Persons with Disabilities

Beyond the customary practices discussed above, there are other practices around education, work and employment, accessibility, safety and accommodation that are discriminatory against persons with disabilities. Firstly, consider education. One way in which persons with disabilities are discriminated against in education is in the availability or lack thereof of financial resources and educational institutions to cater for their needs. Presently, there are only a few educational institutions that exist for children with disabilities across the country. Furthermore, persons with disabilities more generally find it hard to access government scholarships for their studies.[11] Another way is when schools fail to provide facilities that are inclusive of and accessible to persons with disabilities. The impact of such exclusionary practise on persons with disabilities can be seen from the comments by Nkechi Nwokeke, a law student at the University of Ibadan. She mentions the effect on her studies of the lack of reasonable accommodation for wheelchair users in her university. According to her, she often has to depend on colleagues and friends to commute around. She describes this as frustrating and dehumanizing and notes that the situation prevents her from going to the library to do research and to study sufficiently well for exams (Adelaja, 2011).

Secondly, there are practices that exclude accessibility aids in the construction and modification of public buildings, roads, and other facilities. These practices discriminate against persons with disabilities and make life difficult for them. The case of Lekan Ajayi, a wheelchair user helps to illustrate this. Ajayi is unable to move around and has to rely on others to do the simple things in life like going to the bank. According to him, since the bank facilities are not accessible by wheelchair, he has to send friends to the bank whenever

---

11 In November 2009, students with disabilities and graduates staged peaceful protests in several Nigerian cities over what they consider unjustified discrimination against them by the government in the areas of employment and scholarships. See Fatunde, 2009.

he needs to do any transaction. He says: "I don't have any privacy....The way things are designed in this society makes me feel bad" (Adelaja, 2011).

Thirdly, consider work and employment. Persons with disabilities are discriminated against in work and employment when they are either overlooked in job selection or not given the due consideration that they deserve. So take the example of David Okon who was demoted from the position of a bank training manager to telephone operator because of his disabilities. Commenting on this case, Lanre Adebayor notes[12]: "the fact that you are deformed physically or mentally will be used against you even when you are qualified and apply like any other person. [An] employer will explain it in two ways; it will be difficult for you and we don't have the facilities for you" (Azu, 2002; *Next.com Nigeria*, 2009b). He adds: "Nigeria is guilty of nonchalance to the plight of these individuals...a situation of being turned back from a job interview on account of being disabled is not just nor is it pleasant to be denied access to housing by landlords merely on account of being a disabled person" (Azu, 2002; *Next.com Nigeria*, 2009b).

6 On Social Justice

Generally, the concept of social justice is taken to be about the distribution of wealth, opportunities, and privileges within a society, on the one hand, and about rights or human rights and equality and the treatment of people, on the other. This will imply that when one talks of social justice we are talking of the application of justice on a social level.[13] This means then that social justice is not limited to what happens in the law courts, but finds application in all aspects of society. The obligation or principle of social justice is one that requires that people and indeed everyone be treated fairly and justly, that the distribution of advantages and disadvantages in society be egalitarian and as fair as possible, that there been a level playing field for everyone. The nub of the norm of social justice can therefore be said to be concerned with the fair and egalitarian allocation of resources in society (e.g. rights, privileges, advantages and disadvantages, etc.).

Ever since Plato argued in *The Republic* that an ideal state rest on four cardinal virtues: wisdom, courage, moderation, and justice philosophers have extensively discussed the concept of social justice (Plato. 1950. See especially Bk. V). One of the prominent discourse on the concept of social justice is John

---

12 Adebayor is a journalist with visual impairment and served as spokesperson of "Club 2 – 12 of Nigeria", an association of people with disabilities based in Lagos State, Nigeria.
13 For some rigorous discussion of the concept of social justice in the context of privatization in Nigeria, see Etieyibo, 2011, 37–44.

Rawls in his highly influential book, *A Theory of Justice* (1971 and revised in 1999) and in *Political liberalism* (1993). Rawls' discussion of social justice takes a different tangent form that of Plato in *The Republic*. While for Rawls, justice is to be found in the notion of *fairness* expressed in the two principles of justice, Plato's conception of justice *qua* virtue arises from a harmony of all the other three virtues. In particular, and on the first principle of justice for Rawls, which he calls the liberty principle individuals are said to possess an inviolability founded on justice. That is, each person ought to have the same indefeasible claim to a fully adequate scheme of equal basic liberties, which scheme is compatible with the same scheme of liberties for all (Rawls, 1971; Rawls, 1993).

One can say that this notion of justice informs more or less and to some degree the various United Nations' human rights instruments—from the International Bill of Human Rights to the Convention on the Rights of Persons with Disabilities for which Nigeria is a state party and which in some sense informed the passing into law of the Disabilities Act. The claim that we make here is that the principle of social justice which places an obligation on government to promote fairness and a level playing field for every member of society and to maintain a social minimum for its citizens is not been meet by Nigeria. The next section takes up this idea about Nigeria not doing enough to ensure the fair and equal treatment of people with disabilities.

7 Nigeria and the Fair and Equal Treatment of People with Disabilities

In the context of the above discriminatory practices against persons with disabilities, it is penitent to ask if Nigeria is doing enough to ensure fair and equal treatment of people with disabilities. More specifically, the question is whether the country is heeding the norm of social justice in the fair and egalitarian allocation of resources in society (e.g. rights, privileges, advantages and disadvantages, etc.). I claim that Nigeria is not heeding the norm and more broadly that the country is not doing enough when it comes the equal and fair treatment of persons with disabilities.

In the rest of the chapter, I will try to argue for this claim. The crux of the argument that I present is that in order to ensure fair and equal treatment of people with disabilities Nigeria must aggressively take appropriate measures, including legislation, to modify or abolish existing laws, regulations, customs and practices that constitute discrimination against persons with disabilities, but that it is not doing so. This argument will be developed along four lines. The first two lines relate to having a functional legalisation on disability, the third is about the content of the Disabilities Act, and the fourth concerns its implementation.

In terms of the first line, besides the Federal Government only six states (out of thirty-six) of the Federation have pushed for the enactment of disabilities legislation. The message that this seems to send is that the remaining thirty states are not yet committed to accommodating the needs and rights of persons with disabilities. It is difficult to see how those states without disabilities legislation are going to give force and expression to the CPRD or even aspects of the yet to be assented Disabilities Act, in particular provisions in those sections that require state funding of public infrastructure in section 74(1) and section 75 according to which unemployed persons with disabilities are to be paid by their states of origin monthly disability allowance not less than the prevailing minimum wage in their respective states of origin.

Secondly, the Disabilities Act has not been passed. Without its passage into law, the Disabilities Act.is gathering dust somewhere in Government House. It is really shocking and incomprehensible for the Federal Government not to have passed into law the Disabilities Act. How are they expected to give force to the CPRD in the Nigerian context if the country lacks any disability legislation at the Federal level that it has to work with?

The third line is with regard to the content of the Disabilities Act, which is silent on issues relating to customs and beliefs that perpetuate violations of the rights of persons with disabilities. Not saying anything about such customs and beliefs can be considered a major flaw in the Disabilities Act. One can interpret its silence on these issues as suggesting that the governments (state and federal) do not consider it important to address customs and false beliefs that Nigerians hold about disability and persons with disabilities. If this is so, then it is not clear how they intend to complement provisions in the CRPD that encourage state parties to modify or abolish customs and practices that violate the rights of persons with disabilities. Pushing to enact the Disabilities Act, which expands on provisions in the CRPD, is an important step in the right direction at providing fair and equal treatment for persons with disabilities. However, since it by itself does not effectively shape prevalent beliefs and attitudes towards persons with disabilities, it can be consider wholly inadequate in complementing the objectives and provisions of the CRPD.

The fourth line of argumentation relates to the implementation of provisions in the Disabilities Act. Firstly, the Disabilities Act states that the Federal Ministry of Information shall issue regulations and guidelines "for the purpose of giving effect to the provisions of the Act" (Disabilities Act, section 13). However, it is neither clear what the participatory planning and implementation strategy is for the Ministry in "giving effect to the provisions of the Act" in ways that are complementary to the objectives of those of the CRPD. The Disabilities Act also states that the Ministry "shall make provisions for the promotion of awareness regarding (a) the rights, respect and dignity of persons with disabilities; and (b) the capabilities, achievements and contributions of persons with disabilities to the society" (Disabilities Act, section 2). It is not obvious how it intends incorporating into its broader policies provisions that will promote awareness regarding the rights of persons with disabilities and their capabilities, achievements, and contributions in society.

Secondly, there is no mechanism in place to help deal, on the one hand, with exclusionary practices in areas of accessibility, safety and self-determination for persons with disabilities, and on the other, with patent discriminations and violations of the rights of persons with disabilities. Simply put, it is not clear what the machinery is for preventing broad discriminatory practices and violations of the rights of persons with disabilities in the areas of exclusionary practices such as education, employment, safety, accessibility and accommodation. So for example, section 6 of the Disabilities Act provides a transitory period of five years for the modification of buildings and automobiles to allow persons with disabilities to be able to access them. This is in line with requirements of the CPRD regarding accessibility for persons with disabilities. Even though the Disabilities Act is not yet in force because of the refusal to sign it into law by the last two Presidents of Nigeria, there are no signs of such modifications of buildings and automobiles whether those owned by governments or by natural or legal persons (at least in line with requirements of the CPRD regarding accessibility for persons with disabilities). Additionally, sections 4 and 5 of the Disabilities Act have clear provisions with regard to accessibility and safety, but buildings, roads, and other facilities continue to be constructed without taking into account the accessibility and safety of persons with disabilities, clearly in violations of the requirements of the CPRD regarding accessibility for persons with disabilities.

Thirdly, there is the issue of the punishment for those that discriminate against persons with disabilities or violate their rights. Violations of the rights to life, liberty, the physical and mental integrity of the person are hardly punished, prosecuted or brought to justice. Going by the provisions of the CRPD and the yet to be signed Disabilities Act in the areas of life, liberty and security and mental integrity of the person it is clear that the above customary practices violate the rights of people with mental illness, oculocutaneous albinism, and angular kyphosis in Nigeria. The practices violate their rights to life because they deprive person with disabilities the time and space to expend themselves in activities that they find valuable. In addition, the rape of women with mental illness violates their rights to privacy, liberty and security of the person. It could also be said to violate their rights to personal integrity, dignity and life particularly when one considers the intrusive nature of acts of sexual violence and the possibility of them contracting HIV/AIDS. The lack of investigations of these cases and the prosecution of those that violate the rights of persons with disabilities is a testament to the view that Nigeria is not doing enough in ensuring fair and equal treatment of people with disabilities.

It is important to note that commenting on these rights the Human Rights Committee (HRC) of the International Convention on Civil and Political Rights[14] emphasis that they should not be interpreted narrowly, and that state parties should (a) take measures to prevent and punish deprivation of life by criminal acts, (b) take specific and effective measures to prevent the disappearance of individuals; (c) establish effective facilities and procedures to investigate thoroughly cases of missing and disappeared persons in circumstances which may involve a violation of the right to life (HRC, articles 6(1), 9(1), 17(1)). It further notes that "the right to liberty and security of persons is applicable to all deprivations of liberty, whether in criminal cases or in other cases such as, for example, mental illness, vagrancy, drug addiction, educational purposes, immigration control" (HRC, General Comment 16 (1988), paragraphs 1, 3–5 & 11) and that violation of the right of the physical and mental integrity of persons with disabilities as contained in article 17 of the CRPD broadly prohibits making human body and its parts as such a source of financial gain. Cleary then, with regards to these rights Nigeria is not doing enough in ensuring fair and equal treatment of people with disabilities given that it does seem to take a lukewarm attitude towards practices that prevent people with mental illness, oculocutaneous albinism, and angular kyphosis the time and space to engage in activities that are of value to them.

The same conclusion can be reached regarding discriminatory practices in employment, accessibility, safety and accommodation. The Disabilities Act contains clear punitive provisions for violations of these.

In terms of employment, section 67 prohibits all forms of discrimination against persons with disabilities in a labour market. Section 68 states that persons with disabilities are not be discriminated against in "the job application procedure; the terms and conditions of employment; opportunity for promotion and advancement; and accommodation." Section 70 requires that "employers of labour employing up to 100 persons shall reserve at least 10% of such workforce for qualified persons with disabilities." 68(1) states that a person that

---

14 References to the HRC of the of the International Convention on Civil and Political Rights are to the United Nations, 1982 HRC General Comment 6, 1982 HRC General Comment 9 and 1988 HRC General Comment16.

discriminates against persons with disabilities in a labour market 'shall on conviction be personally liable to damages of N100, 000 (US $250) payable to the affected person with disability.' Where a company is in breach of the section 68(1) states that it 'shall be liable on conviction to N500, 000 (US $1,500) damages payable to the affected person with disability' and if the violation involves any principal officer of the company that person 'shall be liable on conviction to N100, 000 damages payable to the affected person with disability.'

With regards to accessibility, safety and accommodation section 1(2) outlines the punishment for those that contravene section 1(1). Violation by an individual carries with it a fine of N100, 000 Naira or six months imprisonment or both, while violation by a corporate body carries a fine of 1,000,000 Naira (US $3, 000). Section 9(3) states that "A person, organisation or corporate body in control of a public parking lot who fails to provide for the reserved spaces" as outlined in 9(1) 'commits an offence and is liable on conviction to a fine of 1,000 Naira' (US$3) for each day of default.

These are laudable provisions. However, they are useless and of no benefit to anyone (including persons with disabilities), if no clear mechanism for their implementation is provided. More importantly, if the Disabilities Act that contains these provisions is not passed into law Nigeria will continue to be business as usual with people (natural or legal) continuing to discriminate against persons with disabilities. It could be said then that Nigeria's response to discriminatory practices and the violations of the rights of persons with disabilities in the above areas diverges from the clear recommendations of the CRPD and the HRC. A more cynical way of putting it would be that the county does not even take seriously the recommendations of the CRPD and it being a state party to it. What all of this boils down to is that, as a country, it does not have any regard for the fair and equal treatment of persons with disabilities. If as has been noted, the trafficking, killing, and rape of persons with disabilities either for personal or communal rituals, on the one hand, and practices around education, employment, and accessibility violate their rights, and given that such violations are tragic and that mechanism needs to be put in place to prevent the violations (but since Nigeria has refused to put them in place), the conclusion that the country is not taking seriously its commitment of ensuring fair and equal treatment of persons with disabilities seems warranted. It is important to note that these practices do not only deprive persons with disabilities the time and space to employ their lives and bodies for purposes that they consider valuable. But by doing little in preventing the violations of their rights the governments can also be said to contribute to the terror engulfing persons with disabilities that are alive and thus undermine the exercise of their rights to life and freedom of movement.

7   Conclusion

This chapter is about social justice and persons with disabilities. In particular, it is about practices that are discriminatory against persons with disabilities and that violate their rights and by so doing violates the core norm of social justice, which is about fairness or the fair and egalitarian allocation of resources in society (e.g. rights, privileges, advantages and disadvantages, etc.). I examined, on the one hand, how some various practices in Nigeria discriminate against persons with disabilities and violate their rights, and on the other, why it can be said that as Nigeria, as a party to international instruments on rights, is not doing enough to ensure fair and equal treatment of persons with disabilities. Some of these practices are reflected in community and personal rituals, namely, the trafficking and killing of people with mental illness, albinism, and angular kyphosis, and the rape of women with mental illness. Others are in the areas of work and employment, accessibility accommodation and safety. Because most of these practices treat persons with disabilities as mere means to the end of some other people, they ought to be wholeheartedly denounced.

Like everyone else in society, people with disabilities ought to be treated as equal and with respect and dignity. As human beings, they are ends-in-themselves and not mere means or objects that can be manipulated or exploited for other ends that others may have.[15] They are entitled to the full rights that have been expressly recognized in the CRPD, other human rights instruments, and the Disabilities Act. These rights place a limit on others in society with regards to how to treat persons with disabilities. Even though persons with disabilities may have different abilities, such differences are not reasonable grounds for discrimination against them or violation of their rights. Furthermore, as equal members of society we have a duty to ensure that they enjoy the same and equal treatment that everyone else enjoys in society. As Ramphal (1981) notes "the world community must continue to assert its legitimate role in the advancement of human rights through the rule of law world-wide; and it must be in the vanguard of enlightened response to the insistent limitations of our common humanity that so characterise our time" (Ramphal, 1981, 10).

Given that society at large has a moral obligation to ensure that a level playing field is provided so that persons with disabilities can realize their rights and goals in life and given the level of commitment of Nigeria to issues affecting people with disabilities it could be argued that it is not taking seriously its

---

15 For some argument as to why it is morally wrong and unjust to treat individuals as mere objects or simply as means-to-an-end see Etieyibo, 2006, 403–419.

commitment to ensuring fair and equal treatment of persons with disabilities as it should. It must be noted that the enactment and passing into law disabilities legislation is important for the protection of person with disabilities. Nigeria has not managed to do this, i.e. pass into law the Disabilities Act. Even when it does eventually do this (if it ever it will), one must note that the passage into law of disabilities legislation is not an end in itself. It is but one important step in the many steps required in the protection of the rights of persons with disabilities. The existence of laws on rights does not in and of itself guarantee that citizens' rights would be protected. There has to be a proper mechanism in place to translate such laws into ways that are meaningful to the public, but in this case for persons with disability.

References

Abang, T.B. 1988. "Disablement, Disability and the Nigerian Society." *Disability, Handicap & Society* 3(1):71–77.

Abosi, C.O. and Ozoji, E. D. 1985. *Educating the Blind: A Descriptive Approach*. Ibadan: Spectrum Books.

Adelaja, A. 2011. "Providing Equal Opportunities for Persons with Disabilities." *Next. com Nigeria*. May 24, 2011.

Audu, I. A., Idris, S. H., Olisah, V. O. and Sheikh, T. L., 2013. "Stigmatization of People with Mental Illness Among Inhabitants of a Rural Community in Northern Nigeria. *International Journal of Social Psychiatry*, vol. 59, pp 55–60.

Azu, M. 2002. "Job Placement." *Daily Times*. June 21.

Canadian Mental Health Association. 2011. *What is Mental Health and Mental Illness?* Available at https://reddeer.cmha.ca/wp-content/uploads/2017/04/mental-health-and-mental-illness.pdf. [Accessed on 12 June 2019].

Central Intelligence Agency (n.d). *The World Fact Book*. Available at https://www.cia.gov/library/publications/the-world-factbook/geos/print_ni.html. Accessed 12 March, 2020.

Christianson, A. L., Howson, P. and Modell, B. 2006. *The March of Dimes: Global Report on Birth Defects: The Hidden Toll of Dying and Disabled Children*. New York: March of Dimes Birth Defects Foundation.

Coleridge, P. 1993. *Disability, Liberation and Development*. Oxford: Oxfam.

Desta, D. 1995. "Needs and Provisions in the Area of Special Education: the Case of Ethiopia." Report on the 2nd South-South-North Workshop, Kampala, Uganda.

Etieyibo, Edwin. 2006. "Libertarianism and the Dichotomy Between Positive and Negative Rights." In Patricia Hanna et al (eds.), pp 403–419. *An Anthology of Philosophical Studies*. Athens: Athens Institute for Education and Research.

Etieyibo, Edwin. 2011. "Privatization in Nigeria, Social Welfare, and the Obligation of Social Justice." *Journal of Economics* 2011 2(1): 37–44.

Etieyibo, Edwin and Omiegbe, Omiegbe. 2016. "Religion, Culture, Discrimination against Persons with Disabilities in Nigeria." *African Journal of Disability* 5(1):1–6.

Etieyibo, Edwin and Omiegbe, Omiegbe. 2017. *Disabilities in Nigeria, Attitudes, Reaction and Remediations*. Mary Land USA: Hamilton Books.

Etieyibo. 2020. "Rights of Persons with Disabilities in Nigeria." *Afrika Focus*.

Fatunde, T. 2009. "Disabled Protest at Discrimination." *University World News*. 15 November, 2009, Available at http://www.universityworldnews.com/article.php?story=20091113141506713. Accessed 13 December 2018.

Fishbien, M. and Ajzen, T. 1975. *Belief, Attitudes, and Intentions and Behaviour: An Introduction to Theory and Research*. Manila: Addison Wesley Publishing Company.

Grønskov, K., Ek, J. and Brondum-Nielsen, K. 2007. "Oculocutaneous Albinism." *Orphanet Journal of Rare Diseases* 2(43):1–8.

Gureje, O., Lasebikan, V.O., Ephraim-Oluwanuga, O., Olley, B.O., and Kola, L. 2005. "Community Study of Knowledge of and Attitude to Mental Illness in Nigeria." *The British Journal of Psychiatry*, vol.186, pp436–441.

Houreld, K.2009. "African Children Denounced as 'Witches' by Christian Pastors." The *Huffington Post*, 18 October 2009, Available at http://www.huffingtonpost.com/2009/10/18/african-children-denounce_n_324943.html. Accessed July 15, 2017.

Igwe, Leo. 2011. *Ritual Killing and Human Sacrifice in Africa, International Humanist and Ethical Union*. Available at http://www.iheu.org/ritual-killing-and-human-sacrifice-africa. Accessed 11 March 2020.

Livneh, H., 1982. "On the Origins of Negative Attitudes toward People with Disabilities." *Rehabilitation Literature* 43: 338–347.

Madu, Fabian and Yahaya, Ibrahim.2004. "Deaf Persons Raise Alarm Over Future." THISDAY. 8 October 2004.

McVeigh, T. 2007. "Children Abused, Killed as Witches in Nigeria." *The Observer*, 9 December 2007.

Munyi, *Chomba Wa.*, 2012. "Past and Present Perceptions Towards Disability: A Historical Perspective." Disability Studies Quarterly 32(2). http://dsq-sds.org/article/view/3197/3068.

Next.com Nigeria. 2009a. "Police Calls for Sensitization against Kidnappers." 25 May 2009.

Next.com Editorial, 2009b. "The Lost Ones." *Next.com Nigeria,* 10 December 2009.

Nigeria. 2009/2011/2016. Discrimination Against Persons with Disabilities (Prohibition) 2009 Act.

Nigerian Tribune. 2011. "Albinos as Endangered Species." 23 March 2011.

Nwanze, P. 1999. "Albino Baby Saga: Suspects Confess." Weekend *Pointer*, 14 March 1999.

Odejobi T. 2010. "The Worth of the Nigerian Life. *Nigerian Tribune*, 7 February 2010.

Okafor, Leonard. 2003. *Enhancing Business-Community Relations – Sir David Osunde Foundation Case Study, Nigeria*. Sir David Osunde Foundation. UNDP, www.undp.org.ng.

Okhomina, O. 2004. "Ozalla: Royal Father Justifies Witchcraft Screening Exercise." *Vanguard*, 30 November 2004.

Oko, E. O. 2003. "Extra-judicial Killings in Nigeria: The Case of Afikpo Town. Paper presented at the 17th International Conference of the International Society for the Reform of Criminal Law, 24–28 August 2003, The Hague: Netherlands, http://www.isrcl.org/Papers/Elechi.pdf.

Okoro A. N. 1975. "Albinism in Nigeria: A Clinical and Social Study." *British Journal of Dermatology* 92(5):485–92;

Olupona, J. K. 1991. *Kingship, Religion, and Rituals in a Nigerian Community*. Stockholm: Almqvist & Wiksell International.

Omiegbe, Odirin. 1998. *An Introduction to Special Education*. Bellco Publishers: Benin.

Omiegbe, Odirin. 2001. Superstitious Beliefs Associated with the Handicapped in Africa, in Orubu, A. O. (ed), African Traditional Religion: A Book of Selected Readings, Benin: Institute of Education.

Onyejekwe, N. 2003. *Witchcraft: Myth of a Curious Institution, Niger Delta Congress*. Available at http://www.nigerdeltacongress.com/warticles/witchcraft_myth_of_a_curious_ins.htm). [Accessed 13 December 2018].

Ozoji, E. D. 1991. *Psychology of Attitudes towards the Disabled: The Nigerian Perspective*. Jos: University of Jos Press.

Pfeiffer D. 1993. "Overview of the Disability Movement: History Legislative Record, and Political Implications." *Policy Studies Journal* 4(21): 724–34

Plato. 1950. *The Republic*. London: Macmillan and Co.

Pritchard, D. 1963. *Education and the Disabled*. London: Routledge.

Punch. 2001. "Instant Richness Guaranteed." Saturday Punch, 21 February, 2001.

Purefoy, C. 2010. "Children are Targets of Nigerian Witch Hunt." *CNN*, 28 August 2010. Available at http://www.cnn.com/2010/WORLD/africa/08/25/nigeria.child.witches/index.html. Accessed July 15, 2017.

Ramphal, Shridath. S. 1981. "Keynote Address." *Development, Human Rights and the Rule of Law*. Report of a Conference held in The Hague on 27 April-1 May 1981, pp.9–24. Convened by the International Commission of Jurists Toronto: Pergamon.

Rawls, John. 1971 (Revised in 1999). *A Theory of Justice*. Cambridge, MA: Harvard University Press.

Rawls, John. 1993. *Political liberalism*. New York: Columbia University Press. Paperback edition, 1996; Second edition, 2005.

Sky News. 2008. "Albino Girl Killed for Witchcraft." 1 October, 2008, p2, Available at http://news.sky.com/home/world-news/article/15125431. Accessed 13 December 2018.

Teaching for Diversity and Social Justice, 2007. *Perspectives on the Historical Treatment of People with Disabilities*, Available at http://www.life.arizona.edu/residentassistants/programming/diversity/Ability/Ability.Hist.pdf. Accessed on 12, June 2019.

The Sun News. 2008. "Fear of Ritualists: Albinos go Underground." 11 October, 2008.

The Sun News. 2009. "Murder of Hunchback: Senator Ogunwale Moved to Abuja." 11 October 2009.

The Sun News. 2010. "Ritualists After Us, Albinos Cry Out." 12 May, 2010.

THISDAY. 2002. "Police Kill Seven Robbers, Arrest 30 Others." 5 May, 2002.

THISDAY. 2005. "Group Flays Sexual Abuse of Mentally Ill Women." 4 January 2005.

THISDAY. 2009. "Senator Quizzed Over Alleged Murder." 7 October, 2009.

THISDAY. 2010. "Breaking the Sound Barrier." 16 August, 2010.

Triandis, H. C. 1994. *Culture and Social Behaviour*. New York: McGraw-Hill.

United Nations, 2006a. *Convention on the Right of Persons with Disabilities*. Available at https://www.un.org/disabilities/documents/convention/convoptprot-e.pdf. Accessed 21 July 2018.

United Nations. 2006b. *Optional Protocol to the Convention on the Right of Persons with Disabilities*. Available at https://www.ohchr.org/EN/HRBodies/CRPD/Pages/OptionalProtocolRightsPersonsWithDisabilities.aspx. Accessed 21 July 2018.

United Nations, 2011a. *Universal Declaration of Human Rights*. Available at http://www.un.org/en/documents/udhr/index.shtml. Accessed 15 December 2018.

United Nations, 2011b. *International Covenant on Economic, Social and Cultural Rights*. Available at. http://www.ohchr.org/EN/ProfessionalInterest/Pages/CESCR.aspx. Accessed 15 December 2018.

United Nations. 2011c. "International Convention on Civil and Political Rights". Available at http://www.ohchr.org/EN/ProfessionalInterest/Pages/CCPR.aspx. Accessed 13 December 2018.

Van der Vyver, J. D. and Green, M. C. 2008. "Law, Religion and Human Rights in Africa: Introduction." *African Human Rights Law Journal* 8(2):337–356.

Vanguard. 2010. Albinos Have Suffered Neglect, Says Shagari." 19 July, 2010.

Winship, W. S. 2003. *Handbook of Genetic and Congenital Syndromes*. Oxford: Oxford University Press.

World Health Organisation (n.d). *Disabilities*. Available at https://www.who.int/topics/disabilities/en/. Accessed 15 May, 2020.

World Health Organisation, 2011. *Word Report on Disability*. Available at https://www.who.int/disabilities/world_report/2011/report.pdf. Accessed 18 May, 2020.

World Health Organization. 2018a. *Disability and Health*. Available at https://www.who.int/news-room/fact-sheets/detail/disability-and-health. Accessed 15 May, 2020.

World Health Organisation. 2018b. *International Classification of Functioning, Disability and Health (ICF)*. Available at https://www.who.int/classifications/icf/en/. Accessed 18 May, 2020.

CHAPTER 8

Poverty and Persons Living with Disabilities in Nigeria

Odirin Omiegbe

1   Introduction

Disability is a world-wide phenomenon. It cuts across countries, sex, age, religion, race, social status, economic and political positions. Its prevalence and then incidence in the contemporary world are high and worrisome. It is estimated that there are more than 2 billion persons with disabilities world-wide and majority are from developing countries. The Nigerian National Assembly in 2013 estimated that there are over 20 million persons living with disabilities in Nigeria (National Assembly, 2013). However, this number has increased with a wide margin, because, according to the Center for Disability and Development Innovations (CEDDI, 2016), the approximate number of disabled people in Nigeria is 25 million. The United Nations (UN) projected that in every ten people in Nigeria, one person is suffering from one type of disability or the other (NILS, 2010).

2   Defining Disability and Poverty

2.1   *Disability*

Definitions of disability is complex. Disability is defined differently depending on the paradigm that is being considered. The medical model of disability is strongly normative, based on the individual and his or her medical condition and people are considered to be disabled on the basis of being unable to or less able to function as 'normal" persons (Mitra, 2006). Disability is sometimes defined as a medical condition in which an individual has a defect—structural and biochemical abnormality; a physical pathology or aberration, and interference with normal growth or development or capacity to learn, caused by continuing disability to the body, intellect or personality to such a degree to need extra care or treatment from medical, nursing social and educational services (Oppe, 1972). Persons with disabilities include those who have long-term physical, mental, intellectual or sensory impairments, which in interaction with various barriers may hinder their full and effective participation on equal basis with others (Article1)-(United Nations, 2006) and are they are the visually impaired, speech impaired, hearing impaired, physical and health impaired, intellectually retarded, emotionally disturbed, learning disabled, gifted and talented. The categories of persons living with disabilities that are perennially associated with poverty are the visually impaired, speech impaired, hearing impaired, physical and health impaired, intellectually retarded, emotionally disturbed, and learning disabled.

2.2   *Poverty*

Economists have traditionally measured poverty by the lack of income or low levels of consumption. Welfare economists and social policy makers consider the poor as those individuals whose income is below a referenced subsistence level, known as poverty line. However, such measures fail to distinguish between income and livelihood in a cashless society. Two traditional poverty measures (the head count ratio and the income gap ratio) have been criticized by Sen (1992) because they do not take into consideration the distribution of income among the poor or the change in total poverty induced by a worsening of the situation of people already poor. Other authors argue that poverty cannot be measured by a single indicator of well-being, but that other factors such as food intake, shelter, life expectancy, education, provision of public goods must be taken into consideration (Atkinson & Bourgugnon, 1982; Kolm, 1977; Maasouumi, 1986; Tsui. 1995).

3   Economic or Income Poverty

Economic or income poverty could be measured by levels of household income or assets, type of housing, or per capita consumption expenditure. Monetary or economic poverty can be conceptualized in absolute or relative terms depending whether estimates are made in comparison to a subsistence income level or to an average income in a given context. Absolute or extreme poverty can be defined as the economic incapacity of an individual to satisfy basic needs such as food, clothing, shelters, health and education. However, KAR Report (2005) asserted that "poverty is not simply a matter of incomes that are low to meet the basic subsistence needs. It is above all, a symptom of imbedded structural imbalances, which manifest themselves in all dominants of human existence. As such, poverty is highly correlated with social exclusion, marginalization, vulnerability, powerlessness, isolation and other economic, political, social, and cultural dimensions of deprivation….it results from limited or no access to basic infrastructure and services, and is further compounded by people's lack of access to land, credit, technology and institutions and to other productive assets and resources needed to ensure sustainable livelihoods" (1995 Poverty Assessment Study Report, cited by Dube and Charowa, 2005). However, in a nut shell, poverty can be measured in terms of lack of income and access to human basic needs such as food, clothing, shelter, health, education and recreation.

4   Disability and Poverty

The relationship between disability and poverty is often described as a vicious circle. Here, it is argued that in fact, both disability and poverty are often manifestations of the same processes. If the commonalities are recognized then the need to build horizontal alliances becomes apparent (Yeo, 2005). It is evident that, compared to non-disabled person, people with disability have legal protection and live in extreme poverty and poor health, as well as poor educational achievement and are rarely involved in social, cultural and political participation. Disability mostly affects vulnerable and marginalized people with a high level of prevalence among lower income people in particular women, children and older people. Disability consists poverty and vice versa. Thus, disability is both a cause and a consequence of poverty. There is a strong relationship between the two with a cyclical tendency. Thus, disability is both a cause and a consequence of poverty. Thus, poverty makes an individual more vulnerable to disability and disability reinforces and deepens poverty. Therefore, disability along with old age, gender, and low socio-economic status interacts to make people poor (Mitra, Alexander & Brandon, 2011). Both disability and poverty are symptoms of the way that society is organizing, marginalizing and isolating certain people (Yeo, 2005). The claim that disability is both a cause and consequence is quite debatable. However, there are some exceptions. There are disabilities not traceable or related to poverty such as industrial hazards, automobile and natural disasters. In addition, there are many poor people who are not in any way disabled. Simply put, clearly not all disabled people are poor, nor are all poor people disabled. Therefore, one fact that should not be disputed is that with some exceptions 'disability is both a cause and consequences of poverty' and 'if there are such similarities between the characteristics of poverty and of disability (not impairment) then perhaps the relationship would be better described as interlocking circles as shown in Figure 8.1 (Yeo, 2005).

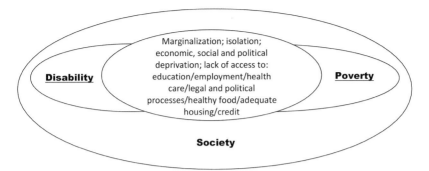

FIGURE 8.1   Relationship between poverty and disability in society
SOURCE: YEO, R. 2005. *DISABILITY, POVERTY AND THE NEW DEVELOPMENT AGENDA. DISABILITY, KNOWLEDGE AND RESEARCH PROGRAMME*

A multitude of studies have also shown to demonstrate a significant rate of disability among individuals living in poverty. Persons with disabilities were shown by the World Bank to comprise 15 to 20 percent of the poorest in developing countries (Elwan, 1999). Former World Bank President, James Wolfensohn, has stated that this connection reveals a link that should be broken (World Bank, 2011). The link between disability and development has been further stressed by Judith Henmann, the World Bank's first adviser for international disability rights, who indicated that of the 650 million people living with disabilities today eighty percent live in developing countries (Office of Policy Planning and Public Diplomacy, 2012). According to the United Kingdom Department for International Development, 10,000 individuals with disabilities die each day as a result of extreme poverty, showing that the connection between these two constructs is especially problematic and deep-seated (Yeo, 2005). This connection is also present in developed countries, with the Disability Founders Network reporting that in the United States alone, those with disabilities are twice more likely to live below the poverty line than those without special needs (Dickson, 2011). Statistics affirm the mutually reinforcing nature of special needs and low socio-economic status, showing that people with disabilities are significantly more likely to become impoverished and people who are impoverished are more likely to become disabled. Barriers presented can lead individuals to be deprived of access to essential resources, such as opportunities for education and employment, thus causing them to fall into poverty (Yeo, &Moore, 2003). In a systematic review on researches on poverty and disability in low-and middle-income countries (-LMICs) ten electronic data bases were searched to retrieve studies of any epidemiological design, published between 1990 to march 2016 with data comparing the level of poverty between people with and without disabilities in LMICs (World Bank Classifications). Results indicated that there is a strong evidence for a link between disability in low-and middle-income countries (-LMICs) and an urgent need for further research and programmatic/policy action to break the cycle (Banks, Kuper & Polack, 2017).

5 Disability and Poverty in Nigeria

Despite the fact that Nigeria has massive oil wealth and revenues and endowed with human capital resources, its citizens are still enmeshed in abject poverty. Nigeria's population estimated at 181.6 million has a high proportion of 62% of Nigerians living below poverty using Poverty Headcount ratios, Poverty Gap at $ 1.25 a day (PPP) and Poverty Gap at $ 2 a day (PPP).It ranks among the low human development index (HDI) countries, on 152nd position as against 188 countries (UNDP, 2015) and for persons living with disabilities their condition is worse off due to societal negative attitude and government policies towards their wellbeing. Numerous studies that have been reviewed which show significant rate of disability among individuals living in poverty in developing countries also correlates with that of individuals living with disabilities in Nigeria. A study conducted by Leprosy Mission of Nigeria and reported by Smith (2011) on persons living with disabilities in Nigeria asserts that "in Nigeria 70% of the population earn below U S $I a day. With 64% of the survey population earning approximately U S $15 per month, and another 20% earning between U S $15—U S $38 per month. The majority of people with disabilities fall within this socio-economic grouping. The 16% earning more than U S $38 a month comprised primarily people with disability". Similarly, Olusanya and Ruben (2006) found that disabled people with vocational training earn less than US $35 a month. The findings of Smith (2011) and Olunsanya and Ruben (2006) depict the state of poverty in Nigeria. With the state of poverty in Nigeria, what would be the fate of persons living with disabilities; one may likely ask? Their fate is indeed pitiable. More odds are against their living above poverty and they are discussed follows:

Firstly, typical traditional Nigerian families has large number of children and relatives staying in the home and are all engaged in contributing to the upkeep of the home through either farming or taking to a trade. Parents who find it difficult to cater for the financial needs of their household; the birth of a child with disability is an added financial burden. This-thus prevents the child with disability from enrolling in school or learning a vocation. Some parents send their children with disabilities to beg for alms to meet their financial needs because begging for alms seems lucrative due to the societal attitude and religious beliefs as Christianity and Islam encourage it. Ogunkan (2009) articulates the functional perspective of begging as a product of poverty. He argues that "begging performs some identifiable functions seem needed by the society. The existence of beggars helps the society to "fulfill" social, religious, and economic obligations. By giving alms to beggars, most Nigerians perform religious obligations as major religions in Nigeria encourage the giving of alms to the poor and needy. Beggars are readily available in meeting this religious responsibility." No wonder Olawole (2007) asserts that "in Nigeria, people living with disabilities flood the streets and soliciting alms from passersby, motorist, cyclist, foreigners and the general public" and that "these are people who ought to be in schools but are still roaming the streets begging for alms".

Secondly, the birth of a child with disability in a Nigerian family is received with mixed blessing; sadness and joy. It is also accompanied with societal stigma. This thus account for their being kept from public glare. To buttress further, Etieyibo & Omiegbe (2017) assert that "various beliefs about negative attitudes and behaviour towards people with disabilities can be attributed to beliefs about disabilities. Some of these beliefs are superstitious and are embedded in traditions and cultural practices. In general, and in respect of such beliefs, persons with disabilities are looked down upon; they are seen as a curse to their families and society or punishment from god for an offence committed by them or their families. These beliefs account for inadequate care and attention that people with disabilities receive from society and their being discriminated against or non-inclusivity. The treatment of people with disabilities sometimes explains why a number of them in Nigeria are generally found at entrance to churches, mosques, shops, and street junctions begging for alms. This is not to talk about those that are locked up in private homes away from public glare, as well as those that have been abandoned in special and regular schools".

Similarly, Children with disabilities often constitute the most marginalized and isolated segment of the Nigerian society as they face discrimination not only from family members, but also from wider society due to myths. Various myths have been developed to justify the society's ill-treatment of children with disabilities. The most common myth prevalent in Nigeria community is the view that children born with disabilities are witches or bewitched (Abosi & Ozoji, 1985). Other common myths include the belief that the child's condition is as a result of an evil act perpetuated by the parent. Religion has also played a role in reinforcing these myths. Religious leaders are very important pillars of the Nigerian society. They are often viewed as intermediaries between gods and man. Consequently many Nigerians consult them on various issues. Very often parents take their child with disabilities to these religious leaders to find out God's thoughts regarding the child. Once the religious leader makes this claim, the child is likely to become marginalized from society. One of the most serious consequences of the accusation of witchcraft against children with disabilities is the severity of violence inflicted upon them. They are sometimes subjected to physical abuses such as severe beatings, doused with acid, hacked with machetes or forced to drink dangerous hallucinogenic portion. They also face exclusion from society as a result of this stigmatization. The exclusion of a child with disability from society is more likely to lead to deterioration in the child's condition (National Teachers' Institute, 2011).

Thirdly, some children living with disabilities who reside in rural areas would have been able to enroll and attend schools but could not due to the reason that most of the special schools that are equipped to take care of their type of disabilities are located in the urban areas. While those that reside in urban areas; the location of the special schools could be far from their home and as such they remain at home.

Lastly, government attitude towards the care of persons living with disabilities is very poor in aspect of education, health, social welfare and employment. In a study conducted by the Leprosy Mission in Nigeria and reported by Smith (2011) state thus:

> The Leprosy Mission in Nigeria conducted a disability survey in Kogi and Niger States in 2005, investigating the demographic characteristics of people with disabilities, including gender, age religion, marital, education, occupational, employment and economic status on 1093 respondents over half of them had no education, 20% had primary education, 8% secondary education, 2% had secondary education, 2% had tertiary education and 18% had Islamic education. The majority (61%) of them were unemployed due to their disability. Over 70% of them were not able to access disability specific health services.

Similarly, in a disability survey conducted in Nigeria it was revealed that the common occupations of persons living with disabilities were begging, studying, farming, and trading, but the majority (60%) were unemployed due to their disability and only 4% have access to economic improvement (UNDP, 2005). Children with special needs are denied access to special education because it is expensive for families to bear the cost and the environment is unsafe and not people friendly for the disabled to move freely. The transportation of children with special needs from school is extremely difficult that some of the poor families fail to pick up their children during the holiday. The financial cost of educating a child with special needs in Nigeria, where the government support is insufficient, is more than four times compared to that of a non-disabled child. It is observed that the incentive of household to enroll their disabled children is discouraged by lack of appropriate schooling options, poor accessibility of facilities, long distance to school and lack of transportation, school fees and cost of uniforms and/or low expected returns to schooling for disabled children (Johnson & Wiman, 2001).

People with disability in Africa are usually extremely poor people who often live in rural and other areas where medical and other services are scarce, or even totally absent, and where disabilities are not detected in time. When disabled people receive medical attention, if at all, the impairment may have become irreversible (WHO, 2012). It is very common in Nigeria to see disabled persons on the streets holding prescription cards asking for money to purchase medicine. It is common to hear the voices of the disabled denied medical treatment because of their inability to settle the bill and as a result a number of them seek for financial assistance from members of the public without, which will continue to live and die under suffering. This problem is more pronounced among disabled children who, due to their condition of disability, miss out on vaccinations on treatment for simple fever, diarrhea, easily curable illness, which can become life-threatening if left untreated. For those children with severe disabilities many of them may not survive childhood because of lack of access to basic primary health care facilities which may not be readily available in some rural settings. Sometimes a number of medical decisions made have come to convey that the life of a child with disability is considered to be worthless than that of a child who has no disability. There are documented cases of physicians in both income-rich and income-poor countries who have chosen to deny children with disabilities access to essential operations because of the inability to pay the medical bills (Mohammed, 2008).

6 Disability and Poverty Reduction Effort in Nigeria

There has been noticeable change in the attention paid to persons with disabilities in recent years. As the disability movement has grown in strength, so the language of the mainstream establishment has also changed. Many governments have passed new legislations, as well as noting the need to include persons with disabilities in their international programmes with the United Nations and its agencies. Many international development organizations also known have some form of guidelines or policies regarding the need to include persons with disabilities in their work. Among those organizations specifically dedicated to working with persons with disabilities internationally, the majority now refer to the social model of disability and to disabled rights as central to their work. However, the extent to which changes in legislation and documentation reflect change in practice is more debatable (Yeo, 2005). In the last thirty years, Nigeria has become a signatory to a plethora of International Conventions, which are all aimed at securing the interest of disabled Nigerians. Federal Government of Nigeria enacted the Nigerians with Disability Decree, 1993, the first and only legislation aimed at catering for the needs of the categorized persons with disabilities to "provide a clear and comprehensive legal protection and security for Nigerian with disability, as well as establish a standard for the enhancement of their rights and privileges, guaranteed under this decree and other laws applicable to the disabled in Nigeria". Consequently, following the advent of democracy and the passage of the 1999 Constitution of the Federal Republic of Nigeria, more cogent provisions were included to cater for the rights of the Nigerian child (National Teachers' Institute, 2011). The Disability Act was passed into law by the Nigerian Senate on March 10, 2009. Following this development, six other states of the federation passed into law disability legislation (Etieyibo & Omiegbe, 2017). One of such states is Lagos State. The Special Peoples Law, (SPL) 2011 incorporates many of the obligations under the Convention on the Rights of Persons with Disabilities (CRPD), including the non-discrimination, education, health and the data collection provisions. Furthermore, Section 23 (1) SPL, 2011 states that "all levels of government shall take appropriate steps to ensure that persons living with disability have good standard of living for themselves and their families including adequate food, clothing and housing, and continuous improvement of living conditions" Section 24 (3) of the law also mandates the modification of accommodation so as to provide access to such property for persons with disability. The law also establishes the office of Disability Affairs in Compliance with the provision of CRPD (National Teachers' Institute, 2011). After the passing to law the SPL Bill, Aruya (2017) comments thus:

> "Street begging has reached an alarming dimension in Lagos State in spite of the regular rescue operations being carried out by the rescue team of the State Rehabilitation Department of the State Ministry of Youths and Social Development. The Department rescued a total of 531 beggars destitute. In addition to reduce this number, the government stepped up on its welfare packages for people living with disabilities in the state as it is apparent that an average percentage of beggars and physically impaired turned to begging in the bid to survive. Through the Lagos State Office of

Disability Affairs (LASODA), the Lagos State Government has been able to reach out this group by ensuring that their needs for infrastructure development, social welfare and amenities, employment opportunities and inclusiveness are met".

Likewise, Isah (2017) on the effort of some state governments to rehabilitate persons with disabilities from begging writes thus:

A community-led approach to ending the menace of street begging by disabled people at the grassroots in Northern Nigeria through skills acquisition programmes for disabled is helping to keep them off the street and help them achieve self-reliance. Ending street begging in Northern Nigeria which is more associated with Special needs like the lepers, the blind, the deaf, and the crippled; this has always been a contentious issue. In a bid to check this menace in 2013 Kano State Government enacted a law prohibiting child and adult begging in streets, roundabouts, motor parks and shop corners. Thus in the aftermath of the law banning street begging in Kano State, the people of Dawakin Tofa Local Government Area of the state, which is home to a government owned skills acquisition center for the blind, decided to make better use of the skills acquisition center; to provide empowerment opportunities for the community's teeming disabled people and therefore help to keep them off the street as well as to make them self-reliant.

Despite these efforts that have been identified, made by the Nigerian government, state governments, local governments, governmental and non-governmental organizations and individuals in assisting persons living with disabilities to be self-reliant and live above poverty, which is indeed commendable, but it is just a tip of the ice berg. According to Etieyibo & Omiegbe (2017), "these are steps in the right direction. However, there are legitimate worries about the level of commitment of the country as a whole with regard to the protection of rights of persons with disabilities (Including efforts at making them live above poverty). Besides the federal government, only six states (out of thirty-six) of the federation have enacted disability acts. What does this say? That the remaining thirty states are not yet committed to accommodating the needs and rights of persons with disabilities". Persons living with disabilities are in the streets, at every corner of the major roads, under the bridges, in the traffic begging for alms, and living in shanties (Aruya, 2017), are at homes from public glare, without education, proper health care, employment and living in abject poverty.

7 Conclusion and Remedy Recommendations for Poverty Reduction for Persons Living with Disabilities

Yeo (2005) notes that "despite many policy and manual statements which have been produced both regarding disability and poverty reduction the rhetoric has changed somewhat, but disabled people are still among the most marginalized and tens of thousands of people still die from extreme poverty. Many development agencies have done much beneficial work relieving human suffering among some of the most disadvantaged people around the world. This can only be a good thing, unless the result is to focus on a particular wound, delivering attention from the fact that the body is being continually lacerated from the spotlight" What then should we do? The root causes of poverty for persons with disabilities have to be tackled and are discussed as follows:

7.1 *Education*
An adage has it that "If you teach a child how to fish; you will feed him for life". The root of unemployment which is a major cause of poverty for persons with disabilities is education which is speculated to begin with discrimination at an early age. UNESCO reports that 98 percent children with disabilities in developing countries are denied access to formal education (UNESCO, 1995). Although, there is a lack of data on the rate of education of people with disabilities in Nigeria, a survey carried by UNICEF shows that at 1993, there were 1.51 million children with disabilities and only 4.23 percent of the children were enrolled in formal school, suggesting that about 95 percent had no access to formal education (UNICEF, 2000). According to the World Bank, at least 40 million children with disabilities do not receive education thus barring them from obtaining knowledge and skill essential for gainful employment and forcing them to grow up to be financially dependent upon others (The Office of Policy Planning and Public Diplomacy, 2012). This is also reflected in a finding obtained by World Development Report that 77 percent of persons with disabilities are illiterate (Elwan, 1999). This statistics is even more jarring for women with disabilities, with the United Nations Development Programme, reporting that the global literacy rate for this population is a mere 1 percent (United Nations, 2012). This may be attributed to the fact that, according to the World Health Organization, boys with disabilities are significantly more likely to receive an education than similarly non-disabled girls. Beyond simply the skills obtained, experts such as former World Bank advisor Judith Heumann speculate that societal value of education and the inability of schools to accommodate special needs children substantially contributes to discrimination of these individuals (Office of Policy Planning and Public Diplomacy,

2012). It is important to note that the deprivation of education to individuals with special needs may not be solely an issue of discrimination, but an issue of resources. Children with disabilities often require specialized educational resources and teaching practices largely unavailable in developing countries (Action on Disability and Development, 1998). Therefore, People with disabilities should also be provided financial resources to facilitate their education as most of them are too poor to afford expenses relating to education. In view of this, financial aid/services in the form of bursaries, grants, scholarships, small loans or student loans could also be granted to them to assist them in their educational needs (Ofuani, 2011). Government should invest in the education of children with special needs by ensuring that their education is free at all levels and providing them with the enabling environment and basic learning facilities that would cater for their individual educational needs. Human rights issues and subjects on disability should be included in the curriculum to address the myths about disabilities and the societal negative attitude towards persons living with disabilities.

7.2 Healthcare

There is a popular adage that says "Health is Wealth". Another reason individuals living with disabilities are impoverished is the high medical cost associated with their needs. One study, conducted in villages in South India, demonstrated that the annual cost of treatment and equipment needed for individuals with disabilities in the area ranged from three days of income to upwards of two year's worth, with the average amount spent on essential services totaling three months worth of income (Erb & Harriss-White, 2001). This figure does not take into account the unpaid work of caregivers who provide assistance after these procedures and opportunity cost leading a loss of income during injury, surgery, and rehabilitation. Studies reported by Medical Anthropologists Benedicte Ingstad and Susan Reynolds Whyte have also shown that access to medical care is significantly impaired when one lacks mobility. They report that in addition to the direct medical costs associated with special needs, the burden of transportation falls most heavily on those with disabilities. This is especially true for the rural poor whose distance from urban environments necessitates extensive movement in order to obtain health services (Ingstad & Whyte, 2007). Due to these barriers, both economic and physical, it is estimated that only 2 percent of individuals with disabilities have access to adequate rehabilitation services (Depouy, 1993).Therefore, government should invest in the health care of persons with special needs by ensuring that their health needs are catered for through free health scheme, because when they are healthy they will be able to attend school and when they are healthy they will be able to work diligently in their various occupations.

7.3 Employment

An adage has it that "Enjoy the fruit of your labour". This statement can be true if a person is gainfully employed. Some sociologists have found a number of barriers to employment of individuals with disabilities. These may be seen in employer discrimination, architectural barriers within the work place, pervasive negative attitudes regarding skill, and the adverse reactions of customers (Walters & Wilder, 2005). For example, persons with disabilities are especially vulnerable to discrimination and disadvantaged in employment in Nigeria. They often experience unequaled employment opportunity, limited rights to work place and reduced job security. Even when they are well educated, they are generally denied employment because of their disabilities. Most employers are reluctant to employ persons with disabilities believing how they will be unable to perform their roles and/or that it would be too expensive due to fear and stereotyping, thus focusing more on the disability than on the abilities of individuals (UN, 2010). According to Sociologist Edward Hall "more disabled people are unemployed, in lower status occupations, on low earnings, or out of labour market altogether, than non-disabled people (Butler & Parr, 1999). The International Labour Organization estimates that roughly 386 million of the world's working population have some forms of disability, however, up to eighty percent of these employable individuals with disabilities are unable to find work. Statistics show that individuals with disabilities in both industrialized and developing countries are generally unable to obtain work. In India, only 100,000 of the country's 70 million people with disabilities were employed, with two-thirds of those unemployed (United Nations, 2012). Similarly, in Belgium, only 30 percent of persons with disabilities were able to find gainful employment (Metts, 2000) and in the United Kingdom 45 percent of adults with disability were found to live below the poverty line (Barnes & Mercer, 2003. However, reliable data on the rate of unemployment for persons with disabilities has yet to be determined in most developing countries (Wikipedia, 2018).The International Labour Organization estimates that the current exclusion of employable individuals with special needs in employment is costing possible gains of 1 to 7 percent of their GDP (Gross Domestic Product). Employment is seen as a critical agent in reducing stigma and increasing capacity in the lives of individuals with disabilities. The lack of opportunities currently available is shown to perpetuate the vicious cycle, causing individuals with disabilities to fall into poverty. To address these concerns many recent initiatives have begun to develop more inclusive employment structures (International Labour Office, 2012). One example, of this is the Nitro Project in South Africa, the project aims to eliminate segregationist models prevalent in the country through coordinated efforts between districts, NGO,s and community organizations. The model stresses education and pairs individuals with intellectual disabilities with mentors until they have developed skills necessary to perform their roles independently. The programme then matches individuals with local employers. This gradualist model ensures that people who may have been deprived of the resources necessary to acquire essential skills are able to build their expertise and enter the workforce (Parmenter, 2011). Therefore, all efforts should be made to encourage employers, particularly, those in the private sector to employ persons with disabilities and the government should gainfully employ the disabled persons and create the enabling environment for those with skills to put them into use and subsequently become employer of labour. The Nitro Project in South African and others that have been used to make persons with special needs to be self reliant should be replicated to make them to be gainfully employed. Statistics of persons with disabilities should be taken and those that are not employed should be placed on social security benefits.

7.4 *Vocational Rehabilitation*

When it is not possible for person with disabilities to be educated or employed, another means to assist them to live above poverty is through vocational rehabilitation. "Vocational rehabilitation refers to a continuous and coordinated process of rehabilitation which involves the provision of vocational services such as vocational guidance, vocational training and selective placement" (SAINDS, 1997). It is a means through which people with disabilities can be reintroduced into society to function socially and economically according to their capability. It entails the transfer of power and control over their lives from external entities to the individuals themselves based on their individual needs and prepares people with disabilities to achieve a lifestyle of independence and integration within their workplace, family and local community (Kosciuleck, 2004). The purpose of vocational rehabilitation is to secure, retain and advance in suitable employment and thereby to further such person's integration into society (ILO, 1983). It includes education, training, vocational guidance and counselling, and rehabilitation services such as medical, psychiatric, social and psychological assessments, vocational assessment and restoration, job preparation and placement and assistive technological services (Dupes, 2005). Vocational rehabilitation could be community-based or institutional-based. Community-based rehabilitation involves meeting the needs of people with disabilities through the combine efforts of people with disabilities, their families and communities. On the other hand, institutional-based rehabilitation is rehabilitation of people with disabilities at or through institutions, often away from homes (Arora, 2010). However, there are few vocational centers in Nigeria. The government has implemented a community-based vocational rehabilitation project in some states in the country and some of such centers are supported by CMB. For instance, the CMB project 'services for people with disabilities' supports about 100 persons a year in its economic empowerment and livelihood unit by vocational training and small loans or grants for those that have achieved vocational skills to set up their own micro-business (CBM World Wide, 2010). Nevertheless, there is a lack of commitment by the government to provide the requisite manpower and resources to ensure the functioning of such centers. The Nigerian government should therefore be more committed to reducing poverty and unemployment by establishing more vocational centers and providing such centers with resources to function effectively (Ofuani, 2011).

7.5 Provision of Financial Services/Resources

Persons with disability who have been trained in educational institutions and vocational rehabilitation centers can be helped to become self reliant through the provision of financial services/resources. "Financial services are products, facilities and services including savings, credit, leasing, and such which are provided by banks, credit unions and financial institutions, government and non-governmental organizations (South Africa's Draft Code...2011). It is indisputable that financial service providers have largely failed in providing services that include people with disabilities (Ofuani, 2011). Microfinance is the best way to address the financial needs of persons with disabilities because it lacks the usual difficulties involved in accessing other financial products such as the provision of security. It also has features like doorsteps delivery and product flexibility such as access to rental services to ensure that people with disabilities are not sidelined (South Africa's Draft Code...2011). In the 1970's, microfinance was instrumental in the dramatic shift from seeing the poor as not bankable and the provision of financial services to them as a losing proposition and business folly, this is because not only did the poor prove bankable, but they were bankable in a sustainable and profitable way. The provision of financial service to people with disabilities in the twenty-first century also faces similar skepticism, some of it based on real service delivery challenges and some rooted in misconception (Goldstein, 2010). People with disabilities ought to be given access to financial services/resources to assist them to become self-reliant and to realize their social-economic needs such as education, self-employment, and social security. The right of persons with disabilities to financial services should be facilitated as it could be a means of empowering them. Indeed, the Convention on the Rights of Persons with

Disabilities (CRPD) recognizes persons with disabilities right to control their own financial affairs and to have equal access to bank loans, mortgages and other forms of financial credit (CRPD, 2010). Nevertheless they are not given access to financial services because of the belief that they are not bankable and providing them financial services is not cost-effective (Ratnala, 2009). The provision of financial resources to persons with disabilities is important as not all of them can be educated, trained, rehabilitated or employed by the public and private sectors. So they ought to be provided with financial services to be able to cater for themselves. Hence, persons with disabilities that have successfully completed their education or vocational training/rehabilitation but are yet to secure wage-earning jobs should be given access to financial services, especially microfinance, to enable them set up workshops or suitable income-generating enterprise in order to earn a living (Ofuani, 2011).

7.6 *Financial Aid to Families with Disabled Persons*

Research show that families who lack adequate economic agency are unable to care for children with special medical needs, resulting in preventive deaths (Yeo &Moore, 2003). In times of economic hardship studies show that families may divert resources from children with disabilities because investing in their livelihood is often perceived as investment caretakers cannot afford to make (Ashton, 1999). Benedicte Ingstad (1977) an Anthropologist, who studied families with a member with disabilities, asserts that "what some may consider neglect of individuals with disabilities was mainly a reflection of the general hardship that the household was living under" (Ingstad, 1997). A study conducted by Oxfam found that the rejection of a child with disabilities was not uncommon in areas of extreme poverty. The report went on to show that neglect of children with disabilities was far from a deliberate choice, but rather a consequence of a lack of essential resources. The study also demonstrated that services necessary to well being of these children "are seized upon" when they are available. The organization thus concluded that if families had the capacity to care for children with special needs they would do so willingly, but often the inability to access crucial resources bars them from administering proper care (Coleridge, 1993). Therefore, government should be at the fore front to provide financial assistance to families with a disabled child as this will in a long way help in taking care of the child's health, educational, and social needs. However, such financial aid should not be provided only by the government but rather the government can initiate a trust fund for persons with disabilities where by individuals, organizations and companies could contribute to it through the payment of taxes for such purpose.

7.7   Enforcement of Compliance of Disabilities Legislations

Initiatives on the local, national and international levels and addressing the connection between poverty and disability are exceedingly rare. According to the United Nations, only 45 countries throughout the world have anti-discrimination and other disability-specific laws (United Nations, 2012). Additionally, experts point to Western World as a demonstration that the association between poverty and disability is not naturally dissolved through the development process. Instead a conscious effort towards inclusive development is seen by theorist, such as disability policy expert Mark Priestly as essential in the remediation process (Priestley, 2001). The United Nations has been at the forefront of initiating legislation that aims to deter the current toll disabilities take on individuals in society, especially, those in poverty. In 1982, the United Nations published the World Programme of Action Concerning Disabled Persons, which explicitly states that "particular efforts should be made to integrate the disabled in the development process and that effective measures for preventive, rehabilitation and equalization of opportunities are therefore essential" (UN. Org, 2012a). This doctrine set the stage for the United Nations Decade of the Disabled persons from 1983 to 1992, where at its close the General Assembly adopted the Standard Rules of Equalization of Opportunities for Persons with Disabilities (UN. Org, 2012b). The Standard Rules of Equalization of Opportunities for Persons with Disabilities encourage states to remove social, cultural, economic, educational and political barriers that bar individuals with disabilities from participating equally in society (United Nations, 2012). Proponents claim that these movements on behalf of the United Nations helped facilitate more inclusive development policy and brought disability rights to the fore front (Yeo, 2005). Yes indeed, such effort is laudable, but it is not enough. Effort should be made by the United Nations to ensure full compliance by member nations on the legislations made for persons with disabilities by proper monitoring and evaluating compliance; sanctioning non-performance; and commending effective performance.

7.8   Incorporate the Voices of Individuals with Disabilities into the Decision-Making Process

An adage has it that "He or she who wears the shoe knows where it pinches". Disabilities advocate James Charlton asserts that "it is crucial to better incorporate the voices of individuals with disabilities into the decision making process". His literature on disability rights made popular the slogan "Nothing about Us without Us" evidencing the need to ensure those most affected by policy have an equitable hand in its creation. This need for urgency is an issue particularly salient for those with special needs who are often negatively stereotyped as dependent upon others (Charlton, 2000). Furthermore, many who are part of the disability rights movement argue that there is little emphasis on aid designed to eliminate the physical and social barriers those with disabilities face. The movement asserts that unless these obstacles are rectified, the connection between disability and poverty will persist (Dickson, 2011).Therefore, it is necessary that the United Nations, governments-and non-governmental organizations involved in the care and welfare of persons with disabilities involve them in decision making process affecting them because they know how it is to being disabled and what can be done to assist them. Their contributions will in a large measure help to remove the barriers that make them to be poor and thus ultimately live above poverty.

References

Abosi, O. C. and Ozoji, E. D. 1985. *Educating the Blind: A Descriptive Approach*. Ibadan: Spectrum Books.

Action on Disability and Development (ADD). 1998. Uganda Annual Report, Kampala: ADD.

Albert, B. and Miller, C. 2005. *Mainstreaming Disability in Development: Lesson from Gender Mainstreaming*. Disability Knowledge and Research Programme. http://www.disabilitykar.net.research/revpov.html

Albert, B. 2004. *Is Disability Really on the Agenda? A Review of Official Disability Policies of Major Government and International Development Agencie*s, Disability Research Programme. Available at http://www.disabilitykar.net/research/revpov.html

Albert, B. Dube, A. K. and Riss-Hansen, T. C. 2005. *Has Disability Been Mainstreamed into Development Cooperation?* Disability and Research Programme. http://www.disabilitykar.net/research/redpov.html

Arora R. 2010. 'National Programme for Rehabilitation of Persons with Disabilities—A Blend of CBR and IBR' http://www.aifo.H/english/resources/online/apdrj/frimeet202/national.doc (Accessed 20 October, 2010).

Aruya, T. 2017. "The Menace of Street Beggars in Lagos." *Business Day*. http:businessday-online.com/exclusive/analysis/sub/erticle/menance-street-beggars-lagos/ Accessed 15 August, 2018.

Ashton, B. 1999. "Promoting the Rights of the Disabled Children Globally." *Disabled Children Become Adults: Some Implications*. Frome: ADD.

Atkinson, A.and Bourgnon, F. 1982. "The Comparison of Multidimensioned Distributions of Economic Status," *Econom Stud,* 49:183–201.

Banks, L. M. Kupper, H. and Polacks, S. 2017. "Poverty and Disability in Low-and Middle-Income Countries: A Systematic Review." *US National Library of Medicine Health*, 12 (12): e.018996 10.1013//journalpone 018996.ecollection

Barnes, C.and Mercer, G. 2003. *Disability*. Malden MA: Blackwell Publishers.

Buttler, R. and Parr, H. 1999. *Mind and Body Spaces: Geographies of Illness, Impairment and Disability*. New York, NY: Routledge.

CBN World Wide, 2017. "Others are not so Lucky-Vocational Training in Nigeria." http://www.cbn.org.en/general/CBN.EV.EN.general_article415191.html (Accessed 5 January, 2011).

CeDDI, 2016. Number of Disabled Persons in Nigeria (Center for Disability and Development in Nigeria. Cited in Mohammed, A H. 2017. "The Problems of Living with Disability in Nigeria." *Journal of Law, Policy and Globalization*, 65, www.ijste.org.

Charlton, J I. 2000. *Nothing about us Without Us: Disability Oppression and Empowerment*. Berkeley, CA: University of California Press.

Coleridge, P. 2012. *Disability, Liberation and Development*. Oxford: Oxfam.

Despouy, L. 1993. *Human Rights and Disabled Persons*, (Study Series 6) Centre for Human Rights. Geneva and New York.

Dickson, J. 2011. *Philanthropy's Blind Spot: The Disability Rights Movement*. National Committee for Responsive Philantrophy.

Dube, A. K. and Charowa, G. 2005. Are Disabled Peoples' Voices from both South and North Being Heard in the Development Process? A Comparative Analysis Between the Situation in South Africa, Zimbabwe and the United Kingdom. Available at: http://www.disabilitykar.net/research/thematic-voices.html

Dupes B. 2005 Vocational Rehabilitation: Helping People with Disability in Jobs and Careers. http://www.amputee.coalition.org/easyread/first_step_2005/voc_rehab-ez.pdf (Accessed 20 September, 2010).

Elwan, A, 1999. *Poverty and Disability: A Review of Literature*. The World Development Report. Washington DC: World Bank.

Erb, S. and Harriss-White, B. 2001. *The Economic Impact and Developmental Implications of Disability and Incapacity in Adulthood: A Village Study in India*. Cambridge: Welfare, Demography, and Development.

Etieyibo, E. and Omiegbe, O. 2017. *Disabilities in Nigeria, Attitudes, Reaction and Remediations*. Lanham, Maryland: Hamilton Books.

Goldstein J. 2010. "Making International Microfinance Institutions Disability Inclusive: A Call to Action." http://www.wid.org/employment-and-economic-equity/access-to-assets/equity/equity-e-newsletter-November-2010/feature. (Accessed 5 January, 2011).

ILO, 1983. Vocational Rehabilitation and Employment (Disabled Persons) Convention No 159 1983 Part 1, art 1 (1) http://www.ilo.otg/ilolex/cgi-lex/convde.pl?c159 (Accessed 20 November, 2011).

Ingstad, B & Whyte, S.R 2007. *Disability to Local and Global Works*. Berkeley CA: University of California Press.

International Labour Office, 2012. Employment of Social Justice and a Fair Globalization overview of ILO Programmes. Web accessed: http://www.ilo.org/wcmsp51groups/public/edemp/documents/publication/wcms-140958.pdf

Johnson, T and Wiman R 2001. "Education, Poverty, and Disability in Developing Countries: A Technical Note. Http://siteresources.worldbank.org/Disability/Resources280658-117201312075/education., Accessed 22 July, 2008.

Kolm, S. C.1977. "Multidimensional Egalitarianisms." *Quart J Econn,* 91:1–13.

Kosciulek J. F 2004 "Empowering People with Disabilities through Vocational Rehabilitation" *Counselling. American Rehabilitation. See also Vocational Rehabilitation.* http://www.minddisorders.com/py-z/vocationa-rehabilitation.html (Accessed 20 September, 2010.

Maasoumi, E. 1996. "The Measurement and Decomposition of Multidimensional Inequality." *Econometrica*, 54:771–779.

Metts, R. 2000. Disabilities Issues, Trends and Recommendations for the World Bank.

Mitra, S. 2006. "The Capability Approach and Disability." *Journal of Disability Policy Studies*, 16 (4): 236–247.

Mitra, S. Alexander, P. & Bradon, V. 2011. "Disability and Poverty in Developing Countries: A Snap shot from the World Health Society." S P Discussion Paper No 11.

Mohammed, A. H. 2017. "The Problems of Living with Disability in Nigeria." *Journal of Law, Policy and Globalization.* 65, www.ijste.org

National Assembly, 2013. The Senate: National Assembly Federal Republic of Nigeria. Available at http//.www.nassnig.org/nass/news 01/04/2014.

National Teachers' Institute. 2011. "National Teachers' Institute, Kaduna Manual on Special Needs & Disabilities (SENDS) Millennium Development Goals (MDGS) Project 2011." Lagos, Nigeria: Axiom Learning Solutions.

NILS (Nigerian Institute of Legal Studies). 2010. Available at http//www.nailsnigeri.org-editedbookcover 02/08/2011.

Office of Policy Planning and Public Diplomacy. 2012 Special Advisor Heumann's Remarks on Inclusive Development. Webaccessed: "Archived Copy" Archived from the Original on 2012-03-11, Accessed 26 October, 2012.

Ofuani, A. I. 2011. "The Right to Economic Empowerment of Persons with Disabilities in Nigeria: How Enabled?" *African Human Rights Law Journal*, 2:639–658
http://www.ahrij.up.ac.za/images.ahrij/2011/ahrij_vol_no2_2011_anwuli_i_ofuani.pdf (Accessed 12 August, 2018).

Ogunkan, D.V. 2009. Socio-economic Implication of Begging Ogbomoso, Nigeria. Unpublished B.S.C Dissertation. Department of Sociology, University of Ilorin, Nigeria.

Olawole, S. G. 2007. "Aetiological Perceptions of Alms Begging Behaviour among People with Special Needs in Oyo State: Counselling Towards Solution." *The Counsellor* 23(1):44–53.

Olusanye, S and Ruben L. 2006, "Reducing the Burden of Communication Disorders in Developing World: An Opportunity for the Millennium Development Project." *The Journal of the American Medical Association*, 4:441–444. Doi.10.1001/jama.296.4.441 PMID. 16868302

Oppe, T. 1972. Unpublished Working Paper on Risk Registers.

Parmenter, T. R. 2001. Promoting Training and Employment Opportunities for People with Intellectual Disabilities. International Labour Office.

Poverty Assessment Study Report, cited in Dube, A. K. & Charowa, G. 2005. Are Disabled Peoples' Voices from both South and North Being Heard in the Development Process? A Comparative Analysis Between the Situation in South Africa, Zimbabwe and the United Kingdom. Available at: http://www.disabilitykar.net/research/thematic-voices.html

Rischewski, D. Kuper, H. Atijosan, O. Simms, V. Jofret-Bnet, M. Foster, H et al. 2008. "Poverty and Muscuskeletal Impairment in Rwanda." *Transactions of the Royal Society of Tropical Medicine and Hygiene* 102(6): 608–617.

SAINDS, 1997. South Africa's Integrated National Disability Strategy-A White Paper, Appendix B, http://www.info.gov.za/whitepappers/1997/disability.htm (Accessed 20 September, 2010).

Sen, A. K. 1992. *Inequality Re-examined*. Oxford: Clarendon Press.

Smith, N 2005. "The Face of Disability in Nigeria: A Disability Survey in Kogi and Niger States." 11.92.pp (2)pdf www.dcidj.org.Disability, CRB *and Inclusive Development*, 22(1), 2011 Doi 10.5463/acid,v22:1.11. Accessed August 15, 2018.

South Africa's Draft Code of Good Practice on Disability in the Workplace. http://www.labour.gov.za/legislation/codws-of-good-practice/employment/code-of-good-practice-on-disability-in-the-workplace (Accessed 05 January. 2011).

Thomas, P. 2005. Disability, Poverty and Millennium Development Goals: Relevance, Challenges and Opportunities for DFID. Disability Knowledge and Research Programme. Available at http://www.disabilityKar.research/policydfid.html

Tusi, K. Y. 1995. "Multidimensional Generalizations of Relative and Absolute Indices: The Atkinson-Kolm-Sen Approach." *J Econ Theory*, 67:251–265.

United Nations. 2010a. UN Enable International Day of Disabled Persons http://www.un.org/disabilities/default.asp?id=110 (Accessed 15, September, 2010).

United Nations, 2010b. *Convention on the Rights of Persons with Disabilities*. http://www.uni.org/disabilities/documents/conventions/convopt-prot-e.pdf (Accessed 20th April, 2010).

United Nations, 2012 Fact Sheet on Persons with Disabilities. Web accessed: http://www.un.org/disabilities/toolaction/pwdfs.pdf

UN.org, 2012a. www.un.org.disablities/defaultasp?id=23

UN.org, 2012b. www.un.org/esa/soded.enable.dissreOO.htm

UNDP. 2005. World Population Prospects: The 2004 Revision. New York: UN Population Division.

UNDP, 2015. Nigeria-Human Development Reports-UNDP hdr.undp.org-hdr.theme .country-notes>NGR Accessed 15 August 2018.

UNESCO, 1995. Review of the Present Situation in Special Education. Web accessed. http://www.unesco.org/p4objcache/pvobjidc133ADOAFO5E62AC54C2DE8EEICO2 6DABFAF3000/FILENAME/28179pdf

UNICEF. 2007. Nigerian Children's and Women's Rights in Nigeria: Renewing the Call-Situation Assessment and Analysis.

Walters, W. H.and Wilder, E. I. 2005. *Voices from the Heartland: The Needs and Rights of Individuals with Disabilities.* Brookline MA: Brookline Books.

WHO, 2012. "Disabilities" http:www.who.int.topics/disabilities/en/ Accessed 25/11/12.

Wikipedia, 2018. Disability and Poverty. https://en.wikipedia/disabled_and_poverty. Retrieved 11th August 2018. United Nations (2012) Fact Sheet on Persons with Disabilities. Web accessed: http://www.un.org/disabilities/toolaction/pwdfs.pdf

World Bank, 2012. Disability: Overview. Web accessed. http://web.Worldbank.org/ WEBSITE/EXTERNAL/TOPICS/EXTSOCIALPROTECTION/EXTDISABILITY/ 10.Content/MDK.21151218-menuPK.282706-PagePK.21OO58-PIPK21O462-thesitePk .282699.00html

Yeo, R. 2005. Disability, Poverty and the New Development Agenda. Disability, Knowledge and Research Programme. Web accessed: http://www.dfid.gov.uk/r4d/PDF/ outputs/Disability/Red/Pov-agendapdf

Yeo, R. and Moore, K. 2003. Including Disabled People in Poverty Reduction Work: Nothing about Us.

CHAPTER 9

Poverty and Illicit Drug Use among Youths in Lagos Metropolis, Nigeria

Adekunle Victor Owoyomi

1   Introduction

Globally, the dramatic increase in youths' involvement in illicit drug use is attributed to several factors in which poverty has been increasingly recognized, though poorly documented in most low-income countries including Nigeria, as one of the key enablers (Ward, 2015). For decades, the phenomenon of poverty and illicit drug use among youths has been under-theorized and insufficiently documented, using mixed methods in Nigerian empirical literature. However, gaining insight into the linkage between poverty-deprivation and widening inequalities in income, are significant enablers that need to be given sufficient attention within the drug policy debate and programs. A UNDP (2015) report indicated that a considerable portion of the Nigerian society live below one U.S. dollar per day. This is disturbing given Nigeria's available natural resources; it is observed that mismanagement and coupled with bad leadership have been the bane to her quest for development.

Nigeria is the largest African country, with a population of over 150 million people. Out of this, the youth population is above 42. 54% of the aggregate (NPC. 2006, NBS, 2012). The country is blessed with abundant natural and human resources - demographic dividend. However, there is lack of political will to develop the necessary technological, industrial, managerial, political and technocratic tools to pull its resources together into a vibrant economy that can ameliorate the condition of most essentially her teeming young population. Unfortunately, the introduction of Structural Adjustment Programmes (SAPs) in the late 1970s and early 80s, rather than save the day, marked the watershed of the pervading economic hardship in the country. The Naira was grossly devalued; many manufacturing industries in Nigeria were shut down because they could not compete favourably in an open market. Sadly, poverty and unemployment have continued to eat deep and wide into the socioeconomic life of people, including the youths, even as the country faces rapid population growth (Emeh 2012: 33, ILO, 2010), galloping inflationary gaps, ethno-religious conflicts, slow industrialization and attempts modernization. The data set from the Nigerian Bureau of Statistics (NBS) show that unemployment rate in Nigeria increased to 23.10 percent in the third quarter of 2018 from 22.70 percent in the second quarter of 2018 (NBS, 2018). With the current overarching impact of economic hardships many Nigerian youths are contending with, a sizeable number of them feel pressured to indulge in illicit drug use and trafficking as either a means of escaping economic reality or sustaining their livelihood (UNODC, 2017). Meanwhile, this situation has weakened the social fabric, overburdened health care facilities and increased crime rates in the country. Hence, posing a grave concern to both national and international organizations in recent times.

To stress further, a report from the National Drug Law Enforcement Agency (NDLEA) cited from the reports of the National Survey on Drug use, conducted by the National Bureau of Statistics (NBS), in partnership with the Centre for Research and Information on Substance Abuse (CRISA), sponsored by the United Nations Office on Drugs Control (UNODC), and the European Union (EU), indicated that Nigeria has about 14.3 million illicit drug users aged between 15–64 years (NBS, 2018) The revelation from the key findings of this study further revealed that 10.6 million Nigerians abuse opioids while 2.4 million youths and adults abuse codeine based syrup with 92,000 more using cocaine (NBS, 2018). In addition, the submission from the 2018 Global report on Drug indicated that both Nigeria and India are the countries with worrisome prevalence abuse of illicit drugs like Opium and Tamadol which is a wakeup call for the relevant stakeholders (UNODC, 2018). The report from the National Survey on Drug prevalence pattern of illicit drug use based on gender disparity showed that men abuse drug more than women and the data set further revealed that any drug used by men is estimated to be 21.8% while women is 7.0%, high risk drug use is 0.6% for men and 0.12% for women, people who inject drug is estimated for about 0.12% for men and 0.04% for women, prevalence by drug type estimated men of 18.8% abuse cannabis and 2.6% women while Opioids is 6.0% men and 3.3% women, Pharmaceutical opioids (tramadol, codeine, morphine) is 6.0% for men and 3.3% for women, Cocaine is among the lowest abuse drug in Nigeria with 0.1% and 0.04%, Tranquilizers/Sedative 0.5% men and 0.4% women, Amphetamines (Pharmaceutical amphetamine and illicit amphetamine) is 0.2% of men and 0.1% of women while Methamphetamine is 0.1% of men and 0.04 of women, Ecstasy is 0.4% of men and 0.3% of women, Haccucinogens is 0.03% of men and 0.02% of women while solvent/inhalant is 0.5% of men and 0.1% of women, Cough Syrups is 2.3% of men and women is 2.5%. However, a critical look at this report indicates that women tend to abuse cough syrup than men (NBS, 2018) and that cannabis is most prevalent illicit drug use in Nigeria with an estimated 10.8% of the population or 10.6

million people had abused cannabis in the past year and to make it worst, the average age of initiation of cannabis use among the general population is 19 years (NBS, 2018). The implication of this is that young people are more vulnerable to the most common type of drug abuse-cannabis in Nigeria. Thus, about 40 percent of young people in Nigeria engaged in illicit drug use NDLEA report cited from (NBS, 2018).

Poverty and crime such as illicit drug use have a very intimate relationship that has been described by experts from various fields such as Sociology and Economics (Ward, 2015, Urdang, 2012, Danziger and Haveman, 2001: 6). For instance, the UN and the World Bank both ranked crime high on the list of obstacles to a country's development. This means that governments that intend to tackle poverty often have to face the issue of crime as they try to develop their country's economy and society (Ward, 2015). According to Urdang (2012), crime like illicit drug use is often perceived as a problem common in areas with a high level of poverty. In a country with high level of social inequality, limited access to quality education will most likely increases criminal tendencies among the young people (Danziger and Haveman, 2001: 6). Poverty itself is increases the likelihood of engaging in violence acts, criminal damages, as well as drug use, as a catalyst for violence (Ward, 2015). Impoverished places with high population of poor people usually engage in criminal activities compared to places where middle income or high income individuals reside. (Danziger and Haveman, 2011: 6).

It is instructive to note that illicit drug use is one of those criminal activities among the Nigerian youths that are traceable to harsh socioeconomic conditions (Siegel, 2008: 131). Sadly, the world ATLAS of Substance use disorder (SUD) cited from WHO (2010) report indicated that Nigeria's profile on the illicit drug use policy and law did not make provision for availability of programs for the diversion of clients/consumers from the criminal justice system into treatment. However, it suffices to say that this policy is more punitive in nature and culture, and does not speak well for social justice especially for many youths in Nigeria (WHO, 2010). Hence, this lacuna in policy suggests to us one among other reasons why it has not made any considerable achievement in reducing illicit drug use in Nigeria. However, it is of interest to this current study to advocate for a more comprehensive corrective approach rather than a punitive approach to reduce the currently overwhelming and burdensome illicit drug use especially among the youths in Nigeria. In other words, while efforts to curtail the increasing illicit drug use through policy action has been proven abortive, an urgent review of the current policy is needed to accommodate diversion from mere criminal justice system into an organized treatment system that is not just corrective but also preventive in nature and culture. This is very germane for this current study.

Against this backdrop, the current effort of this paper is an attempt to investigate, analyse and critically discuss within the context of empirical juxtaposition and theoretical illustration the nexus between poverty and youths involvement in illicit drug use in Lagos metropolis, Nigeria. This intellectual discourse is very germane as Nigeria attempt to attain the world largest economy by 2030. The study aims to provide insights on available social inclusive drug policy options for policymakers and stakeholders alike on adequate and appropriate interventions for the youths and social development that can enhance a sustainable national development programme in Nigeria.

2 Aim and Objectives of the Study

Given the lacuna in both research literature and drug policy in Nigeria, the current study aimed to build on Siege's (Siegel, 2008: 131) research and WHO's (2010) policy brief by critically analyzing the correlation between poverty and youth involvement in illicit drug use in Lagos metropolis, Nigeria. This is done by considering two variables of poverty in the specific objectives. Therefore, the following are the specific objectives of the study:
1. To examine the relationship between youth unemployment and their involvement in illicit drug use in Lagos, Nigeria.
2. To find out the correlation between low family income status and youth involvement in illicit drug use in Lagos, Nigeria.
3. To examine the extent to which young people involved in the illicit drug use in Lagos, Nigeria.

3 Theoretical Underpinning

The relevant theory considered for this study is the Relative Deprivation Theory (RDT). The theory of relative deprivation was proposed by Sociologists Judith Blau and Peter Blau cited from (Passas, 1987: Chap.4). They combined concepts from anomie theory and social disorganization models (Siegel, 2008: 133). This theory states that people who are economically deprived may form the negative self-feelings and hostility which can motivate them to engage in deviant and criminal behaviours (Stiles, Liu and Kaplan, 2000: 64). Morenoff, Sampson and Raudenbush (2001: 518) opined that neighborhood-level income inequality is a significant predictor of the neighbourhood crime rate. A sharp contrast between the rich and the poor create an atmosphere of envy and mistrust that often lead to violence and aggression (Kruger, Huie, Roger and Hummar, 2004: 224).

Criminal motivation according to Braithwaite (1991, in Siegel 2008: 131) is fueled by perceived humiliation and the perceived right to humiliate a victim in return. This is further buttressed upon by the psychologists, as Wilson and Daly (1991: 572) noted that under these circumstances young males will begin to fear and envy "winner" who are doing very well at their expense. If they fail to take risky aggressive tactics, they are surely going to lose out in social competition and have little chances of future success. These general feelings of relative deprivation are pre-cursor to high crime rates (Blau and Blau, 1982) cited from (Passas, 1987: Chap. 4).

One can conclude that if the youth are socioeconomically deprived, they can be indulging in several anti-social behaviours like illicit drug use in order to alter their mind and escape from the social reality of their extant deprived socioeconomic conditions as a way of compensating as well as coping with their inability to attain certain standard of human conditions.

4 Research Hypotheses

H1: there is no significant relationship between youth unemployment and their involvement in illicit drug use.
H2: there is no significant relationship between low family income and youth involvement in illicit drug use.

5 Methods and Data Source

Lagos as an urban city in Nigeria has the highest prevalence rate of drug abuse among other states in the south-western part of Nigeria (NBS, 2018). However, there are some locations like Ajegunle, Okoko, Bariga, Idi Oro in Mushin Local Government Area (LGA), Oshodi Under-Bridge and Ojota Motor Park in Kosofe (LGA) where many young people especially the vulnerable street youngsters do engage in illicit drug use and this aroused the researcher interest to examine the correlation between low economic status-poverty and illicit drug use among the youths in Kosofe LGA of Lagos State.

This study is an empirical analysis of the nexus between poverty and illicit drug use among Youths in Kosofe Local Government of Lagos Metropolis Nigeria. A non-experimental research design which consists of cross-sectional survey research method was adopted to evaluate the nexus between poverty and illicit drug use in Lagos State, Nigeria. The correlation of key enablers like youth's employment status and low family income are important independent variables tested against the involvement in illicit drug use to enhance the clarity and accuracy about the characteristics of each factor and its correlation with illicit drug use. A self-structured questionnaire was used for the quantitative primary data collection. While an In-depth Interview guide was equally adopted for the qualitative primary data collection. These enabled the researcher to tap into the advantages of the strength of face-to-face and in-depth information from the respondents and to complement the robust findings from the survey.

6   Study Location

The study location is Kosofe Local Government Area, Lagos, Nigeria. Kosofe is situated in Lagos State, Nigeria, in the continent of Africa, and came into existence on 27th November 1996. The LGA has a population of 682,772 (National Population Census, 2006), with a geographical area of 17,85sq/km. The Kosofe community is viewed from different perspectives. It is a crowded community that boasts of hustling and bustling inhabitants, at least in the majority. Kosofe is one of the populous communities in Lagos State with inhabitants from the East, West, and Northern part of the country. This area can be seen as the hub for economic and commercial nerve of Lagos State as well as West Africa. This area consists of the middle, lower class men and few higher income earners. Kosofe L.G.A. consists of seven (7) wards of the Independence National Electoral Commission (INEC): Oworonshoki I, Oworonshoki II, Gbagada, Ifako/Sholuyi, Anthony Village-Ajao Estate, Mende, Ojota and Ogudu.

7   Study Population and Sample Size

The population of the study consists of male and female youths residing in Kosofe Local Government Area of Lagos-state. A sample of 90 youths were recruited for the quantitative data survey. However, the proportion of the respondents selected was based on simple random sampling and specifically lottery due to the non-existence of sample frame (the list of all the youths between the ages of below 18- 40years in Lagos State) in the study area as at when the study was conducted. 10 respondents among selected security agencies - the Nigeria Police Force (NPF) and National Drug Law Enforcement Agency (NDLEA) in Lagos State - were purposively recruited using convenience sampling technique for the In-depth Interviews (IDIs) based on their knowledge of the general and specific objectives of the study.

8 Sampling Techniques

Four multi-stage (Local Government Area, Wards, Street and Household) and simple random sampling techniques were utilized to select a sample size of ninety (90) respondents for the quantitative data. The lack of sampling frame for the inclusion of the selected respondents necessitated the adoption of this sampling technique. However, convenience and purposive sampling technique was adopted for the qualitative data collection.

9 Research Instrument/Data Collection

A structured self-completed questionnaire was employed to collect data in the survey. A total of 100 copies of the questionnaire was administered to the study population through a method of a personal interview but only 90 instruments were found useful for the analysis. This was appropriate since the method avails the researcher an opportunity to fill out the questionnaire accordingly in order to avoid misleading responses. However, the survey was structured in such a way that adequate information was elicited on the research objectives and hypotheses. The instrument was divided into two major sections, namely section A and B. Section A of the questionnaire was designed to collect information on respondents socio-demographic variables, while section B was designed using scales in accessing responses to statement made to answer the stated research questions. Prior to the main study, a pilot study was conducted in Shomolu LGA to ascertain the validity and reliability of the instrument and a result of 0.88 was obtained using Cronbach-Alfa. The instrument was administered with the help of trained research assistants. Informed consent, anonymity and confidentiality of the respondents were considered during the course of the data collection. In addition, Newspaper and Magazines, Published Articles, Journal papers and books were used for the secondary data.

10 Data Analysis

The quantitative (self-completed questionnaire) method of data collection was adopted for this study. The Statistical Package for Social Sciences (SPSS) version 20.0 was employed in the analysis of the variables of the study. The researcher ran the frequency for all the variables by way of univariate analysis and for the bivariate analysis; the cross-tabulation of the hypotheses of the study was carried out using the Chi-square (x^2) tool. However, content analysis was adopted for the analysis of the qualitative data.

TABLE 9.1 Socio-demographic status of the respondents

Responses	Frequency	Percentage
Sex		
Male	68	75.6
Female	22	24.4
Total	90	100.0
Religion		
Christianity	36	40.0
Islam	12	33.3
Traditional	15	16.7
Others	9	10.0
Total	90	100.0
Age group		
18-23	22	24.4
24-29	26	28.9
30-35	24	26.7
36-40	18	20.0
Total	90	100.0
Mean age = 34.45, Min. = 19, Max. = 62.		
Marital status		
Single	48	53.3
Married	36	40.0
Divorced/Separated	6	6.7
Total	90	100.0
Educational attainment		
Formal Education	63	70.0
No Formal Education	27	30.0
Total	90	100.0
Employment status		
Employed	22	24.4
Unemployed	68	75.6
Total	90	100.0

SOURCE: FIELD SURVEY, 2016

11 Data Analysis and Discussion of Findings

The socio-demographic characteristics of the respondents in Table 9.1 above reveal that 75.6% (68) of the respondents were male, while 24.4% (22) were female. The data on the religious affiliation of the respondent reveal that majority 40% (36) were Christians, 33.3 (12) were Muslims, 16.7% (15) were traditionalists, while 10% (9) belong to other religion. The result of the distribution indicates that Christianity and Islam are dominant in the area of study. Also, their age range shows that 24.4 (22) of the respondents were in the age range of 18–23 years; 28.9% (26) were in the age range of 24–29 years; 26.7% (24) were in the age range of 30–35 years; 20% (18) were in the age range of 36–40. The age distribution of the respondents indicates that majority of the respondents were of active ages. The data on the marital status of the respondents show that majority 53.3% (48) of the respondents were single, 40% (36) were married while 6.7% (6) were divorced/separated. Data on the educational background of the respondents reveal that 70% (63) attended formal schools, while 30% (27) has no formal education. The data on employment status indicates that majority 75.6% (68) were unemployed as at the time of conducting the research while 24.4% (22) were employed.

TABLE 9.2 Respondents' involvement in illicit drug use

Illicit drug use	Response	Frequency	Percent %
Have you ever used any substance without a professional medical prescription before?	Yes	57	63.3
	No	33	36.7
	Total	90	100.0

SOURCE: FIELD SURVEY, 2016

Data from Table 9.2 show distribution of the respondents' involvement in the use of illicit drug as the majority 63.3% (57) of the respondents have used illicit drug before while 36.7% (33) of the respondents have not. The implication of this result is that majority of the young population in the study area have used illicit drug before. Similarly, this study corroborate with the Drug Use in Nigeria report cited from the NBS (2018) data that show that many young people in Nigeria get initiated into substance abuse like cannabis as early as 19 years and more so, 40% of the young people in Nigeria are indulging in illicit drug use. Another study conducted among young the secondary school students in the southwestern Nigeria show that many students have abused illicit drug like cannabis, alcohol among others before (Fatoye and Morakinyo, 2002: 301).

12   Hypothesis One

Ho   There is no significant relationship between youth unemployment and their involvement in illicit drug use.
H1   There is a significant relationship between youth unemployment and their involvement in illicit drug use.

TABLE 9.3   Distribution of respondents by youth unemployment and involvement in illicit drug use

What is your employment status?	Have you ever used any substance without a professional medical prescription before?		
	Yes	No	Total
Employed	9 (10.0%)	2 (2.2%)	11 (12.2%)
Unemployed	59 (65.6%)	20 (22.2%)	79 (87.8%)
Total	68 (75.6%)	22 (24.4%)	90 (100.0%)

χ^2 = 14.27, df = 4, sig (p-value) = 0.006.
SOURCE: FIELD SURVEY, 2016

As indicated above, the calculated value (x^2) is 14.27 and the 'P' value is 0.006 which is lesser than the level of significance of 0.05. Hence, the Alternative hypothesis (Ho) is rejected and the Null hypothesis (H1) is accepted. Then, there is a significant relationship between youth unemployment and youths involvement in the illicit drug in the country. From the table above, we can analyze the difference between the youth unemployment rate and their involvement in illicit drug use. About 68 (75.6%) stated "yes", while 22 (24.4%) of the respondents said "no". The implication of this is that youth unemployment has a significant relationship with

Similarly, data from qualitative study show that majority of the participants were of the opinion that high rate of unemployment in the country is one those factors that motivate many youths into illicit drug use. According to one of the participants during IDIs:

> "Youth unemployment increases youth involvement in illicit drug use and trade because of the inability of some young boys and girls to get good job with good pay. This creates the need to step into the drug business and invariably illicit drug use for the majority of the youths in our country-Nigeria."

This finding corroborate with the theoretical proposition of Judith Blau and Peter Blau who combined the two concepts of Anomie theory and social disorganization models (Siegel, 2008: 133) while arguing that people who are socioeconomically deprived may develop a negative self-feelings and hostility which can then motivate them to engage in deviant and criminal behaviours (Stiles, Liu and Kaplan, 2000:64) like illicit drug use or trade. This proposition suggest that the high rate of youth unemployment in Nigeria has created negative self-feelings and hostility which invariably have motivated a significant number of Nigerian youths to be indulging in illicit drug use as a means of responding to the stress and strains that accompanying living as a young member of a given society with high level of economic deprivations.

13 Hypothesis Two

Ho: There is no significant relationship between low family income and youth involvement in illicit drug use.
H1: There is a significant relationship between low family income and youth involvement in illicit drug use.

As indicated above, the calculated value (x^2) is 14.113 and the 'P' value is 0.001 which is lesser than the level of significance of 0.05. Hence, the Alternative hypothesis (Ho) is rejected and the Null hypothesis (H1) is accepted: there is a significant relationship between low family income and youth's involvement in illicit drug use in the country. From the table above, we can analyse the difference between family income and youth involvement in illicit drug use. About 64 (71.1%) stated "yes", while 26(28.9%) of the respondents said "no". The implication of this is that family income has a significant relationship with the use of illicit drug use.

In the same vein, data from the qualitative study gave credence to the above finding. For instance, one participant during the IDI state thus:

TABLE 9.4   Distribution of respondents by low family income and youth involvement in illicit drug use

Do you generate enough income that caters for your household?	Have you ever used any substance without a professional medical prescription before?		
	Yes	No	Total
Yes	24 (26.6%)	6 (6.7%)	30 (33.3%)
No	40 (44.5%)	20 (22.2%)	60 (66.7%)
Total	64 (71.1%)	26 (28.9%)	90 (100.0%)

χ^2 = 14.113, d.f = 2, sig (p-value) = 0.001.
SOURCE: FIELD SURVEY, 2016

> "There are several young illicit drug users that said they take for instance, alcohol and cannabis because of the nature and culture of the job that they do which is a low cadre jobs like public transport Task Force. For instance, those young boys who work as a member of the National Union of Road Transport Workers (NURTW) have told me severally that they have to take cannabis and mixed it up with alcohol so that they can be bold enough to harass anyone- referring to commercial Danfos' Driver who may like to prove stubborn when forcefully tasking them to pay their daily dues. So, one may like to ask that what if these teeming youths have a better employment opportunities, perhaps they will have no cause to be indulging themselves in illicit drug use such as alcohol, tramadol, cannabis among others."

Evidently, this finding gave credence to the theoretical principles of the relative deprivation theory as Morenoff, Sampson and Raudenbush (2001: 517–560) opined in their study that neighborhood-level income inequality is a significant predictor of the neighbourhood crime rate. A sharp contrast between the rich and the poor create an atmosphere of envy and mistrust that often lead to violence and aggression (Kruger, Huie, Roger and Hummar, 2004: 224). The implication of this is that the wide range of inequality in the family income levels in Nigeria is a predisposing factors for some criminal behaviours like use of illicit drug for many young people in Nigeria. For instance, relative deprivation theory states that people who are economically deprived may form the negative self-feelings and hostility which can motivate them to engage in deviant and criminal behaviours like illicit drug use (Stiles, Liu and Kaplan, 2000: 54–90). As such, many Nigerian youths especially those who work in low income jobs that are associated with stress and frustrations have a high tendency of engaging in criminal activities like use of illicit drugs in Nigeria as indicated in this study.

14   Conclusion

In conclusion, the outcome of this study indicates a correlation between poverty and illicit drug use among young people in Nigeria. Thus, factors like unemployment and low family income are part of the key enablers of illicit drug use among the youths in Nigeria. More so, to some reasonable extent, many young people in Nigeria at their tender age are getting initiated into illicit drug use as a coping mechanism to escape their low socioeconomic reality or an alternative means to sustain their livelihood. It is however incumbent on the government and stakeholders alike to jointly work together to ameliorate the Nigerian youths' socioeconomic condition by employing the following recommendations in order to achieve the quest for a sustainable development goals.

15   Recommendations

The essay then recommends that:
- The government should intensify efforts in providing employment opportunities for the teeming youths in the country. Hence, there is a need to develop a comprehensive drug policy that will be more socioeconomically inclusive and drug treatment friendly.
- The government should find ways to bridge the inequalities in workers' income to make it suitable for the economic realities in the country. It is obvious that most youths from the low-income population in Nigeria involve in illicit drug use and other associated criminal activities to complement their meagre income. Hence, reducing inequalities in income, may lower the high rate of illicit drug use and other associated criminal activities.
- Finally, social worker, youth workers, school counselors should intensify effort to offer professional and youth friendly counselling for young secondary school children who are constantly vulnerable to abusing all forms of illicit drug use in Lagos, Nigeria.

References

Braithwaite, J. 1981. "The Myth of Social Class and Criminality Reconsidered." *American Sociological Review*, 46: (1), 36–57.

Danziger, S & Haveman, D. 2001. *Understanding Poverty*. New York: Russel Sage Foundation. doi: https://www.irp.wisc.edu/publications/focus/pdfs/foc212.pdf.

Emeh, I. E. J. 2012. "Tackling Youth Unemployment in Nigeria: The Lagos State Development and Empowerment Programmes Initiatives." *Afro Asian Journal of Social Sciences*, 3:34.

Fatoye FO, Morakinyo O. 2002. "Substance Use Amongst Secondary School Student. In Rural and Urban Communities in South Western Nigeria East." *African Medical Journal* 79: 299–305.

International Labour Organisation (ILO). 2010. "Global Employment Trends", Available Online: http://www.ilo.org/public/english/region/eurpro/ankara/areas/youth.htm.

Kruger, P. M.; Huie, S. A.; Rogers, R. G. and Hammer, R. A. 2004. "Neighborhood and Homicide Mortality: An Analysis of Race/Ethnic Differences." *Journal of Epidemiology and Community Health*, 58, 223–230.

Morenoff, J.; Sampson, R and Raudebush, S. 2001. "Neighborhood Inequality, Collective Efficacy, and the Spatial Dynamics of Urban Violence." *Criminology*, 39 (2001). 517–560. Doi: https://onlinelibrary.wiley.com/doi/abs/10.1111/j.1745-9125.2001.tb00932.x

National Bureau of Statistics. 2018. *Drug Use in Nigeria 2018 Survey Report*. 437749. Nigeria https://www.proshareng.com/news/General/NBS-Publishes-Drug-Use-in-Nigeria-2018-Survey-Report/43749.

National Bureau of Statistics. 2012b. *Statistical News: Labor Force Statistics No. 476*. Abuja: The NBS Publication.

National Population Commission. 2006. *Nigeria Demographic and Health Survey 2006*. Calverton, Mary land: National Population Commission and ORC/Macro.

Passas, N. 1987. "Anomie and Relative Deprivation." Paper Presented at the Annual Meeting of the Eastern (American) Sociological Society, Boston, U.S.A.

Siegel, L.J. 2008. *Criminology: The Core*. Belmont, Wadsworth, Cengage Learning. 130–492

Stiles, B., Liu, X. and Kaplan, H. 2000. "Relative Deprivation and Deviant Adaptations: The Mediating Effects of Negative Self-Feelings." *Journal of Research in Crime and Delinquency* 37(1):64–90. DOI: 10.1177/0022427800037001003

Udama, A. R. 2014. "The Risk Factors of West Africa Illicit Drug Trade." *International Journal of Scientific and Research Publications*, Vol. 4, Issue 11.

UNDP. 2015. *Human Development Reports*. UN House New York, U.S.A.

United Nations Office on Drugs and Crime (UNODC, 2017) *Document on Drugs Organised Crimes in Nigeria*. Online Material. www.unodc.org/nigeria/en/drug-prevention.html.

UNODC. 2019. Document/data and analysis/statistics/Drugs/Drug Use Survey in Nigeria. https://www.unodc.org/documents/data-and-analysis/statistics/Drugs/Drug_Use_Survey_Nigeria_2019_BOOK.pdf

Ward, M. 2015. *Poverty and Crime. National Dialogue Network*. http://www.nationaldialoguenetwork.org/poverty-and-crime/

Wilson, T. and Daly, A. 1991. "Life Expectancy Economic Inequality, Homicide, and reproductive Timing in Chicago Neighborhoods." *American Sociological Review*, 57, 570–589.

WHO. 2010. ATLAS survey on resources for the treatment and prevention of substance use disorders. Country profile: Nigeria.

World Bank. 2001. "Voice of the Poor" World Development Report, Washington D.C.

CHAPTER 10

The Politics of Poverty in Sub-Saharan Africa

Jonathan O. Chimakonam

1   Introduction

The problem of poverty is a serious subject which demands concrete programmes aimed at addressing it. But since the last quarter of the 20th century, poverty in sub-Saharan Africa has become an issue in political campaigns and intellectual debates by African and western politicians, intellectuals and global institutions who would instead trade blames than proffer pragmatic solutions. As a result, the problem is not decreasing. What is required to address the issue of poverty in sub-Saharan Africa are concrete programmes that would create opportunities for a decent income and equip people living in poverty with relevant skills to take up such opportunities. Examples of such practical programmes would include but not limited to capital investment, public infrastructure, loans to SMEs and the big manufacturing industries which will create wealth in sub-Saharan countries. But this appears not to be happening in most countries severely affected by the problem of poverty in sub-Saharan Africa. Discussions on the subject seem to take different directions in policy and action. Most policy documents like the MDGs, SDGs, UNDP and foreign policies of developed nations often spell out programmes, but what is available in terms of action and implementation is different, less concrete and a lot of arguments.

The national and international efforts at fighting poverty in sub-Saharan Africa which involve various commitments to reduce the phenomenon or even eradicate it are often not concrete. Some of these efforts which crystallise in aids by foreign governments, multinational institutions, agencies and corporations, distributed through the assistance of national agencies and NGOs translate to mere palliative measures rather than reduction, let alone eradication of poverty. The preceding is because these aids do not aim at creating wealth, redistributing wealth and creating opportunities for decent income but at temporary easing of the burden of poverty. In a recent paper (Chimakonam 2020), I have discussed the psychological effects of aid programmes on the poor and as such will not belabour it here.

When one surveys prominent international and national programmes implemented in some parts of sub-Saharan Africa, especially in the post-Cold

War era, they will observe that while these governments and agencies actually commit to poverty reduction or eradication, they manage to accomplish temporary placebo in most cases. Also, most of these programmes have one thing in common; they are aids that provide social services like health care, basic education, food handouts, provision of water, the supply of medical equipment and drugs and various forms of social orientations.

The question that looms large therefore is: are the various national and international efforts at fighting poverty in Africa politicised? I argue that these social services are not equivalent to wealth creation, redistribution of wealth or the creation of opportunities for a decent income, etc., which are some of the concrete strategies that can lift people out of poverty. Contrarily, the fiery debates that wind up in blame games, unfulfilled promises, accusations and counter-accusations are merely politicising the subject of poverty in Africa. Employing the conversational thinking technique, I examine three major hypotheses associated with the discussions on poverty in Africa.

2   Poverty as a Philosophical Problem

What makes poverty a philosophical problem? It is not merely the hardship it imposes on victims; it is (1) because it is a phenomenon that is often created more by human actions and inactions than by nature which would amount to anyone of injustice, breaking promises, failure to uphold duties and responsibilities, human rights abuses or violation, (2) and the fact that poverty robs victims of their human dignity. But what makes poverty a problem for sub-Saharan Africa is precisely 'number.' The number of people who live in poverty in sub-Saharan Africa is more than the number of those who do not, which explains why addressing the issue becomes urgent. The concern of this section, therefore, is to find out what makes poverty a philosophical issue as well as a problem in the sub-Saharan region. I will address these two issues one after another.

Moral philosophers generally have problems with human actions and inactions, which cause pain to other humans. Libertarians (Nozick 1974; Vallentyne 2014) say no person should take an action that infringes upon the liberty and dignity of another person. So, 'A' does not have the right to infringe upon the liberty and dignity of 'B.' Unfortunately, foreign governments, global institutions and local politicians are not committed to taking concrete steps that will lift people out of poverty. Instead, they take palliative measures that remand people in poverty and rob them of their dignity. Most of those who scrape by through aids distributed by NGOs are still homeless. A good example is the case of the Skolombo or the homeless people in the city of Calabar in eastern Nigeria. In a recent work, I investigated the losing battle which these people fight with poverty which leaves them dehumanised (See Chimakonam 2020, 433-446). What the handouts which the Skolombo occasionally receive from foreign-sponsored NGOs amount to is a palliative measure that compromises their dignity. One often notices the dismay on their faces when their benefactors take pictures as they eat or receive food and clothing.

Bentham (1789/1907), Mill (1861/1998), and Driver (2014) speaking from utilitarian perspective, say that actions which do not bring happiness to the greatest number or which do not amount to a greater good for an affected individual are immoral. Put differently, actions which impose a cost on the greatest number or which amount to greater cost for an affected individual are morally repugnant. For example, when local politicians and dictators loot public funds meant for projects, and that action later leads to many citizens losing their jobs, or being underemployed, or unable to access opportunities for income, the implication might be that the majority of the citizens will sink deeper into poverty. Also, deontologists, according to Alexander (2000) argue that morally upright acts are obligatory. If politicians are tasked with rooting out poverty from African nations, and they have promised to do so if elected, then they are duty-bound to take concrete measures like investing public money in building industries and public infrastructure, creating wealth and redistributing it, and enacting and implementing policies that prioritise loans to SMEs and big industries over financial speculators, even if it means they would not be able to buy private jets and fancy properties abroad. And for the teleologists, the moral worth of an action can be measured by the value of the action or its output. If foreign governments, global institutions and local politicians claim to care for the teeming population who are grinding in poverty in sub-Saharan Africa and have drafted wonderful policies for poverty reduction or eradication, the moral value of those gestures can only be measured by the outcome of such programmes. A situation where the action is not as concrete as policy and the plight of poverty victims continues to worsen despite such programmes, suggests that there might be a need, therefore, to call to question the morality of those initiatives.

It is immoral for those saddled with the responsibility of deploying public resources into programmes that can reduce or eradicate poverty in their countries or in a foreign country not to do so creditably for selfish reasons. Whether the agents involved are foreign governments, global institutions or local politicians, the moral weight is the same. If you have a moral commitment to discharge a certain duty, then you have no reason to deviate from that purpose. Doing so, especially with the phenomenon of poverty, would mean that those already in poverty will continue to wallow in it, and those on the verge might end up falling into it. And since poverty robs its victims of their human dignity as Odera Oruka (1976/1985) suggests, the actions or inactions of those who failed in their commitment to take concrete steps to address the problem are morally condemnable.

This argument about human dignity can even be extended to palliative aid programmes that foreign governments and global institutions oversee. It is easy for some critics to lose sight of the moral damage of certain aid programmes. Some of these aid programmes available in sub-Saharan Africa take different forms, like the distribution of used clothes to recipients and food handouts to poverty victims. Oruka (1989/1997) shows why such palliative measures are not good for the victims of poverty. As he suggests, humans are animal species with rationality and dignity. Certain gestures could devalue the dignity of an individual even if they are supposed to benefit by such. He argues that foreign aids as an international charity could subject their recipients to humiliations (1989/1997, 84). No reasonable individual would be glad to (for being made to) survive by food handouts, or depend on donor agencies for their clothing, especially when such clothes have been used by some individuals in other parts of the world. So, even though the aid programmes soothe the physical pain of poverty; they also inflict more devastating psychological pains by devaluing the dignity of victims.

As I indicated earlier, sub-Sahara Africa has the highest number of people living in poverty among other regions of the world. "We talk of poverty as a problem militating against development in sub-Saharan countries not just because of its presence but its depth. Poverty is everywhere, but in the sub-continent, it has become endemic" (Chimakonam 2019, 143). Statistics show that sub-Saharan Africa is home to the largest number of those living in poverty (Kharas et al 2018). It is also home to the largest number of people living in extreme poverty in the world (Müller-Jung 2018).

Current statistics from World Bank's *Poverty and Shared Prosperity 2018: Piecing Together the Poverty Puzzle* (2018) indicate that whereas the number of those living in extreme poverty has declined globally, from 1.9 billion in 1990 to about 736 million in 2015, the figure has gone up for sub-Saharan Africa. The report has it that sub-Saharan Africa is the only region of the world where the numbers of extreme poverty have been on the increase, and forecasts show that 9 out of 10 extremely poor people in the world by 2030 would live in sub-Saharan Africa (Wadhwa 2018). According to Friederike Müller-Jung (2018, *World Bank report*) "…an estimated 413 million people in Africa currently live in extreme poverty — more than half of the world's total." Writing for the *Brookings Institution*, Nirav Patel (2018, "Understanding poverty in Africa") explains that "The average poverty rate for sub-Saharan Africa stands at about 41 per cent, and of the world's 28 poorest countries, 27 are in sub-Saharan Africa, all with a poverty rate above 30 per cent. Projections by the World Bank also show that extreme poverty is showing few signs of improvement in sub-Saharan Africa..."

From the above statistics, it is clear that if poverty is a big problem in the world, then it is a bigger problem in the sub-Sahara Africa; worrisome elsewhere but threatening and dire in the African sub-region. It is not just a problem for sub-Saharan Africa; it is the number one problem for the region. Ironically, few people on the continent realise this. Even fewer researchers on the continent dedicate research effort to the problem. It is as if it is a sole concern for the 'government people' who are often blamed for creating the problem, and who alone possess the power to address it if they genuinely wish to. If one probes a little further; they will find a bit of cynicism and conspiracy theory shared among academics and activists in sub-Saharan Africa. That conspiracy theory is that 'the politicians in sub-Saharan countries are wicked crooks who intentionally subject the people to poverty to disarm them of any power and zeal to mount a challenge against corrupt governments while enriching themselves and their cronies.' The philosopher, or specifically, the African philosopher must not be caught in this web of conspiracy theory. It is not the lot of the philosopher to give up hope or abandon their moral duty and debt to the society. The dearth of research effort on the subject of poverty in Africa by African philosophers is worrisome.

There is a crisis of thought in African philosophy. This crisis stems partly from the grooming of many African philosophers in western institutions. The affected African philosophers are thus trapped in a double-bind whether to advertise their western education or to creatively reassess Africa's situation. Partly, it also stems from the fact that actors have been distracted, if not disconnected from the real problems far too long. In addition, there is an unnecessary overwhelming attention being paid to despicable remarks by western philosophers against the mind(s) of African(s) that a few African philosophers in the last five decades or so have had the consciousness to tackle some of the real issues confronting the continent. The recent World Bank Report affirms that Africa is a cesspool of poverty, the world's poverty capital, and the forecasts are saying that in as little as a decade from now, 9 out of every 10 persons living in extreme poverty would be found in sub-Sahara, if that is not already the case. The reported scenario is critical and deserves urgent and dedicated attention from Africans from all walks of life, especially the intellectuals.

However, the type of action required to confront the menace of poverty on the continent is not happening at the moment. Much of the academic effort directed at fighting poverty in our world today, and even in sub-Sahara comes from the west, Asia and the Americas. Very little in terms of academic research and publications is taking place in Africa. The African philosopher who should awake the consciousness of the people and governments on the issue of poverty is rather docile, if not unconcerned. The poverty of the mind, therefore, entrenches poverty of the body. It takes the mind to appreciate the challenge posed by poverty to society. But where there is widespread ignorance, under-education or miseducation, it is difficult to generate ideas, let alone to deploy concrete programmes geared towards tackling the problem of poverty.

It is imperative to view and treat poverty as a serious philosophical problem. Those who are living in conditions of poverty, whether extreme or normal, are victims whose rights must be protected.[1] They are victims not only of the phenomenon of poverty but of the society that has failed them in terms of policy and implementation. Justice is about the distribution of resources as it is about rights and liberties. Poverty excites our imagination about the possibilities of moral concepts like 'food justice,' 'financial justice,' as so on, in which a section of the society who experiences great disadvantage in the distribution of wealth and resources can be regarded as victims and are entitled to certain claims.

Poverty is a problem in Africa and as well as being a philosophical issue. The preceding is made worse by the crisis of thought in Africa (as) earlier mentioned. The African philosophers who should know better are at war with themselves on where their priorities should lie. On the one hand, is the question of identity mounted by western detractors, and on the other hand, is the question of dignity posed by the terrible condition of life on the continent. Much as we could agree that cultural identity is a feature which a people should not toy with, yet, it is empty without dignity. There is a way in which terrible conditions of life could distort and negatively reconstruct a people's identity. Nowadays, Africa conveys an image of diseases, HIV/AIDS, and chronic poverty. Conditions of life play a major role in identifying or even disidentifying a people. African philosophers, therefore, must rise and begin to fulfil their duties and responsibilities to the continent and its peoples. One of the ways of doing the preceding would be to raise public consciousness on the wrongheaded discussions on the problem of poverty on the continent. The subject of poverty which arguably represents the number one problem facing the continent today, appears to be heavily politicised.

---

1   UO Egbai and JO Chimakonam (2019, 608-623), recently addressed the question of rights of victims in light of transitional justice. But protecting the rights of victims of poverty is also something we can consider seriously in the poverty debate.

3 The Politics of Poverty in Africa

We must not ignore the fact of the Igbo maxim, 'onye rijuo afọ, ọrụba ụka,' which roughly translates to, 'it is when one has eaten that he will be able to philosophise properly.' This does not really proscribe philosophising or declare the impossibility of doing so on an empty stomach. It simply draws attention to the fact that poverty can be an impediment to different progressive activities, including philosophising. There is a Latin proverb that corroborates this idea: 'mens sana in corpore sano,' meaning 'a healthy mind is to be found in a healthy body.' This does not actually mean that unhealthy or sick or hungry people possess unhealthy or sick minds, no. What is meant by this saying is that certain conditions of life could constitute a serious obstacle for some progressive activities that characterise life in society. Poverty is one of such conditions, and it affects life in the sub-Sahara deeply. If poverty then can be as threatening as described in the preceding paragraphs, why would anyone politicise it?

It is not assumed here that certain politicised discussions are inappropriate. The point I want to make is that there might be many things that can be politicised without harm. Still, the experience of poverty which robs victims of their dignity, and which is the most devastating problem facing sub-Saharan Africa, should not be one of those subjects. Unfortunately, as I shall argue, it is being politicised. To score petty political, cultural, intellectual and ideological advantage, different actors and interest groups drag the subject to the discourse arena intending above all else, to undermine some perceived opponents and score personal victories. Making poverty a subject of discussion in the public sphere and in ways that are not geared towards practically and concretely addressing the problem, but paying lip service, identifying fault lines, apportioning blames and perhaps, at best, sprinkling in palliative measures is a problem in itself. It is my claim in this work that there is a way in which the efforts to address the poverty problem in sub-Saharan Africa, by governments, global institutions and intellectuals could be viewed as political.

To discuss the issue concerning the politicisation of poverty, I identify three hypotheses, namely; neo-colonialism, dictatorship and ineptitude. The neo-colonial hypothesis can be associated with some African intellectuals and academics who often claim in their books, scientific papers, newspaper columns and news media (TV, radio, social media, blogs), that the colonial west (and now they include China and the global institutions), run a neo-colonial programme through which they exploit, intimidate, manipulate and dictate for African governments, thereby impoverishing Africa. Books such as Kwame Nkrumah's *Neo-colonialism: The Last Stage of Imperialism* (1965); Walter

Rodney's *How Europe Underdeveloped Africa* (1972); Chinweizu's *The West and the Rest of Us* (1975); Ali Mazrui's *The African Condition* (1980), etc. are examples of such literature.

The argument is that colonialism never really ended. It was transformed into neo-colonialism which is an indirect colonialism,[2] or colonialism without boots on the ground — postage colonialism if you like. Under this new frame, political power was transferred to indigenes, and the political independence of their country was declared by the departing colonial west. But the claim here is that the colonial west did not just leave. Britain, for example, is often accused of sowing seeds of conflict between indigenous peoples or using a more suitable group for colonial administration and handing over power to those they earlier considered less fit to rule, who then depend on Britain for guidance (Achebe 2012). Anyone of these strategies naturally would create room for ethnic conflicts and wars, thereby opening the newly independent country to western exploitation. The west sells weapons of war to destabilise the country, then move in for cheap raw materials and natural resources. In destabilising the new state, development of infrastructure and industrialisation are made difficult, thus from the onset, the new nation cannot develop industrial and technological capacity making them dependent on the west for literally everything from policy to manufacturing. The west then controls the economic policies in the nations of sub-Sahara, and also controls the political policies both directly and through the global institutions.

Another claim by the neo-colonial group is that, where there is a government or a leader who refuses to kowtow to western dictates, such a government or a leader is made a target. And a programme of regime change is set in motion to flush out such a recalcitrant government or leadership and bring in western puppets. Examples are often cited with Kwame Nkrumah in Ghana, Patrice Lumumba in the Congo, Idi Amin Dada in Uganda, Thomas Sankara in Burkina Faso, etc. If, however, a puppet regime is installed and it remains loyal to the west, the west turns a blind eye and even protects the agenda of life presidency. Some examples include, Mobutu Sese Seko in Congo, Dawda Jawara in Gambia, Yoweri Museveni in Uganda, Paul Biya in Cameroon, Blaise Compaore in Burkina Faso to name just a few. Where a puppet becomes recalcitrant along the line, they are marked for removal by any means necessary, examples include, Laurent Gbagbo of Ivory Coast, Robert Mugabe of Zimbabwe, etc. The list is long.

---

2 See Santos, S. Boaventura, "Epistemologies of the south and the future," *European South* 1 (2016): 17-29.

The point which is made by the neo-colonialism group is that the ideology is real and accounted for bad post-colonial governments in sub-Sahara with massive abuses of power and human rights, looting of public resources, clueless leadership, control and exploitation by western powers, etc. These translate to the destruction of local economies and impoverishment of sub-Saharan peoples.

The problem with the neo-colonialism hypothesis is that they transfer blames to western governments and global institutions as if to say the African despots and corrupt regimes play no part in the problems of their countries. We are talking of nations that fought and secured their independence from western colonial powers. It is not completely correct to claim that they do not have the influence to organise and run their governments the way that would make those nations prosper. We must have the courage and sincerity to place part of the blame at the feet of African leaders and the bad, most times, visionless regimes that crippled and continue to under-develop the nations of sub-Sahara. Several despots and their cronies have been known to loot dry the coffers of their national treasury. Some good examples include Nigeria's military dictators like Yakubu Gowon, Olusegun Obasanjo, Muhammadu Buhari, Ibrahim Babangida, Sani Abacha, Abdulsalami Abubakar, etc.; Congo's Mobutu Sese Seko, Laurent Kabila and his son Joseph Kabila; Cameroon's Paul Biya; Togo's Gnassingbé Eyadéma, to name just a few.

The neo-colonial group erroneously apportion the blame for the massive poverty in Africa today to neo-colonial forces as if to say the post-colonial African leaders and their regimes have been spotless. This seeming assumption is incorrect.

Then, there is the dictatorship hypothesis which can be associated with western governments and global institutions. This group blames the dictators in various African countries for being corrupt, mismanaging the economies and impoverishing their people. Through global institutions like the World Bank, IMF, UNDP, etc., they promote the ideology that dictatorship is 'bad' for the economies of nations. Democracy to them is the only system that is good for business. The belief is that if a dictatorial regime ran a government in sub-Saharan Africa, the economy of such a country would inevitably collapse, and the people would plunge into poverty due to corruption and high-handedness. They give examples of Robert Mugabe's Zimbabwe, Sani Abacha's Nigeria, etc., without mentioning that Western-imposed sanctions contributed to the destruction of the economies of those nations such as Zimbabwe

This group tells the sub-Saharan governments to adopt economic and political policies drafted by global institutions such as the World Bank, IMF, HRC, FAO, WHO, etc. The argument is that these institutions are neutral bodies, made up of specialists who know better than their counterparts in sub-Saharan nations.

However, the problem with this group is that those nations that do not adopt foreign-drafted policies are treated somewhat as rogue nations. Their homegrown policies are condemned, and sanctions may be imposed on them. In many cases, especially during the Cold War, programmes of regime change can be called in, and internal uprising and conflicts may be sponsored to destabilise the nation. Coup d' état was also a regular option used in effecting regime-change in Africa. With the threat of economic and political sanctions, many African governments have been tamed and brought under the direct control of western powers whose bidding they must do or face penalties.

As for the accusation of corruption, there can be little objection that many dictatorial regimes in Africa were corrupt. Most of the dictators and their cronies lived and continue to live extravagant lifestyles squandering the resources of their countries. Needless to cite examples as almost all dictators — military or democratic, in the post-colonial Africa were and are guilty of corruption. But there is something which some western governments and global institutions do not talk about concerning corruption in Africa. It is the fact that all corrupt African leaders worked and conspired with some western governments and institutions to loot and steal the resources of the countries in sub-Sahara. Monies looted from Africa have ended up in Swiss, British, American banks, etc., to lubricate those western economies. There is a silent cooperation of some of these western governments which turn a blind eye as their financial institutions collaborate with corrupt African politicians to empty the treasury of their countries. What this entails is that the criticism by the dictatorship group also applies to the critics of the group. Corruption is not peculiar to sub-Saharan Africa; in fact, one can even argue that it was imported from the west. It is easy to see different African leaders being accused of corruption by these same western governments that provide safe heaven to wealth stolen from Africa. A higher percentage of Africa's stolen wealth is stashed in financial institutions or invested in real estates in the west. One would think that a well-meaning criticism of the corruption in Africa should begin in the west.

In recent times, the International Criminal Court (ICC) is used to tame many African recalcitrant leaders, sometimes, for the good of the nations they rule, but at other times, to their disadvantage. Because some of these leaders have their hands soiled with blood and other atrocities in their desperate bid to seize power or keep their nations under firm control, it is easy to threaten them with the ICC into becoming puppets to foreign powers. Whereas a number of African despots and military commanders like Charles Taylor of Liberia and Bosco Ntaganda of Democratic Republic of Congo have been tried and convicted at the ICC for crimes against humanity. It is widely believed that the ICC usually turns a blind eye to several human rights violations committed by leaders and armies of western governments. It is worth noting that the call for American military officials to be prosecuted by the ICC has been met with the threat of sanctions by the American government.[3] The preceding raises serious questions with regards to the neutrality and sincerity of some of the so-called global institutions and western governments, which claim to uphold global justice.[4] The accusation that institutions such as the ICC are neo-colonial weapons which the west uses to check recalcitrant leaders and governments from the global south cannot be ignored. In fact, at a point, all the cases at the court involved people from Africa prompting the widespread suspicion that the ICC was designed to witch-hunt leaders in Africa.[5]

Fatou Bensouda, an ICC prosecutor from Africa in 2017 submitted what was deemed a credible request to prosecute US Army/CIA war crimes in Afghanistan. But the ICC panel of judges rejected the application claiming that "the current circumstances of the situation in Afghanistan are such as [sic] to make the prospects for a successful investigation and prosecution extremely limited" (Kennedy 2019, "World Criminal Court Rejects Probe Into U.S. Actions In Afghanistan"). This generated uproar in the human rights and international corners, especially in Africa. It was the first solid confirmation that the ICC might indeed be partial and might never have been established to treat all peoples fairly. When in 2019 the ICC announced its willingness to allow the investigation, the American government through the Secretary of State Mike Pompeo announced that they would sanction the ICC prosecutors if they dared look into the cases of American human rights violations in Afghanistan (See footnote 3).

So, for the dictatorship group, the poverty in various parts of Africa can be blamed on the dictatorial regimes that have run or are currently running such countries. But this is incorrect as my discussions so far have shown.

Let us address the third hypothesis, which for lack of a better word, I describe as the ineptitude hypothesis. This can be associated with some western and African intellectuals as well as some African and western politicians. There is a crisscrossing pattern of claims here. Some intellectuals (Africans

---

3   See, Al Jazeera, "US bars entry to ICC members probing 'war crimes' in Afghanistan," last modified March 15, 2019, https://www.aljazeera.com/news/2019/03/bars-entry-icc-members-probing-war-crimes-afghanistan-190315191933901.html
4   In (Chimakonam 2017, 120-137), I engaged and demonstrated the lopsidedness that characterises research on global justice.
5   See, Fatou Bensouda, "Is the International Criminal Court (ICC) targeting Africa inappropriately?" last modified March 17, 2013, https://iccforum.com/africa.

and westerners), some western governments and global institutions claim that African politicians are corrupt and or inept at governance and management of local economies. Some African politicians also claim that the populace is corrupt and or inept at playing their roles for good governance and effective management of economies, (whether as civil servants, skilled workers or even as responsible citizens).

The problem here is that those who are in the position to develop viable policies and ensure effective implementation of policies on the fight against poverty in sub-Sahara are more interested in arguments and blame games than in taking concrete action. Some intellectuals would theorise and comment on who did what or failed to do what, instead of developing and implementing effective policies. Some western governments and global institutions are more concerned with showcasing dirty linens and ineptitudes of African politicians and governments and playing the politics of foreign aids which, they use to achieve multiple selfish goals. First, by providing aids, they present themselves as charitable nations to whom the ordinary person in sub-Sahara should genuflect in gratitude. Second, it proves incorrect, the claim of the neo-colonialism group that western powers are exploiters that do not want the progress and development of the sub-Sahara region. Third, they use aids to arm-twist politicians in the countries in sub-Sahara. Fourth, they dictate to the governments in sub-Sahara how and where to channel the aids, thus ensuring that such aids go back to the west through western contractors and serve only palliative measures against poverty while subverting the goals of poverty reduction and eradication. Fifth, through regular aids that serve palliative measures, they perfect a structure that allows them to withdraw the aids and cause a crisis or use it to influence the beneficiary masses to rise against a government that has become recalcitrant.

On their part, some politicians and governments in sub-Saharan Africa are more concerned with spreading propaganda against the opposition and manipulating the people rather than implement concrete measures to combat poverty in their countries. One often hears such mantra as 'government cannot do everything.' Recently, Nigeria's government has switched from fruitless campaigns against high-level corruption to a new jingle, 'change begins with you.' This new jingle blasting through the radio waves and TV channels is targeted at the ordinary citizen. A corruption free society would have to start with the poor Nigerian on the street no longer with the stupendously rich politicians and their business cronies who loot the national treasury. In fact, the civilian government of Muhammadu Buhari wasted the first four years (2015-2019) blaming the erstwhile government of Goodluck Jonathan for the bad economy and ended up not only crippling Nigeria's economy but making Nigeria the poverty capital of the world. His first four years keeps the unenviable record of the worst economic period in Nigeria's history. One of the most respected Newspapers in Nigeria, *The Guardian* of October 16, 2019 reported that in the last three years of Buhari's government, Nigeria has borrowed more than it did in the previous 30 years (Adepetun 2019). By 2018, Nigeria overtook India and became home to some 87 million people living in extreme poverty. By 2019, that number had climbed to more than 90 million. Mass emigration, unprecedented corruption and rise in crime currently define his regime which has become dictatorial than democratic. This is also the story in many countries in sub-Sahara, including the ones that are supposed to be democracies.

Overall, my hunch is that dragging a serious problem as poverty to the media where the subject becomes politicised is appalling. Trading blames and accusations and evading measures for concrete actions have characterised poverty discussions on and about the continent. Powerful countries in the west discourage practical steps such as serious capital investment, infrastructure, loans to SMEs and the big manufacturing industries which will create wealth in sub-Saharan countries. They often cite reasons such as instability and conflict, most of which are created by western power blocs directly and indirectly. Global institutions appear more like tools which western power blocs use to manipulate and control the sub-Saharan region. Some politicians and governments in the region seem to care about individual interests as against those of the people. Amidst these, poverty continues to have a free reign as it decimates the ordinary peoples of sub-Sahara. The African philosopher is, at this moment, called to duty to expose these sneering politics and awaken the consciousness of stakeholders to their moral responsibilities to the peoples of sub-Saharan Africa.

4   Conclusion

As various global institutions publish poverty statistics, the subject becomes further driven into the public space for all kinds of political interpretations. Tavis Smiley (2014, "The Politics of Poverty"), argues that the politicisation of poverty discussions might not be completely bad "…if it means that policy-makers are truly committed to eradicating poverty in our nation, but it's worse than cynical if our most vulnerable citizens are being used as pawns in a high-stakes political chess match." Smiley (2014, "The Politics of Poverty"), goes on to caution that poverty discussions often become a debate about aids, "handouts, lack of will or parental responsibility," mismanagements, bad leadership and corruption, but,

> Instead of playing the blame game and assigning fault to the victims of an economic system and political structure that has done precious little to help lift them out of poverty, it is essential that politicians, activists, businesses, faith- and community-based organisations and concerned citizens take advantage of the marginal-but-better-than-usual media attention now being paid to issues surrounding poverty. Now is the time for us to mount a coordinated, targeted and effective war on poverty. (Smiley 2014)

This war on poverty for sub-Saharan Africa must transcend the richness of blue papers such as MDGs and SDGs and involve concrete measures that would transform policies into actions. What is most dangerous about the politicisation of the problem of poverty is that it soon takes a new shape, making the problem appear less threatening, and making those who are in a position to fight the menace to lose sight of the dangers it poses to the victims. In such political climate, debates and arguments over who was right or wrong about conceptual issues; who has the magic wand to lift the people out of poverty if elected; who is to be blamed and who should be applauded, take centre stage and displace the discourse on what can and should be done to practically address the challenges posed by poverty to millions of people on the subcontinent. The time has never been more urgent for the philosopher to wade in and put the discourse in proper perspective.

References

Achebe, Chinua. 2012. *There Was a Country: A Personal History of Biafra.* New York: Penguin Group.

Adepetun, Adeyemi. 2019. "Nigeria borrowed more in last three years than it did in 30 years," *The Guardian,* 16 October, 2019. https://guardian.ng/business-services/nigeria-borrowed-more-in-last-three-years-than-it-did-in-30-years/

Alexander, Larry. 2000. "Deontology at the Threshold." *San Diego Law Review* 37: 893–912.

Al Jazeera, 2019. "US bars entry to ICC members probing 'war crimes' in Afghanistan," last modified 15 March, 2019, https://www.aljazeera.com/news/2019/03/bars-entry-icc-members-probing-war-crimes-afghanistan-190315191933901.html

Bensouda, Fatou. 1789/1907. "Is the International Criminal Court (ICC) targeting Africa inappropriately?" last modified March 17, 2013, https://iccforum.com/africa.

Bentham, Jeremy. *An Introduction to the Principles of Morals and Legislation.* Oxford: Clarendon Press.

Chimakonam, O. Jonathan. 2019. "Addressing the Problem of Mass Poverty in the Sub-Saharan Africa: Conversational Thinking as a Tool for Inclusive Development." *Filosofia Theoretica: Journal of African Philosophy, Culture and Religions* 8: 141-162 DOI: https://dx.doi.org/10.4314/ft.v8i1.10

Chimakonam, O. Jonathan. 2020. "Othering, Re-othering, and De-othering: Interrogating the Skolombo's Fight-Back Strategy," Handbook of African Philosophy of Difference, E. Imafidon (ed.). Cham: Springer, 433-448.

Chimakonam, O. Jonathan. 2020. "Where Are We in the Global Poverty Measurement? The Human Minimum Model as a Veritable Option," *Journal of Asian and African Studies* 55: 509–521.

Chimakonam, O. Jonathan. 2017. "African Philosophy and Global Epistemic Injustice," *Journal of Global Ethics* 13: 120-137, DOI: 10.1080/17449626.2017.1364660

Chinweizu, Ibekwe. 1975. *The West and the Rest of Us: White Predators, Black Slavers and the African Elite.* New York: Random House.

Driver, Julia. 2014. "The History of Utilitarianism," *The Stanford Encyclopedia of Philosophy.* Edward N. Zalta (ed.), last modified. Assessed October 12, 2019. https://plato.stanford.edu/entries/utilitarianism-history/

Egbai, O. Uti., and Chimakonam, O. Jonathan. 2019. "Protecting the Rights of Victims in Transitional Justice: An Interrogation of Amnesty," *African Human Rights Law Journal* 19: 608-623. http://dx.doi.org/10.17159/1996-2096/2019/v19n2a3

Kharas, Homi, Hamel, Kristofer and Hofer, Martin. 2018. "The Start of a New Poverty Narrative," *Brookings Institutions* Blog, last modified, 19 June, 2018. Accessed, 6 August, 2018. https://www.brookings.edu/blog/future-development/2018/06/19/the-start-of-a-new-poverty-narrative/

Kennedy, Merrit. 2019. "World Criminal Court Rejects Probe into U.S. Actions in Afghanistan," last

modified, 12 April, 2019. Assessed, 12 October, 2019. https://www.npr.org/2019/04/12/712721556/world-criminal-court-rejects-probe-into-u-s-actions-in-afghanistan

Mazrui, A. Ali. 1980. *The African Condition: A Political Diagnosis.* London: Heinemann.

Mill, John Stuart. 1861/1998. *Utilitarianism*, Roger Crisp (ed.). Oxford: Oxford University Press.

Müller-Jung, Friederike. 2018. "World Bank report: Poverty rates remain high in Africa," last modified, October17, 2018. Retrieved October 11, 2019. https://www.dw.com/en/world-bank-report-poverty-rates-remain-high-in-africa/a-45926382.

Nkrumah, Kwame. 1965. *Neo-Colonialism, The Last Stage of Imperialism.* London: Thomas Nelson & Sons, Ltd.

Nozick, Robert. 1974. *Anarchy, State and Utopia.* Cambridge: Blackwell.

Oruka, H. Odera. 1989/1997. "The Philosophy of Foreign Aid: A Question of the Right to a Human Minimum." Reprinted in Oruka Odera, *Practical Philosophy: In search of an Ethical Minimum.* Nairobi: East African Educational Publishers, 81-93.

Oruka, H. Oruka. 1976/1985. *Punishment and Terrorism in Africa: Problems in the Philosophy and Practice of Punishment*, 2nd Edn. Nairobi: Kenya Literature Bureau.

Patel, Nirav. 2018. "Understanding poverty in Africa." *Africa in Focus Series. The Brookings Institution,* Wednesday, 21 November, 2018. Assessed, 11 October, 2019. https://www.brookings.edu/blog/africa-in-focus/2018/11/21/figure-of-the-week-understanding-poverty-in-africa/.

Rodney, Walter. 1972. *How Europe Underdeveloped Africa.*London: Bogle-L'Ouverture Publication.

Santos, S. Boaventura. 2016. "Epistemologies of the south and the future," *European South* 1: 17-29.

Smiley, Tavis. 2014. "The Politics of Poverty." 23 May, 2014. Assessed, 10 September, 2018. https://talkpoverty.org/2014/05/23/redlener/.

Wadhwa, Divyanshi. 2018. "The number of extremely poor people continues to rise in Sub-Saharan Africa," 19 September, 2018. Assessed, 11 October, 2019. https://blogs.worldbank.org/opendata/number-extremely-poor-people-continues-rise-sub-saharan-africa.

The World Bank. 2018. *Poverty and Shared Prosperity 2018: Piecing Together the Poverty Puzzle.* Washington DC: International Bank for Reconstruction and Development.

Vallentyne, Peter. 2014. "Libertarianism," *The Stanford Encyclopedia of Philosophy.* Edward N. Zalta (ed.), last modified, 2014. Assessed, 12 October, 2019. https://plato.stanford.edu/archives/sum2014/entries/libertarianism/.

CHAPTER 11

Informality, Marginality and the State: A Case Study of Low-Income Households in Budiriro, Harare, Zimbabwe

Tafadzwa Chevo

1   Introduction

Urbanisation in Sub-Saharan Africa (SSA) continues to increase, accelerate and expand. In SSA, urbanisation is twice the global average, making it the highest in the world (Manjengwa, et al 2016). Estimates project that by 2030, Cairo, Kinshasa and Lagos will have populations that exceed 20 million while Johannesburg, Luanda and Dar es Salaam will add 10 million inhabitants in the same year (Bjarneseen and Mats, 2008). At the same time, the world's population living in urban areas is expected to increase from 53% to a projected 70% by 2050 (Mpanje, 2018). This urbanisation translates into the intensification of varied livelihood activities, the intersection of bodies and technologies (Simone, 2004; UN-Habitat, 2016). Most of the urbanisation is taking place informally and concentrated in high-density low-income urban areas where the infrastructure is in most cases, half-built, underdeveloped, overused, fragmented and makeshift. Services are also expensive, erratic with this inefficiency resulting in the urbanisation of diseases such as cholera (Simone, 2004; Muscmwa, 2010).

As with other African urban contexts in Zimbabwe, the urbanisation of poverty is worsened by the failure of decision-making centres such as local and central governments to formulate and implement social, economic and political policies that generally contribute to the alleviation of poverty (Mlambo, 2017). The governments are engaged in as noted by Simone (2004) endless trickery, pronouncements of progress combined with sophisticated new ways of taxing the population. Consequently, urban residents encounter institutions, policies, and services that are inadequate, inaccessible, indifferent, unaffordable and hostile to their needs. Everyday living is characterised by over crowdedness, unhygienic conditions and lack of clean water (Woolcock, 2005; Manjengwa et al 2016).

In response to these dynamics, a significant amount of literature has emerged examining the nature and form of livelihood practices in difficult and challenging contexts such as those in urban Zimbabwe. For example, a study by Gukurume (2015) on livelihood resilience traces the lived experiences of individuals involved in money-burning activities and explores the dynamics and challenges of trading in foreign currency during the era of hyperinflation in Harare. In another study by Tawodzera and Zanamwe (2016), the authors examine various livelihood and income-generating activities amongst poor urban households in Harare in the context of economic crisis. The researchers show how these households are deriving their incomes from part-time and full-time employment, informal sector activity, remittances, rent, pensions, gifts and aid, among other livelihood strategies. In a different study on urban poverty in two low-income neighbourhoods (Highfield and Epworth) located in and near Harare, (Manjengwa et al, 2016) found high levels of income-based poverty mainly associated with family size, low education level of the household head, lack of income from permanent employment, and low cash transfers. Further, Kamete (2010) demonstrates the oppositional spatial practices of urban youth in an authoritarian environment by highlighting how they defend their 'illicit' livelihoods, challenging the dictates of the planning systems through localised non-confrontational struggles that disrupt existing institutional arrangements and spaces.

These, and other, studies are legitimate and valuable studies, but they display a minimum attempt in exploring the production and source of informality and marginality among low income urban households. According to Gatzweiler et al (2011) marginality is an involuntary position and condition of an individual or group at the margins of social, political, economic, ecological, and biophysical systems, that prevent them from access to resources, assets, services, restraining freedom of choice, preventing the development of capabilities, and eventually causing extreme poverty. In this chapter, I argue empirically that the state, through its functioning, is the source of marginality and the resultant informality and territorial stigmatisation of relegated and dishonoured areas.

I employ Wacquant's (2019) theoretical framework on marginality. In this work, Wacquant (2019), adapts four concepts, from the work of Pierre Bourdieu (1997). These are symbolic power, bureaucratic field, social space and habitus. Wacquant (2019) through a trilogy of books, demonstrates that the state is a stratifying and classifying agency imbued with symbolic power to constitute the given by enunciating it. The state imprints itself on social space by granting authority and distribution of resources to different categories of agents. The bureaucratic field, which is the field that has monopoly over physical force, economic, cultural and symbolic capital, validates or amends the distribution of resources that results in the marginality of actors in contexts such as

Budiriro. The framework therefore sheds light on how public policies contribute to the production of both urban reality and its hierarchies. The structure of social space and distribution of resources within the urban setting is objectified in the built environment and embodied in the cognitive and affective categories that direct the practical strategies of agents in everyday life, in their social circles, on the labour market and in their dealings with public institutions.

2 Methodology and Study Context

Methodologically this chapter draws and relies on the data collected during my doctoral fieldwork using a mixed-methods research design that combined the life histories, focus group discussions and a household survey in Budiriro, Harare (Chevo, 2018). Budiriro is a low-income, high-density urban area located in the south-western part of Harare. It has a population of about 129,280 with 32,929 households (Dodge 2011; PoZ, 2010). Budiriro is generally known to be characterised by extreme poverty, inadequate infrastructure and deficient service delivery mechanisms, much like other high-density, low-income urban areas within Harare specifically, Zimbabwe generally and sub-Saharan Africa even more broadly (Boakye-Ansah et al., 2016). Indeed, the depth of poverty and poor service delivery led to a cholera outbreak in the year 2008 in Zimbabwe; over four thousand people died from the disease, with Budiriro being seen as the epicentre of this epidemic (Musemwa, 2010; Kone-Coulibaly et al., 2010). In the following section, I examine how state activities have influenced the livelihood practices of low-income households located in Budiriro and then go on to the discussion of findings and conclusion sections of the chapter.

3 Economic Decline and Informal Sector Livelihoods

Since the year 2000, Zimbabwe's economy has experienced a continuous decline. During fieldwork, the decline of the national economy of Zimbabwe was one of the significant contemporary influences shaping people's livelihoods, including in Budiriro. When asked how the economic decline had impacted on their livelihoods, participants in the study observed that their livelihoods had been negatively impacted. In the focus group discussions, for example, participants generally perceived and experienced a drop in their household livelihoods and well-being, which was understood in terms of the broader economic crisis. One FGD respondent had the following to say:

The main reason our businesses are not performing well is that everyone these days does not have money. There is no money; the person you are selling to has no money. What is needed is money. For example, I am into fish vending. Ten years ago, after working for three months, I was able to work and generate enough profit that allowed me to purchase a cow. I worked for another two months and bought another cow. If I am to work for three months with the way things are today, I will not do the same. Back then a landlord would order fish worth $30 per month, those formally employed would do the same. Those in South Africa with children here [Zimbabwe] would even place orders worth $50. Nowadays the situation is different; those living in South Africa will say that their money is not enough, those formally employed will tell you that they have not yet been paid and others buy goods on credit but will not honour their debts; and those that used to order fish for $30 now order fish for $3. Those that are formally employed will say they will pay you when they get paid, but their payday never arrives. (Focus Group Discussion)

In another focus group discussion, respondents mentioned that before 2005 they were able to pay school fees for their children and purchase enough food for household consumption. This is not possible because of either loss or lack of employment, or jobs simply not paying a living wage. Blaming the economy for her current hardships, a woman who was a street vendor stationed in Budiriro asserted that, before the economic decline, she was able to survive and look after her children using the profits that she made from her small business: "I am one of those who was able to sell goods worth over a $100 in a week. We were able to buy food and pay school fees for our children; this is now in the past. Now we only come here just to get a dollar to buy relish for our families. The economy is to blame for our hardships" (Interview).

The economic troubles impacted profit margins in the informal sector since the purchasing power of clientele also reduced. A related issue was the all-around inability to save money to meet future household needs. Budiriro residents hence stressed that they could not save enough money as capital to start new businesses or even to expand and grow existing businesses. As one person said: "We are facing challenges in accessing capital to start new businesses; the money that we are supposed to use to expand our businesses ends up being used for rent and other basic commodities hence leading us into bankruptcy" (FGD). This was reiterated in another FGD: "People are just able to survive. They cannot save their money and do anything tangible; they just work to meet basic food needs in most cases" (FGD). All this implies that people involved in informal economic activities have entered into a survivalist mode of livelihood existence as a result of the poor performance of the economy.

4 Formal Sector Jobs Non-viable?

Concerning formal sector livelihoods (or work within the formal economy), a majority of respondents stated that they once had access to a formal sector salaried or wage-earning job, mostly in private companies. Formal employment was seen in the past as the conventional pathway out of poverty. With the collapse of the national economy, however, this is no longer the case such that the normal became exceptional. During data collection, five people spoke of being promoted in their place of employment in days gone by, including from a general hand to middle and even senior-level positions. One respondent named Daniel (Interview) is currently a trader of second-hand household products (such as refrigerators and electric stoves). When he initially moved to Harare, he was a general hand at the Dairy Board (the largest milk company in the country) and rose to the position of boiler operator after the company sent him for training and attained the necessary certificate. Another respondent (Interview) had joined a construction company as a general hand and rose through the ranks to become site clerk after working for 17 years with the company. A general thread within these (and other) stories was that, although they had been promoted, they felt compelled eventually to leave formal employment because the purchasing power of their income was declining. For many workers, transport costs consumed an increasing portion of the monthly wage, leading to voluntary resignations from employment. A resident who had moved from the rural areas and worked as a shopkeeper in an Indian-owned shop had the following to say about why he left his job and moved into the informal sector after only eight months of employment: "I left the job in 2008 when the economic situation had declined. Economic hardships led me into this desperation [vending]. I was working for an Indian owned electrical shop, and during those days, the Indians were not paying sustainable and viable salaries. I could not even afford to come to work with the salary they were giving me" (Interview).

Thus, the deteriorating economic trajectory, characterised by hyperinflation and employment contraction, shaped people's livelihoods by driving them from the formal economic sector into informal sector livelihoods. It seemed that participation in the informal sector (through for example buying and selling goods) became the only sensible and rational activity to undertake to eke out a living by selling any commodity they could get their hands on. One respondent had this to say:

> It is not that buying and selling are much more lucrative than formal sector jobs, it is just that there is not much to do and vending has become the last resort. You cannot just sit; one has to do something. Vending these days is not even that rewarding. You will be lucky if you get 10 per cent profit. In the past, for instance, you would buy a suit or dress at $20 and sell it at $100. These days even one South African Rand profit is possible, and you have to be content with that type of profit. It is actually better to get one rand (R1) profit than to incur a loss'. (Focus Group Discussion)

The decline in formal employment as a useful livelihood activity challenged prevailing norms and assumptions about livelihoods. This in a sense, entailed a crisis in habitus, insofar as habitus is the product of an ingrained history which produces collective practices following schemes engendered by history. Deeply-embedded expectations around livelihood practices, therefore, were disrupted by the context of economic turmoil, and this led to a re-evaluation of what are suitable livelihood strategies under changed circumstances. It seems clear that, to some extent, Budiriro residents still prefer formal employment which (ideally) would pay a living wage or at least provide a regular source of income. With formal employment being scarce, insecure and irregular in the face of a decrease in real wages, the status of employment became regarded, however, as a drain on household resources which could be better used elsewhere.

5 Dollarising Livelihoods

Dollarisation introduced in Zimbabwe in 2009 is credited with stabilising the economy (including lessening price fluctuations), eliminating hyper-inflation and improving incomes for working Zimbabweans when compared to the days of the Zimbabwean dollar (Nkomazana and Niyambanira, 2014; African Development, Bank 2015). Nevertheless, the Budiriro study shows that, under dollarisation, some companies were unable to recapitalise, leading to a loss of formal employment. As well, dollarisation sometimes limited the ability of people to save and invest. One Budiriro woman in the informal sector mentioned that, during the hyper-inflation era, she was able to save money from her business (in foreign currencies) and this enabled her to purchase a residential stand (plot of land). However, after dollarisation, she has not been able to save or invest as earnings have declined. Quantitative evidence from the study shows that Budiriro working people lost employment as the Zimbabwean economy worsened and that this was particularly prevalent after the economy was dollarised. Figure 11.1 shows the trend of Budiriro people leaving employment from 1970–2015 (either voluntarily or through compulsion) as the economic situation declined. In total, 87 people reported leaving employment and the proportion of those who left by year is shown below. Important to note is that the number of household heads leaving paid formal employment increased significantly between 2000 and 2015, and this was particularly dramatic from the year 2010 onward

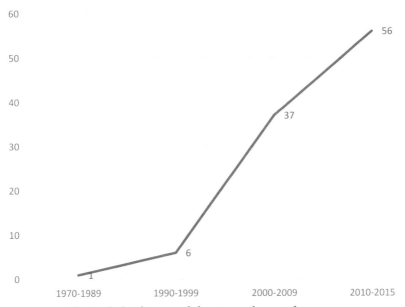

FIGURE 11.1 The trend of Budiriro people leaving employment from 1970–2015

6 Economic Institutional Arrangements and the Nature of Livelihoods

In addition to the factors discussed thus far, the study also revealed that economic institutional arrangements play a crucial role in the shaping of livelihood activities in Budiriro. According to Autio and Fu (2014), economic institutional arrangements and regulate the conditions for conducting business transactions within a given national economy. Where there are reliable and high-quality economic institutions, then operating a business becomes more straightforward and streamlined (Acs, Autio and Sqerb, 2014). At the same time, strict regulations might be seen and experienced as troublesome and cumbersome, particularly for those trying to start up a business.

In this respect, respondents in the Budiriro study involved in informal economic activities described their experiences with economic institutional arrangements as bureaucratic and laced with red-tape such that some even abandoned or avoided any efforts to formalise their income-generating activities. In this sense, they preferred to operate under the radar of the state. The following points from one focus group discussion are illustrative:

TT: There are a lot of legal procedures to be followed when opening up a company that makes it difficult, cumbersome and costly for most people here in Budiriro to open up a company. There is what they call tax clearance; you ought to have a tax clearance form if you are to supply large organisations.

KC: There is also what is called the vendor number, which supermarkets want when you are about to sell products to them. You should pay again in order to have it.

WD: If you happen to get all things done, operating licenses are too exorbitant again.

EM: You need at least $500 to open up a new business if you are to follow the rules. (Focus Group Discussion)

All this is further complicated by what was also said in this FGD, namely, the need for up-front funds for such charges (in addition to start-up capital for the business itself) when – simultaneously – small business owners are refused loans from mainstream financial institutions because of the lack of collateral as security. In a separate FGD, respondents spoke not only about the costs incurred for licensing purposes, but also the bribes that are usually demanded by officials issuing the licenses as well as other forms of extraction and extortion (for example, by the police):

> The licensing of small grocery shops should be made easier rather and much more transparent. Huge sums of money are being demanded, making it very difficult to open a new legal business. In addition to the bribing that we have to do, the municipal police make expansion and formalising of our businesses impossible. (Focus Group Discussion)

This corruption is complicated by other aspects of their interaction with regulatory authorities (including customs officials for cross-border traders) in combination with the overall declining economic environment:

> The opportunities are plenty; people can cross the border to go and get wares from Zambia or South Africa for resale here in Zimbabwe, but the

customs officials at the border are very corrupt. They take money from you there, and when you come here [Budiriro] people take things and promise to pay up in instalments, but it is increasingly becoming difficult for them to pay in time. (Focus Group Discussion)

The economic institutional arrangements put in place by the state within Zimbabwe do not provide for a conducive business environment for lower-income households and even for official entry into business activities. The extraction of various forms of rent by state officials certainly adds to the potential burden for Budiriro residents. It is not surprising then that Budiriro households seek to operate outside the grip of state regulations by side-stepping them, thereby avoiding the time and effort (and money) involved in fulfilling and abiding by various state requirements as embodied in economic institutions. Operating beyond the regulations at least frees up money which is then directly used in the informal economic activity, including the purchase of supplies in the case of traders.

7   Disappearance or Death of Social Security

Another significant influence on the livelihoods of households in Budiriro is the absence of, the decline in, or even the complete disappearance of social protection for those involved in the formal economic sector. Within the formal sector, workers are entitled to social protection schemes such as pensions, severance packages, unemployment insurance and cash transfers. These schemes have the function of protecting levels of household consumption and shielding households when they experience various covariate and idiosyncratic shocks such as unemployment, illness or death within the household. As a result of the economic decline and hyperinflation between the years 2000 and 2008, respondents indicated that these entitlements often simply fell away. For example, one Budiriro household head mentioned that upon retirement, and after working for 42 years, he did not receive his retirement benefits. When asked why he did not obtain any retirement benefits after working for such a long time, he indicated that something unknown to him happened at the company, which led to him and a number of his colleagues not getting their benefits. He said that they sought legal assistance on this matter, but to no avail. He, however, receives a monthly pension (of only $16USD) from the National Social Security Authority (NSSA), which he supplements by working as a tailor and a security guard.

Though in the past the option of suing a company for benefits lost may have been a viable alternative, in the hyperinflationary environment it seemed to formal sector workers that the labour laws governing the formal sector effectively had been suspended or abandoned. Even if a retirement package was forthcoming, the value of the package under hyperinflationary conditions was minuscule and did not provide any long-term post-employment household security. Either way, there were desperate attempts via the informal economy or casual employment to make ends meet under harsh circumstances. Hence, the collapse of Zimbabwe's economy not only had a significant influence on household-based livelihoods but also shaped the kinds of livelihood strategies they could pursue as alternative livelihood options.

8 Credit, Capital and Clients

Lack of financial capital, which arises in part because of ongoing employment and wage challenges amongst Budiriro households, has clear implications for income-generation activities within the informal economy. Household heads thus highlighted that low levels of financial capital inhibit any capacity to expand their informal economic activities. This absence of sufficient capital relates to the survivalist character of the Budiriro informal economy, as low-end, low-capital, low-profit businesses. This is further complicated by the problems faced in accessing loans from formal financial institutions, and the expensive and arduous task of registering a business. In the quantitative survey, close to 90 per cent of the households running an informal enterprise indicated that they faced various constraints in their operations. These constraints included lack of access to credit, lack of capital, inputs and technology, issues related to transport, access to markets, the irregular supply of inputs, strict state regulations, dwindling clientele base and bad debts amongst customers purchasing on credit. The three most essential constraints were lack of credit, lack of capital and insufficient clientele base. During the life history interviews and focus group discussions, these constraints were also highlighted. Lack of capital and lack of credit were intimately connected, as credit could not be used as a source of capital for kick-starting or expanding informal businesses. To emphasise, the absence of collateral for loan security was a determining factor in this regard. Budiriro heads indicated that, unlike civil servants or those who are employed in the corporate economy and receive a salary regularly, financial firms always stress the lack of collateral security as the basis for denying them any line of credit. Lack of access to loans is reflected in the survey data, with more than 90 per cent of those running informal businesses having no access to loans of any kind. The following comments from an FGD bring this to the fore:

> We cannot borrow any money because some of us are indigenous business people; money lenders do not lend us money because we do not have any collateral security and that is different from civil servants. Banks cannot lend us money even under the numerous government schemes for small businesses because we just cannot fulfil the required prerequisites. In most cases, they require a payslip and other papers that we do not have. There are small money lenders in Budiriro, but the way they do business and the kind of interest rates they charge are too much; money should be paid back daily which is not easy for some of us. The way they do business makes us entangled to them because you will not be able to separate yourself away from them. After all, the interest rates are too high. (Focus Group Discussion)

Hence, though informal lenders based in Budiriro are an alternative to formal financial institutions, the former charge interest rates far above the market-rate and hence are not a suitable option for low-income Budiriro households. Because of low levels of capitalisation (and of profit) within the Budiriro informal economy, the chances of embarking on an expansion of businesses is almost nil, particularly given the dire state of the national economy. Even ensuring that operational costs are met daily becomes a severe challenge. Any profit generated, which ideally should be in part ploughed back into the business, is used for consumption purposes in paying housing rent and purchasing essential household commodities. Any loan funds which may be available for the informal economy is, according to Budiriro heads, inaccessible unless the head has connections or contacts within the disbursing agency.

9 Fast Track Land Reform

Even the unconstitutional taking over of white commercial farms, which the state articulated as a pro-poor and pro-redistribution measure, had direct and indirect implications for Budiriro livelihoods. In a smaller number of cases, the effect was very direct. For example, one respondent directly linked the loss of his employment as a research assistant to the land reform programme:

> I worked from 1995–1999 on a research project which was led by a Zimbabwean but involved volunteers from America, including American doctors and lawyers. The research project stopped because of the land reform programme. It was affected by the political situation that attained at the time. Some white farmers were being murdered, and so the sponsors

of that research decided to withdraw. We had to stop because we were working in rural areas. They [project leaders] feared their volunteers and staff would be caught up in what was happening in the country at that time. ... There was a lot of tension and so the research team I was working decided to leave due to concerns about their security (Interview)

Indirectly, land reform contributed to a downsizing 'of the national (including urban) economy and the loss of employment for urban households in Harare and elsewhere. Those employed in the agro-industrial sector, either up-stream or down-stream, experienced more directly the undercutting of agricultural production on commercial farms. In this regard, one head had been employed at a company selling irrigation pipes but then lost his employment because of land reform: "We were paid on a weekly basis, and I think we were getting 80–100 dollars per week... My life changed because the money I was now getting was far much better than what I could get whilst I was in Domboshava. The company closed soon after the land reform programme in 2003" (Interview).

The Interviewee said that, because of his employment in the agro-industry and the estimated equivalent of US$100 he was earning, his life had improved significantly. He was able to buy cattle and some household goods (such as a kitchen unit and bed) as well as to pay part of his bride price. However, as indicated, after the fast track land reform programme was implemented in the early 2000s, the company closed down. This was a turning point in his life as his life worsened and never improved after he lost this job. Subsequently, he moved and started working at a nearby farm as a general hand and later decided to leave his job when the inflation rate had reached 217 million per cent. It had become senseless to continue working, earning an income that could not sustain him and his family. Finally, he found himself on the streets of Harare in the informal economy as a pushcart driver. The devastating ripple effects from the massive drop in agricultural production in the immediate years after fast track, and particularly given the significance of irrigation equipment to commercial farmers, were clearly evident in the life and livelihood of this Budiriro resident.

In fact, according to Chimhowu (2010), before the year 2000, the agricultural sector in Zimbabwe was the largest employer and earner of foreign currency, generating 30 per cent of formal employment inclusive of the agro-industry. Significantly, the sector accounted for between 13 and 19 per cent of the Gross Domestic Product of the country, provided 60 per cent of the raw materials for the manufacturing industry and generated between 40 to 50 per cent of the total export revenues (of which 50 percent of this came from tobacco sales). The fast track programme had mainly political and social objectives, with its implications for the agrarian and national economies not pronounced in its formulation and implementation. In an unmediated or mediated fashion, the fast track was to have repercussions for the livelihood trajectories and pathways of Budiriro households, and they had to scramble to cushion these repercussions through seeking alternative livelihood options.

10   Pernicious Urban Planning and Household Livelihoods in Budiriro

Other government policies and actions also influence people's livelihoods in Budiriro. Where policies are pro-poor and less prohibitive, urban people can make a living more efficiently; however, when policies are not conducive to easing livelihood burdens, any ability to make a living in urban spaces becomes curtailed. In various focus group discussions and life history interviews, respondents indicated that central government and local municipal officials in Harare make their livelihood activities difficult. One head had the following to say: "For me starting a business was not that difficult. It was after I started being a vendor that I began to have problems with the police. My goods are confiscated all the time. But I have to keep on doing this business. I have no other means for survival. I have financial problems that persist" (Interview).

Another case from the study clearly illustrates how government through policy pronouncements illegalises certain activities which were once legal; it closes down a deeply-rooted livelihood strategy which urban poor have depended upon historically. Thus one household head had been engaged in the informal public transport sector (using Peugeot 404s) and highlighted that the decision by the government to ban these cars in 1995 from the road dramatically affected his livelihood:

> I will not mince my words on this one, but I wish the government had given us alternative projects to do when they gave that directive to ban all Peugeot 404s on the roads. I am sure my life would be much better today if that had not happened. Owning and driving those cars was the direction I had taken in terms of sustaining my livelihood. But it all ended when the government gave that directive to ban the cars of the road. Today my brothers are destitute. I actually paid for their education until they went on to get their driver's licenses. Now one is selling petrol somewhere in Harare and the other is growing sugarcane for resale in Nyanga. I can tell you, if that directive had not been given, I would have been able to elevate my immediate family's livelihoods. Had the government offered us loans to purchase the approved sixteen-sitter mini buses, then I am sure things

would be different for my family and me. It was just a sudden directive by the government and suddenly we had no income.... I just had to come up with another plan. I started to think about my future, how was I to survive when the time came for me to retire. It was very apparent that no one was going to look after me. (Interview)

The case, of course, demonstrates the importance of the informal sector in its capacity to provide employment and livelihood to people. However, a central state policy cascading down to urban spaces closed down a long-term viable informal economic activity (transport) in a period of heightening economic decline. The government shut down a significant dimension of the public transport system in Harare, even though it was widely recognised as a critical source of employment and part of the solution to the urban transport shortage (Mutizwa-Mangiza, 1995). The government had claimed that the Peugeot 404s (known colloquially as emergency taxis) were not well-maintained and were the cause of the high vehicular accident rate in urban areas. A study undertaken by Maunder and Pearce (1999) noted that the total number of reported accidents increased in Zimbabwe from 21,150 in 1992 to 38,777 in 1996, with 1,066 and 1,205 fatalities, respectively. But they concluded that only 7 per cent of the accidents were due to vehicle defects, with over 80 per cent arising from driver misjudgments. A supposed attempt to decrease vehicular accidents by phasing out emergency taxis led, to the contrary, to phasing out a crucial livelihood activity.

The ramifications for the Budiriro head (quoted above) and his household were utterly devastating, and he was unable to recover from this shock. His experience illuminates the findings of Baulch and Davis (2008) who established that upward and downward movements in livelihood trajectories regularly take on different forms. In particular, upward movements are gradual and incremental, while downward movements tend to be more abrupt and jagged. In the case of this Budiriro head, his upward movement had entailed a lengthy process of exploring the transport gap through working for an employer, years of saving, a supportive employer, and supportive rural-urban linkages, all in combination with an enabling government public transport policy. The outcome was a viable and secure livelihood activity. He had thus moved from being a public transit driver at a company to become an owner in his own right, able even to train his brothers and employ them. He was in the process of building a house where his family could live and also generate rental income through this. With the government's shift of policy on public transport, his processes of accumulation and his condition of security came to an abrupt and immediate end.

11 Operation Murambatsvina and Its Impact on Livelihood Strategies

While policies that prohibit people from conducting business in unauthorised places, or constructing houses without seeking urban council's permission, are meant to protect the urban environment, such policies can also be detrimental to the livelihoods of poor people if these are indiscriminately applied. For example, a respondent named Patrick who owned a barbershop in Harare before Operation *Murambatsvina* (Restore Order) had expanded his barbershop into a saloon and was able to pay his house rent, purchase a bed and a wardrobe, and pay school fees for his sibling. He invested his savings from this effort into equipment and other necessities for his saloon. His business expanded, and he was able to maintain his client base. After five years of business growth, in 2005 his building was demolished by Operation *Murambatsvina* because it had been constructed without the necessary permission and approval from the city council. After the demolition, he sold his equipment and downgraded his operation from a salon which employed other people to an individually-run barbershop; from working in a saloon with brick walls and a roof to operating from a shack made of cardboard boxes adjacent to a busy minibus terminal in Budiriro. The shop near the terminal was meant to enable him to obtain as many walk-by customers as possible. The makeshift cardboard shelter was also meant to protect him against losses similar to those he incurred if an operation such as Operation Restore Order was launched again. Ten years after the operation, Patrick was simply unable to recover from the effects of the operation. Policies such as Operation *Murambatsvina*, which are supposedly designed to maintain orderliness and cleanliness, may have unintended longer-term consequences. In the case of Patrick, he was not prepared to reinvest in fixed structures and expand his business because of fears concerning losses arising from future state 'urban renewal' programmes.

12 Discussion of Findings

What is clear from findings presented above is that the functioning of the state in Zimbabwe has produced a social space that has driven urbanites such as those from Budiriro into social, economic and political marginality. The marginality is often characterised by a heavy reliance on informal sector livelihoods and practices (Mlambo, 2017; Chevo 2018). The state, through its network of national and local administrative agencies, has produced a contracting national economy. The institutional deficiencies within the state do little to guarantee property rights and promote investment through policies such as the fast track land reform and urban renewal programmes. Even well-intentioned policies such as dollarisation might have stabilised but it did not lead to any economic upturn. For Budiriro household-heads, dollarisation meant an absolute drop in urban employment (particularly of stable, permanent employment), a burgeoning of the informal economy and the pursuit of a diversified livelihood portfolio – often consisting of erratic, precarious and short-term activities – as a way of managing risk for many households. Within this sector, economic constraints highlighted included insufficient access to financial credit and commodity markets, which undermined the possibility that informal economic activities would be able to move beyond being low capital and low profit, survivalist businesses. In almost all cases, Budiriro households indicated that the declining performance of the formal economy increased competition within the informal sector, a decline in the purchasing power of customers and a decrease in the number of sales per day. Given the growing significance of the informal economy for Budiriro households, this thwarted their effort in maintaining a living while also trying simultaneously to guard against both idiosyncratic and covariate shocks.

The actions and inactions of the state have impacted on the social space, habitus, agency and livelihood practices of households in Budiriro in multifaceted ways. This chapter has attempted to show the utility of Wacquant's cartography on analysing the production of marginality in low income high density urban areas within a sub-Saharan African context. The analysis points to the functioning of the state as the producer of social, economic and political marginality. The symbolic power and the bureaucratic field possessed and controlled by the state generate a juxtaposition of social positions arranged along the volume of economic and cultural capital social actors possess. It is clear that these interactions are objectified in the poor infrastructure and deficient service delivery occurring in Budiriro which led to the epicentre of the cholera epidemic in 2008. Not only does this stigmatise the territory, but it also shapes the livelihood practices, human experience and actor's relationship with the state. Given the monopoly the Zimbabwean state has over physical force and judicial power, it is also clear from this study that the state has a significant role to play in the determination of livelihood paths followed by residents in low income areas such as Budiriro. Livelihood practices in Budiriro have resulted from and are constituted by an ongoing crisis marked by conjunctures that necessitate some form and level of conscious reasoning in making livelihood decisions and pursuing livelihood options. Consistent with Wacquant's view that the habitus propels lines of action that reaffirm or alter the structures of social space, in Budiriro, reflexivity rarely comes into play.

13 Conclusion

This chapter has argued that the functioning and workings of the state have impacted in numerous ways on the nature of livelihood practices adopted by household heads in Budiriro and thereby having an implication on the household's capacity to respond to poverty and inequality. Utilising Wacquant's (2019) analytic cartography allows one to illuminate and detect state activities directed at producing marginality upstream and how the state treats marginality downstream within a context of deindustrialised urbanisation. This is a field characterised by deprivation and marginalisation in the context of multiple and shifting political and economic crises. It is also a field which, despite changes over time, remains stable in its crucial political and economic factors and to which households in Budiriro have become accustomed. Households exist within this urban livelihood field and drawn upon available assets in a manner which does not seek to challenge or dismantle this field; rather, they work within it and, if possible, work it to their best advantage.

References

Acs, Zoltan J, Erkko Autio, and László Szerb. "National Systems of Entrepreneurship: Measurement Issues and Policy Implications." *Research Policy* 43, no. 3 (2014): 476–94.

Autio, Erkko, and Kun Fu. "Economic and Political Institutions and Entry into Formal and Informal Entrepreneurship." *Asia Pacific Journal of Management* 32, no. 1 (2015): 67–94.

Bjarnesen, Jesper, and Mats Utas. "Introduction Urban Kinship: The Micro-Politics of Proximity and Relatedness in African Cities." *Africa* 88, no. S1 (2018): S1-S11.

Chevo, Tafadzwa. "The Construction of Household Livelihood Strategies in Urban Areas: The Case of Budiriro, Harare, Zimbabwe." (2018).

Gatzweiler, Franz W., and Heike Baumüller. "Marginality—A framework for analyzing causal complexities of poverty." In *Marginality*, pp. 27–40. Springer, Dordrecht, 2014.

Gukurume, Simbarashe. "Livelihood Resilience in a Hyperinflationary Environment: Experiences of People Engaging in Money-Burning (Kubhena Mari) Transactions in Harare, Zimbabwe." *Social Dynamics* 41, no. 2 (2015): 219–34.

Jones, Jeremy L. "'Nothing Is Straight in Zimbabwe': The Rise of the Kukiya-Kiya Economy 2000–2008." *Journal of Southern African Studies* 36, no. 2 (2010): 285–99.

Kamete, Amin Y. "Defending Illicit Livelihoods: Youth Resistance in Harare's Contested Spaces." *International journal of urban and regional research* 34, no. 1 (2010): 55–75.

Lourenço-Lindell, Ilda. "Walking the Tight Rope: Informal Livelihoods and Social Networks in a West African City." Acta Universitatis Stockholmiensis, 2002.

Manjengwa, Jeanette, Collen Matema, and Doreen Tirivanhu. "Understanding Urban Poverty in Two High-Density Suburbs of Harare, Zimbabwe." *Development Southern Africa* 33, no. 1 (2016): 23–38.

Mlambo, Alois S. "From an Industrial Powerhouse to a Nation of Vendors: Over Two Decades of Economic Decline and Deindustrialization in Zimbabwe 1990–2015." *Journal of Developing Societies* 33, no. 1 (2017): 99–125.

Mpanje, Desire, Pat Gibbons, and Ronan McDermott. "Social Capital in Vulnerable Urban Settings: An Analytical Framework." *Journal of International Humanitarian Action* 3, no. 1 (2018): 4.

Musemwa, Muchaparara. "From 'Sunshine City' to a Landscape of Disaster: The Politics of Water, Sanitation and Disease in Harare, Zimbabwe, 1980–2009." *Journal of Developing Societies* 26, no. 2 (2010): 165–206.

Nkomazana, Lionel, and Ferdinand Niyimbanira. "An Overview of the Economic Causes and Effects of Dollarisation: Case of Zimbabwe." *Mediterranean Journal of social sciences* 5, no. 7 (2014): 69.

Potts, Deborah. "Making a Livelihood in (and Beyond) the African City: The Experience of Zimbabwe." *Africa* 81, no. 4 (2011): 588–605.

Simone, AbdouMaliq. "People as Infrastructure: Intersecting Fragments in Johannesburg." *Public culture* 16, no. 3 (2004): 407–29.

Tawodzera, Godfrey, and Lazarus Zanamwe. *The State of Food Insecuritity in Harare, Zimbabwe.* Southern African Migration Programme, 2016.

Wacquant, Loïc. "Class, Ethnicity and State in the Making of Urban Marginality." In *Class, Ethnicity and State in the Polarized Metropolis*, 23–50: Springer, 2019.

Woolcock, Michael. "Calling on Friends and Relatives: Social Capital." *The urban poor in Latin America* (2005): 219.

PART 3

Marginalization, Terrorism and Intolerance

CHAPTER 12

Intolerance: The Activities of Ethnic Militias in Nigeria

Adeshina Francis Akindutire

1   Introduction

Nigeria as a country is made up of different and diverse communities spiced along various ethnic, religious groupings, persuasions, and different social orientations both in the rural and urban enclaves, having about 395 ethnic groups (Osaghae, 2001). Ethnicity however, is a cultural characteristic that connects a particular group of people to each other. The concept of ethnicity is rooted in the idea of societal groups, marked especially by shared tribal affiliation, religious faith, shared language, cultural and traditional origin. Ethnic groups as "human groups (other than kinship groups) held together by the belief in their common origins, provides a basis for the creation of a community" (Mbaku, 2001). However, ethnicity can be seen as referring to differences in language, religion, colour, ancestry and culture to which social meanings are attributed and around which identity and group formation occurs (Nagel, 1995).

Ethnicity can result from choice or ascription, either an individual chooses to be identified with a recognized ethnic group, or membership in a certain ethnic group can be imposed on him by the greater society (Barth, 1969). This implies that while individuals can choose their ethnicity, the choice must be acceptable to society. Ethnicity is a combination of individual choice and social imposition (Mbaku, 2001). Furthermore, ethnicity is not a permanent trait but a changing group characteristic, which means that the boundary of an ethnic group as a social category can change (Barth, 1969). By definition and features, ethnicity in its true sense has got no relationship with violence or conflict of any type as it has become with regards to the crisis in Nigeria, where the influence of two foreign religions (Islam and Christianity) have given ethnicity a different meaning. Imperatively, ethnicity and religious differences ought to bring along solidarity and support among a people who share a common ancestral linage or history irrespective of location and not the reverse.

2 What Is Ethnic Militia?

It is imperative to first and foremost understand the concept of ethnicity before we can conceptualize ethnic militias. The word ethnic can be traced to its Latin and Greek origin "Ethnos" which means nation or race. (Toland, 1993) defines ethnicity as the sense of people hood held by members of a group, sharing a common culture and history within the society (Thomson, 2000) in the same vain defines ethnic group as a community of people who are convinced that they have a common identity and based on issues of origin, kinship ties, traditions, cultural uniqueness, a shared history and possibly a shared language. Babawale (2001) see ethnicity as a highly inclusive group identify based on some notion of common origin, recruited commonly primarily from kinship and typically manifesting some measure of cultural distinctions. Ethnic militia as a concept cannot be boxed in a single definition. This implies that divergent conceptualization of the term abound. In the words of (Olukotun, 2003) ethnic militias are paramilitary forces that performed police functions within their locality while the government considers militia group as insurgent groups that engage in subversive activities against the state.

To Falana (2003) Ethnic militia in the Nigerian context is viewed as a militant organization set up to protect the interest of a particular nationality within the Nigerian Federation. In this paper, ethnic militias can therefore be seen as paramilitary actors in a given community who make political demands on the state as citizens. They are also particularistic in nature and are characterized by subversion of the capacity for deliberations, usurpation and incivility. (Adejumobi, 2002) sees these organizations as 'youth based formations that emerged with the intention of promoting and protecting the parochial interests of their ethnic groups and whose activities sometimes involve the use of violence'. Ethnic militias therefore are organized violence-oriented groups populated by diverse elements, cutting across different age strata, but drawing membership exclusively from an ethnic group and established to promote and protect the interests of an ethnic group. Ethnic militias are an extreme form of ethnic agitation for self-determination and occur when the ethnic group assumes militant posture. They serve as a social pressure group designed to influence the structure of power to the advantage of and call attention to the deteriorating material condition or political deprivation and perceived marginalization of their group or social environment.

Also, ethnic militia can be defined as the youth wing or the constabulary of an ethnic group, which has been mandated by their elders or has arrogated to themselves the duty of protecting the ethnic group. Usually ethnic militia are psychologically predisposed to thinking that their cause is just, never mind even if other people suffer in the process. Also an ethnic militia movement can be described as an extreme form of ethnic agitation for self determination as various ethnic groups assume militant postures and gradually metamorphose into militia groups which rely on ethnic identity and purport to act as machinery through which the desires of the people are actualized. The common characteristics of these ethnically inspired groups are: the resort to violence, a preponderance of youth membership and an ethnic identity affiliation (Ijomah, 2011).

From the foregoing explanations and definitions, an ethnic militia can be described as youth organization formed for the struggle against deprivation and marginalization which have transformed into violent militant youth some of who, have also changed their objectives from struggles for ethnic desires into criminal activities.

3 Theoretical Framework: Social Identity Theory

Theoretical framework refers to a postulation that guides a research. Social Identity Theory has been adopted as the theoretical framework for this study. Social identity theory was first postulated by Tajfel in 1972 to show how people perceive themselves in any group context (McNanara, 1997). He explains that group formation gives an individual a sense of social identity and people tend to ally with their in-group identity against another out-group. According to (Ashforth and Mael, 1989), social identity theory, explains how people develop a sense of membership in a particular group in the society. The major concept behind social identity theory according to (Stets and Burke, 2000) is the categorization or grouping of people in the society. The idea is that people categorize one another consciously or unconsciously to create sets of groups. Social identity is described as the category and attributes that a person is deemed to possess in relation to others. These attributes sometimes are categorized as an individual's-gender, age, profession, religion, social class and ethnic group among other values and all these form the various social identities in the society. (Imobighe, 2001)

Furthermore, social identity is based on the society and the in-group an individual finds himself or herself either by birth, sex, ethnic, race, profession and other social formations (Stets and Burke, 2000). Identity varies as an individual can be initiated by origin or created via socialization in the society. The interesting thing about identity grouping is that people can be part of multiple groups, and the part of their identity that is most dominant can override the other identities, depending on which group exacts greater influence on the individual (Hornsey, 2008). Central to the understanding of identity theory are phenomena such as, ethnicity and nationalism. Social identity theory expresses the collective or group measures in achieving certain goal(s).

Social identity theory also describes how a system of social categorizations creates and defines an individual's place of social construction in any society (Hogg, 2001). This then shows that identity is the individual's knowledge that he belongs to certain groups together with values significant to the individual's group membership. For the fact that groups only exist in relation to other social groups, they therefore, tend to derive their descriptive and evaluative properties, and their social meaning in relation to other groups. People tend to seek out social group membership as an affirmation of self–esteem and belongingness which fosters social capital and identity as capital utilization in the society. Thus, through identity, social capital is created and the group identity creates social links in which trust, bond and love are built (Baum and Ziersch, 2003; Omobowale and Olutayo, 2009).Hence social identity is also a form of social capital. In essence, social identity theory indicates that the individuals and groups also have social capital values. Social identity theory shows the utilization of identity notion, ideology, intent and value as capital for achieving social and development ends. This illustrates how people of the same identity in a society tend to exploit every means of group cohesion in achieving their aims. The utilization of identity to generate and achieve social link, uniformity, understanding, ideology and cohesion is thus referred to as *identity-capital*. Thus, identity-capital provides the ties for individuals and creates the ability to interact with their members. Identity-capital emphasizes the use of identity formation to achieve social capital. Identity-capital acts as a social tool for development and for harnessing the unity of a formed group, example an ethnic group. Social identity as capital explains the use of identity by an individual or group of individuals in realizing and accomplishing set goal(s) in the society. This explains the social link and bond of identity that is used to achieve necessary action in a group or among people in a given society. The fact about Identity-capital is that individuals of same identity tend to use their identity in cohesion to achieve a particular goal (capital).

For this study, identity is narrowed to the context of Biafra identity and its utilization as capital. Social identity explains the use of Biafra identity and consciousness as constructed among the contemporary Igbo of South-Eastern Nigeria who are currently embracing *Biafraism*, aiming to achieve Biafra symbolism and capital for social and developmental purposes. This somewhat indicates the conscious drive by the Igbo ethnic group in the construction of a new identity (that is, *Biafra*) which cohesively spurs them into action in the actualization of Igbo for self-determination in Nigeria's democratizing society. Although social links are intentionally created in social capital, social identity tends to utilize the 'unconsciously' and consciously created Biafra identity as capital.

The *Biafran* identity construction in the South-Eastern Nigeria thus generates the cohesion of oneness, understanding and creation of a network for achieving set goal (self-determination) among the people. Biafra identity creates unified bond for identity network for the general Igbo, above the 'mere' Igbo identity, thus encouraging a possible the drive for an independent nation. Ethnic identity as 'Biafrans' has created social consciousness, social link and bond among the Igbo wherever they find themselves, these have facilitated the cohesion for the continuous contest in Nigeria for Biafra renaissance in recent time. Social identity as capital, therefore, draws meaningful relationship with persons from same ethnic group (identity) to incorporate the concept of group activity as a central component in identity processes and construction in achieving set goal(s). This study adopts social identity theory to demonstrate how Biafra identity and consciousness possibly create social link for Biafra resurgence and possibly serves as capital for development in South-Eastern Nigeria. The idea of Biafra consciousness conceptualizes identity as capital in the investigation of a group's interaction for ethnic/group identity and accomplishment. Identity-capital goes beyond individual utilization; it is a wider group context that is spurred by social resource mobilization, identity cohesion and social development. In connection with identity as capital, the Biafra identity drive is used to project the Biafra resurgence and sustaining strong *Biafra* consciousness in the South-Eastern Nigeria.

4 Various Ethnic Militias in Nigeria

The various ethnic militias and social movement groups in contemporary Nigeria are undoubtedly associated with an ethnic group. They include the following, Oodua People's Congress (OPC)-Yoruba, was formed in the year during June 12, 1993. While, the Movement for Actualization of the Sovereign State of Biafra (MASSOB) was founded in the year 1999 and Movement for the Survival of Ogoni People (MOSOP)-Ogoni The Movement for the Survival of Ogoni People (MOSOP) is an Ogoni-based non-governmental, non-political apex organisation of the Ogoni ethnic minority people of South-Eastern Nigeria and was founded in 1990 with the mandate to campaign non-violently to: · Promote democratic awareness; · Protect the environment of the Ogoni People; · Seek social, economic and physical development for the region; · Protect the cultural rights and practices of the Ogoni people; and · Seek appropriate rights of self-determination for the Ogoni people.

The Movement for the Emancipation of the Niger Delta (MEND) founded in January 11th, 2006. The group's efforts are directed towards knocking down oil production in the Niger-Delta region and claims to expose exploitation and oppression of the people of the Niger-Delta and devastation of the natural environment as a result of public-private partnerships between the Federal Government of Nigeria and corporations involved in the production of oil in the Niger Delta. Its composition includes members of the *Ijaw* who accuse the government and overseas oil firms with promoting massive economic inequalities, fraud, and environmental degradation. MEND's methods include kidnap-for-ransom of oil workers, staging armed assaults on production sites, pipeline destruction, murder of Nigerian police officers, and draining off of oil and sell it to the black market. And for, The Indigenous People of Biafra (IPOB) is a group that leads the calls for Biafrans freedom from Nigeria. Its main aim is to restore an independent state of Biafra for the people of old Eastern Region of Nigeria through a referendum and was founded in the year, 2012 among others (see Adekson, 2004, Ayokhai, 2013). The sociological study of these ethnic movement groups indicate their quest and struggle for self-determination, political relevance and socio-political interest of their ethnic groups. The South-Eastern based social movement known as Movement for the Actualisation of the Sovereign State of Biafra (MASSOB) championing the struggle for Igbo ethnic nationalism. MASSOB announced that it had embarked on a non-violent exercise to re-enact the aborted secession of Biafra as an emerging nation from Nigeria.

At the launch of MASSOB in year 2000, the leader, Ralph Uwazuruike, an Indian-trained lawyer, in his message stated that the Igbo nation had not fared better since they were forcibly reunited with Nigeria following a bitter 30-month civil war (Onuoha, 2012), and should therefore, return to Biafra. This appeared impracticable, especially as the Igbo people were participating fully in the contemporary democratic dispensation. Before the emergence of MASSOB, the Oodua People's Congress (OPC) which espoused the hope of pulling the Yoruba nation out of Nigeria into an Oduduwa Republic had emerged, as a result of what they perceived as injustice (Akinyele, 2001). The Yoruba people felt highly marginalized under the various military regimes (1976–1978; 1983–1998). This perceived marginalization got to its peak following the annulment of the election believed to have been won by a Yoruba candidate, M.K.O Abiola during the June 12, 1993 presidential election (Akinyele, 2001). Thus, some Yoruba activists under the leadership of Dr. Frederick Fasheun formed the OPC to achieve the goal of actualising the sovereign state of Oduduwa Republic. The quest for self-determination is active in their also ethnic groups in the country in the post-1999 dispensation.

5   Emergence of Biafran (Ethic Militia in Nigeria)

The coming of white men gave birth to many new territories in Africa, annexation and extinction of the existing ones. A good example is, the territory known as Nigeria today was invented by the British through the annexation of different existing territories. This geographical invention precipitated the historical distortion and geographical extinction of certain territories. Biafra among other territories lost their sovereignty to this colonial arrangement. Alaba-Isama. (2013). The pre-independence political arrangements by the colonial masters divided Nigeria in to three parts; the North with 60% of the land mass, while the East and West together amounted to less than 40%. This scenario was replicated in the major political partly's power base with the NPC (Northern Peoples Congress) in the north, AG (Action Group) in the West and NCNC (National Council of Nigeria and Cameroon) mainly in the East. The NPC had an opposition party mainly based in Kano – the NEPU (the Northern Elements Progressive Union) led by Mallam Aminu Kano, and there was the party of Benue people UMBC (The United Middle Belt Congress) led by Joseph Taka. The party was in opposition to the NPC of the North and supported mainly by the people of Benue, and was ally of the Action Group in the West. All these political parties were tribal based. The NCNC, however, which was more nationally organized, though, had its stronghold mainly in the East and was Ibo-led with wide support across the country…..(Alaba-Isama, 2013).

For Chinua Achebe (2012), Biafra territory was deduced from "the bight of Biafra, the vast expanse of water covering the Continental shelf into which the Niger empties before flowing into the gulf of Biafra." In John Mitchell comprehensive map intrinsically made for resolving border disputes, it's also elucidated that the pertinent estuaries from where the rivers flew into the Ocean is called "Ephraim town" located at 60miles from River Num presently in the South-South Nigeria today. The river is named after Nun, Joshua's father, the tribe of Ephraim. In a nutshell, some researchers held the view that Biafra was inhabited by Ephraim descendants.

The emergence of ethnic militia groups in the Nigerian state can be examined under the following themes: Identity Crises, crises of distribution, Political exclusion and crises of legitimacy.

5.1   *Identity Crises*
Those scholars who discuss the crises of Identity argue that the bane of most developing countries in Africa is due to attachment to primordial grouping. This in turn creates many shades of identities. In places like Ruwanda and Burundi, it is the Tutsis and Hutus; in Kenya, it is the Kikuyu and other tribes; in South

Africa, it is the Zulus and Xhosas. Here in Nigeria, people pay more attention to their primary groups at the expense of the nation's identity. Afenifere (Yoruba grouping) the Northern Elders Forum (an Hausa/Fulani grouping) the Eastern Mandate Union or the Ohaneze Ndi-Igbo (the Igbo grouping) are examples. This and others make it difficult to have a true national identity as what is called the national identity is more of a lip service. People prefer to identify first with such groupings before that of the nation. It naturally follow that those in power identify first with their groups (who probably sponsor them) before the nation, (Agweda and Akindutire, 2017) The various socio-political problems affecting the country can be trace to this crisis. Here, the-sociological perspective is relevant. In Nigeria, there are; many shade of identities. This has made it difficult for the entire polity to have a national identity. People identify more with their primary groups and they readily give their loyalty to such grouping than, they give to the nation state. On the issues requiring the cultivation of national identity, it has been most difficult. What we find is competing shades of identities, each group seeking advantages over, the other.

Identity explains the underpinning social factor for inclusion and/or exclusion among social groups (Obianyo, 2007; Nnoli, 1994; Adekson, 2004). Identity as a social phenomenon cuts across races, ethnicities, tribes and religions, among other social groups (Horowitz, 1985). Identity distinguishes the social construct of individuals or groups of people in a given society, thus giving a notion and reality of heterogeneity. Heterogeneity has implications for socio-political interactions especially on issues relating to political power and resource distribution (Suberu, 1996) in a society. In any large society with schismatic ethnicities, identity provides clear lines of decision making in determining who will be included or excluded (Horowitz, 1985; Azam and Mensard, 2003). This entails some sort of politics of inclusion and exclusion, within a geographical or social space (example, ethnicity, tribe nation etc.).

In Nigeria, ethnic groups, interests and ethnic identities come into play in the political space (Nnoli, 1994). This is often characterized by inter-ethnic contests and strife for political inclusion and recognition across the country. Ethnicity is in fact a central factor in Nigeria's political processes. The quest to access political power especially at the 'center' has often resulted to overt inter and intra ethnic/regional political contest. Thus, ethno-regional identity is an extant factor influencing Nigeria's socio-political space, pitching groups against one another along ethnic divides (Adekson, 2004; Ojukwu, 2005; Kalu, 1996). Literature generally describes Nigeria's experience within the discourse of politics of supremacy and marginalization (Adekson, 2004; Obianyo, 2007). Just as in the case with Nigeria, the conceptual description of ethnic groups as minority (Bello-Imam, 1987) is an important indication of exclusion from privileges, access to political power and resources in the overall political manipulation which often yields to marginalization. The politics of marginalization has negative implication to social and political cohesion in Nigeria as diverse ethnicities contest to access national resources (Nnoli, 1994; Akinyele, 2001). Over the years, in Nigeria, there has been unavoidable synergy between selection of individuals for political and administrative positions and ethnic identity such as state of origin as in the Federal Character Principle (Dibua, 2011). Ethnicity based selection of administrative and political appointments, notwithstanding these have generated notions of marginalization and exclusion in Nigeria's socio-political discourse (Suberu, 1996; Akpan, 2005; Obianyo, 2007). Ethnic identity, therefore, interferes and influences the instigation of marginalization consciousness and notions of supremacy against so called 'majority' ethnic groups and that is why the Igbos we like to identify with ethnic group first before any other ethnic in Nigeria.

Also, in any large society with schismatic ethnicities, identity provides lines of argument on who will be included or excluded in the political space (Horowitz, 1985; Azam and Mensard, 2003). This most times, has resulted in civil wars or contests for self-determination especially among the minorities.

Furthermore, Collier and (Hoeffler, 2002) observe that issues of discrimination, racism, exploitation, inclusion and exclusion have heightened in-group consciousness which has resulted in ethnic strife and Civil Wars in Africa and some other Third World nations. The story is not different from the Rwandan Civil War of 1994 between the Tutsi and Hutus ethnic groups, where thousands of Tutsi were massacred (Hintjens 1999; Verwimp, 2004; White, 2009). It is important therefore, to note that marginalization, ethnic chauvinism, self-determination and contest for social inclusion among other issues are major factors that instigate civil wars, just as it was the case of the Nigerian Civil War.

5.2 *Crises of Distribution*

Both Pye and Huntington (1957), agree that when the power of a government are used in such a way that there is disparity in term of benefits and distribution of values and interesting among the various sections of the polity, such a system faces distribution crises. In other words, when governmental powers are used in recourses or values allocation as to make one section or group benefit extensively at the expense of other section/group, there will be crises of distribution. Critical analyst of the politics of new nations often agree that distribution crises is one of the 3 principal factors responsible for military intervention in politics. In Nigeria, a major problem has to do with how the various groups see themselves in relation to other groups on issues relating to the distribution of recourses, economic development and opportunity of participation in socio-political process.

When the power, resources and wealth of a nation are manipulated in such a way that there is disparity in which some components of the polity are better favoured than others, there is bound to be distribution crises. The distribution of resource and wealth should be such that there is a sense of belonging from the various components of the state. For this, distribution crises have always been a problem in Nigeria. Political and economic powers are not equally distributed. Economic inequality cannot be separated from the root of all these developments. Nigerians are frustrated because they can see economic inequality growing at a faster pace than ever before and no one seems to be doing anything about it.

Take for instance, the pervasive feature of the fiscal arrangement in the years between 1960 and 1966 was the lessening of emphasis on derivation principle and greater emphasis on principles of need, population, continuity and balanced growth all of which inadvertently favoured the Northern region. Thus a cursory look at the fiscal profile of the 3 major regions, comparatively in revenue terms revealed that the Northern region received £246.44 million or 255.68% of statutory revenues allocated to the regions from the centre, the West got £209.68million or 230.48% and the East £191.81million or 197.66% N.I.A (1981)

5.3 *Political Exclusion*

Political exclusion describes group of people/ethnic groups that are not equally represented in the system of government and governance in a country. Gergen (1999) and Kenny (2004) describe this situation as identity politics. Identity politics entail the exclusion and inclusion of groups in the distribution of political power and governance in an organized society. Thus, (Obianyo, 2007) posits that, identity (ethnicity) is used as an integral aspect of government in contemporary politics. Also, identity politics can be describes as a structure in which the oppressed and marginalized groups in any heterogeneous society generate self-designated recognition. Implicitly, in multicultural society, governance is often characterized by dominance and marginalization (Orji, 2001 and Ikpeazu, 2000), which, results in the quest for political recognition and inclusion. Identity politics is especially common in most developing countries, particularly in Africa, where ethnicity and tribal contests play crucial roles in governance and democratization process (see for example, Udogu, 1999; Reynal-Querol, 2000; White, 2009; Cooke, 2011). Across Africa, the politics of inclusion and exclusion have also resulted in political crises in countries like

Sudan, Rwanda, Ivory Cost, South Africa, Eritrea and Burundi (Uvin, 1999 and Madibbo (2012), posit that in Sudan, the political process is rooted in ethnic identity. Madibbo also hold that identity influenced Sudanese socio-political issues which border on exclusion and marginalization.

The politics of inclusion and exclusion in Sudan pitted the predominant Arab population in North Sudan against the predominant Black population of the South. The Blacks were the marginalized while the Arabs were the dominant group, controlling the national resources. The contest for political power and resources resulted to the country's Civil War of 1955 to 1972 and also, from 1983 to 2005. Similar system of politics existed in Ivory Coast in year 2002 such that, there was an exclusion policy towards the northern citizens and in Burundi in 1988 the exclusion of Hutu majority by a Tutsi government (Rocco and Ballo 2008). Same identity politics was recorded in Rwanda before the 1994 crises (Hintjens, 1999, Cooke, 2011) between the Tutsis and Hutus ethnic groups where the Tutsi were politically marginalized. Identity politics also played-out in South Africa, Eritrea and Nigeria (Mimiko, 1995).

Someone can say that, the political structure of Nigeria's federal government, as the most potent source of domination among various ethnic groups in the country. This dominance invariably promotes competitive ethnicity, which intensifies the politics of exclusion. Unless majority dominance and minority marginalization is addressed, politics in Nigeria will tend to be based on ethnicity. To address this, (Adekson, 2004) argues that policies should be made to ensure equal and inclusive political process in the country. Though, the Nigeria government in the year 1979 came up with Federal Character principle to address marginalization (Bello-Imam, 1987; Maduagwu 1999), the principle, however, has grossly failed to produce the desired result (Lambert, 2011) as the politics of exclusion and inclusion remain critical in socio-political and economic processes in Nigeria. The present socio-political situation in Nigeria is similar to the political experience in the First Republic which eventually led to the Nigerian Civil War (Forsyth 1982 and Adekson 2004). Duruji, (2009) argues that the resurgence of the post-war Igbo secessionist campaign groups is a reaction to a continual marginalization and alienation of the Igbo from the Nigerian polity (Chiluwa, 2012). In attempting to explain the word 'marginalization' as it applies to the Igbos, West (2017) writes: 'The Igbo, in particular, believe that they are not receiving a fair deal in the union despite all the talk about reconciliation, rehabilitation and reconstruction.

5.4   *Crisis of Legitimacy*
This simply refers to an open questioning of the validity or the basis of authority and power of a regime. When the basis of power and authority of any regime

faces challenges, crises of legitimacy arise. In other words, any rule without a popular mandate is at a serious deficit in terms of legitimacy. For example, where people are supposed to have the right to vote for their leader and they are robbed of such a right, then there is a question of legitimacy, which often brings about military intervention (since civilians do not have arms).

A government is supposed to be representative of the people who elected them into such positions. When a government lacks such peoples mandate, it faces legitimacy crisis. Most military regimes routinely have this problem because they were not voted in the first place. When the interim National Government(ING) headed by Chief Earnest Sonekan, 1993 was declared illegally by the court, it faced legitimacy crisis. When Abacha took over in place of a supposed winner of an election the crisis followed him to the grave, (Agweda and Akindutire, 2017).

Because of emergence and proliferation of ethnic militia group on perceived injustice, perceived exclusion of various forms, such a political injustice, deprivation and marginalization of some ethnic nationalities and contended that "The ethnic militant organisation arose in Nigeria because of perceived injustice, perceived exclusion of various forms, such as political injustice, ethnic marginalization and economic exclusion in terms of access to social services (Aja, 2012).

Futthermore, according to Aja (2012), "These organization are products of several reasons, several areas of mis-governance of our country. OPC came scuttling of the June 12 (1993) election."

6 Secession in Nigeria

According to (Ijomah, 2011) the secession in Nigeria can be trace to when Major General Aguyi-Ironsi abolished all the regional agents in the United Kingdom which had given the impression that the country was not united. A number of decrees were issued; many of them had their demerits. Perhaps what frightened the Northerners into a state of riotous indignation was the decree that sought to centralize the administration and unify the civil service. Obviously, this would have exposed the northerners to competition with their more advanced and qualified Southern counterparts on the basis of merits. It is pertinent to point out that in the civilian regime, appointments to the civil service were heavily influenced by political pressure.

No sooner was the decree issued than some students at the Ahmadu Bello University (ABU) Zaria, and some other Northerners revolted against the Federal government. Many Igbos in the North were killed in May 29th, 1966.

The tension in the country was so high that the Ibos in the north began their exodus to the South. Major-General Ironsi and the governor of eastern region appealed to them to go back in the interest of one Nigeria, and assured them that, that would be their last act of sacrifice in the of interest national unity. Perhaps this was a test case. The Federal Government did not do anything to punish those who were responsible for killing Ibos in the North. A commission was set up to investigate the massacre. Towards the end of June, the Northerners were ready for retaliation. This time, most of the Army Officers who were of Ibo origin, were rounded up and killed (Ijoma, 2011).

The supreme commander of the Armed Forces and Head of State of the Federal Government (Major-General Ironsi), along with the Military governor of Western Region, Lt. Col, Adekunle Fajuyi were assassinated July 29, 1966. The Northerners headed to by Lt. Col. Yakubu Gowon took over the Federal Government. Whether Lt. Col. Yakubu Gowon was personally involved in the July 29th, coup is a matter for historical speculation. There followed a period of uncertainty. The Northerners at first wanted secession from Nigeria. It was stated that Lt. Col Yakubu Gowon's "first inclination on taking power last July was to drop all semblance of a strong central government...." His decision to form a "loose league tied together only by common currency, post office and diplomatic services...." was based on the advice of some Northern permanent secretaries who warned that a secession of the North from Nigeria was 'suicide' since the North would have no access to the sea and would be the least viable. (Alaba-Isama, 2013)

The killing of the Army Officers of Igbo origin did not begin the agitation for the Biafran secession, but in September 1966, there followed what the Biafrans described as a Pogrom in which it was reported that more than 30,000 Igbo living in the Northern Region were massacred. It became apparent that they were no longer needed in a country for whose independence they made incalculable sacrifices. Col. Odumegu Ojukwu followed the September blood bathing with and appeal to the Easterners that they should remain calm. He did however observe that it appeared as a calculated move by the Hausa's to push the Igbo out of Nigeria. But the Igbo would not break away unless they were pushed. He later in one of his speeches inferred that the push had started (Alaba-Isama, 2013)

More than four decades after the Civil War and five decades after independence, Nigeria is still bedeviled with ethnic schism (Salawu, 2010). Just as late Chief Obafemi Awolowo in 1963 reportedly described Nigeria as a *"mere geographical expression"* with many ethnic nationalities (Onwubu 1975 and Mimiko 1995), he, further emphasized that ethnic diversity and multicultural state of the country serve as the underlying factors for ethnic schism, mutual suspicion, and contest which question the status of Nigeria as a nation. Within Nigeria, the Biafran phenomena and diverse inclusion and exclusion contests by ethnic groups have continued to haunt contemporary democratization process and state-building in the country. Also, ethnic groups in the country through organized social militias, tend to seek recognition and inclusion. Citizens, thus, derive their identity in the Nigerian states through their ethnicities.

7 Biafra Agitations

The Nigerian Civil War, commonly known as the Biafran War (7 July 1967 – 15 January 1970), was a war fought between the government of Nigeria and the secessionist state of Biafra. ... Immediate causes of the war in 1967 included a military coup, a counter-coup and persecution of Igbo living in Northern Nigeria. Seven years after the independence of Nigeria from Great Britain in 1960, Nigeria went to war with one of its key regions - the southeast region – located in an area formally known as the of South-East Region of Nigeria. The Nigeria-Biafra war started on July 7, 1967 and ended on January 15, 1970. The massacre of 1966 was after the independence of Nigeria from Great Britain, and its motivation and the events that surround it may have been the drivers for Biafra secession in 1967 (Madimbo, 2012)

Two important catalyzing events at that time were the January 15, 1966 coup d'état orchestrated by a group of military officers dominated by the Igbo soldiers which resulted in the killing of top civilian government and military officials mainly from the northern Nigeria (Hausa/Fulani) including a few south-westerners (Yoruba). The effect of this military coup on the Hausa-Fulani ethnic group in the northern Nigeria and the negative emotional stimuli – anger and sadness – fueled by the killing of their leaders were the motivations for the counter coup of July 29, 1966. The July 29, 1966 counter-coup which in some quarters called a coup of attrition against the Igbo military leaders was planned and executed by the Hausa-Fulani military officials from the northern Nigeria and it left the Nigerian head of state Maj Gen.Ironsi (of Igbo ethnic origin), some top military Igbo leaders and the military governor of western region Col. Adekunle Fajuyi (Yoruba) dead. Also, in revenge for the killing of the northern military leaders in January 1966, many Igbo civilians who were residing in northern Nigeria at a time were massacred in cold blood and their bodies were brought back to the eastern Nigerian (Alaba-Isama, 2013)

As a result of this ugly development in Nigeria, Col. Chukwuemeka Odumegwu Ojukwu, the then military governor of the eastern region decided to declare the independence of Biafra. His argument was that if the Nigerian government and law enforcement were unable to protect the Igbos residing in the other regions – northern– then it is better for the Igbos to return to the eastern region where they will be safe. The declaration of the independence of Biafra caused a bloody war that lasted almost three years (from July 7, 1967 to January 15, 1970), because the Nigerian government did not want a separate Biafran state. Before the end of the war in 1970, it is estimated that over three million people died and they were either directly killed or starved to death during the war most of whom were Biafran civilians including children and women. To create the conditions for the unity of all Nigerians and facilitate the reintegration of Biafrans, the then military head of state of Nigeria, General Yakubu Gowon, declared "no victor, no vanquished but victory for common sense and the unity of Nigeria." Included in this declaration was a transitional justice program popularly known as the "3Rs" – Reconciliation (Reintegration), Rehabilitation and Reconstruction. Unfortunately, there were no trusted investigations into the gross violations of human rights and other atrocities and crimes against humanity committed during the war like the Asaba Massacre in the present day Delta state (Mimiko, 2012)

The flag of the former Republic of Biafra consists of a horizontal tricolour of red, black, and green, charged with a golden rising sun over a golden bar. Red represents the blood of those massacred in northern Nigeria and in the consequent Nigeria-Biafra war. Black is for mourning them and in remembrance. Green is for prosperity and the half of a yellow/golden sun stands for a glorious future. The sun has eleven rays, representing the eleven provinces of Biafra. (Znaimerowski 2001).

FIGURE 12.1
Biafra flag
SOURCE: HTTPS://COMMONS.WIKIMEDIA.ORG/WIKI/FILE:FLAG_OF_BIAFRA.SVGMYSID / CC BY-SA (HTTP://CREATIVECOMMONS.ORG/LICENSES/BY-SA/3.0/)

The declaration of the independence of Biafra caused a bloody war that lasted almost three years (from July 7, 1967 to January 15, 1970), because the Nigerian government did not want a separate Biafran state. Before the end of the war in 1970, it is estimated that over three million people died and they were either directly killed or starved to death during the war most of whom were Biafran civilians including children and women. To create the conditions for the unity of all Nigerians and facilitate the reintegration of Biafrans, the then military head of state of Nigeria, General Yakubu Gowon, declared "no victor, no vanquished but victory for common sense and the unity of Nigeria." Included in this declaration was a transitional justice program popularly known as the "3Rs" - Reconciliation (Reintegration), Rehabilitation and Reconstruction. Unfortunately, there was no trusted investigations into the gross violations of human rights and other atrocities and crimes against humanity committed during the war. There were instances where communities were completely massacred during the Nigeria-Biafra War, Running head: for example, the Asaba massacre at Asaba located in the present-day Delta state. Nobody was held accountable for these crimes against humanity. History and Memory: Consequences of not addressing the past – history repeats itself because the postwar transitional justice program was inefficient, and failed to address the human rights abuses and genocidal crimes committed against the southeasterners during the war, the painful memories of the war are still fresh in the minds of many Biafrans even fifty years after. War survivors and their families are still suffering from intergenerational trauma. In addition to trauma and yearning for justice, the Igbos in the southeast of Nigeria feel

FIGURE 12.2   Nigeria flag
SOURCE: JON HARALD SØBY, HTTPS://COMMONS.WIKIMEDIA.ORG/WIKI/FILE:FLAG_OF_NIGERIA.SVG, PUBLIC DOMAIN

completely marginalized by the federal government of Nigeria. Since the end of the war, there has not been an Igbo president in Nigeria. Nigeria has been ruled for over forty years by the Hausa-Fulani from the north and the Yoruba from the southwest. The Igbos feel they are still being punished because of the aborted session of Biafra.

The flag of Nigeria was designed in 1959 and first officially hoisted on 1 October 1960. The flag has three vertical bands of green, white, green. The two green stripes represent Nigeria's natural wealth, while the white band represents peace.

8 The Resurgence of Biafra

The resurgence (renaissance) of Biafra consciousness among Igbo people represents a socio-political context of the post-war experience. There has been an increasing agitation to reinstate the defunct Biafra nation in the recent years. It is generally accepted that the Movement for Actualization of Sovereign State of Biafra is the contemporary harbinger of the Biafra cause especially in Nigeria's Fourth Republic and contemporary democratization process. *Biafra* is somewhat a social reconstruction of the contextual Nigerian Civil War experience. Lasting between 1967 and 1970, the Nigerian Civil War was a phenomenal national experience in the making of post-colonial Nigeria (Ademoyega 1981). The preceding inter-ethnic violence and the resultant civil war created a consciousness of Igbo marginalization within the Nigerian state (Obianyo 2012). Although the resurgence of Biafra consciousness in contemporary Igboland has been linked with the pre and post Civil War experience of the Igbo within Nigeria.

9 The Movement for Actualization of Sovereign State of Biafra

After 30 (Thirty) years of Biafra war came another raising group, the Movement for the Actualization of the Sovereign State of Biafra (MASSOB) is a secessionist movement in Nigeria, associated with Igbo nationalism, which supports the recreation of an independent state of Biafra. … There are two arms to the group the Biafra Government in Exile and Biafra Shadow Government. Failure of the post-war transitional justice, generational of the trauma, removal of history education from the school curricula in Nigeria through the policies of oblivion – have created the conditions for the reawakening and revitalization of the old agitation for the independence of Biafra. Although the actors, the political climate, and the reasons may be different, the goal and propaganda are still the same. The Igbos claimed that they are the victims of an unfair relationship and treatment at the center. Therefore, a complete independence from Nigeria is the ideal solution.

Beginning in the early 2000s, new waves of agitation started when the military handed over the country to a newly elected civilian government. The first non-violent social movement to gain public attention is the Movement for the Actualization of the Sovereign State of Biafra (MASSOB) formed by Ralph Uwazuruike, a lawyer who was trained in India. Although the activities of MASSOB led to confrontations with the law enforcement at different times and the arrest of its leader, it received little attention from the international media and community.

MASSOB launched the Biafran passport in 2009 as part of the program to celebrate its 10th anniversary. MASSOB leader, Ralph Uwazuruike, said the introduction of the Biafran passport was in response to persistent demands from Biafrans in diaspora, (Vanguard 20 March, 2015).

10   Re-introduction of the Old Biafran Currency

In 2005, MASSOB re-introduced the old Biafran currency into circulation. This sparked a lot of excitement at the time especially as one Biafran pound was said to exchange for two hundred and seventy naira at the border communities of Togo and the Republic of Benin. In his reaction, the then President of Nigeria, Olusegun Obasanjo, likened the Biafran pounds to a collector's item and attributed its high exchange value to its relative rarity.

11   Introduction of the Biafran Passport

11.1   *Arrests and Trials*
Irked by MASSOB's growing popularity, the Nigerian government began clampdowns on the group. Uwazuruike was arrested on several occasions on charges of unlawful gathering and disturbance of public peace. He was often eventually released within a few weeks. On one occasion, he was arrested in Lome, Togo, for storming the 36th Organisation of African Unity (OAU) Summit which had in attendance several African Heads-of-State (Duruji, 2009).

Uwazuruike's longest spell in detention was to come in 2005 when he was arrested in his Okwe hometown by men of the Nigerian Police. He alleges to have been flown to Abuja aboard a private jet and remanded in an underground sss facility. He remained in prison detention for two years after a protracted bail hearing at the Federal High Court, Abuja. Justice Binta Nyako eventually granted him three-month bail to enable him bury his mother who had died during his incarceration. Again in 2011, Uwazuruike and 280 MASSOB members were arrested in Enugu at an event in honour of Ojukwu. He was released on orders of Nigerian President, Goodluck Jonathan. (Duruji, 2009)

11.2   *Treason Trial*

Uwazuruike was charged with treason in 2005 at the Federal High Court, Abuja, before Justice Binta Nyako. The then Attorney-General of the Federation, Bayo Ojo, SAN, appeared in person for the government while Mike Ahamba, SAN, represented the defendant before being replaced by Festus Keyamo. The case however did not proceed to the trial stage as the first two years were spent hearing Uwazuruike's bail application. He was finally granted bail in November 2007. In April 2013, the Supreme Court held that the trial could commence after rejecting contrary submissions by Festus Keyamo. Soon or later, the activities died off and not much was heard of it. (Thisday 23rd march, 2018)

12   The Indigenous People of Biafra

After MASSOB, came another agitation group, the Indigenous People of Biafra (IPOB) lead by Mr Nnamdi Kanu, a Nigerian-British based in London and who was born at the end of the Nigeria-Biafra war in 1970 decided to use the emerging mode of communication, social media, and online radio to drive millions of pro-Biafra independence activists, supporters and sympathizers to his Biafran cause.

This was a smart move because the name, *Radio Biafra* is very symbolic. Radio Biafra was the name of the national radio station of the defunct Biafran state, and it operated from 1967 to 1970. At a time, it was used to promote the Igbo nationalist narrative to the world and to mold the Igbo consciousness within the region. From 2009, the new Radio Biafra aired online from London, and has drawn millions of Igbo listeners to its nationalist propaganda. To draw the attention of the Nigerian government, the director of Radio Biafra and self-proclaimed leader of the Indigenous People of Biafra, Mr. Nnamdi Kanu, decided to use provocative rhetoric and expressions, some of which are considered to be hate speech and incitement to violence and war. He continuously aired broadcasts that portrayed Nigeria as a zoo and Nigerians as animals without rationality. The banner of his radio's Facebook page and website read: "The zoo called Nigeria." He called for the supply of arms and ammunitions to wage war against the northern Hausa-Fulani people if they oppose to the independence of Biafra, stating that this time, Biafra will defeat Nigeria in war (Basi, 2017).

Basi (2017), further went further to say, because of his hate speech and violence inducing messages that he was spreading through Radio Biafra, Nnamdi Kanu was arrested in October 2015 upon his return to Nigeria by the State Security Service (SSS). He was held in detention and released in April 2017 on bail. His arrest charged the atmosphere in Nigeria and within the diaspora abroad, and his supporters protested in different states against his arrest. President Buhari's decision to order the arrest of Mr. Kanu and the protests that followed the arrest led to a rapid spread of the pro-Biafra independence movement after his release in April 2017.

In addition to the support the pro-Biafra independence movement has gained, Kanu's activities through his Radio Biafra and IPOB have inspired a national debate about the nature of the federal structure of Nigeria. Many other ethnic groups and some Igbos who do not support the independence of Biafra are proposing a more decentralized federal system of government whereby the regions or the states will have more fiscal autonomy to manage their affairs and pay a fair share of tax to the federal government. His whereabouts is still unknown until today after the federal government introduction of what is referred to as PYTON DANCE in the eastern part of the country (West, 2017)

13 Implication

The arousal of these emotions, feelings or strong sentiments tend to cloud and suppress a rational national debate on the Biafra issue. As the pro-Biafra independence activists leverage on the affective state of their members, supporters and sympathizers, they also confront and suppress negative sentiments directed against them by the Hausa-Fulani and others who do not support their movement. An example is the June 6, 2017 eviction notice given to the Igbos who are living in the northern Nigeria by a coalition of northern youth groups under the umbrella of Arewa Youth Consultative Forum. The eviction notice enjoins all Igbos residing in all the northern states of Nigeria to move out within three months and asks that all Hausa-Fulani in the eastern states of Nigeria should return to the north. This group openly stated that they will engage in acts of violence against the Igbos who refuse to obey the eviction notice and relocate by October 1, 2017. (BBC.com 2017)

14 Conclusion

This chapter has shown that, the Nigerian governments approach to the problem of ethnic militia is flawed. It has criminalized militia groups most especially the IPOB, and branded them most especially the IPOB, and branded them as disgruntled and misguided elements or terrorist groups rather than looking at the underlying issues. The emergence of ethnic militias and their violent activities has posed a serious threat to security in Nigeria. The violence and arbitrariness associated with militia created a society in which violence having been cultivated over a long period of time. Ethnicity and the conflicts associated with it oftentimes are directly related to the centralization of power. At the end of the day resolving the conflicts boils down to the creation of the conditions that can enable conflicting interest and forces to accept arrangements and procedures for addressing social and political contradictions. There is the need for the creation of an enduring framework for the domestic resolution of disputes, and this is only possible when all stakeholders agree on this framework through a national dialogue whose outcome will be binding on all. For Nigeria, a country with immense human and material resources, the future will be assured and democracy consolidated when its leaders and elite decide that it is now time to build a nation based on justice for all. With the kind of pressure emanating from the civil populace such as the activities of ethnic militias, this decision must either be made now by the political elite and their representatives or others will make it on their behalf.

15 Recommendations

As a strategy of dowsing the tension generated by activities of ethnic militia groups in Nigeria, this paper suggests the following recommendations:
– Good governance: Elected leaders should devout the resources in their disposal to improve the quality of life of their citizen.
– The government should opine that fundamental issues bordering on social deprivation, inequality in the distribution of Nigeria state wealth, and marginalization related to the region minority status should be look into.
– The government should build a spirit of oneness which the citizen cannot build by themselves. Meaning we should learn how to accommodate each other.
– Efforts should be made to constitute formal third party intervention void of interest that will assist in the transformation of conflict elements

- Also, efforts should be made to constitute formal mechanism that will be responsible for formal grievance handling (joint committees)
- Fiscal federalism is recommended along with restructuring which will enable the various component in Nigeria to have its pride of place.
- Finally, there is also the need for imaginative and far-reaching initiatives in the areas of job creations, poverty alleviation and refocusing of youth energy towards constructive endeavours.

References

Adedayo, O. A. 2004. *The 'Civil Society' Problematique: Deconstructing Civility and Southern Nigeria's Ethnic Radicalization*. Routledge.

Adejumobi, Said. 2002. "Ethnic Militia Group and National Question in Nigeria." Social Science Research in Africa. Available at www.ciaonet.org/wps/ads01.

Adekson O. 2004. *The Civil Society Problemtique: Deconstrating Civility and Southern Nigeria Ethnic Radicalization*. Routledge: London and New York.

Ademoyega A. 1981. *Why We Struck (the Story of the First Nigerian Coup)*. Ibadan: Evans Brother Limited.

Agweda. T.O and Akindutire., A.F. 2017. *The Military in Developing Nations: A Sociological Approach*. Gsplus Int: Benin City

Akinyele. R. T. 2001. *Ethnic Militancy and National Stability in Nigeria: A Case Study of the Oodua People's Congress*. Oxford Academic.

Akpan, G. E. 2005. "Natural Resource Control: A Market View." *The Nigerian Journal of Economics and Social Studies*, 7, 1. 21- 44.

Alaba-Isama. G. 2013. *The Tragedy of the Victory (on-the-sport Account of the Nigeria-Biafra War in the Atlantic Theatre)*. Safara Books Export limited: London.

Aja, A. 2012. "Basic Concepts of Conflict." In Ikejiani-Clark (ed.), *Peace Studies and Conflict Resolution in Nigeria: A Reader*: Spectrum Books Limited: Ibadan.

Ashforth, B.E and Mael, F. 1989. "Social Identity Theory and Organization." *The Academy of Management Review*, 14(1): 20–39

Ayokhai, F.E.E. 2013. Natural Resource, Identity Politics and Violent Conflict in Post-independence Nigeria." *African Journal of History and Culture*, 5(2): 32–40

Azam. J. P and Mesnard. 2003. "Civil War and Social Contact." *Public Choice*, 115: 455–475.

Babawale, T. 2001. *The Rise of Ethnic Militias, De-legitimisation of the State and the Threat to Nigerian Federalism*. West Africa Review: Ibadan.

Basi. U. 2017. International Center for Ethno-Religious Mediation. https://www.icermediation.org/.

Barth, F. 1969. *Ethnic Groups and Boundaries: The Social Organisation of Culture Difference.* Little Brown: Boston.

Baum, F. E. and Ziersch, A. M. 2003. "Social Capital." *Journal of Epidemiology and Community Health,* 57, 5. 320–323

Bello-Imam. I.B. 1987. Local Government Election: Challenge of Grassroots in Nigeria (NISER).

Chiluwa.I. 2012. "Citizenship Participation and CMD: The Case of Nigeria." *Pragmatic and Society,* 3(1): 61–88

Chinua. A. 2012. *There Was a Country: A Personal History of Biafra.* Penguin: London

Collier, P and Hoeffler, A. 2002. "On the Incidence of Civil War in Africa." *The Journal of Conflict Resolution,* 46(1): 13–28.

Cooke J.G. 2011. *Assessing Risks to Stability.* Centre for Strategic and International Study (CSIS) Washington DC.

Dibua. J.I. 2011. "Ethnic Citizenship, Federal Character and Inter-group Relations in Postcolonial Nigeria." *Journal of the Historical Society of Nigeria,* 20:1–25

Duruji, M.M. 2009. "Social Inequity, Democratic Transition and the Igbo Nationalism Resurgence in Nigeria." *African Journal of Political Science and International Relations,* 3: 1, 54–65.

Falana, F. 2003. "Democracy, Constitutionalism and the Phenomenon of Ethnic Militias." In Tunde Babawale (ed), *Urban Violence, Ethnic Militias and the Challenge of Democratic Consolidation in Nigeria.* Malthouse Press Ltd: Lagos.

Emma. I. Orji. 2001. "Issues on Ethnic and governance in Nigeria: A Universal Human Right *Perspective." Fordhan International Law Journal.*

Gergen, J.K. 1999. "Social Construction and the Transformation of Identity Politics." In Newman and L. Holzman (eds.), *End of knowing: A New Developmental Way of Learning.* Routledge: New York.

Hintjens, H.M. 1999. "Explaining the 1994 Genocide in Rwanda." *Journal of Modern African Studies,* 37: 2, 241–286.

Hogg, M.A. 2001. A Social Identity Theory of Leadership. *Personality and Social Psychology Review,* 5, 3, 184–200.

Hornsey. M.T. 2008. "The Social Identity and Self-categorization: A Historical Review." *Social and Personality Psychology Compass,* 2(1): 204–222.

Horowitz D.L. 1985. *Ethnic Groups in Conflict:* University of California Press: Berkeley.

Huntington. S. P. 1957. *The Soldier and the State.* Cambridge: Harvard University Press.

Ijomah B.I.C. 2011. Nigerian Nationalism and the Problem of Socio-Political Integration. Blue Prints Ltd: Onitsha.

Ikpeazu, N. 2000. "Post–Biafran Marginalization of the Igbo in Nigeria." In Amadiume, I and An-Naim, A. (eds), *The Politics of Memory: the Truth, Healing and Social Justice.* Zeb Books: London.

Imobighe, T. A. 2001. "An Overview of the Theoretical Issues in *African* Security." In Akindele. R. A and Massey E. Ate (eds.), *Beyond Conflict Resolution: Managing African Conflict in 21st Century*, pp 39–56, Ibadan: Vantage Publishers.

Kalu, K.A. 1996. Political Economy in Nigeria: The Military, Ethnic Politics and Development. *International Journal of Politics, Culture and Society*, 10, 2, 229–247.

Kenneth. G. 1999. *An Invitation to Social Construction.* Sage Publication

Kenny, M. 2004. *The Politics of Identity.* Polity: Malden: Cambridge, MA.

Mbaku J, Pita, A. and Kimenyi, M. 2001. *Ethnicity and Governance in the Third World.* Ashgate Publishing Company: Aldershot.

Madibbo A.I. 2012. "Conflict and the Contention of Nations of Identities in Sudan." *Current Sociology,* 60(3):302–319.

Maduagwu M.O. 1999. *Globalization and its Challenges on National Culture and Values: A Perspective from Sub-Saharan Africa.*

McNamara, T. 1997. "Theorizing Social Identity: What do we Mean by Social Identity? Competing Frameworks, Competing Discourses." TESOL *Quarterly*, 31(3): 561–567.

Mimiko N.O. 1995a. "From Reform to Neo-regulation: An Assessment of Recent Political Economic Development in Nigeria." *Thunderbird International Business Review*, 37(5): 513–532

Mimiko, N.O. 1995b. "Between Yugoslavia and Czechoslovakia: the Abacha Coup, the National Conference and Prospect for Peace and Democracy in Nigeria." *Social Justice*, 22(3): 129–142.

Nagel J. 1995. "American Indian Ethnic Renewal: Politics and the Resurgence of Identity." *American Sociological Review*, 60(6):947–65

N.A.I. 1981. Auditor Generals' Report of Statutory Allocation to regions by Central Government, Various Years.

Nnoli. O. 1994. "Ethnic Conflict and Democracy in Nigeria: The Marginalization Questions of African." *Journal of Social Development in Africa*, 15(1): 61–78.

Nnoli, O. 1994. *Ethnicity and Democracy in Africa. Intervening Variables.* Malthouse Press: Lagos.

Obianyo, N.E. 2007. Citizenship and Ethnic Militia Politics in Nigeria - Marginalization or Identity Question: The Case of MASSOB. Paper presented at the 3rd Global Conference on Pluralism Inclusion and Citizenship, at Salzburg Austria. November 18–19, 2007.

Ojukwu, C.C. 2005. "The Politics of Integration and Marginalization in Nation-building: The Igbo Question in Nigerian Politics." UNILAG *Journal of Politics.* 2(1): 130–153

Olukotun, A. 2003. Ethnic Militias and Democracy: A Media Perspective." In Tunde Baawale (ed.), *Urban Violence, Ethnic Militias and the Challenge of Democratic Consolidation in Nigeria.* Malthouse Press Ltd: Lagos.

Omobowale A. O. and Olutyo A. O. 2009. "Social Capital and Human Development in Nigeria: A Study of Lalupon Community." *African Identities,* 7(1): 77–88.

Onuoha G. 2013. "Cultural Interfaces of Self-determination and the Rise of the Neo-Biafran Movement in Nigeria." *Review of African Political Economy*, 40(137): 428–446.

Onwubu, C. 1975. "Ethnic Identity, Political Integration and National Development: Igbo Diaspora in Nigeria." *The Journal of Modern African Studies*, 13(3): 399–413

Orji, E.I. 2001. "Issues on Ethnicity and Governance in Nigeria: A Universal Human Rights Perspective." *Fordham International Law Journal*, 25: 431.

Osaghae, E. 2001. 'Exiting from the Existing State in Nigeria'. In Bekker, S.B., Dodds, M., and Khosa, M. (eds.), *Shifting African Identities*. Human Sciences Research Council.

Reynal-Querol Marta. 2002. "Ethnicity Political System and Civil Wars." *Journal of Conflict Resolution*, 46(1): 29–54.

Rocco, Lorenzo, and Zié Ballo. 2008. "Provoking a Civil War." *Public Choice*, 134 (3–4): 347–366.

Toland, T.Y. 1993. *The Concept of Ethnicity*. Yabe University Freer: New Haven

Samuel H. 1957. *The Soldier and the State*. Harvard University Press: Cambridge.

Stets, J.E and Burke, P.J. 2000. "Identity Theory and Social Theory." *Social Psychology Quarterly*, 63(3): 224–237.

Suberu R. 1996. *Ethnic Minority Conflicts and Governance in Nigeria*. Spectrum: Ibadan.

Tajfel, H. 1972. "Interindividual and Intergroup Behaviour." In Tajfel, H. (ed.), *Differentiation Between Groups: Studies in the Social Psychology of Intergroup Relations*, Academic Press: London.

Thomson, A. 2000. *An Introduction to African Politics*. Routledge: London

Salawu, B. 2010. "Ethno-religious Conflicts in Nigeria: Causal Analysis and Proposals for New Management Strategies." *European Journal of Social Sciences*, 13(3): 1–9.

Udogu, I.E. 1999."The Issue of Ethnicity and Democratization in Africa: Toward the Millennium." *Journal of Black Studies,* 29: 790–809.

Verwimp, P. 2004. Death and Survival During the 1994 Genocide in Rwanda. *Population Studies*, 58(2): 233–245.

Uvin, P. 1999. Ethnicity and Power in Burundi and Rwanda: Different Paths to Mass Violence. *Comparative Politics*, 31(3): 253–271

West. I. 2017. "Biafra is not a Dirty Word." *The Cable*. 28 May, 2017. Available at https://www.thecable.ng/biafra-not-dirty-word. Accessed 27 May 2020.

White, K.R. 2009." Scourge of Racism: Genocide in Rwanda." *Journal of Black Studies*, 39(3):471–481.

Znaimerowski, Alfred. 2001. *The World Encyclopedia of Flags*. Anness Publishing Ltd: London.

CHAPTER 13

A Complementarity Reflection on Human Interest and Common Good in Africa: Examples of Nigeria's Ghana-Must-Go and South Africa's Xenophobia

Phillip A. Edema and Adewale O. Owoseni

1   Introduction

According to Hare (1965), to have an interest is, crudely speaking, for there to be something which one wants or is likely to want. Interest could also be a means necessary or sufficient for the attainment of want. Simply, this suggests that human interest presupposes the essential nature of human persons, in terms of preference and aversion for course of events, actions, and state of affairs toward an anticipated end. Aristotle's locution, *Eudaimonia,* conveys the notion of human interest as the pursuit of happiness or flourishing existence which is an outcome of practical wisdom or rationality. Given the imprecise nature of what constitutes happiness or flourishing existence of human persons, that is what, how, and who defines happiness, the idea of human interest becomes conflated and ambivalent. Hence, it may also refer to the dialectical privation of alternative desires, or happiness of individuals towards specific ends.

In this connection, the idea of common good that implies the appropriation of justice for individuals, groups, society or state, seems not far removed from the basis of human interest. In other words, human interest and common good are intertwined concepts; the former is characterized by ambivalence, while the latter is discerned by contemplation and dispensation of justice in socio-political, religious, economic, and other contexts. In the bid to make sense of such complex connections between common good and human interest, this discourse attempts a complementarity reflection on the concepts, hinging on an African philosophical outlook. This is done by drawing on the example of xenophobic manifestations in South Africa and Nigeria. Here, the intent is to impress that contemporary African nations are trapped in autochthonous and foreign exertions in the course of attaining common good, which is underscored by the ambivalence of human interest in terms of the crisis of self-definition, ethnocentric nationalism, and economic determination, among others. This chapter shows that the ambivalence of human interest, which conditions the attainment of common good in Africa, is depicted through the missing link of reality as emphasised by an African philosopher, namely, Innocent Asouzu. It is worthy of note that reference to contemporary Africa is in terms of post-colonial African nations' crisis, with specific emphasis on xenophobic happenstances in South Africa and 'Ghana-Must-Go' incident in Nigeria respectively.

2   Human Interest and Common Good in Africa: South African and Nigerian Examples

It has been clarified from the above that the discourse of common good is implicated by the notion of human interest. Etzoni (2004, 2015) presents a historical conception of common good from Greek and Roman philosophical, economic and legal thoughts. Etzoni proffered a descriptive conception of common good that impresses that there are contested paradigms of what is supposed as common good in varying contexts. This includes objective versus subjective good, private versus public good, liberal versus communitarian good (Rand and Branden 1986) and so on. Basically, Etzoni suggests that while the concept of common good connotes public interest or good, it is one with a long and contested history. Situating this observation within the confine of the USA and the United Nations is apt here. It has been noted in the case of the USA, that the public are favorably disposed towards the 'invisible hand' of free market (Etzoni 2015, 2). This is engendered by liberal capitalism that propels economic conservatives to clamour for public policies that restrain governmental control of individual rights and liberties in the pursuit or maximisation of common good. Common good in this sense refers to unlimited creation of wealth, security from state sanctions and sobriety measures as well as unhampered individual privacy. Put differently, in the USA, common good is a struggle to attain equilibrium between public interest supposed to be promoted by the state/*polis* and individual rights. Within the context of the United Nations, common good of member states are subjected to dominant interest of certain prioritised member states, as spelt out within the organogram and role ascription in the UN.

United Nations' organizational structure reflects a sort of prioritised categorisation of developed-developing member states relation. For instance, its Security Council which consists of 15 member-states comprises five permanent member states (China, France, Russia, U.K, and United States) while the remaining member states occupy temporary seats (Angola, Chad, Chile, Jordan, Lithuania, Malaysia, New Zealand, Nigeria, Spain, Venezuela and so on). The permanent member states hold veto power over UN resolutions, which also allow them to block adoption of any unsatisfied resolutions, while the temporary seats are voted in by General Assembly on a regional basis. Also, official languages recognised in UN seating are majorly six; Arabic, Chinese, French, English, Russia, and Spanish. The instrumentality of language in safeguarding interests should not be underrated. Hubert Igboanusi (2017) indicates the extent of employing language as a tool to perpetuate interest within sects, groups, or organisations. Among other uses of language, Igboanusi asserts the use of language as an instrument of identity, control, or access to power, as well as a tool of exclusion in some cases. There is a suspicion that this sense of the instrumentality of language plays out in the UN as hinted. This is not to suggest that the entire operations of the UN do not in any way benefit other member states. The instances of the USA and UN indicate the contention about the notion of common good and the complexity of human interest.

Africa is no exception in this regard. Drawing insights from xenophobic expressions in South Africa (also known as the Rainbow Nation) and Nigeria would illustrate the complexity of human interests in view of common good. According to the South African Human Rights Commission's (SAHRC cited in Solomon and Kosaka 2013), xenophobia is "the deep dislike of non-nationals by nationals of a recipient state." Deep dislike in this sense could manifest in physical attack or threat. The trend of xenophobic attacks since 1998 till date and the repatriation of Ghanaians and other non-Nigerians back to their home country in 1983 indicate the ambivalence of human interests in the pursuit of common good. This would be clarified as the work progresses. Many diverse reasons have been adduced for the outbreak of xenophobic attacks in the Rainbow Nation (Harris 2002; Crush et al 2008; Coplan 2008; Misago 2011; Crush and Ramachandran 2009). Notably, the causal factor of presence of migrants or non-South Africans from neighbouring countries like Nigeria, Somalia, Mozambique, Zimbabwe, who are mainly alleged to be responsible for high levels of crime wave, burden of border control, unemployment, spread of HIV/AIDS, house/shelter difficulty, among others, have been emphasised. This factor is popularly held by a number of South Africans as responsible for the slow pace of substantive transformation since 1994 as well as the improvement of the poor living conditions of South Africans (Williams 2008). The national statistical representative survey conducted by Southern African Migration Project (SAMP cited in Williams 2008) in 1997 reports that:

> 25% of South Africans wanted a total prohibition of migration or immigration and 22% wanted South African government to return all foreigners presently living here to their own countries. 45% of the sample called for strict limits to be placed on migrants and immigrants and 17% wanted

migration policy tied to the availability of jobs. In the same survey, some 61% of respondents agreed the migrant put additional strains on the country's resources.

The above South African disposition about extradition of migrants and immigrants from South Africa has taken the form of expressive persuasions through violence and non-violent campaigns and popular sloganeering like "Buyelekhaya" (Go back home). Similarly, in January 1983 in Nigeria, the popular slogan "Ghana-Must-Go" was championed as Nigerian government, under Shehu Shagari in the 1970s, repatriated over one million Ghanaians and other non-Nigerians to their home countries for reasons that include illegal paper work, gaining popularity with Nigerians for election sake, stabilising Nigerian economy, vendetta feelings (since in 1969, Ghanaian government repatriated Nigerian immigrants from its territory – the Alien's Compliance Order) among others. Information that was gathered at the time on the matter suggests that most Ghanaians feared that xenophobic attack would be unleashed if they refuse to leave Nigeria. The report of the official statement made by Shehu Shagari in a press conference and the narrative from a Ghanaian, namely, Charles Ekwere, who was technically an illegal immigrant that worked as an assistant sales manager in a chemical firm in Lagos, depicts this fear about xenophobic attack:

> If they don't leave they should be arrested and tried and sent back to their homes, illegal immigrants in fact under normal circumstance should not be given any notice whatsoever, if you break a law, then you have to pay for it – Official statement from Nigerian authority. (Chia 2015)

> Someone told me that there was a deadline. That minister is about to handover every power to every civilian. That any civilian could do anything to any alien in the country. And it was that threat that after the deadline every Nigerian citizen could take action against foreigners. After deadline he gave power to every Nigerian citizen. We had nowhere to hide in Nigeria because wherever you're staying you are staying with Nigerians. So that made everyone scared. – Ghanaian sales manager in Nigeria. (Solomonov 2016)

However, it seems that the Ghanaian government also leveraged on this past experience that their citizens encountered in Nigeria, since a recent report also shows that between January 2018 and 2019, the Ghanaian government, through its Immigration Service, deported about 723 Nigerians back to Nigeria for reasons of alleged overstay, cybercrime, and prostitution among others (FG Protests Inhuman Treatment of Nigerians as Ghana Deports 723, 2019).

One could state that in the case of Nigeria, latent xenophobia is signaled as in the official statement released by Shehu Shagari rather than active xenophobia as perceived in the case of South Africa, though this distinction is not central to the focus of this discourse. It could be stated that the analogy of events in both nations as regards the rationale of the eviction of foreigners are decisions fueled mainly by economic and socio-political interests. This is underscored by ethno-nationalism and economic conservatism. Ethno-nationalism and economic conservatism imply intentions to secure autochthonous interest and development, while obliterating what is perceived as the impact of external accretions or the presence of foreigners in the course to achieve common good. This simply means safeguarding South African or Nigerian resources for South Africans or Nigerians' interests respectively. From a fictional point of view, Taiye Selasi's (2013) novel titled "Ghana Must Go" tells the story of how stereotypes of immigrant identities influence national and trans-national safeguards of interest in terms of social interaction or discrimination. Selasi's novel narrates the ordeal of the Sai family, that is, Kweku (husband) and Fola (wife), in terms of struggle for survival. It is a narrative about the influence of family structures and identities on the livelihood of Scottish, Nigerian, American, Chinese and Ghanaian immigrants. In this novel, Selasie often makes allusion to the character of Olu, the eldest Sai's son, in order to emphasise the factor of stereotypical identities and its influence for human interpersonal relationship as driven by human interest. This is captured in the drama that unfolds in Selasi's work when Olu, one of Sai's sons, approached his girlfriend's father, Dr. Wei, to ask for her hand in marriage. Dr. Wei, who seems not to be comfortable with the proposal, cites accounts from Africa about the incidence of rape, child soldiers and ethnic conflict. Dr. Wei, in his curiosity, questions Olu; "How can you value another man's daughter, when you don't value your own?

Though fictional, Selasi's novel suggests that the nature of human interest is informed by stereotypical identities or perceptions about immigrants by host nations and, even among fellow immigrants. One can further make reference to other recent significant events unfolding within the Nigerian space that are instances of the ambivalent nature of human interest such as the secessionist movement of Biafra – MASSOB, IPOB – in Eastern Nigeria, the agitation for commensurable derivation principle in South-South Nigeria and the faith-triggered insurgent movement of Boko Haram in North-East Nigeria, among other emerging ones. However, the explication of the details of these instances is beyond the scope of interest here.

The expedient concern at this point is whether there is any plausible approach that can engender surmounting the challenge of ambivalence of human interests as seen, for instance, in the threat of xenophobic manifestations in South Africa and 'Ghana-Must-Go' in Nigeria. Importantly, shifting attention to the focus of the discourse in terms of complementarity approach is expedient. It follows that there is an essential need to inquire the rationale of complementarity of human interest in the pursuit of common good. Thus, the next section would embark on a brief exposition of the complementarity approach as nuanced in the philosophical thought of the African philosopher, Innocent Asouzu.

3   Asouzu's Complementarity Approach

Innocent Asouzou's (2005, 2006, 2007a, 2007b) collection of writings among others expound the approach of complementarity or, as it is often called, *Ibuanyindada* philosophy. For the purpose of this section, this discourse refers to Asouzu's (2011) complementarity approach as concisely conveyed in the 50th Inaugural Lecture delivered by him at the University of Calabar, Nigeria, titled "Ibuanyindada and the Philosophy of Essence." Innocent Asouzu's complementarity approach is a dialectical engagement of Aristotle's metaphysics of substance/essence and accident (which is a critique of Plato's theory of 'form'). In Asouzu's opinion, Aristotelian metaphysics conceives of reality from the mindset of exclusive relationship between human (as substance) and the world (as accident). According to him, Aristotle's philosophy of substance stipulates that substance does not need accidents to subsist, rather accident needs to rely on essence to subsist (Asouzu 2011, 17). Asouzu conceives that this sort of metaphysical or ontological understanding of reality, also known as 'joy of being', presupposes a disjointed and polarised mindset. Asouzu's conception of complementarity proposes that the point of entry to understanding the world is a mutually inclusive mindset that does away with the demarcation between substance and accident, that is, human and the world. It is through this mindset that we can understand and appreciate reality as a whole.

For Asouzu (2011, 13), mindset means trying to understand and explain reality, seeking to inculcate the correct type of disposition in our relationship with the world. For him, this is what simply constitutes the philosophy of essence or reality. Asouzu's notion of mindset suggests a contrary position to Aristotle's understanding that places premium on superiority of ideology and knowledge in the course of human relationship with the world. Asouzu (Ibid, 18) notes that "fidelity to Aristotle's metaphysics has resulted in a tendency to see reality as something disjointed, bifurcated and polarised; where what is essential or substantial is easily equated with what is superior, whereas what is accidental is equated with what is inferior and inconsequential." Speaking of the effect that Aristotelian philosophy of essence has on the vocation of philosophy as a pursuit of truth, Asouzu (2011, 19) further notes that:

> ... Instead of philosophers speaking with one voice based on a unified subject matter, most philosophers soon found themselves defending scientific propositions in keeping with the demands of their inclinations and localized interests. Without prejudice to very honest efforts invested in the cross-fertilizations of ideas beyond national boundaries and other mundane considerations, there were visible signs of segmentation of ideas along ethnic, ideological and religious lines. It is in this that rationalism, for example, became heavily associated with French-rationalism, empiricism, with British-Empiricism and Idealism with German-Idealism. We shall have American Pragmatism later on.

The above suggests that mindset in the Aristotelian sense instigates theoretical schisms about reality, human interpersonal relationship, and the world. Such mindset fosters the 'irrationalism of reason' (which simply means the privation of reasoning) consequent upon what is called the phenomenon of concealment, according to Asouzu (2011, 30). Phenomenon of concealment refers to that which has the capacity to becloud our intellect, twist consciousness and induce us to perceive and interpret reality always depravedly, as well as interpreting situations only to our advantage. This means outrightly ignoring the interests of others and some of the most severe consequences of our actions (Asouzu 2011, 30). In its Igbo rendition, *ihe mkpuchi anya* (phenomenal of concealment), metaphorically means 'the thing that covers the eyes or impairs vision' (Asouzu 2011, 31). Being beclouded by phenomenon of concealment suggests that the mindset of understanding reality would become ambivalent and mismanaged. This erodes the possibility of mutual complementarity and harmony in mindset (Asouzu 2011, 29). In the absence of a complementary mindset, it follows that human interpersonal relationship would be trapped in the pursuit of negation and isolation from others and the world. Asouzu suggests that this leads to a solitary and lonely life and captured this through the Igbo expression of *ka so mu di* which means 'to be is to be alone.' Negation and isolation from others subsequently amount to undue rivalry of mindsets. This can be addressed by complementarity approach according to Asouzu:

the asymmetrical situations of power imbalance, those who have the advantage of power (essence/substance) to lord it over those they perceive as weak, unwise and inconsequential (accident) while redefining those things designated as accidental to align with interests guiding human beings in society to appear substantial and vice versa. (Asouzu 2011, 21)

The impression of the above for human interest and common good in this discourse would be addressed soon in the next section. In Asouzu's view, enhancing a complementarity worldview of reality means forging a unity of being, that is, coexistence that would reinforce the relationship between essence and accident as mutual complements. This is also called the missing link of reality that refers to all fragments, units, components, and combinations that enter into our understanding of any aspects of the world, which constitutes the diverse mode of being in history (Asouzu 2011, 41). This missing link of reality forms the basis of *Ibuanyindada* philosophy that explores a method and principle for coalescing the real and the ideal, the essential and accidental, into a system of complementing units. *Ibuanyindanda* is derived from the allegory of mutual complementation, dependence or interdependency strategy of the ants (*danda* in Igbo language) in carrying a heavy load bigger than individual self (an ant). This notion is coined in Asouzu's view to descriptively convey the point that, since through such mutual complementation devised by the ants, they can move heavy loads, it follows that through mutual complementation, human interests could be harnessed to surmount difficult problems or challenges (Asouzu 2011, 41). In concrete terms, *Ibuanyindada* attempts at showing how the ego/self/human can relate with reality in a mutually harmonized non-absolutistic mode (Asouzu 2011, 38–39). In Asouzu's terms, *Ibuanyindada* is a philosophical assertion that portrays that to be is to be in mutual complementary relationship with all missing links in reality (*ka so mu adina*).

The foregoing exposition only grants a limited consideration of concepts adopted in Asouzu's explication of the philosophy of *complementarity*, as derived from Igbo ontological conceptions. However, this exposition is not error-free. There are appraisals of Asouzu's worldview like those of Ozumba (2011), Heinz Kimmerle (2016), Akpan and Etta (2013), Bisong and Udo (2014), as well as Mendie (2015). Also, there is a suggestive stance that Asouzu's reading of Aristotle's metaphysics may not be error proof. For instance, Annas's (1977, 146–160) interpretation of Aristotle's metaphysics suggests that Aristotle does not foreclose the idea of complementarity, rather emphasizes that 'form' (that is the notion of the Universal in Plato's worldview) is the basis of substance and attribute/accident. Annas impresses that Aristotle's notion of 'form' as substance is not one intended for a relational engagement with attributes. In Annas's opinion, Aristotle mainly criticized Platonic understanding of 'form' and emphasized the need for the rejection of Plato's theory of 'forms' entirely. In other words, Aristotle's metaphysics of 'forms' could be conceived as the basic nature of both substance and matter. The understanding here is that 'form' is essential for the substance (it is a form of) but accidental for the matter it informs. Exhausting the discourse on 'form' and matter in relation to substance/essence and attributes would demand attention beyond this discourse. Importantly, Asouzu's interpretation of Aristotle's metaphysics conceived above is taken for granted for the purpose of the discourse here.

One cogent utility of Asouzu's approach is the bequest of its complementarity approach that emphasises mutual coexistence. Thus, one could state that *Ibuanyindada* philosophy proposed by Asouzu to address the missing links of reality, to forge complementation of relationship between humans and the world, as well as self and the other, is incisive. Though metaphysical and ontological in nature, it indicates the expedient need to address the ambivalence of reality or being (existence and co-existence). Extending this to the course of common good would substantiate the need for mutual complementarity of interests, especially in the case of xenophobic expressions and intentions in South Africa and Nigeria.

4   Complementarity of Interest in Contemporary Africa: A Considerable Panacea?

Asouzu (2011) posits that a polarised, exclusive, and non-conciliatory mindset mainly seek self-interest that intends to negate, alienate, and annihilate other interest through any conceivable strategy. Asouzu (2011, 28–29) notes that:

> Fundamentally human beings tend to secure their interests first, in the course of which they tend to negate the interests of others due to the challenges of … primitive instinct of self-preservation. They devise all thinkable strategies to secure that interest first… in seeking to preserve their interest first at the cost of other stakeholders, human beings at the same time devise measures to negate the interest of those others adjudged as a threat to their most cherished interests and for this reason become exclusivist and intolerant.

The above quote aptly explains the intricacy of the xenophobic expressions and intentions in South Africa and Nigeria. It gives support to Asouzu's connection of mindset with human interest. In other words, one could link the discourse of mindset with reality or world through the idea of human interest. This would be on the basis that human interest are constitutive mindsets or dispositions intended for the attainment of anticipated ends or goals like self-preservation. As hinted previously, the pursuit of such end or good is laced with the negation of alternative interest, which denotes the exclusivity of interests that is disjointed, disharmonious and polarised (to use Asouzu's words). This signifies the ambivalence of human interest, hence the absence of complementarity of interests. Lack of complementarity enhances extreme expressions, which result into the endless list of theoretical schisms noted by Asouzu such as British empiricism, German idealism, Afrocentrism, and so on. These ideological schisms have practical implications in terms of superior *vs.* inferior complex, white *vs.* black, developing *vs.* underdeveloped, and indigenes *vs* foreigners, among others. The implication of indigene vs. foreigner identity plays out boldly in the case of xenophobic expressions.

Xenophobic threats and attacks in Nigeria and South Africa, motivated by economic conservatism and ethno-nationalism, imply the dichotomy of self-interest (as essence/substance) against other interest like migrant/alien/foreigner interest (as accident). This reality of dichotomy of interests is characterized by the absence of complementarity. Human interest in the two contexts is edged by the irrationalism of reason, alongside the twin intent of alienation and isolation. This is depicted in the xenophobic events in South Africa and Nigeria through violent attack and non-violent (threat) campaigns that are meted out on foreigners/migrants. Non South-Africans have been subjected to active alienation and negation such as maiming and undue killing, while Ghanaians and other foreigners in Nigeria have been compelled to return to their homelands following government's fiat that Nigeria be left alone (*ka so mu di* syndrome in Asouzu's worldview). These dynamics in South Africa and Nigeria reinforce the category of indigenous identity or interest against foreigners. The need to rethink this category of foreigner identity as accidents and indigenous identity as essence is the emphasis in complementarity approach.

As Asouzu proposes, through the idea of complementarity, such categorization should rather be obliterated by considering all parties of interest that are indigenes and foreigners as potential essence or stakeholders. This would engender mutual recognition, respect and rights, where appropriate. The mutuality of recognition does not ultimately confer on immigrants' rights of claims over host nation's resources or autochthonous horizon of identity that could be material and immaterial which may include claims to land, ancestry, national cultural identity, artefacts, and population control among others. Otherwise, such mutual recognition ought to serve the course of reckoning immigrants as fellow humans that are subjected to vulnerable conditions as aliens/foreigners, and hence should be so treated from this point of privilege to exercise some rights of self-preservation and livelihood within the permissive limits of international guarantees of minimal protection and movement that do not constitute a strain or threat to host nations and their citizens (Khalil 2018, 8–10). This preceding way of thinking is aptly captured in Peter Singer's (1972, 229–243) notion of positive duty and Thomas Pogge's (2005) negative duty. Positive duty emphasises that affluent/developed nations (in this context, the host nations) ought to act in ways that would alleviate others or broadly put, those in need or in vulnerable circumstances (that is the immigrants) of suffering while negative duty reiterates the need of such nations to repress the circulation of inequalities or harm towards others in need or vulnerable conditions. While discerning the basis of justification for what constitutes host nations' duty (positive or negative) toward immigrants within their borders remains difficult to resolve, Singer's and Pogge's conceptions of duty mainly recall the imperative of the Kantian categorical maxim on the side of host nations to foreigners. The Kantian maxim basically suggests that actions or policies should be made or enacted in a way that those making them implicitly prescribes them as a universal law (Koorsgaard 1985, 1), applicable to all similar circumstances/situation involving persons and state within the context of this discourse. Put simply, policies or actions of host nations, with reference to South Africa and Nigeria, according to the Kantian paradigm, requires that both states should advance a minimal sense of recognition of the common humanity and aspirations of immigrants within their borders to foster global security and stability, as long as it does not render the host nations worse-off. The rationale of this is that whichever part of the world besides their country, that Nigerians and South Africans also find themselves, they are likely to also enjoy same measure of recognition in lieu of global security and stability. While such proposal seems desirable, it is far-fetched from practical reality of the global order, though it is doubtful that it suggests that citizens and foreigners should be subjected to equal measures of treatment in terms of rights and privileges within the host nations.

Given such preceding understanding, host nations are to be reasonably tolerant (understanding as well that there are limitation of tolerance) in terms of interaction with immigrants from a sense of moral obligation and reciprocity of alleviating them (immigrants) from the position/condition of vulnerability, as well as preventing foreigners from intense discrimination, violence or harm. In the South African xenophobic example, the preceding suggestion would translate to extending such moral reciprocity of protection and prevention of active harm toward immigrants from neighboring African and non-African countries that include Zambia, Angola, Zimbabwe and

Nigeria among others, whose government had provided solidarity in terms of financial, moral-psychological and Pan-African support in the past towards the repression of apartheid regimes (Egbedo 1987, 33–39; Reddy 1992; Abegunrin 2009, 5–27; Ogunsanwo 2015). Similar expectation is applicable to the Nigerian case, in terms of the shared history of colonial exploitation, (that is, the common expediency of historical reparation) regional, and communitarian ties between Nigeria and Ghana as co-member in the Commonwealth of Nations as well as the ECOMOG. UN General Assembly Resolution 45/158 act of 1990 and ECOWAS free movement accord that prioritise the rights and protection of nationals/indigenes and immigrants in terms of securing fairness and, equality in treatment as well as work conditions, are noteworthy exemplars of the idea of complementarity in concrete terms. The view that UN and ECOWAS' resolutions or accords are exemplars of complementarity could be explained on the basis that the world is gradually molding into a single global border of political and economic exchange or relations, in which foreigners in host nations are perceived as substantial partners for the vitality of host nations.

Embracing counter dispositions to such complementarity effort would mean reviving the Aristotelian ghost of disjointed or disharmonious mindset of interests and reality. In this regard, Asouzu (2011, 22) clarifies that an endorsement of Aristotle:

> Elevates the human innate urge to put one's interest first, at the cost of the interests of other stakeholders... thereby, underrated and even ignored in fact the asymmetrical situations of power imbalance, those who have the advantage of power tend to interpret this in keeping with their most cherished interests and use the means at their disposal to secure their interests first in keeping with the promptings of our fundamental primitive instinct of self-preservation.

Within the context of xenophobic expressions in South Africa and Nigeria, ambivalence of human interest is signified in the host nation's interest to negate the interest of foreigners. The host nation's interest is mainly to alienate the perpetuity of foreigners or migrants in the bid to secure the national resources for their citizens or indigenes. For the host nation, this is the benchmark of safeguarding the idea of common good. On the other hand, the interest of the non-South Africans and Ghanaians as foreigners is basically the search for greener pastures and integration into the viable nations. Again, it needs to be reiterated that while such immigrants' aspiration is desirable in lieu of the furtherance of self-preservation and better livelihood, it may constitute a strain for host nations' socio-political and economic resources or opportunities. In such situation, it is expedient for host nations to advance restriction of immigrant flow or what is commonly called limited immigration (Khalil 2018, 40–45; Miller 2005, 194–206). It is likely that advancing such restriction would surmount the application of international resolution and accords of free movement pertaining to immigrants. However, it safeguards immigrants from undesirable consequences of vulnerable conditions in the form of violence and non-violent expressions as in the case of South Africa and Nigeria. In such critical situation where host nations' government are not proactive to reasonably consider the alternative of limited immigration and foreigners' uncontrolled access into host nations, ambivalence as well as conflict of human interest is bound to occur with grievous outcomes in form of xenophobic intentions and attacks from some indigenes/citizens of host nations. Given this ambivalence, managing human interest due to the incompatible intention of the host nations with that of the foreigners becomes difficult, and relegate each side of interest to the condition of phenomenon of concealment emphasized by Asouzu.

At this juncture, understanding that this ambivalence could be addressed when considered as missing links of reality is the central claim of complementarity approach. This simply demands that actors involved, that is, those with vested interests, need to make sense of the missing link of reality to overcome the ambivalence inherent in human interest. Asouzu (2011, 51) emphasises that:

> This is precisely why in order to uphold their authenticity, actors have to encounter all missing links in full awareness of their relativity, historicity, and fragmentation, while at the same time bearing in mind their ultimate determination to absoluteness, universality, comprehensiveness, unity, totality and future reference.

Furthermore, drawing upon Asouzu's idea of unity of being is expedient for addressing the bane of ambivalence in human interest. Asouzu's (2004, 367–380) emphasis on the unity of being, also called 'transcendental complementary unity of consciousness' or transcendental goodwill, illustrates that goodness or common good lies in the reciprocity of being. However, due to the ambivalent moments in interest or mindset, humans often overreact in the bid to protect the natural inclination of their interests. Asouzu conceives that a goodwill that is premised on the unification of missing links of reality would aid overcoming the ambivalence of interests. In clearer terms, he argues that once there is the understanding that the condition that favors personal autonomy or self-preservation is the same condition that would aid complementarity of interest and harmonious coexistence, then common good could be realized. In this sense, the dichotomy of indigenous identity versus migrant/foreign identity as exemplified in the South African/Nigerian government against non-citizens would be blurred. In other words, in the absence of the understanding about the sameness of condition for preservation of self and other interests, there would be the limitation of being as suggested in Asouzu's opinion. Limitation of being simply connotes a strain in compatible interest in terms of coexisting together in harmonious relationship. It follows also that limitation of being frustrates the attainment of common good or ends for both sides that are indigenes and foreigners.

Be that as it may, there is the crucial need to explicate what common good means within the context of South Africa and Nigeria, given the background of xenophobic event. In both nations, common good would translate to protecting the reasonable interests of legitimate migrants or foreigners (as stakeholders in host nations) that are compatible with the vitality of the nation. This understanding is essential for the forging of a common humanity in a fast growing global world to mitigate the perpetuation of undesirable consequences issued from discriminatory category such as national/indigene *vs* migrant or foreigner identity. More so, even South Africans and Nigerians enjoy the benefits of global (naturalized or second class at least) citizenry in many parts of the world. In concrete terms, the missing link of reality (complementarity) translates to the need for the delimitation of 'self against other' perception, that is, an indiscriminate mindset and proactive action or intervention of the states (South Africa and Nigeria) to discourage and criminalize violent expressions from nationals towards foreigners/migrants. Sensitizing citizens that the presence of foreigners is also a mark of global livelihood is equally important. In other words, the global reduction of world borders from one nation to another renders the presence of non-indigenes or foreigners almost inevitable.

The foregoing proposal is mainly to emphasize the essence of complementarity of interest in contemporary Africa, which is drawn from mutual relations and reciprocity of interest and recognition, in terms of respect and rights to common good for indigenous people and foreigners. Perpetuating the ECOWAS free movement accord, *Braamfontein Statement* and the United Nations' resolution of minimum degree of protection even for illegal immigrants from the angle of complementarity is to promote common good. *Braamfontein Statement* is a by-product of the pact between South African Human Rights Commission (SAHRC) and United Nations High Commission for Refugees (UNHCR) in 1998, which states among other things that:

> No one, whether in this country legally or not, can be deprived of his or her basic or fundamental rights and cannot be treated as less than human. The mere fact of being an [alien] or being without legal status

does not mean that one is fair game to all manner of exploitation or violence... Foreigners in our midst are entitled to the support and defense of our law and constitution... [The] manifestation [of xenophobia] is a violation of human rights. (Williams 2008, 3)

The pact seems to correlate with the basic requirement of the United Nations' Resolution and ECOWAS freedom of movement accord regarding migrants and immigrants. Compliance to these provision would indubitably prevent indigenes from picking on foreigners/immigrants as scapegoat. The idea of picking on the other seems inconsequential for the goal of attaining development in South Africa or Nigeria. Given this, where complementarity of interest is perpetuated, the first step to linking the missing links of reality is enhanced.

In a concise manner, the discourse above could be illustrated in a table to show clearly that Asouzu's complementarity approach, as a critique of Aristotle's metaphysics of essence and substance, could be deployed as a framework for understanding the ambivalence of human interest in view of common

TABLE 13.1   Asouzu's complementarity approach: human interest in view of common good in contemporary Africa

South African/Nigerian government	Non-Nigerians/Non-South Africans
– Essence/Superiority: rights claim to privilege position as indigenes/nationals – Mindset (Autochthonous Identity/Interest): Self-identity/Interest – Missing Links of Reality: Securing country's resources for the indigenes or nationals only, that is, economic conservatism and ethno-nationalism (Elimination of Burden) – Phenomenon of Concealment: Social emancipation, reclamation of socio-economic empowerment, illegality – Irrationalism of Reason: Alienation and annihilation of foreign presence, banishment/repatriation	– Accident: Dependency on viable economy/nations, zeal for integration – Mindset (Immigrant/Migrant Interest): Search for the golden fleece – Missing Links of Reality: Expectations of privileges/rights of protection, working condition, vulnerability (Zeal of Being) – Phenomenon of Concealment: Global village assumption, diplomatic ties – Irrationalism of Reason: Object of xenophobic attack, security threat consequent in either cases of legality or illegality (entry)

good in contemporary Africa, using xenophobic expressions in South Africa and Nigeria as examples.

5 Conclusion

The attempt so far is not to offer a normative conception of human interest and common good, or to arrive at a (moral) judgmental stance of what is good or bad. The discourse attempted to portray the yardstick of complementarity as a proximate thrust for the attainment of common good for indigenes and foreigners. Thus, the discourse emphasised that the ambivalence of human interest is the bane of the attainment of common good, in lieu of the dynamics of relationship between host nations' indigenes and foreigners. It explains this through the instances of xenophobic expressions in South Africa and Nigeria. In other words, the discourse reflects on the ambivalent nature of human interest, adopting Asouzu's complementarity approach to inquire how this ambivalence conditions the realisation of common good, as seen in the example of South Africa and Nigeria. Given this, the study shows that the conceptualisation of common good as the aggregation of individual or group interest, and state formulation of public interest, is not devoid of ambivalence. In light of this, the discourse placed premium on the need to embrace Asouzu's notion of complementarity of human interest(s) as missing links in reality to address this ambivalence.

The practical manifestation of embracing a complementarity approach is thus stressed in the discourse. In light of the above, the attempt so far is to heed Asouzu's (2011, 27) call on the expedient need to dispense the philosophical duty of demolishing all forms of ideology and ethnocentric inspired understanding of the world that negates the idea of mutual complementary relationship between all persons and realities.

References

Abegunrin, Olayiwola. 2009. "Nigeria and the Struggle for the Liberation of South Africa." In *Africa in Global Politics in the Twenty-First Century*. New York: Palgrave Macmillan. https://doi.org/10.1057/9780230623903_2.

Akpan, Chris O. and Etta, Peter T. 2013. "Asouzu's Complementary Ontology as a Panacea to the Problem of Ethnic Idolization in Nigeria." *British Journal of Arts and Social Sciences*, 15(2).

Annas, Julia. 1977. "Aristotle on Substance, Accident and Forms." *Phroenesis*, 22(2).

Asouzu, Innocent. 2004. *The Method and Principles of Complementary Reflection in and Beyond African Philosophy*. Calabar: Calabar University Press.

Asouzu, Innocent. 2005. *The Method and Principles of Complementary Reflection in and Beyond African Philosophy*. Münster: Lit Publishers.

Asouzu, Innocent. 2006. "Redefining Ethnicity within Complementary System of Thought in African Philosophy." In *Re-Ethnicizing the Minds? Cultural Revival in Contemporary Thought*, edited by Botz-Bornstein, Thorsten and Habermas Jürgen. Amsterdam: Rodopi Publishers.

Asouzu, Innocent. 2007a. *Ibuanyidanda: New Complementary Ontology: Beyond World-Immanentism, Ethnocentric Reduction and Impositions*. Münster: Lit Publishers.

Asouzu, Innocent. 2007b. *Ibuarụ: The Heavy Burden of Philosophy beyond African Philosophy*. Münster: Lit Publishers.

Asouzu, Innocent. 2011. *Ibuanyidanda and the Philosophy of Essence: Philosophy, the Science of Missing Links of Reality, 50th Inaugural Lecture*. Calabar: Calabar University Press.

Bisong, Peter B. & Udo, Inameti L. 2014. "Absolute Certainty and Asouzu's Transcendental Unity of Consciousness." *American Journal of Social and Management Sciences* 5(2).

Chia Anne. 2015. "Ghana Must Go: Nigeria's Expulsion of Immigrants." Accessed 29 February, 2017. https://annechia.com/2015/04/20/ghana-must-go-nigerias-expulsion-of-immigrants/

Coplan, David B. 2008. "Crossing Borders". In *Go Home or Die Here: Violence, Xenophobia and the Reinvention of Difference in South Africa*, edited by Shireen Hassim, Tawana Kupe, and Eric Worby. Johannesburg: Wits University Press.

Crush Jonathan, McDonald David A., Williams Vincent, Lefko-Everett Kate, Dorey David, Taylor Don and la Sablonnière Roxanne. 2008. *The Perfect Storm: The Realities of Xenophobia in Contemporary South Africa*. Southern African Migration Project, Migration Policy Series, 50. Cape Town: Idasa.

Crush, Jonathan and Ramachandran, Sujata. 2009. "Xenophobia, International Migration and Human Development." *Human Development Research Paper 47, United Nations Development Programme*. http://ideas.repec.org/p/hdr/papers/hdrp-2009-47.html

Egbedo, Ihebom. 1987. "Nigeria and Apartheid." *Round Table: The Commonwealth Journal of International Affairs*, (76)301.

Etzoni, Amitai. 2004. *The Common Good*. Cambridge: Polity.

Etzoni, Amitai. 2015. "Common Good". In *The Encyclopedia of Political Thought*, edited by Micheal T. Gibbons. John Wiley & Sons Ltd.

"FG Protests Inhuman Treatment of Nigerians, as Ghana Deports 723." 2019. *Premium Times* Agency Report February 19. Accessed 5 August, 2019. https://www.premiumtimesng.com.

Hare, Richard M. 1965. *Freedom and Reason*. Oxford: Oxford University Press.

Harris, Bronwyn. 2002. "Xenophobia: A New Pathology for a New South Africa?" In *Psychopathology and Social Prejudice,* edited by Derek Hook and Gillian Eagle. Cape Town: UCT Press.

Heinz Kimmerle, Zoetermeer. 2016. "The Methods and Principles of Complementary Reflection in and Beyond African Philosophy." *IGWEBUIKE: An African Journal of Arts and Humanities*, 2(4).

Igboanusi, Hubert S. 2017. *The Conflicts and Politics of Language. An Inaugural Lecture Delivered at the University of Ibadan*. Ibadan: University of Ibadan Press.

Khalil, Selma. 2018. *Ethics Beyond Borders: The Nature of Our Responsibility Towards the Refugee Population*. A Long Essay in Partial Fulfilment for Honours in the Department of Philosophy, Wellesley College. https://repository.wellesley.edu>...

Koorsgaard, Christine M. 1985. "Kant's Formula of Universal Law." Pacific Philosophical Quarterly, 66(1–2). http://nrs.harvard.edu/urn-3:HUL.InstRepos:3201869

Mendie, Patrick J. 2015. "Asouzu's Critiques of Philosophy of Essence and Its Implication for the Growth of Science." *Philosophy Study*, 5(5).

Misago, Jean P. 2011. "Disorder in a Changing Society: Authority and the Micro-Politics of Violence." In *Exorcising the Demons Within: Xenophobia, Violence and Statecraft in Contemporary South Africa*, edited by Loren B. Landau. Johannesburg: Wits University Press.

Ogunsanwo, Alaba. 2015. *Selected Essays on Politics and International Relations*. Ibadan: Concept Publications Limited.

Ozumba, Godfrey. O. 2011. "Integrative Humanism and Complementary Reflection: A Comparative Analysis." *Filosofia Theoretica*, 1(1).

Pogge, Thomas. 2005. "World Poverty and Human Rights." *Ethics and International Affairs*.

Rand, Ayn and Branden, Nathaniel. 1986. *Capitalism: The Unknown Ideal*. New York: Penguin Books.

Reddy, Enuga S. 1992. *Struggle for Liberation in South Africa and International Solidarity: A Selection of Papers published by the United Nations Center Against Apartheid*. New Delhi: Sterling Publishers Private Limited.

Selasi, Taiye. 2013. *Ghana Must Go*. New York: The Penguin Press.

Singer, Peter. 1972. "Famine, Affluence, and Morality." *Philosophy and Public Affairs*, 1(1).

Solomon, Hussein and Kosaka, Hitomi. 2013. "Xenophobia in South Africa: Reflections, Narratives and Recommendations." *South African Peace and Security Studies*, 2(2).

Solomonov, M. 2016. "Ghana Must Go Exodus from Nigeria Remembered." Accessed on 1 March, 2017. https://yen.com.gh›16384-gha...

Williams, Vincent. 2008. "Xenophobia in South Africa Overview and Analysis." *Perspectives, Political Analysis, and Commentary from Southern Africa* 3.

CHAPTER 14

Boko Haram Terrorism and Out-of-School Children in North East Nigeria

Temitope J. Owolabi

1   Introduction

One of the most pressing concerns facing our current generation is the geometric rise in the incidence and notoriety of terrorism and terrorist activities. Unfortunately, Nigeria has in recent years become the epicenter of violent terrorist and militant attacks. These incessant terrorist attacks by the extremist group – Boko Haram – have claimed several lives and limbs, and have remained complex threats to peaceful existence in Nigeria (Okolo and Akubo, 2019). The North east is one of the geo-political zones in Nigeria, and it consists of six (6) states, namely; Adamawa, Bauchi, Borno, Gombe, Taraba and Yobe; but terrorist activities have been profound in Borno and Yobe states. Since the emergence of this insurgency (2002 till date) in these north east states (Borno and Yobe) of Nigeria, where it is running on the abhorrent philosophy – 'western education is evil', the group has been confronted by the Nigerian authorities. The ensuing conflict has claimed closed to 5000 lives and destroyed private and public property worth billions of naira (Adesoji, 2010, 98).

Apart from this, the group has been deliberately and systematically using violence to destroy, kill, maim, and intimidate the innocent in order to achieve a goal or draw national or international attention to demands which ordinarily may be impossible or difficult to achieve under normal political negotiation or on the battlefield against a government's army. This was why Obioma (2012, 97) noted that some of these terrorist attacks are politically motivated even though some may have other ancillary motives such as religious, economic or social. But Abiye (2011) documented that domestic terrorism arose in Nigeria because emergent militant groups took advantage of government's inefficient action and inactions in dealing with the fundamental elements of nationhood such as internal security, resource control, injustice, corruption, ethnicism, sycophancy, favouritism, over-lordship, and marginalization. These factors have made terrorism to be ethicised in Nigeria.

Currently, the nation is witnessing high spate of insecurity by this group of terrorists, especially in northern Nigeria; and this is why we would conceptualise, for the purpose of this chapter and in the context of Boko Haram insurgency, terrorism is the unlawful use of force or violence by a person (at the command of a group) or organized group (with misguided religious and political ideologies) against a government and its citizens to achieve its desired objectives (Shabayany, 2012, 41). Giving a brief history of the group, Boko Haram is a strong pseudo-Islamist terrorist group which has its base in north east Nigeria. The group has been in existence since 2002, but did not become popular until 2009 when they participated actively in the sectarian violence which occurred in northern Nigeria (Musa, 2011, 19). The name Boko Haram is a Hausa statement, which, upon translation into English, means 'Western education is sinful'. This group is opposed to everything that is of western origin, especially western education; its ideologies and systems.

Etymologically, 'Boko' in Hausa language means animist, western or otherwise non Islamic education, and the Arabic meaning of 'Haram' figuratively means 'sin'. Boko Haram opposes not only western education but western culture and modern science as well. For example, Yusuf (2019, 39–40) stated that the belief that the world is a sphere is contrary to Islam and should be rejected along with Darwinism and the theory that rain comes from water evaporated by the sun. Being under the control of Ustaz Mohammed Yusuf, the group set up a base called 'Afganistan'. This base was used to attack nearby police outposts, killing police officers, burning Churches and schools with a vow that the war will continue unless there is change in the political and educational systems (Oladunjoye and Omemu, 2013, 7). They vowed that they would rather have a separate Islamic state carved out of Nigeria where they can practice their religion unhindered.

The Federal Government of Nigeria saw these demands as treasonable, unreasonable and unacceptable, and in an attempt to purge the group of its excesses, Mohammed Yusuf, the leader, was killed in 2009. Adamu (2019, 33) stated that from that year and following the assumption of a new leadership headed by Abubakar Shekau, Boko Haram reinvented violence and began what can best be described as the bombardment of northern Nigeria with such frequency and intensity that are quite unprecedented in the history of Nigeria. These have had implications on the socio-economic and political spheres of not only the north-east, but on Nigeria as a whole. Terrorism has always had huge financial implications and burden to Nigeria. For example, annual budgets of billions of naira have always been earmarked to combat terrorism in Nigeria, and these could have been deployed to development programmes that the nation desperately needs.

Apart from the economic and monetary costs associated with terrorism, there are also social and psychological costs. Terrorism erodes inter-communal trust and destroys the reservoir of social capital that is so vital to building harmonious societies and pooling together community energies for national development. The attendant proliferation of small arms and the militarisation of society results in a vicious cycle of violence, which hampers national cohesion and stability. Also, the tragedy is that the collapse of local economies and the erosion of social capital reinforce a downward spiral of further impoverishment, which in itself sows the seeds of further conflict. Boko Haram's impact on education has affected thousands of students by stealing what is rightfully theirs (Seetanah, 2019, 142). For a nation that has the lowest school attendance nationwide, the attacks on the educational system have been severely damaging for Nigeria (O'Mally, 2010, 2).

The high displacement occasioned by Boko Haram has forced school-aged children to be placed in IDP camps, private homes and communities. In such environments, schools are made up of students of the same age congregating in large rooms or under trees for about three to four hours a day. However, these children do not have access to textbooks and their teachers must teach without any teaching aids. In Borno, one of the devastated states, schools at all levels have been closed in 22 out of the 27 local government areas for a minimum of two years (Human Rights Watch, 2016). With this gridlock on education, children are more vulnerable to becoming trapped in a cycle of poverty (Olofin, 2012, 124) This study, therefore, assesses terrorism in Nigeria and out-of-school children in north east Nigeria, with special consideration of its magnitude, coping strategies adopted by parents and measures taken by the government to address these problems. Secondary sources were used to gather data in order to ascertain the magnitude of the problem as well as proffer solutions for meeting the educational needs of the victims of Boko Haram.

2 Theoretical Framework

This chapter examines the systems theory in relation to the magnitude of out-of-school children as a result of terrorism in North East Nigeria. The theory was articulated by Ludwig von Bertalanffy in the 1940's (Davidson, 1983, 49) and grew out of his view of organism. The theory attempts to view the human society from the point of view of irreducibly integrated systems like an organism. Von Bertalanffy believed that all things, whether living or non-living, could be regarded as systems (Joshua and Olanrewaju, 2016, 61). It focuses attention on the whole system and also gives awareness to the relationships among its fundamental parts. On the basis of this, he drew a contrast between living organism and social organizations (Laszlo and Krippner, 1998, 57–59). Systems theory proposes that there is a resemblance between the organization of the human body and the social organizations (Fremont, and Rosenzweig, 1972, 51).

The theory posits that just as the human body functions in unity to ensure the survival of the whole body, individuals, organizations and various agencies depend on each other for the survival of individual unit and the society at large. The implication with regards the magnitude of the children that are out-of-school in North east Nigeria due to terrorism can be best understood within the framework of this theory because of the core assumptions of the theory. The presumption is that there exist a relationship between terrorism, education and other aspects/institutions of the Nigerian society. In this context, a system according to McLuhan (2014, 74) is a group of interrelated and interacting units that form a unified whole. One of the core assumptions of this theory is that anything that affects a part affects the entire whole and vice versa.

Nigeria as a country is a social and political system and anything that impacts a state has implication on the entire country. Studies by Erne and Ibietan (2012, 26), Oladunjoye and Omemu (2013, 6), Soriwei, et al (2014, 10) show that since the prominence of Boko Haram in north east Nigeria, educational institutions at all levels have come under the attack of the group, leading to the closure of schools in various parts of the northern region as well as the displacement of these children, making them out-of-school. The theory therefore helps in the understanding of the effects the terrorist group has on education in North East Nigeria. As these activities of terrorists increases, displacement would also be on the increase.

3   Magnitude of Out-of-School Children in North East Nigeria

The list of the various attacks by Boko Haram is endless. They have unleashed fear and terror in the minds of the people staying in these parts of the country, thereby affecting every aspects of their social and economic life. Such insecurity has led to massive migration from such troubled areas to other parts of the country which is believed to be less vulnerable to Boko Haram's attacks. According to the Global Terrorist Index (2016), published by the Institute for Economics and Peace, the group was responsible for the deaths of over 6,644 people in Nigeria and Cameroon in 2014 alone. Further findings by Human Rights Watch (2016) showed that an estimated 10,000 civilians have died in Nigeria since the group began its attacks in 2009. The group's brutal insurgency has affected every strata of life in Nigeria's north east region, including education, which has become the fault line of the conflict.'

Indeed, education is worst hit by the Boko Haram activities, and apart from the fact that the fight is directly against western education, which is widely practiced in Nigeria with schools established in every nook and cranny of the country, western education has remained the bedrock of human and capital developments in Nigeria. Despite the imbalance in education in northern and southern Nigeria, northern Nigeria still suffers low enrolment rate especially at the primary level of education. Ruquyyatu (2013) blamed this on the effect of long-standing effect of Islamic education as most parents are yet to embrace western education. To such parents, western education is tied to the Bible and it is an indirect way of changing their religion. Secondly, the security situation in northern Nigeria also comes to play, due to this, there is the fear of death, terrorist attacks and violence, and children often suffer disruption to daily routines or school.

In most cases, children are either lost or their parents are not available or do not feel safe enough to take them to school. This aside, the Boko Haram group has so far burnt down or destroyed more than fifty primary schools in northern Nigeria in a staunch campaign to shut down all western-oriented schools. Reports from (Human Rights Watch, 2016; Oladunjoye and Omemu, 2013, 5; Ruquyyatu, 2013) suggest that students and teachers have had to stay at home for fear of attack. A study by Nigeria DHS Education Data survey (2012, 31) aptly describes a picture of education in the north east parts of Nigeria. According to the report, 12 percent of children in Borno state are not in primary school while in Zamfara state, the percentage of out-of-school children is 68 percent. The two states have the highest number of out-of-school children in Nigeria, which is a consequence of terrorist activities in the Northern region.

Boko Haram has targeted and killed teachers, education workers and students. At least 611 teachers have been deliberately killed and a further 19,000 have been forced to flee since 2009 (USAID, 2015, 15). The report narrated that more than 2,000 people are females and they have been abducted by the group, many from their schools from the beginning of the conflict. Thousands more students and teachers have been injured, some in deadly suicide bombings in the same period. According to Sanni (2015, 54), between 2009 and 2015, attacks in north east Nigeria have destroyed more than 910 schools and forced at least 1,500 to close. By early 2016, an estimated 952,029 school-age children had fled the violence (Ohiwerei, 2017, 165). They have little or no access to education, likely blighting their future for years to come.

These findings can be supported by Voice of Africa (2018), that Nigeria has more out-of-school children today than any country in the world (estimated at 20 million), with 13.2 million currently in Nigeria. The findings further show that 60 percent of this figure are girls living in the north; the over 200 Chibok girls is a case in point. Thus, it is obvious that Northern Nigeria remains a volatile area subject to an armed insurgency contributing to a growing population of IDPs and out-of-school girls, boys, and youth. The education situation in this region is dire (Owoeye and Yara, 2011, 69). These states are among the worst performing in the nation on a series of education indicators, thus reflecting the broader political, economic and social crisis in the region. For instance, In May 2013, Boko Haram took control of part of Borno state, and by January 2015, over nine-thousand deaths were reported due to Boko Haram related violence. Estimates suggest a rate of approximately one-thousand deaths per month in 2015 and 2016 with over nine-million people affected by the violence.

There is an estimated 1.5 million IDPs in Borno, Yobe and Adamawa (Human Rights Watch research, 2016). The attacks are not only interrupting children's learning and putting them at risk of grave injury, but it is also leaving them susceptible to long-term risks. Advocates have long held that education is the number one guarantor of income, wealth, status and security. Education also comes with the reduced risk of infant mortality, contracting HIV and being forced into child marriage. The increased risks come just as the United Nations recently pledged that by 2030, all children will complete free, equitable and quality primary and secondary education. The declaration was made as part of the U.N.'s Sustainable Development Goals. Despite this, insecurity, fear of violence and attacks are preventing many teachers from resuming classes and discouraging parents from sending their children back to school. In Nigeria alone, approximately 600 teachers have been killed since the start of the Boko Haram insurgency (UNESCO, 2011). '

As a result of this, an estimated 2.2 million people, including about 1.4 million children, have fled the fighting in the northeast, this has brought about displaced children of school age to 952,029 (UNICEF, 2015). Out of this, only about 10 percent of the children are in government-recognized displacement camps, where some educational services are provided by volunteer teachers. The remaining 90 percent are with friends and family members, with little or no access to schooling (USAID, 2015). Despite these regular attacks, children are willing to go to school (UNESCO, 2011). However, children, youth and parents remain fearful to go to school because they are afraid of attacks, abductions and kidnappings. In other words, children and youth are willing to go to school but they will not go if they are afraid of the risks they face to get to school.

Addressing the issues related to safety (i.e. transportation and accessible safe learning spaces) is required in order to increase school attendance. As cited in one of the FGD responses conducted by Sanni (2015), a concerned parent supported the fact that out-of-school children face difficulty in retracing their steps back to school after being displaced by terrorist activities.

The issue of out-of-school children and their difficulties have been noted by parents.

Parent (Male) - Benisheik Community, Borno State: "The total number of children who are attending school has drastically reduced, even though we desire education for our children, we do not have the means to provide an education to them."

Parent (Female) - Benisheik Community, Borno State: "We have great concern about the education of our children. The insurgency has seriously affected their education and now they have spent two or three years out of school."

We could also see the concerns of parents for their children's education, and despite the high rate of drop-outs as a result of the activities of these terrorists, they are concerned with the rate at which schools are being burnt and destroyed. Another respondent had this to say: "These terrorists have burnt majority of the schools in this community multiple times. Every time the school is renovated, it is burnt again." – Parent (Male) - Benisheik Community, Borno State.

However, it is not surprising in many of the communities without schools or few schools that fewer children have returned to school. Because secondary data sources from USAID (2015) report the following figures on the status of schools as of November 2014 in Borno area in North East Nigeria:
– There are 324 primary schools out of a total of 1,357 schools open in Borno,
– There are 105 junior secondary schools out of a total of 249 schools open in Borno, and
– There are 46 senior secondary schools out of a total of 86 schools open in Borno.

A recent study by Uthman (2019) showed that 21 mega primary/junior secondary were built and they spread across the safe and secured locations of the state to facilitate the actualization of the commitment of the government towards education. Down the line, Borno state's mega schooling initiative has expanded robustly to orchestrate the construction of not only 42 mega primary/junior secondary schools, 21 more than the initially planned number, but also 13 more educational structures in the mega schooling concept, which adds up to 53. This has been facilitated by the 2019 state budget that allocated N2 billion for the mega schools alone. Out of the 42 mega primary/junior secondary schools, 24 were constructed in Maiduguri metropolis while the remaining 20 were constructed, each one in Bama, Gubio, Ngazai, Monguno, Kwaya Kusar, Hawul, Biu, Shani, Magumeri, Gwoza and other related secured communities.

Despite these findings, the IDP camps have not failed to carry out their expected responsibilities and functions. IDP communities serve multiple purposes. Majorly as shelters for displaced victims and as schools for children (this serves as a coping mechanism for parents and their children). Therefore, when schools are destroyed, there are multiple spill over effects to families in IDP camps. This was corroborated by a respondent in one of the findings by Olamilekan (2014): "In the Dikwa Camp, the school serves two purposes, that of a school in the morning (7–12), where a learning space is provided and also as shelter for IDPs. The school facility has been over stretched" – Parent (Male) - Dikwa IDP Camp, Borno State.

The government has not been able to meet the humanitarian and educational needs of the children in IDPs, probably because their needs outweigh its current capacity to address them, and also its limited understanding of the rights of IDPs. National efforts to respond to displacement and to mitigate its long-term effects on IDPs and host communities tend to be fragmented, uncoordinated and inadequate, and most of the assistance IDPs receive is provided by host communities (Human Rights Watch, 2016).

4 Measures Taken by the Government to Address the Problem of Terrorism in North East Nigeria

Until recently, the Nigerian government has taken a soft-handed measure in an attempt to engage the members of the Boko Haram in political negotiations, as was done with the Niger Delta militants. For instance, In April 2013, former President Goodluck Jonathan established a 26-member Amnesty Committee on Dialogue and the Peaceful Resolution of Security Challenges in the North, with the mandate to convincing the Boko Haram sect within three months to surrender its arms in exchange for a state pardon and social integration. The sect, however, claimed that it had done no wrong deserving pardon, and insisted instead on continuing its violent campaign to establish an Islamic State in Nigeria. This attempt, according to Sanni (2015), was ill advised as the religious motivation of the sect is different from the secular demands of the Niger Delta militants. Although this was initiated, it did not yield the expected results because of the fact that the sect was not thoroughly understood from the point of view of their ideology and overall objectives.

This has made the Nigerian government to shift from a self-implemented approach to a collaborative approach by working together with other neighbouring governments like Chad, Niger and Cameroun; non-profits organizations and other partners. For instance, UNICEF has been able to reach 67,000 students by setting up temporary learning spaces and renovating and expanding schools (USAID, 2015). It has also trained teachers in providing psychosocial support to children who have been uprooted by the conflict as documented by Okoli & Lortyer (2014, 39). In north east Nigeria, UNICEF has additionally supported 170,000 children back into education in the safer areas of the three states most affected by the conflict, where the majority of schools have been able to re-open (UNICEF, 2015). However, many classrooms are severely overcrowded as some school buildings are still being used to house the large number of displaced persons seeking shelter from the conflict.

In these areas, some displaced teachers, who themselves have fled the fighting, are involved in the schooling and classes are often given on a "double shift" basis to help more children attend school (The Cable, 2015). In Yobe, UNICEF has provided temporary learning spaces for the education of IDP children, as well as teaching and learning aids. In Dalori camp in Borno State, the state Coordination Committee, supported by UNICEF, enrolled 4737 children in school. UNICEF provided pedagogical materials to Borno SUBEB for the children enrolled, and also transport to and from school, to meet parent's security concerns. It also established two in-camp temporary learning spaces in UNICEF tents for children aged between 3 and 5 years. As of 1 October 2015, 6300 children have been able to undertake schooling in a more appropriate environment through UNICEF school support programmes. Also, the 'Back to School' campaign in Borno and Yobe has led to the enrolment of 170, 432 children previously out of school (Isokpan and Durojaye, 2016, 12).

However, the support rendered by these bodies is limited to only some camps, reaching just a fraction of the number of IDPs. The major burden lies with the Nigerian government, having regard to its international human rights obligations to address the issues affecting persons displaced by the Boko Haram insurgency. In addition, UNICEF has trained teachers on psychosocial support and provided more than 132,000 children uprooted by conflict with learning materials, including in local schools hosting displaced students. However, security constraints and funding shortfalls hinder access to education services and the delivery of emergency learning materials. So far, UNICEF has received 44 per cent of the funding required in 2015 to respond to the humanitarian needs of children in Niger, Nigeria, Cameroon and Chad (USAID, 2015). Apart from this, government security forces' use of schools for military purposes not only places schools at risk of attack but is contrary to the Safe Schools Declaration, which Nigeria endorsed in 2015.

The declaration urges parties *"not to use schools and universities for any purpose in support of the military effort."* The report documents security forces' abuses against teachers, students, and schools, especially Quranic schools and the response of the Nigerian government, as well as the interventions by government agencies, inter-governmental and non-governmental organizations (NGOs), including humanitarian agencies seeking to restore the right to education for children affected by the northeast conflict. The government established a Joint Task Force (JTF) and deployed 8000 soldiers to the region, which was the largest military deployment since the Nigerian civil war. In 2015, the troops succeeded in reclaiming most of the areas under Boko Haram control. Supported by the Nigerian Air Force, the army has launched attacks against Sambisa Forest, which is considered to be a major stronghold of the sect, rescuing captives, arresting insurgents and destroying their weapons.

The UN High Commissioner for Human Rights (HCHR), however, has documented a series of human rights violations against Nigerians by the JTF, such as extrajudicial and summary executions, torture, arbitrary detention, enforced disappearances, and rape. They are also reported to have carried out the intimidation of residents, arbitrary arrests and searches, and the burning of houses and shops belonging to civilians. In a fire fight between the JTF and the Boko Haram in Baga, a village on Lake Chad, near the Nigerian border with Cameroon, for instance, Ohiwerei (2017, 163) reported that almost 185 people were killed and others were injured. Human rights abuses also exist at the Nigerian military detention facility at Giwa Barracks in Maiduguri, where thousands of Boko Haram suspects (some without concrete evidence to support the suspicion) are detained. Reports exist that due to the overcrowded and unsanitary living conditions, several persons have died, including children (Olamilekan, 2014, 367).

Sadly, the children there are either being detained along with their mothers, or have been born while in detention. This further tells us that instead of this agency to protect the lives and properties of these displaced citizens, the reverse is the case. Hence, this measure introduced by the government has been abortive. The Nigerian government appears to have failed in its obligation to ensure that children do not participate in hostilities, as required by the local and international laws for the protection of children. The JTF, which consists largely of teenagers without basic education, some of whom have lost their parents and siblings to the insurgency, are on a revenge mission. According to UNICEF, Commission for Human Rights, and the Protection Sector Working Group, children are joining the ranks of the JTF in increasing numbers and being used in the fight against the insurgency.

Nigeria has received international support to take care of the increasing needs of those affected by the insurgency. Following the repeated attacks on schools and the abduction of over 200 Chibok girls in 2014, the Safe Schools Initiative was launched by the UN Special Envoy for Global Education and the former United Kingdom Prime Minister, Gordon Brown, at the World Economic Forum in Nigeria, with an initial donation of $10 million (Sanni, 2015). The purpose of the initiative is to strengthen the #BringBackOurGirls campaign and to ensure that all schools in Nigeria are safe from attacks in the future, as it seeks to build community security groups to promote safe zones for education.

5   Conclusion

The study assessed Boko Haram terrorism and out-of-school children in North East Nigeria. Findings from the study reveal that terrorism and insurgency are globally becoming household words as there is no nation that is completely absolved from their effects. This is the reason why Global Terrorism Index (2016) observes that war, terrorism and other forms of transnational political violence are in many ways more threatening today than ever before as civilian casualties have been on increase. Among these civilian casualties are parents and their children who become 'out-of-school'. Hence, Boko Haram sect have rubbished the image of Nigeria and have hampered the quest of achieving the Sustainable Development Goals (SDGs) as well as vision 2020, and access to education is one of the goals that has always called for the attention of the government and the world at large.

Therefore, the federal government should post security personnel to guide all schools from primary to tertiary institutions in Nigeria, most especially in this crisis prone areas. This study also advocates for free bus services to be available for children in these areas to take them to and from school under tight security. The rural schools should not be neglected as security men should be drafted to security risk areas. Most importantly, adequate school attendance record should be kept by teachers to monitor the attendance of children. This measure must be used to forestall any form of kidnaping of children.

This study further suggests that the Nigerian government should partner with international organisations to ensure that funds disbursed by them are effectively utilised to reintegrate affected out-of-school children into the society. It is clear from many successful donor-funded programmes in Nigeria that collaborative interventions with local communities have a more positive impact. Thus, collaboration with community members in such interventions, for example, engaging local skilled workers to make uniforms or school bags can help localise solutions and build a sense of responsibility.

Education is a basic right and its availability in post conflict communities can provide life-saving information, protect children from trafficking, and recruitment by armed groups. Considerable effort is needed to ensure that children deprived of educational facilities as a result of the Boko Haram insurgency are given access to quality education. Development partners should encourage and financially support Nigerian government's effort to ensure that humanitarian education response plans are adequately funded so that interruptions to education caused by the insurgency are minimised.

The present situation in North East Nigeria as a result of the Boko Haram insurgency calls for urgent intervention. The use of the military in fighting the insurgency is commendable, but the government needs to pursue a more comprehensive strategy that addresses the economic and social roots of the crisis. Measures should address the prevalence of poverty and unemployment in this region.

References

Abiye, Solomon. 2011. "The Abuja attacks, Lagos." *The New Telegraph*, 10 May. https://issuu.com/newtelegraphonline/docs/friday__may_10__new_telegraph

Adamu, Idris. 2019. "Ideology of Boko Haram." *Journal of Islamic Education* 2 (2): 31–34.

Adesoji, Abimbola. 2010. "The Boko Haram uprising and Islamic revivalism in Nigeria". *Africa spectrum.* 45(2): 95–108.

Davidson Mark. 1983. *Uncommon Sense: The Life and Thought of Ludwig Von Bertalanffy*. Los Angeles: J. P. Tarcher.

Erne, Osse and Ibietan, Juntes. 2012. "The Cost of Boko Haram Activities in Nigeria". *Arabian Journal of Business and Management Review* 2(2): 10–32.

Fremont, Edwin and Rosenzweig, Jones. 1972. "General Systems Theory: Applications for organization and management". *Academy of Management Journal* 44(7): 46–55.

Global Terrorist Index. 2016. "Measuring and understanding the impact of terrorism". Institute of economics and peace. Assessed 12 November 2016. http://economicsandpeace.org/wp-content/uploads/2016/11/Global-Terrorism-Index-2016.2.pdf

Human Rights Watch. 2016. "They set the classrooms on fire: Attacks on education in north east Nigeria." Assessed November 12, 2016 https://www.hrw.org/report/2016/11/they-set-classrooms-fire/attacks-education-northeast-nigeria

Isokpan, Aisosa J. and Durojaye, Ebenezer. 2016. "Impact of the Boko Haram insurgency on the child's right to education in Nigeria." *PER*. 19(1): 1–43. doi.org/10.17159/1727-3781/2016/v19n0a1299.

Joshua Segun and Olanrewaju Faith. 2016. "The Impact of Terrorism on Education: The North-Eastern Nigerian Experience." *Journal of International Politics and Development* 14(1): 59–74.

Laszlo, Anderson and Krippner, Sorthe. 1998. "Systems Theories: Their Origins, Foundations, and Development" *In Systems Theories and A Priori Aspects of Perception.* Edited by Jordan, Joyce, 47–74. Amsterdam, The Netherlands: Elsevier Science.

McLuhan, Marshall. 2014. "The Hot and Cool Interview". In *Media Research: Technology, Art and Communication: Critical Voices in Art, Theory and Culture,* edited by Moos, Michel, 69–78. New York: Routledge.

Musa, Palter. 2011. "Boko Haram History in Nigeria", *Journal of Arts and Social Science,* 4(2). 18–21.

Nigeria DHS Education data Survey. 2011. Abuja, Federal Government Press.

Obioma, Linda. 2012. Conflict Management. Ikeja, Lagos: Thomas Nelson Nig. Ltd

Ohiwerei Frederick. 2017. "Effects of Boko Haram Insurgency Education in Nigerian Universities" *Scholarly Journal of Education.* 3(9): 161–173

Okoli, Chukwuma. & Lortyer, Philip. 2014. "Terrorism and Humanitarian Crisis in Nigeria: Insights from Boko Haram Insurgency." *Global Journal of Human-social science.* 14(1): 39–49

Okolo, Benjamin and Akubo, Aduku. 2019. "Boko Haram Insurgency in Nigeria." *The Accord,* 12 August. https://www.accord.org.za/ajcr-issues/boko-haram-insurgency-in-nigeria/

Oladunjoye Patrick and Omemu Felix. 2013. "Effect of Boko Haram on School Attendance in Northern Nigeria" *British Journal of Education.* 1(2): 1–9

Olamilekan Adefolarin. 2014. "A Perusal Analyses on Boko Haram Crisis in Northern Nigeria and its Implication on Educational Psychology of School Children and Teachers" *Journal of Education and Human Development.* 3(2): 361–380

Olofin, Osun. 2012. "Defence Spending and Poverty Reduction in Nigeria" *Journal of Social Sciences.* 2(6): 122–127

O'Mally, Brendan. 2010. Education under Attack. *Priorities in Education* UNESCO. Paris 1–4.

Owoeye Joseph and Yara Philias. 2011. "School Facilities and Academic Achievement of Secondary School Agricultural Science in Ekiti State, Nigeria". *Asian Social Science* 7(7): 64–74.

Ruquyyatu, Ahmed. 2013. "Declining Enrolment in Primary Education in Nigeria. Press Conference by *Minister of Education, Abuja.*, March 11.

Sanni Oluyemisi. 2015. "Effects of Insecurity and Challenges of Female's Education in Nigeria" *African Journal for the Psychological Study Social Issues.* 18(3): 51–57.

Seetanah Boopen. 2019. "The Economic Importance of Education: Evidence from Africa Using Dynamic Panel Data Analysis." *Journal of Applied Economics.* 12(1): 137–157.

Shabayany, Barte. 2012. "New Waves of Terrorism in Nigeria not true Expression of Islam". *Jos studies.* 20: 33–47.

Soriwei, Friday, Idowu, Akinsanmi. & Akinloye, Babatunde. 2014. "Boko Haram Abducts Twenty. Women near Chibok". *Punch Newspaper*, 29 October.

The Cable. 2015. "Boko Haram Forces 1m Children out of School" Assessed May 16, 2017. https://web.thecable.ng/boko-haram-put-1m-children-out-of-school

UNESCO. 2011. "The Quantitative Impact of Conflict on Education." A Think Piece Prepared for the Education for All Global Monitoring Report. Paris. Assessed 16 May, 2017. https://unesdoc.unesco.org/ark:/48223/pf0000191304

UNICEF. 2015. "Nigeria Conflict Forces More Than 1 Million Children from School." Assessed 16 May, 2017 https://www.unicef.org/media/media_86621.html.USAID. 2015. Rapid Situational Analysis in Borno State: *Education and Conflict Creative Associates International*. 16(2): 13–17.

Uthman Abubakar. 2019. Borno's mega schools years after. Assessed 24 April, 2020. https://www.pressreader.com/nigeria/weekly-trust/20190105/282054803165805

Voice of Africa. 2018. "In Nigeria, More Than 13 Million School Age Children Out-of – School" Assessed April 24, 2020. https://www.voanews.com/africa/un-nigeria-more-13-million-school-age-children-out-school

Yusuf, Ladsley. 2019. *The Principles and Practice of Islamic Religion*. Lagos: NOK Publishers Nig. Ltd.

PART 4

Minorities and Education

CHAPTER 15

Academic Abuse and Violence against Students in Delta State, Nigeria and Its Impact on Their Learning Behavior

Israel Oberedjemurho Ugoma

1   Introduction

Since formal education (schooling) is perceived as an instrument for the acquisition of appropriate skills for people to earn a living from and to contribute to the development of the society, every parent and nation is eager to key into it without reservations. Meanwhile, schooling is a formal academic training that usually takes place in an institution where pupils and students are instructed in discipline of arts, sciences and languages etc. Schooling involves mental or cognitive processes that require development and maturity, for effective and meaningful learning to take place. This is because the human body is a combination of complex organ system that function differently at maturity and spelt out by nature. But when these organs are forcefully put to use before maturity it amounts to an abuse of that organ. According to neuro-scientists, part of the brain for learning (cognitive) is the prefrontal lobe while the part for social skill such as reading and verbal communication is the parietal lobe. Neuroscientists such as Giedd, Elizabeth and Paul (2002) noted that these parts of the brain when scanned by Magnetic Resonance Imaging (MRI) revealed that they undergo neuronal pruning for development, reinforcement and strengthening for normal functioning from ages 5 years, 8 years, 12 years, 16 years and 20 year in a gradual process.

In addition to the MRI scanning of the brain by Neuroscientists, the Nigeria Educational Research and Development Council (NERDC, 2014) on the national policy on education, spelt out the required years for admission into pre-primary, primary and secondary school. According to NERD (2014), the pre-primary education is the one -year education given to children at ages 4–5 years, and primary education is the education given in institutions to children ages 6–12 years while the secondary education is the education children receive from ages 12–13 years up ward after primary education and before tertiary education. In the light of this, maturity and acquisition of social skills are very important tools for schooling. Today, however, in Delta State Nigeria and possibly, some other countries in the world, observation has shown that most children are forcefully exposed to academic training at an early stage of childhood development. A stage far from the period in which the prefrontal and parietal lobe are yet to undergo developmental pruning and thinning, for effective use.

Hence, academic training in this context is a period in which the child is admitted into school at early childhood between 1 or 2 years pre-primary school, 3 or 4 years primary school, 8 or 9 years secondary school and 14 or 15 years tertiary school. Children who are sent to school at these early years of childhood, face academic violence and academic abuse. Because this is contrary to the stated norm by NERDC (2014). When this is compared with late or normal schooling, it is the period in which the child begins schooling at late childhood between 3 or 4 years pre-primary school, 6 or 7 years primary school, 12 or 13 years secondary school and 17 or 18 years tertiary school; as spelt out by NERDC (2014).

Meanwhile, an abuse by definition according to African Network for the prevention and protection of child abuse and neglect (ANPPCAN 1990) is the intentional, unintentional or well intentional act which endanger the physical health, emotional moral and the educational welfare of the child.While Wikipedia (2018), defines abuse as the improper usage or treatment of an entity, often unfairly or improper gain…through unjust practices and other types of aggression. Hence, Jean Piaget (1962) in his cognitive development theory, outlines four different stages of cognitive development based on the age bracket to guide parents and to avoid academic abuse of the child, these are:

– Sensory motor – from birth to 2 years
– Pre-operational – from 3 years to 7 years
– Concrete operation – 7 years to 11 years
– Formal operation – 11 years to 17 upwards.

Nwankwo (2003) strongly advises that from these stages that are propounded by Piaget, increases in cognitive performance cannot be attained unless both cognitive readiness brought about by maturation and appropriate environmental stimulations are present. Hence, the sensory motor stage in which the child's cognitive development is very low, (0-3 years) with little competence in representing the environment using images, objects permanence, language and lack of social skills, should not be the periods for academic training of the child in the school. Unfortunately, this period set the stage in Delta state, Nigeria in which most parents push their infant children into formal education and schooling. The children are woken up forcefully from sleep by their parents to prepare them for school as early as 5 am, a time when even adults grumble and find it inconveniencing to get up from bed. The tender children will bitterly cry and cry to be allowed to have their sleep back instead of preparing to go to school. The parents who will never allow this, will forcefully with spanking prepare them for the school amidst tears. In addition to this, the parents also make sure that these children are enrolled to attend lesson or extension classes after the normal school hours where they will stay learning till the evening. A child of 2–3 years in the pre-primary school, 3–4 years in the primary school and those of 8–9 years in the secondary school has spent the whole day learning with immature brain. At the end of the day the children are burn-out as observed by the researcher who interviewed parents carrying out school runs of their wards.

In the school, the teacher will hold the tender hands of these children, to force them to write letters of the alphabet and to solve some mathematics, "a task for which the innate disposition or readiness for learning is yet to develop in the children," according to Otubelu[1]. Meanwhile, when the children are not fully coordinating and cooperating with the teachers in the course of writing and solving mathematical problems as a result of lack of cognitive readiness and immature social skill, the teachers will spank them with canes and curses, such as "naughty child", "cockroach brain, shame, shame, shame, shame, wa, wa, wa, wao, fowl shit". To top it all, this same child who has spent almost the whole day in school, will be given home-work assignment, in any of the subject to submit the next day. Failure to solve the assignment of which they have no knowledge of will attract further punishment from their teachers.

To buttress this, the normal primary six class in which the children are expected to be able to read before they are formally admitted into the secondary school, in Nigeria is gradually being phased out in Delta State, so that the child is now made to read up to primary five and is forced to enter into the secondary school. And while in the secondary school, some are made to write the junior secondary certificate examination (JSSCE) from class 2 instead of 3 and are again made to enroll and write the senior secondary school examination (SSCE) with West African Examination Council (WAEC), National Examination Council (NECO), from class 2 instead of class 3. This means that primary 6, JSS3 and SS3 classes are soon to be phased out of the school system, completely in Nigeria. In all this, going by the definition of abuse and violence, the child who is treated this way, is not far from being abused and violated academically. The same way he/she will be abused sexually at early childhood and be forced into child labor. What then characterized the effect of academic abuse and violence of children in school? Naturally, when a force is applied to an object suddenly, it changes the directions or speed of the motion of that object. It is no wonder too an adage says that when a fruit is forced to ripe early, the fruit will also get rotten early. Under-aged children who are admitted to early schooling to face academic training have a lot of negative side effects that tend to make them have problems early. Some of these problems include, low academic achievement effect, emotional imbalance, substance use disorder, indulgent in examination malpractice.

In this study, only the variable on low academic achievement effects, will be considered. On academic achievement, O'Donnell (2007) on national household education survey (NHES) study of school children, said that school readiness, a multi-dimensional concept conveys important advantages. This is because children who enter schools at an appropriate development stage with appropriate skills are more likely than their peers who enter at an inappropriate development stage to experience later academic success, attain higher levels of education and secure employment. According to him absence of these and other poor social skills may contribute to even greater disparities in academic success down the road. According to the (NHES) study, when children are just 3 years old at the time of starting school, only about 17% of them could recognize letters, 47% could count to 20, 34% could write their names and 2% could read letter words. But the reverse is the case, when they are 6 years and above before they started schooling, 60% could recognize letters, 85% could count more than 20, 89% could write their names and 83% could read two letter words. Catherine (2013) advocated that children who start elementary schools at 6 years or 7 years consistently achieve better academic results as well as high level of wellbeing than those who enter at 3 years or 4 years.

A research was carried out to ascertain the damaging effects of children well-being in which Lord Layard (2013) director of the wellbeing programme, pronounced that research has it that early schooling damages the academic wellbeing of the children, instead, according to the research, children must be receiving education by the age of 5, schooling by the age of 6 so that by the age of 7 and 8, they can be subject to the three R sassessment.

Forcing children to 'Read Early' can be very devastating for them. According to Elkind (2010) who reported a reading research carried out onschool children in Winnetka, compared classes of children who were introduced to formal reading instruction in first grade (Early) with those who were first introduced to it in second grade (Late). He said that children who started earlier reading had an initial advantage on the reading test used to assess pupil's progress, but this advantage disappeared by the time the children were in grade four. According to him, most intriguing and interesting part of the study was a long-term follow-up that was made when the children became young adolescents and were in junior high school (secondary school). Observers who did not know which children had been in which group were introduced into the classroom. They were to look and assess all the facets of the young people's reading behavior. The observers found that the adolescents who were introduced to reading late were enthusiastic, spontaneous and more skilled readers than those who were introduced to reading early. This same reading research study was conducted in England, in Russia, Chicago and New York, the educational information from these countries, supported the data and findings by these researchers. Researches on these studies therefore suggested strongly that, "children confronted with the task of learning to read before they have the requisite mental abilities can develop long-term learning difficulties",[2] Elkind (2010). This means that most children who are taught to read at 6 years have more problem in reading later in life than those taught to read at 7 years and 8 years.

It is based on this that the researcher decided to conduct a thorough study on secondary school students to verify the academic abuse and violence against students in Delta State and its impact on their learning behavior.

2 Statement of the Problem

For years now, it was observed by the researcher, the influx of tender children and students admitted into primary school from ages 3–4 years and 8–9 years into secondary school. Meanwhile, there has been a noticeable decline in their academic achievement according Adesulu (2015) and Toscany (2014) who gave the statistical data of West Africa Examination Council (WAEC) from 2007–2017 particularly from 2012–2017 on candidate's performance with credit pass in Mathematics and English language which were 36.7%, 38.30%, 31.28%, 38.68%, 52.97% and 59.22%, with sudden increase in antisocial behavior. This study was therefore purported to verify the cause-effect relationship between age and academic training by comparing early entrants with late entrants into secondary school taking into cognizance the brain development for academic training, which is the prefrontal cortex of the cerebrum.

3 Purpose of the Study

The purpose of the study is to determine the academic abuse of students in Delta State, Nigeria; as a result of early admission into secondary school.

The research question used for the study is:
(1) What is the influence of early and late (normal) schooling on the academic achievement of secondary school students in Mathematics, English Language and Basic Science.

The hypothesis tested at 0.05 alpha level that guided this study is:
Ho: There is no significant different between early and late entrants of secondary school students on their academic achievement in mathematics, English language and Basic science.

4   Method

The study adopted the ex-post facto research design. This design was appropriate for the study because it stands to establish the cause-effect relationship between early and normal academic training of the child and his achievement. The procedure employed for data collection was the academic records of 700 secondary school students who were between 8–9 years at the point of entering into the secondary school. This group of students (early entrant) was compared with another group of 300 secondary school students (late or normal) who were between 12–13 years at the point of entering into the secondary school. Three core subjects offered in the junior secondary school were used for academic achievement. These are mathematic, English language and Basic science. The research question was answered using the mean (∞) and standard deviation (SD), while the t-test was used to test the hypothesis at 0.05 alpha level.

Research Question 1

TABLE 15.1   Mean and standard deviation scores of students in English language, mathematics and basic science.

Age of schooling	No	English (x)	SD	Maths (x)	SD	Basic science (x)	SD
Early : 8–9 yrs	700	40.11	6.33	39.85	6.31	50.4	7.1
Normal (late) 12–13 yrs	300	74.8	8.6	67	8.2	81	9.0

SOURCE: ACADEMIC RECORDS OF 10 SECONDARY SCHOOLS

Table 15.1 above shows the mean and standard deviation scores of students in English Language, Mathematics and Basic Science based on their age of schooling. It shows that those that entered school at the normal school entrance age scored higher than those who entered school earlier in English Language, Mathematics and Basic Science.

Hypothesis

TABLE 15.2　T-test statistics on differences in mean scores of students who entered school at the earlier and those who entered at normal age in English language, mathematics and basic science.

Subjects	Age of students	$\bar{X}$	SD	DF	T-cal	T-crit	Alpha	Decision
Mathematics	Early: 8–9 yrs	39.85	6.31	18	8.060	2.101	0.05	Significant
	Late: 12–13 yrs	67	8.2					
English Language	Early: 8–9 yrs	40.11	6.33	18	8.660	2.101	0.05	Significant
	Late: 12–13 yrs	74.8	8.6					
Basic Science	Early: 8–9 yrs	50.4	7.1	18	8.406	2.101	0.05	Significant
	Late: 12–13	81	9.0					

SOURCE: ACADEMIC RECORD OF 10 SECONDARY SCHOOLS

An independent sample t-test was conducted to compare the Mean differences in the achievement of students who enrolled in school at an earlier age and those are the normal age in English Language, Mathematics and Basic Science. Table 15.2 reveals that there was significant difference in the scores for early, 8–9 years (M-39.85, SD-6.31) and normal 12–13 years (M-67, SD- 8.2) in Mathematics. The table indicates that t- cal> t- crit (t- cal= 8.060, df = 18=α = 0.05). Therefore, the hypothesis that there is no significant difference in their Mathematic achievement is rejected.

Again, the table reveals that there was significant difference in the scores for early 8–9 years (M-40.11, SD 6.33) and normal 12–13 years (M-74.8, SD-8.6) in English Language. The table indicates that t- cal> t- crit (8.660, df=18=α= 0.05). Therefore, the hypothesis that there is no significant difference in their English Language achievement is rejected.

Furthermore, the table reveals that there was significant difference in the scores for early, 8–9 years (M-50.4, SD-7.1) and normal 12–13 years (M-80, SD-9.0) in Basic Science. The table indicates that t- cal> t- cri (8.406, df=18=α= 0.05).

Therefore, the hypothesis that there is no significant difference in their Basic Science achievement is rejected.

5   Discussion

Academic abuse and violence according to this research study is the academic training given to children in primary and secondary schools at a period when they are not maturationally ready for it. Most especially when the prefrontal lobe and the parietal lobe of the brain which are the organs for academic work, are yet to be matured through pruning. Hence, findings from this study in table1indicated that early entrants into academic training in school experience low academic achievement in Mathematics, English Language and Basic Science. Analysis of the hypothesis using t-test indicated too that there is significant difference in academic achievement both in Mathematics, English Language and Basic Science for those that entered school at the normal school entrance age, against those that entered at earlier school entrance age. This finding is in agreement with the finding by O'Donnell (2007) on National Household Education Survey (NHES), that when children are just 3 years old at the time of starting school, only about 17% could recognize letters, 47% could count to 20, 34% could write their names and 2% could read two letter words. But the reverse is the case when they are 6 years and above before they start school, where 60% could recognize letters, 85% could count more than 20, 89% could write their names and 83% could read two letter words.

Again, this finding agreed with the findings of Elkind (2010) and Hockenbury (2011) who reported in their studies that adolescents who were introduced to reading late, were more spontaneous, enthusiastic and more skilled readers than those who were introduced to it at an early stage. This is because the MRI scanning of the brain of children by neuroscientists show that, a developing brain through neuronal pruning that has not reached maturity before being confronted with cognitive task, results in a behaviour that is immature, risky, impulsive and unpredictable.

Since 2011, down to 2018, the Ministry of Basic and Secondary Education, Department of Exams and Standard, continues to give report of rapid decline in academic achievement in all the core subjects such as Mathematics, English Language and Basic Science. This has prompted the Delta State Governor to initiate a reading competition in 2018 to promote a reading culture among the students in Delta State.

6 Educational Implication of the Findings

From the study empirical evidence is provided to show that learning in a formal educational setting is built upon maturity of the organs of the body of humans, especially the brain. School children achieve academically higher when they are cognitively matured than when they are immatured. An immatured use of an organ subjected by adult constitutes abuse and violence. It is therefore imperative that both parents and teachers take into cognizance the age brackets children are expected to be engaged in academic training in the school. The teachers are also expected to know that it is not their duties to hold school children's hands to write.

7 Recommendations

Based on the findings from this study, supported by related studies and governmental efforts in promoting academic achievement through reading cultures among students, it is hereby recommended that:
- Children below 3 years should not be made to start pre-primary schools, those below 6 or 5 years should not be made to start elementary school, while those below 11 years to start secondary school and below 16 years to start tertiary schools.
- Parents should be well guided through awareness campaign on the growth and development of their children to avoid hurrying.
- Teachers should be well informed, especially those teaching nursery schools to avoid early introduction of academic training by forcing the children to write through holding their hands. Children at this level can be stimulated cognitively through plays, socialization and use of toys.
- Government can continue to motivate students to promote reading culture through scholarship, prizes, grants etc. as demonstrated by the Delta State Government.
- Encouraging and sponsoring researches that are bothered on this subject matters, (academic abuse) and other related sensitive topics.
- Having a fair knowledge of the various organs of the body, their functioning and maturing period in order to harness their usefulness to the betterment of the child and the society.
- Training and sponsoring teachers, organizing workshops and seminars for them.

Providing workable rules and regulations on educational ethics to private school owners and parents, by government.

8 Conclusion

The previous period in the 1970s and 1980s in Delta State, Nigeria, lay emphasis on the full growth of the child by having his hand cross over his head to touch his ear before he was admitted into primary school. The age bracket then was between 6–7 years. But the present society tends to hurry children to grow up quickly, in almost all facets of life. The wrong notion behind the hurrying, is the 21st century era, known as the Computer Age. But unfortunately, *nature's clock* has not changed, not for a second. Hence, pregnancy still remains 9 months, (Elkind, 2010), the reproductive organs begins to mature at 10–18 years upward. Motor and physical development of the child becomes manifest between 10–18 years, and too, the prefrontal cortex of the brain meant for academic use (cognitive) begins to undergo pruning from ages 5,8,12 and 16 years upward until 20s. The recognition and proper understanding of these organs and development of the child is the *"Right of the Child"*. The deviation from this is constitute *the abuse and violence against the child academically*. Academic violence against the child of today who becomes the adult of tomorrow is wrong for their development. He or she also carries out these standards as a model on other persons, thereby creating a vicious cycle, referred to as *repetitive compulsion*. These can crumble national growth and development.

References

Adewale, Afigbo E. 2006. *The Demon with Examination Malpractice, Historical Perspective*. Lagos: Examination Ethics Publication.

ANPPCAN, Article 30. 1990. "The U.N. Convention on the Right of the Child. *International Commitment on the Right of the Children 1990*.

Cameron, David. 2013. "Early Schooling Damaging Wellbeing," 12 September. Accessed 4 September, 2018: http://www.the guardian.com/education/2013/Sept/12.

Colman, Andrew M. 2003. *Oxford Dictionary of Psychology*. New York: Oxford University Press Inc.

Hockenbury, Don H and Hockenbury, Sandra E. 2011. *Discovery Psychology* 5th ed. New York: Worth Publishers.

Elkind David. 2006. *Miseducation, Preschoolers at Risk*. New York: Knopf Publishing Company.

Elkind David. 2010. *The Hurrid Child, Growing Up Too Fast Too Soon.* USA: Da Capo Press.

Giedd, Jay N. "The Teen Brain: Prime to learn, Prime to Take Risks": Cerebrum https://www.dana.org/news/cerebrum/detail.aspx?2009.

Layard, Lord. 2013. Early Schooling Damaging Wellbeing," 12 September. Accessed 4 September, 2018: http://www.the guardian.com/education/2013/Sept/12.

Mash, Eric J and Wolfe, David A. 2005. *Abnormal Child Psychology* 3rd ed. New York: Vicki Knight Publisher.

Michael, Koenigs and Tranel, Daniel. 2007. "Irrational Economic Decision-making after Ventromedial Prefrontal Damage: Evidence from the Ultimatum Game." *Journal of Neuroscience*. No. 951–956.

O' Donnell, K. Parents' Reports of the School Readiness of Young Children from the National Household Education Surveys Program of 2007." Washington, DC: National Centre for Education Statistics. Assessed 4 September, 2018, http://nces.ed.gov/pubsearch/pubsinfoasp?pubid-2008051.

Otubelu Joseph C. 2000. *Growth and Development of Children.* Asaba: Ogive Ventures.

Piaget, Jean. 1963. *Intellectual Development from Adolescent to Adulthood.* London: Routledge.

Prisk. Catherine. 2013. "Early Schooling Damaging Wellbeing," 12 September. Accessed 4 September.

Shonekon, Moses O. 1999. *Promoting the Ethnics and Integrity of West African Examination Council* Lagos: Exam Ethics Publishers.

Sowell, Elizabeth R, Thompson, Paul M, Leonard, Christiana M, Suzanne E, Kan Eric and Toga, Arthur W, 2004. "Longitudinal Mapping of Cortical Thickness and Brain Growth in Normal Children." *Journal of Neuroscience*. No. 8223–8231.

The Guardian. 2018: http://www.the guardian.com/education/2013/Sept/12.

Wikipedia. "Concept of Abuse." Accessed 13 August, 2018, https://en.mwikipedia.org/wiki/abuse.

CHAPTER 16

Effects of Lessons on Empathic Response and Perception on Conflict Reduction among Secondary School Adolescents

Peter Kwaja

1   Introduction

Conflict is a natural and inevitable part of the personal and social life of humans. It is one of the most pervasive aspects of human affairs. It exists in almost all social relationships, whether they are personal and informal or impersonal and formal. Conflict according to (Hornby 2007) is a situation in which people, group or countries are involved in a serious disagreement or argument. (Hornby 2007) also defines it as a situation in which there are opposing ideas, opinions, feelings, or wishes; a situation in which it is difficult to choose. (Schellenberge 2001) defines conflict as behaviour in which people oppose one another in their thoughts, feelings and/or actions. (Agulanna 2008) opines that conflict is an antagonistic struggle over certain scarce objects. This brings about injury, destruction and defeat of an opponent. (Agulanna 2008) also reports that conflicts, though destructive, can also have functional and beneficial consequences for a group and community life.

The prevalence of conflicts among Nigerian students as observed by (Anokam 2012) had increased in the past few years in terms of frequency of recorded clashes and number of adolescents involved. Students are quick to resort to conflict to get what they want. Physical and sometimes fatal fights can start at the slightest comment, a sideways glance, or an unintended bump (Cohen & Nordås 2012). (Jehn & Mannix 2001, 240) opine that some conflicts such as interpersonal incompatibilities, disagreements in viewpoints and opinion, disagreement over the group's approach have often resulted in cruel behaviours and no community in the nation, rural or urban, rich or poor is immune to the incidence and tragedies of youth conflicts. (Kalgo 2001) asserts that students tend to have disrespect for their seniors and teachers in schools and that incivility and widespread dishonesty, cheating and violence are on the increase in secondary schools. This was corroborated by (Minchakpu 2002) and (Ademu-Awuja and Kwaja 2013, 187) who observe that students are involved in various forms of cruelty such as bullying, hitting, kicking and assault of both students and teachers, destruction of property and even murder. (World Health Organization 2013) also state that because of the pressure many students face, they tend to put themselves at high risk for intentional and unintentional injuries which result from some sort of conflict among them.

One of the results of these conflicts is that students miss school and participate less in class. (Ojo 2000, 83) asserts that interpersonal incompatibilities, disagreements in viewpoints and opinions and disagreement over the group's approaches had accounted for many incidences of school drop-out, drug addiction, cultism, prostitution and many other social vices persisting today among adolescents. (Ojo 2000) thus, conclude that such a situation is hardly conducive for meaningful learning and academic success. Some of the likely causes of conflicts are quest for recognition, envy jealousy, sectional pride, disagreement, mistrust, corruption, group assertion, selfishness and group staying too long in power. (Agulanna 2008) observed that students' conflict had been associated with a variety of factors, which include difficulty in controlling anger. (Kwaja 2010,144) agreeing with (Agulanna 2008) notes that students injure and kill themselves over incidents that could be considered trivial such as an insult, a dispute over a girlfriend or boyfriend, or a rumour. Economic deprivation had been one of the major causes of youth restiveness in Delta State. This orientation had over time gradually crept into institutions of learning. The spate of adolescents' conflict in secondary schools in Delta State had resulted in the cancellation of internal and external examination results, disruption of academic calendars and eventual close down of some secondary schools within the state (Aghanta 2006). Some students in secondary schools in Delta State and in Agbor in particular engage in various forms of conflicts resulting in violent behaviours which have negatively affected academic activities. In addition, students at the senior secondary school level are entirely adolescents who are experiencing developmental problems.

Adolescent is a young person in the process of developing from a child into an adult. (World Health Organization 2001) describes an adolescent as a person who is between the ages of 10 to19 and observes that the biological determinants of adolescents are fairly universal; however, the duration and defining characteristics of these individuals may vary across time, cultures, and socio-economic situations. (The International Planned Parenthood Federation 2004) defines adolescents as people who are between ages 15 to19. Actually, IPPF also admitted that the age can be as wide as 10 to 19. However, the categorization of adolescents according to the organization varied depending on the individual's situation. For many of these adolescents according to (Kwaja 2014), the only way to vent their anger is by striking out, often with grave consequences and that this is so because the majority of these adolescent who get involved have low empathy.

Empathy is what happens to us when we leave our own bodies and find ourselves either momentarily or for a longer period of time in the mind of the other. The individual observes reality through his or her eyes, feel his or her emotions and share in his or her pain. Lack of empathy is one of the main factors that allows adolescents to abuse their victims in diverse forms. (Thagard 2010, 80) notes that adolescents' inability to feel their victims' pain and accept their victims the way they are encouraged cruel behavours. However, the basic capacity to recognize emotions is probably innate and might be achieved unconsciously for some, yet it could be trained and achieved with various degrees of intensity or accuracy. In view of the fact that the lack of empathy had been blamed for the many conflicts that adolescents in secondary schools engage in. (Ojo 2000, 85) stipulates that there was the need to reduce the damaging effects of these conflicts by increasing the amount of empathy that students possess.

It would be possible to reduce the cruelty and violence of adolescents and keep civility alive in the society through training in empathic responding. The training aim at equipping the adolescent with conflict reduction skills through emotional understanding. The provision of empathic training according to (Cotton 2001) could be used to enhance empathic behaviour in both adolescents and adults. One of the components of empathy training approach according to (Cotton 2001) is lessons in empathic responding and perception.

Lessons in Empathic Responding and Perception, (LERP) is an empathy training programme involving traditional lessons on issues related to empathy such as the meaning of empathy, how it is developed, how to recognize and respond to other's emotive states. (Cotton 2001) in a review of empathy training programmes found studies that conclude that LERP cause an increase in empathy scores of the participants. It is on this premise that this study utilized LERP to find out its effects on conflict reduction among secondary school adolescents.

2   Purpose of Study

The study aim at finding out the effects of empathic responding and perception and role playing on conflict reduction among secondary school adolescents. Specifically, the study sought to:

1. determine the effect of lessons on empathic responding and perception (LERP) on conflict mean scores of adolescents in secondary schools;
2. ascertain the effect of lessons on empathic responding and perception (LERP) on empathy mean scores of adolescents in secondary schools in Delta State;
3. determine the differences in the mean conflict scores of males and females exposed to lessons on empathic responding and perception (LERP).

3 Research Questions

The following research questions are raised to guide the study.
1. What is the effect of LERP on the post test conflict mean scores of adolescents exposed to LERP compared with those in the control group?
2. What is the effect of LERP on the post test empathic mean scores of adolescents exposed to LERP and those in the control group?
3. What is the difference between males and females' post test conflict mean scores of adolescents exposed to LERP and those in the control group?

4 Research Design

The design of this study is a quasi-experimental research design. This experimental research design according to (Egbule and Okobia 2012) involve the investigation of possible cause and effects relationship by exposing one or more experimental groups to one or more treatment conditions and comparing the results to one or more control groups that were not exposed to treatment. This comparison between the two leads to the acceptance or rejection of a research question.

5 Area of the Study

The area of the study is secondary schools in Agbor, Delta State. Agbor is the headquarters of Ika South local government area of Delta State and is bounded by Edo State at the North, West and South, the area is chosen because the town though not metropolitan in nature is situated in the Niger Delta region of Nigeria which is known for militancy.

6   Population of the Study

The target population of this study comprised all Senior Secondary School ii (ss ii) students in public schools in Agbor. The ss ii students' population figure in Ika South Local Government Area was 1,706 while ss ii student population in Agbor town stood at 749. These figures were obtained from the Post Primary Education Board, Agbor Zonal Office in 2013

7   Sample and Sampling Technique

The sample size for this study was 40 students drawn from two of the six public secondary schools in Agbor which is locality in Ika South Local Government Area. The class registers were used to code the Instrument which was used to select twenty students made up of ten males and ten female from each of the two schools. This agrees with (Ali 2006) assertion that for experimental studies, the number of schools as sample size should not exceed four as experiments impose more rigorous demands on the researcher and so in order not to make the study unwieldy or intractable, smaller samples are usually preferred in experiments.

8   Instruments for Data Collection

The instruments that were used for this study were the Davis' Interpersonal Reactivity Index (iri) and the Conflict Prone Instrument (cpi).

The Davis' interpersonal reactivity index (iri), according to (Frias-Navarro 2009) was designed by Davis in 1980 to assess empathy. It is made up of 28 items using 5-point scales. Davis' iri had test-retest reliability coefficient ranging from .62 to .71 and internal reliabilities ranging from .71 to .77.

The second instrument used in this study was the **Conflict Prone Instrument (cpi)**. The questionnaire was structured, having twenty items with a four point rating scale of Strongly Agreed (sa) Agreed (A) Disagreed (D) and Strongly Disagreed (sa). The cpi was used to screen adolescents who were prone to conflict and also served as pre test for the participants before the commencement of the experiment. For the purpose of selecting adolescents who participated in the study, this instrument was coded using the class registers of the intact classes (ss ii A-C) and the responses were analyzed using mean. Students with mean scores of 2.50 and above formed the number required to participate in the study from each of the three schools that were used.

9 Experimental Procedure

The treatment was conducted in three stages; 1. Pre-treatment Stage 2. Treatment Stage and 3. Post-treatment Stage.

9.2 *Pre-treatment Stage*

Prior to the first session with subjects, the researcher first explained the purpose of the study to the two research assistants who served as facilitators for the experimental and control groups involved in this investigation. These research assistants were guidance counsellors in the selected schools. They were chosen because they were already teachers as well as guidance counsellors in the sampled schools who had been attending training programme in different aspects of adolescent well being within the school system. The use of research assistants as facilitators became necessary because the two groups were engaged at the same time (during the school break hours). The research assistant handled one of the two groups within this period; while one handled lessons on empathic responding and perception (LERP), a second handled the control group which received training on life skills.

Secondly, the researcher and the research assistants met with all the subjects and established rapport with them to ensure that they were relaxed throughout the programme.

Thirdly, the structure of the programme was laid out to the subjects. Specifically, the subjects were told that they would be involved in the group's activities for a period of eight weeks. Expectations such as regular attendance, punctuality and cooperation were spelt out. Specific time for the programme was discussed and agreed on. The meetings held between 11.30 am and 12.15pm., reinforcers for the adolescents and preferred snacks such as doughnuts, meat pie, water, and soft drinks were provided since it was supposed to be their break period.

Finally, the adopted Interpersonal Reactivity Inventory (IRI) was administered after the initial screening in a group setting to all the subjects as pre-test before the commencement of the treatment. Subjects completed this instrument and were assigned code numbers to protect their anonymity in their test results.

9.2 *Treatment Stage*

Treatment group received lessons in empathic responding and perception (LERP) while the control group did not receive any training, rather, they received lessons on life skills.

Each group interacted with a facilitator for about 45 minutes every Friday morning for eight weeks (two weeks for pre and post-testing while six weeks was for the treatment programme proper). Neither the treatment nor the control subjects were aware of their group status because they were in separate schools.

9.3 Post-treatment Stage

After the treatment, all subjects – both treatment and control groups were tested again using the adapted IRI and the Conflict Prone Instrument. This was necessary to obtain the post-test scores. There was a formal ending of the experiment where both the researcher and the subjects recounted their experiences and gave votes of thanks to the facilitators.

10 Method of Data Analysis

The data collected were analyzed using descriptive statistics. The mean score differences between the pre and post test (mean gained or loss) will form the basis for the acceptance or rejection of a research question.

11 Results

11.1 Research Question 1

What is the effect of LERP on the post test conflict mean scores of adolescents exposed to LERP compared with those in the control group?

Table 16.1 shows the post test conflict mean scores of adolescents exposed to LERP and those in the control group. The result indicates that adolescents exposed to LERP had pre test conflict mean score of 62.16 and a post test conflict mean score of 34.05. The post test conflict mean score (34.05) is lower than the pre test conflict mean score (62.16). The mean loss score for adolescents exposed to LERP is -28.08 and the mean loss score for adolescents in the control group is -0.75.

The post test conflict mean score for adolescents exposed to LERP is 34.05 and that of the control group is 60.70. The post test mean score of those exposed to LERP is lower than those in the control group. The post test mean score difference is -26.65. The implication of this result is that treatment is effective for adolescents exposed to LERP as compared with adolescents in the control group.

EFFECTS OF LESSONS ON EMPATHIC RESPONSE AND PERCEPTION 315

TABLE 16.1   Mean of post test (conflict mean scores) of adolescents exposed to LERP and control group

Group		Pre test	Post test	Mean score difference	Post test mean score difference
LERP					
	N	20	20		
	Mean	62.16	34.05	-28.08	
Control					-26.65
	N	20	20		
	Mean	61.45	60.70	-0.75	

11.2   Research Question 2

What is the effect of LERP on the post test empathic mean scores of adolescents exposed to LERP and those in the control group?

Table 16.2 shows the pre test and post test empathic mean scores of adolescents exposed to LERP and those in the control group. The result indicates that adolescents exposed to LERP had pre test empathic mean score of 68.10 and a post test empathic mean score of 77.25. The post test empathic mean score (77.25) was higher than the pre test empathic mean score (68.10). The mean gain score for adolescents exposed to LERP is 9.15 and the mean loss score for adolescents in the control group is -7.95.

TABLE 16.2   Mean of post test (empathic mean scores) of adolescents exposed to LERP and control group

Group		Pre test	Post test	Mean score difference	Post test mean difference
LERP					
	N	20	20		
	Mean	68.10	77.25	9.15	
Control					15.95
	N	20	20		
	Mean	69.25	61.30	-7.95	

The post test empathic mean score for adolescents exposed to LERP is 77.25 and 61.30 for those in the control group. The post test empathic mean score of those exposed to LERP is higher than those in the control group. The post test mean difference between LERP and the control group was 15.95. The implication of this result was that treatment is effective for adolescents exposed to LERP when compared with adolescents in the control group.

11.3 Research Question 3

What is the difference between males and females adolescents' post test conflict mean scores of adolescent exposed to LERP and those in the control group?

TABLE 16.3 Mean of post test (conflict mean scores) of male and female adolescents exposed to LERP and control group

Group			Pre test	Post test	Mean Diff.
LERP					
	Male	N	10	10	
		Mean	61.90	34.20	0.31
	Female	N	10	10	
		Mean	62.44	33.89	
Control					
	Male	N	10	10	
		Mean	61.40	59.90	-1.60
	Female	N	10	10	
		Mean	61.50	61.50	

Table 16.3 shows the post test conflict mean scores of male and female adolescents exposed to LERP and those in the control group. The pre test conflict mean score for male adolescents exposed to LERP is 61.90 while the female adolescents had a pre test conflict mean score of 62.44. The post test mean score for male and female adolescents exposed to LERP are 34.20 and 33.89 respectively and that of male and female adolescents in the control group are 59.90 and 61.50 respectively. The post test mean score difference of male and female adolescents in LERP is 0.31 while the mean score difference for male and female adolescents in the control group is and -1.60. The implication of the result is that treatment had no effect on gender.

12 Summary of Findings

The major findings of this study were;
1. Adolescents exposed to LERP had a significant loss in their conflict mean scores as measured by the conflict prone instrument. This implied that there is a reduction in their proneness to conflict
2. Adolescents exposed to lessons in empathic responding and perception had an increase in their post empathic mean scores as measured by the Davis' interpersonal reactivity index.
3. The finding revealed that treatment has no effect on gender.

13 Conclusions

From the findings, the following conclusions are made:
1. Lessons on empathic responding and perception (LERP) as a training technique of empathic responding has a significant effect on adolescents exposed to the treatment as it caused a reduction in adolescents' conflict as the adolescent exposed to treatment has a reduction in their post test conflict mean scores.
2. Adolescents' proneness to conflict reduced notably as there is significant differences in the post test conflict mean scores of adolescents exposed to treatments and those in the control group.
3. LERP has a significant effect as it increased the empathy level of adolescents. There are significant differences in the empathic mean scores between adolescents exposed to treatments and those who were not exposed to it (control group).
4. Treatments has no effect on Gender.

14 Educational Implication of the Findings

The findings of the present study have extensive educational implication. The findings provide useful feedback on the efficacy of the training techniques of empathic responding – Lessons on Empathic Responding and Perception and Role Playing. The results have ascertained that LERP and role playing are effective in the reduction of adolescents' proneness to conflict and also increased the empathy level of adolescents in secondary schools. Consequently, these training techniques could now be used in Nigerian secondary schools with a high degree of confidence to reduce adolescents' proneness to conflict. If this is done, this menace which has been associated among adolescents in schools and the society at large would be reduced significantly.

15 Recommendations

LERP and role playing are found to be successful in fostering empathy and reducing conflict among adolescents in secondary school schools and so the researcher make the following recommendations.

1. LERP could be used by Counsellors and other school personnel as school-based programmes in secondary schools for the development of empathy and its related skills in adolescents. It could also be useful in enhancing interpersonal relationships by guidance counselors in schools through group counseling.
2. LERP could be used by Curriculum experts and planners in developing in-school programmes, which emphasize prevention and equip adolescents with necessary competencies that would enable them, shun conflict and it attendant ills plaguing the nation today.
3. Teachers and Counsellors could be trained by their employers and Non Governmental Organizations (NGOs) in the effective ways of implementing LERP through organization of seminars and workshops.

Bibliography

Ademu-Awuja Samuel and Kwaja, Peter. 2013. "A Panacea for Curbing Violent Behaviours Among Secondary School Adolescents through Empathic Training." *African Journal of Studies in Education (Special Edition)* 9:188–195.

Aghanta, Johnson A. 2006. "The Need for Effective Leadership in our Post Primary Schools Education." *Workshop on leadership for teacher in secondary schools.* Delta State Ministry of Education, June.

Agulanna, George G. 2008. "Effects of three Training Approaches of Empathic Behaviour of Nigerian Adolescents in Secondary Schools." *Ph.D.* Abia State University.

Ali, Anthony. 2006. *Conducting Research in Education and Social Sciences.* Enugu, Nigeria: Tashima Net Works Ltd.

Anokam, Greg. O. 2012. "Prevalence and Correlates of Juvenile Delinquency among Adolescents in Imo State." *M.Ed Dissertation presented to Department of Educational Psychology*. Imo State University.

Cohen, Dara. K. and Nordås, Ragnhild. 2012. "Sexual Violence in African Armed Conflicts: Introducing the SVAC-Africa Dataset, 1989–2009," *unpublished working paper*.

Cotton, Kathleen. 2001. Developing empathy in children and youth. Retrieved 11/12/2008, from http:www.nwrel.org/scpd/sirs/7/cu13/html.

Egbule, Friday J. and Okobia Duke O. 2012. *Research Methods in Education for Colleges and Universities*. Kmensuo Educational Publishers. Onitsha.

Hornby, Albert S. 2007. *Oxford Advanced Dictionary of Current English*. Oxford: Oxford University Press. International Planned Parenthood Federation. 2004. "Understanding Adolescents." *An IPPF Report on Young People's Sexual and Reproductive Health Needs*, London.

Jehn, Karen. A. and Mannix, Elizabeth. A. 2001. "The Dynamic Nature of Conflict: A Longitudinal Study."*Academy of Management Journal* 44: 238–251.

Kalgo, F. A. 2001. Examination malpractice among Nigerian secondary school adolescents: Forms, causes and challenges to educational psychologists. In R.U.N. Okonkwo and R.O. Okoye (eds), *The Nigerian adolescent in perspective*. Awka: Anwuka and Sons Publishers.

Kwaja, Peter. 2010. Empathic Understanding: An Effective Tool for the Reduction of Students' Proneness to Conflict in Nigerian Schools. *Intellectualism* 3 142–147.

Kwaja, Peter. 2014. "Effects of Two Training Techniques of Empathic Responding on Conflict Reduction among Secondary School Adolescents." *Ph.D Thesis,* University of Nigeria.

Kwaja, Peter and Mormah, Felicia O. 2011. Managing Adolescents Maladptive Behaviour in Nigerian Secondary Schools. *Approaches in International Journal of Research Development* 3 281–287.

Minchakpu, Obed. 2002. Chronic violence claims 2000 lives. Retrieved: 9/8/2005 https://www.christianitytoday.com/ct/2002/january7/18.23.html.

Ojo, Olugbenga D. 2000. Influence of solo and double parenting on the adjustment problems of secondary school adolescents. *The Nigerian Journal of Guidance and Counselling* 1 81–92.

Schellenberge, James A. 2001. *Conflict Resolution*: Theory, Research, Practice. New York: State University of New York Press.

Thagard, Paul. 2010. *The Brain and the Meaning of Life*. Princeton, NJ: Princeton University Press.

Thagard, Paul. 2010. "EMPATHICA: A Computer Support System with Visual Representations for Cognitive-affective Mapping." In MacGregor, Susan K. (Ed.), *Proceedings of the Workshop on Visual Reasoning and Representation* (pp. 79–81). Menlo Park, CA: AAI Press.

World Health Organization. 2001. Global Consultation of Friendly Health Services. A Consensus Statement. Department of Adolescent and Child Health Development, Geneva retrieved 8/8/2008.

World Health Organization. 2013. "Maternal, Newborn, Child and Adolescent Health." Avaliable at http://www.who.int/maternal_child_adolescent/topics/adolescence/dev/en. Accessed 1 February, 2014.

CHAPTER 17

Ethical Dimensions in Research: Informed Consent and Female Gender in Nigeria

Olufunke Olufunsho Adegoke

1   Introduction

This essay focuses on the need to reevaluate the place of women or female and their consent in research. Although ethics and ethical research as well as informed consent are discussed generally the aim of the chapter is to say something at the end about women, informed consent and with some focus in Nigeria. Women, as we know, and in any society are germane to its continual existence and development. Therefore, their contribution to development cannot be neglected and undermined. However, there is the persistence of gender inequality in many places in Africa (carried over perhaps from traditional African societies). Such inequality starves the societies from the gains of development. The inequality manifests itself in many areas including in research.

The chapter looks at ethics and then ethics in social research to understand the role of women in research. What it finds is that evidence based researches show that a lot of the women are not well informed and this over shadows their judgment on appropriate decision-making. On the basis of this, the essay calls for the need of culturally competent and sensitive approaches that addresses identity specific barriers in research when designing consent forms. In particular, the argument is that there is the need for gender mainstreaming in research implementation and ethical process especially informed consent given that the attainment of gender equality should not only be seen as an end itself and human right issues, but as essential for the achievement of sustainable growth.

2   Defining Ethics and Social Research

Like every other subject of social science interest, 'ethics' does not have a uniform or universally accepted definition. However, there is a seeming consensus on what ethics means in a generalized context. In general, ethics is the view or idea regarding the 'good' or 'bad' or 'right' or 'wrong' of human conduct in any given situation at a particular time. This understanding of ethics can be said to put ethics or situate it within the purview of moral philosophy. According to Obono, Ajuwon, Arowojolu, Ognundipe, Yakubu and Falusi (2006), ethics implicates 'a theory of moral valuation and evaluation and may, accordingly be defined as 'the study of morality and its effect on human behaviour'. Ethics draws from the norm (the normative) as well as the expected standard of conduct in a given circumstance.

Ethics is a term derived from the Greek word *ethos,* which translates as character. It is the philosophical study of the general nature of morality or morals and of the specific moral choices made by individuals. It is the branch of philosophy that concerns itself with how individuals or group's moral principles guide and inform their actions and behaviour in the society. In this way, ethics can be said to refer to a system of moral principles governing the appropriate conducts for an individual or a group of people. Or simply, an 'ethos' or 'way of life', 'social norms for conduct that distinguishes between acceptable and unacceptable behaviour'" (Akaranga and Ongong'a, 2013; Shamoo and Resnik, 2015; Akaranga and Makau, 2016). Having the conduct of ethics does tend to maintain the integrity of shared cultural values. Over the years, the principle of ethics has metamorphous from Aristotle's view of ideal behavioural pattern aimed at the goal of happiness or well-being to Kantian ethics of duty. Today, we have views of appropriate behaviours and codes of conduct in the context of the ethics of various disciplines.

In African societies, ethical values can be said to be embedded in the philosophy of communalism and social relations. More so, the ideas and beliefs are considered by members to shape social behavior, which are expected to bring social harmony and peaceful coexistence in society. It is the responsibility of society to impress on its members the moral knowledge and principles and rules of the society through various media such as proverbs and folktales. In the literature, some scholars take religion to determine the African way of life, and its moral values and principles as being derived from religion. This assertion by some notable African scholars: Opoku (1978), Busia (1967), Idowu (1962) take religion to be very impactful on Africans, who are held to be highly religious. Although, there are other scholars such as Maquet, Wiredu, Godfrey Wilson and Monica Wilson who do have contrary views on religion being the foundation of morality in African societies (Gyeke, 2010).

To properly situate 'ethics' in 'social research', it is instructive to first understand the concept of social research. Social research is the application of methods or procedures in researching (investigating or making inquiry about) social phenomenon (Jegede, Adegoke and Ushie, 2015). Scott and Gordon (2005) summarily described the 'social sciences' as a general label comprising disciplines that concern with understanding 'society and human relationships', based on the developments (or methods of natural sciences in the 19th Century. Social science research therefore refers to studies or investigations on human behaviour, social processes, events, institutions or structures in relation to human beings as social beings. Disciplines in this purview include sociology, economics, political science, economics and psychology all of which employ approaches, procedures and methods typical of the natural sciences, in the investigation of social phenomena. A common factor to these disciplines is the fact that they involve humans as subjects (respondents, participants) of their investigation.

Human subjects possess values, dignity and preferences; they have feelings, expectations, ideologies and beliefs, which must not be violated on the 'altar' of research. It is based on this that research ethics ensures that best practices and standard procedures are followed to ensure that the right (not the wrong) and the good (not the bad) is done to human subjects, the researcher himself and other stakeholders due to the social research course. Ethics of social research largely overlaps with those of medical research, because it emerged as a 'patient protection' model of medical research. Thus, 'beneficence', 'justice' and 'respect for persons' (of which informed consent is a major principle) are integral, just as they constitute the ethics of bio-medical research (Shamoo and Resnik, 2015).

3   Ethics in Social Research

Research ethics refers to the application of the principles of ethical philosophy to the field of research, referring to a wide variety of values, norms, and institutional arrangements that help constitute and regulate scientific activities. Ethics are largely products of societal moral codes guiding peoples' behaviour in given circumstances. Research ethics is therefore a product of researchers' attempt to scientifically organize behavioural codes among themselves. Hence, research ethics are codified scientific values and norms guiding researchers' conducts. Although research ethics are not law, they are rather guidelines that must be considered when undertaking research activities. Failure to consider research ethics however is not without consequences that can extend to litigations (Yip, Han and Sng, 2016).

These ethical guidelines were developed due to the need to address the ethical lapses while providing answers to emerging moral challenges in the conduct of social research. It is important to say that the Nazi experiments of World War II and the Tuskegee Syphilis Study are notable tragedies in the history of research that provoked the rise of moral movement which culminated in the emergence of ethical questions in the conduct of research. The World War II Nazi experimentation conducted on prisoners at the concentration camps under the deceit of science research documented terrible atrocities. This occurred in the early 1940s, when prisoners inclusive of children were forcefully used to conduct medical torturous experiments without obtaining their consents. The various medical torturous experiments which resulted into death, disfigurement or permanent disability and trauma were Twins experiments, Bone, muscle, and nerve transplantation experiments, Head Injury experiments, Freezing experiments, Malaria experiments, Immunization experiments, Sterilization and Fertility experiment etc.

Another was the Tuskegee Syphilis experimental study conducted on a total of six hundred Black American males (four hundred infected with syphilis and two hundred not infected with syphilis) in Alabama by the United States American Public Health service provider to determine the real cause of syphilis disease in 1932. The study participants did not sign informed consent forms to participate in the study. More so, the experiment was conducted for over forty years. During the course of the experiment, a cure was found for the syphilis disease, however the study participants whom were infected were denied treatment. The health officials watched the progression of the disease affliction on the study participant, as it degenerated to disability and early death. Due to social media exposure, the experiment was stopped in 1972 by the government officials.

It is these processes and issues regarding research and consent and the ethical questions that they raise that ensued and provoked certain outcomes such as the Nuremberg Code (1949), Helsinki Declaration (1964), the Belmont Report (1979) and Council for International Organizations for Medical Sciences (CIOMS, 1993) guidelines, which established fundamental principles for the ethical conduct of research: respect for persons, beneficence and justice. The ethical questions also facilitated the constitution of Research Ethics Committees (RECS) or Institutional Review Boards (IRBS) for carrying out independent review of research proposals and ensuring adherence to ethics in the conduct of social research.

In the year 1966, the University of the Witwatersrand in South Africa established a REC to review African Health Research which was the first to be documented. Other African countries have followed suit in the creation of RECs'. Zimbabwe established Medicines and Related Substances Act in 1974. In Kenya, through the Science and Technology (Amendment) Act of 1979, the Kenya Medical Research Institute (KEMRI) and its national guidelines in 2004. In Nigeria, the national guideline for regulating human subject research led to the establishment of the National Code for Health Research Ethics in 2007 (Yakubu and Adebamowo, 2012). These review boards must determine if the benefits of any research outweighs the risks. They also serve as an enforcement mechanism which are established to see to the proper implementation of activities of subjects in research (Jegede et al., 2015; Yakubu, Hyder, Ali and Kass, 2017). However, an impending issue is controversy on the ethical review process of the social and behavioural research since its inception. There are arguments on fear of disapproval by the ethics review committee which forestall researchers in the submission of proposals (Eyelade, Ajuwon and Adebamowo, 2011). Another issue is precipitated on the fact that the guiding principles of the ethical review committee used on social and behavioural research are those of the biomedical sciences, thus making such guidelines inadequate for social science research review (Wassenaar and Mamotte, 2012).

Generally, there is the training of a social scientist in research ethics that will be a member of the Biomedical Review Committee. In some institutions such as the University of Ibadan in Nigeria there is the establishment of an Ethical Research Review Board (ERRB), which is a body that coordinate and regulate all matters pertaining to research ethics and integrity of the institution. Furthermore, these are sub-committees established to oversee the activities of the Ethical Review Committees. The ERRB comprises of the following committees: University of Ibadan/University College Hospital Ethical Review Committee (UI/UCH-REC); Behavioural Studies Review Committee (BSRC); Animal Care and Use Committee (ACUC); Plant Care and Use Committee (PCUC). These committees review research protocols submitted by staff and students at the institution (University of Ibadan, Research Management Office, 2020)

As already noted, social research involves human participants from whom relevant and reliable data or information are collected. Often times, it also exerts certain costs on participants in terms of physical strength, quality time (which could have been utilized for other productive activities), and exposure to adverse/exploitative circumstances for vulnerable persons, the sick (in health social science research) or socially disadvantaged persons. Research ethics insists that the 'finding' which research is aimed at achieving through investigation must not be done at the expense of respondents' welfare. Adherence to ethical standards from the design/formulation of the study to the publication of research findings determines the integrity of the research. Ethical standards provide that stakeholders are neither harmed, nor their interests violated, while the scale remains balanced between the advancement of knowledge/ practical utility of research and the protection of participants' rights/welfare. The general tenets of research ethics revolve around honesty, objectivity, integrity, carefulness, openness, confidentiality, social responsibility, competence, non-discrimination, legality/lawfulness, and human subject protection (Shamoo and Resnik, 2015). The history in the emergence of research ethics has subsequently brought to existence the use of informed consent which has become mandatory as research subjects must be properly informed and educated with their rights to accept or decline in participation of the study. The informed consent is a core principle of the human subject protection.

The importance of ethics in social research is highlighted by the generated answers to questions like:
– What are the moral principles guiding a social research?
– In what ways does ethical issues guides selection of a research problem?
– Are there ethical issues that may influence what and how research findings that can be published?
– How beneficial is a research to the participants of a research?
– What are the roles of ethical issues in the design of a research?
– 'What responsibility do you have toward your research subjects? For example, do you have their informed consent to participate in your project?' (Bulmer, 2008).

Without these questions being critically answered, a social researcher is not ready to carry out a research. The research process is entirely integrated with ethics which extends beyond identifying the research problem to the conduct of the research, its interpretation and dissemination of the research findings, all which are guided by ethical principles. However, ethical issues in social research are ongoing processes since social researchers are usually faced with peculiar situations that may not be adequately captured by existing ethical codes. This is a result of the subjective nature of human behaviour which is subject to behavioural research. Due to the extent of diversity among different fields of social research, there exist different codes of ethics within the science of social research. Despite this diversity, the bases of ethical principles in social research are essentially the same.

4   Ethical Principles that Ensure Appropriate Interaction with the Society

As each of these ethical principles is discussed, the ethical dilemma associated with each of these principles will also be discussed.

4.1   *Voluntary Participation*

In some circumstances, research procedures interfere with activities of the respondents. As a result of this, people may be unwilling to participate in a research activity. Aside the sometimes interfering nature of social research, there may be other factors that may be responsible for people's unwillingness to participate in social research. Research ethics requires that unwilling individuals should not be coerced against their own freewill into participating in a research endeavour. The principle of voluntary participation not only encourage that individuals willingly agree to be a part of the research, it also encourage that participants be given opportunity to withdraw their participation whenever they feel like they can no longer be part of the research (Marshall, Adebamowo, Adeyemo et al. 2014). Such unwillingness and withdrawal too must be devoid of consequences. Again, this ethical principle negates the principle of generalizability of research. To ensure voluntary participation, Informed consent of respondents must be sought and obtained.

4.2   Confidentiality

Confidentiality as a principle requires that respondents' private information be protected and kept confidential. It is important to guarantee respondents their confidentiality so that information that is sincere and valuable to the research can be obtained (Gibson, Benson and Brand, 2012). When the fear of exposure is eliminated, respondents are more likely to provide sincere and valuable information. To ascertain this, obtained information is used without the possibility of linking it to the respondents. However, due to researchers' obligation to the society and legal constraints, researchers are sometimes faced with the dilemma of keeping their promise of confidentiality and the risk of going against legal provisions when approached by state agencies for research information. To avoid this, researchers are advised to make known the limitation of the promised confidentiality (Sarantakos, 2013).

4.3   Anonymity

As stated earlier, both confidentiality and anonymity overlaps in certain ways. Anonymity requires that the identity of respondents be protected. To avoid identity exposure of respondents, names of respondents must not be allowed to appear on the research instrument or data. Thus the responses are not linked to the respondents' identity (Gibson, Benson and Brand, 2012). However, in situation where informed consent is obtained, it must be kept separately from the research instrument to avoid linking of respondent information with any of the respondents. To ensure this, coding techniques are employed in coding research instrument and data.

4.4   Non-maleficence

Another ethical principle of social research requires that a research must not bring harm or expose respondents to harm of any kind. Sarantakos (2013) identified types of harm that respondents may be exposed to as physical, mental (emotional) and legal harm. In carrying out social research, it is the ethical responsibility of the researcher to ensure respondents are protected from any form of harm as a result of their participation in the research. Again, this presents another ethical dilemma of social research. Whereas, researchers are required to protect respondent from any form of harm, they are often confronted on legal bases by governmental agencies to provide information that can bring harm to the respondents. There are cases of incarcerated researchers who stood their ground on the basis of non-maleficence and confidentiality of respondents. The fundamental question arising is 'how ethical is it for social researchers to deliberately avoid researching phenomena that can present such dilemma'?

4.5   Beneficence

This ethical principle stipulates that a research should yield positive and beneficial outcome for the participants. In ensuring this, researchers are required to weigh the benefit vis-a-vis the potential harm of the research for the participants as well as the society. A research is considered ethical provided the benefits outweigh the possibility of harm to the participants. Furthermore, 'the principle of beneficence refers to making efforts to secure the well-being of research respondents, or maximize possible benefits of the research and minimize its possible harm' (Gallardo, 2012). Hence, researchers may decide to provide financial incentives to ensure participants' well-being in relation to the research is secured. However, this must be appropriately regulated so that such incentive does not become problematic.

4.6   Justice

The ethical principle of justice is included to ensure fairness and equity among participants. It entails the assurance of equity among people (considering different forms of classifications) in the selection of participants and in the distribution of research risks and benefits and participants (Garfield and Yudell, 2019). That is, inclusion criteria must be informed by the research design and not by any form of bias towards any group. Finally, the research report must be fair to all participants and must not bias towards any.

4.7   Deception

Deception refers to any intentional provision of false information regarding any aspect of social research. Ethics of social research requires that a researcher should make the purpose and intention of research known and open to the research participants. This is also expected to be done without any form of vain promises that might give the participants false hope. Deception must not be used to engender the interest of the participants in the research. Deception may be total or partial. Partial or incomplete disclosure of relevant details of the research is considered deception. However, social researchers are sometimes faced with situations that require the use of deception whether partial or complete (Tai, 2012). A researcher may need to employ incomplete disclosure in studying groups of deviants such as militant groups, drug cartels. In some other cases, disclosure of research purpose may encourage respondents' bias. To avoid this, social researcher systematically (with ethical approval) employs deception whether subtly or actively following provisional guidelines.

4.8   *Analysis and Reporting*

This ethical principle is involved in social research to ensure that researchers fulfil their moral obligation to conduct research analysis and reporting in an objective version. Responsible analysis and reporting of research findings allows for easy replication of research and future validation of research findings. Also, responsible reporting reveals unexpected research outcomes based on "rigorously preplanned and organized" research design (Babbie, 2010).

5   Ethics and Informed Consent

One major component or dimension to the ethical conduct of research is informed consent. It involves a wide range of procedures which must follow due process in a study involving human subjects. It is a process situated under respect for persons – one of the fundamental ethical developments in the emergence of research ethics. As the name implies, informed consent refers to a participant's willingness to participate in a research based on proper information that he or she has been given regarding the research. By implication, the human subject must not be lured or deceived into participation, which would have been against their personal wish, if they had adequate knowledge of the research. Thus, informed consent refers to participants' right to be informed about the nature of a research study and its risks and benefits to them prior to consenting to participation (Munung, Marshall, Campbell et al. 2016). The informed consent could be a written letter which the participant would endorse with signature or thumb print after having knowledge of what the research study entails. Such a letter should be well detailed, outlining the potential risks and how the participants' participation will contribute to the research goals. Also, the contact details of the researcher should be provided on the letter. Other relevant information which should be provided to the intending participants' are the duration of the research study and if there will be any compensation for participating. Furthermore, the confidentiality of the information elicited and what the researcher will do with the research findings, such as dissemination in the community, workshops, conferences and or publications.

Educating or properly informing human subjects about what a research entails does not merely make a research ethical, but a major criterion for the responsible conduct of research. More so, having the ability to read does not transcend to understanding of the research study. However, obtaining an informed consent through an interaction is more valued than being able to read. Informed consent sets forth purpose, benefits, risks and other study information necessary to allow the participants to make an informed and voluntary decision before participating in a study (Shamoo and Resnik, 2015). The importance of informed consent in social research cannot be overemphasized as it safeguards the participants from physical or mental harm resulting from their participation in the research study. It "provides sufficient information to a potential participant, in a language which is easily understood by him/her, so that he/she can make the voluntary decision regarding 't'" or 'not to participate in the research study' (Nijhawan, Janodia, Muddukrishna, Bhat, Bairy, Udupa & Musmade, 2013; Nnebue,2010). More so, there is the need for evidence based research and ethical guidelines for informed consents (Tomljenovica and Shaw, 2013). Also, for a consent to be informed, the prospective respondent must have attained the age of accountability and mental capacity to take decisions.

There are basic facts that need to be taken into consideration for an informed consent, these are: the consent should be voluntary; consent should be informed; consent should be in writing or oral (in the presence of a witness); seeking informed consent; research ethics committee approval (Nnebue, 2010). Similarly, three points should be noted in informed consents: detailed information on the proposed research is provided by the researcher; the prospective participant has an understanding and knowledge of the proposed research; with an understanding of the provided information, the prospective participant makes a decision either to participate or not. According to Roache (2014), informed consent engenders trust between the human participants and the investigator(s), a factor which ultimately promotes reliability of the data being collected. Informed consent is therefore a vital part of the research process, and as such entails more than obtaining a signature on a form. Through the informed consent process, participants are also equipped with sufficient knowledge of their rights and privileges which implicates their 'humanity', in spite that they are subjects of a scientific research, while also informing them of the obligations of the investigator. Subjects also get to have prior knowledge of the research procedure as it would evolve sequentially. This way, participants are mentally prepared for successive stages of the research, including foreseeable risks, benefits as well as alternative procedures; and their decision are not necessarily spontaneous.

This further reinstates Weber's notion of 'social action', which, distinct from spontaneous reactions, takes cognizance of Actors' rational capacity. Furthermore, the theoretical framework in social research which are guided by the Belmont Report precipitated on three ethical principles are Respect for persons, Beneficence and Justice are of the Western value system. The African Value systems which is a different clime does considers three principles which are significant for the ethics framework which are Respect for life, Solidarity and Justice. These according to Onuoha (2007) are three values which are embedded in the African values: humanity, community and morality. These principles does have a connection with the culture and value systems of the African. A researcher thus must adapt the ethical principles when conducting research in an African society in the milieu of a local cultural context which is paramount to the conduct of social research. Invariable, it also brings ethical concerns on the adaptability of the ethical guiding principles of the western clime to the African clime.

6 Blind Spot in Social Research

It has been observed that providing effective communication is the key to enabling potential participants to make informed decisions about their involvement in research. Information may be presented verbally or in a written format and consent could be given verbally, signed or stamped. Important as it is, informed consent is often faced with certain challenges which undermine its ethicality. These include language barrier, religious influence, false expectation, patient's perception (in health-related social research), vulnerability of persons (Nijhawan et al., 2013). According to the Council of International Organizations of Medical Sciences [CIOMS] (2006), the notion of vulnerability of persons such as children, prisoners, patients with mental health problems and or incurable ailments, elderly persons, refugees, homeless people, stigmatized persons (homosexuals, commercial sex workers, drug addicts), learning disability persons and female gender are challenging which requires special consideration. The CIOMS Guideline describes them as persons who are relatively or absolutely incapable of protecting their own self interests. They tend to be deficient in intelligence, education, financial resources etc. Empirical and theoretical findings have documented on women in most developing nations to be susceptible to abuse resulting from their cultural practices and the patriarchal family structures (Ushie, Eneji, Ugal et al. 2019; Sumola, Mayungbo and Ashefor et al. 2019). In the case of the vulnerable persons, the researcher have to take considerable steps in protecting and forestalling any harm to such persons as a virtue of their participating in the research. This also concerts obligation on the Research Ethics Committee, that risk is minimized while the consent validity process is maximized.

Decision making in social research is very crucial to the conduct of informed consent, especially in the African clime where communitarianism with family and or community members is the rule (Wassenaar and Mamotte, 2012). Furthermore, empirical findings have documented the difficulty in obtaining informed consent in Africa (Aderibigbe and Chima, 2019; Bassey, Ugbem, Akpan et al. 2019). Researchers should be informed that knowledge and decisions are negotiations emanating from social and communal construct acts which should be understood. Aside this, research ethics demand a comprehensive understanding of participants before giving their full and informed consents. Participants' potentiality in understanding the informed consent is tied to their individual maturity, level of reasoning, intelligence and comprehension of language. However, in situations where it is observed that the potential participants' does not understand the relevance of the research study, permission is sought from family members or guardians (CIOMS, 2006) who have close emotional relationship with such participant. Thus cultural sensitivity within the local context is important when conducting a social research. Paramount on this is the space or context in which Social Science Research is carried out. With reference to Max Weber's 'Social Action Theory', there exist the problem of dominant/mainstream perception and implication for agency (persons) which is in lieu of women informed consent in social research. Evidence based researches have disclosed that women are not well informed and this over shadows their judgment on appropriate decision making (Osamor and Kass, 2012).

7   Women, Gender and Society

Women in any society are germane to its continual existence and development. This has inevitable being a matter of concern globally in scholarly discourse. Their contribution to development cannot be neglected or overshadowed. However, persistence of gender inequality most especially in the developing nation is such that the female gender is discredited or marginalized from the gains of development. In legal rights: women in many countries still lack independent rights to own land, manage property, conduct business, or even travel without their husband's consent (Duflo, 2012). The level of inequality is rooted within the socio-cultural context of such society. The inequality being faced by the female gender can be traced back to the Bible, namely, passages such as Genesis 3:16, which says: 'unto the woman he said, I will greatly multiply thy sorrow and thy conception; in sorrow thou shalt bring forth children; and thy desire [shall be] to thy husband, and he shall rule over thee'. There are also other references in the Bible that refer to the female gender subjugation to the male gender (See Ephesians 5:22-24; 1 Peter 3:1-7; 1 Timothy 2:11-12; 1 Corinthians 11:3; Colossians 3:18).

Besides the Bible, we have such ideas about women's subordination to men articulated in in places like Africa and other societies in the world that are notoriously patriarchy. For the most part, the African culture has its fair share of incidences of injustice, inequality and discrimination with restricted fair ground of opportunity and power between men and women. The discrimination aspect in African culture does forestall female gender from attaining same status with the male gender. In Nigeria for example, women are faced with marginalization from childbirth where the birth of a baby boy receives more jubilation and from when the sex of the bay is identified and given birth to. The value placed on the sex of children or the subordination of women not just at birth seems very intensified in some ethnic groups like the Yoruba of Southwest, Nigeria. According to Olabode (2009:136),

> Subsequently after the birth of a child, then comes the inquiry on the sex of the new born baby which disregards on the health status of the postpartum woman. If the sex of the baby is female, the mother is not celebrated and is seen as a lazy woman. However, if the sex of the new born baby is male, the woman is praised and celebrated. What is never considered is the Biological evidence that male gender determines the sex of the unborn child or offspring.

Other discrepancies are seen in inheritance of property where the female gender are disadvantaged. More devastating is situation where a married woman bear only female children, she is denied of inheriting her husband's property most especially in Igboland. It could also be inheriting of the woman after the demise of her husband by her husband siblings. Widowhood practices which varies amidst different cultures, has been documented to be dehumanizing to the female gender. In extreme cases, the woman is accused of her husband's demise and made to undergo rituals in bid to vindicate herself of such accusations (Adegoke and Owoseni, 2018). There are issues of taboos which has imposition on the female gender restricting them to perform equal rights with the male gender. These are moral codes where the society expresses disapproval of social behavior which should not be exhibited by the female gender. Such is their restriction in performing rituals when she is menstruating as such is seen as defiling the shrine or place of worship. The woman is depicted as been unclean (Adegoke and Owoseni, 2018). Although, there still exist some exception as some women are religion priestesses who are given roles to participate such as Osun, Oya, Ayelala who are worshipped in Yoruba culture (Familusi, 2012). Also, when considering or making reproductive choices, the male gender are most often at the centre of taking the decisions such as should family planning be used and the choice of family planning, when to get pregnant, number of children to bore, the place of childbirth delivery (Yusuff, 2019; Ushie, Eneji, Ugal et al. 2019).

The situation and observation arises for their emancipation in different spheres be it religious, political and or economic. Such is the dilemma which exhibit itself in any epistemological research when there is the need to align with the ethics guiding a research. There are issues of contention which varies from the context of the local environment, the spousal consent and of importance is the level of education with the contextual understanding of the informed consent in any research. This is seen in most African cultures where a woman cannot single handedly give their assent to partake in a study, despite being older than the age one can give consent. Aside giving their assent to partake in a study, male researchers are not permitted to elicit information from women in some cultures. Furthermore, in some African culture women are not expected to talk unless in the presence of their husband or family. Similarly, for some women informed consents need to be culturally sensitive because there exist cultural and religious norms aside from the challenge of low level in literacy (Howell and Obado-Joel, 2016).

jIn Nigeria, a patriarchal nation, womanhood is reduced to a second-class citizen, which has resulted in the misrepresentation of women right at the level of the family and society at large. It is a system of social stratification and differentiation on the basis of sex, which provides material advantages to males while simultaneously placing severe constraints on the roles and activities of females (Makama, 2013). Also, there is the problem of educational attainment, in which girl child is denied basic education irrespective of implementation of programme put in place to elevate the educational status of the girl child. She is subjected to education that will groom her into motherhood. A situation replica in most developing nations. Unlike most western countries where the female gender have been able to achieve some level of autonomy and parity with their male counterparts (Kilawi, Khidir, Elnashar, Abdulrahim, Hammoud et al. 2014), usually as a result of many years of feminism intellectual adventure, Nigeria and Africa at large still have a very long way to go in ensuring gender equity. Sadly, the obtainable low rate of gender parity prevalent in the society remains noticeable even in social researches across Nigeria (Osamor and Kass, 2012).

8 Women and Research

To overcome one of the blind spots in research and in bid to get women to have more say in research as well as to safeguard the right of research participants to self-determination on whether to be a participant of a research exercise, the concept of informed consent that has become an essential part of ethical requirements must be pursued. In this sesen, informed consent can only be considered ethically valid when it is established that participants of a research exercise made autonomous decision to voluntarily engage in that research usually without any element of pressure and/or coercion. However, findings from researches have established that participants' decisions are rarely autonomous and usually with degree of variation along gender difference due to sociocultural factors like social influence from spouses, family members, friends aside level of education and other factors such as the nature of research being conducted (Bhan, Majd and Adejumo, 2006; Mystakidou, Panagiotou, Katsaragakis, Tsilika, and Parpa, 2009; Lobato, Bethony, Pereira, Grahek, Diemert and Gazzinelli, 2014).

There doesn't seen to be that much about gender relations in research in Nigeria, which I'm focusing on. And it might be the same in many other African countries, given the patriarchal nature of such societies. The point here is that there seem to be limited empirical studies on decision-making and informed consent on the female gender in Nigeria. For further clarification on the issue of informed consent in the dominant space of SSR below are some case studies.

9 Case Study One

In a research conducted on 100 adults (50 men and 50 women) to investigate on how participants' make decisions to partake in biomedical research while also assessing factors influencing their autonomy on decision making in an urban Nigerian community. It was observed that 78% which is over three quarters of the participants' had a discussion with someone else before enrolling in the study. Furthermore, 39% indicated obtaining permission from spouse or family member. Women were more than twice reported than men to have obtained permission from their spouse to participate (Osamor and Kass, 2012). Hence, the above case indicate the high impact of spousal influence (social influence) on women inform consent and women participation in studies in Nigeria. This is owing to both religious practices as well as restrictive sociocultural practices on women autonomy (Makama, 2013).

10   Case Study Two

In another study on voluntary participation and comprehension of informed consent in a genetic epidemiological study of breast cancer in Nigeria, although only 19% of the married participants reportedly sought their husbands' permission to participate in the study, further analysis revealed that 'women with less education were more likely to ask their husband's permission' (Marshall, Adebamowo, Adeyemo, et al. 2014). Thus, there exist a direct relationship between low literacy and low voluntariness to participate in a research for most women. That is, it is more likely for a poorly educated woman to seek for her husband permission before participating in a research than for a more educated woman, where culture and religion is not a factor. In this case, although inform consent is directed at these women, it only become relevant upon the approval of their husbands to participate in the study. For this cohorts of women (uneducated/under-educated), lack of adequate and depth knowledge of what inform consent entails casts a shadow on whether they are truly aware of the import of consenting to participate in a study (Mbonera and Chironda, 2018) either based on their own voluntary decision or spousal decision. Such is the situation of most uneducated/under-educated women on issues of informed consent.

Technically, from the above two case studies some clarity is given to the notion that in reality what really obtains is 'Tailored' consent rather than 'Informed' Consent. The indication that the 'other' gender (woman), in a dominant space is a constrained agency. This constitutes an epistemological imbalance or inequality in research and knowledge production, which is a challenge in social research ethics and any social research that is still stepped in the status quo or old ways of doing research.

11   Conclusion

How do we make sense of the problem concerning the instance of informed and gender ethics in the context of a dominant space of social research? And what is the implication for securing women informed consent in such dominant or mainstream space of research? From these questions, it is pertinent that a cultural environment of gender equality is needed and has to be put in place especially in a patriarchal structure which is evident in most developing society, where male dictates the line of human action. Furthermore, there is the need for a reconstructive gender theory (that draws on the principle of equality) as against Gender Identity Theory or Gender Socialization Theory that often presume stereotypical roles and identity of women participation in social research. A reorientation of some cultural practices which are seen to undermine or hinder on the progress of the female gender should be abolished. While caution is observed in the process of their liberation, some African cultural values should not be destroyed in the process of civilization. This observation calls for the need of culturally competent and sensitive approaches such as a Behavioural Change Communication strategy as well as a community engagement (where everyone is seen as a stakeholder) that addresses identity specific barriers in research when designing the informed consent forms. Also, gender mainstreaming should be considered in research implementation and ethical process especially the informed consent. In this way, the attainment of gender equality will not be seen as only an end itself on human right issues, but as a prerequisite for the achievement of sustainable development.

References

Adegoke, O. O and Owoseni, A. O. 2018. "Social Perception of Menstrual Cycle: Implication for Women's Role in Development". *African Journal for the Psychological Studies of Social Issues,* 21(1):136–146.

Aderibigbe, K. S and Chima, S.C. 2019." Knowledge and practice of informed consent by Physiotherapists and therapy assisants in Kwazulu-Natal Province, South Africa". *S Afr J Physiother.* 75(1): 1330.

Akaranga S.I. and Jude Ongong'a. 2013. "Work Ethics for University Lecturers: An Example of Nairobi and Kenyatta". *International Journal of Arts and Commerce*, 2(8): 8–22.

Akaranga S. I and Makau B. E. 2016. "Ethical Considerations and their Applications to Research: a Case of the University of Nairobi". *Journal of Educational Policy and Entrepreneurial Research.* 3(12): 1–9.

Babbie, E. R. 2010. *The Practice of Social Research.* 12th ed. Bemont, CA: Wadsworth Cenegage.

Bassey, I. E., Ugbem, T. I., Akpan, U. O., Anyanwu, S. O., Glen, E. E. et al 2019. Overcoming Barriers in conducting a Transatlantic Prostate Cancer Familial study in Africa: Best practice from CaPTC Cohort study.

Bhan, A., Majad, M and Adejumo, A. 2006. "Informed consent in International Research: Perspectives from India, Iran and Nigeria". *Medical Ethics*, 3(1): 36–41.

Bulmer, M. 2008. *The ethics of social research*. In N. Gilbert (Ed.), *Researching social life* (3rd ed., pp. 145–161). Sage: London.

Busia, K. A. 1967. *Africa in Search of Democracy*, New York: Praeger.

Council for International Organizations of Medical Sciences (CIOMS), 2006. International Ethical Guidelines for Biomedical Research Involving Human Subjects.

Duflo, E. 2012. "Women empowerment and economic development". *Journal of Economic Literature*. 50(4), 1051–1079.

Eyelade, O. R., Ajuwon, A. J and Adebamowo, C. A. 2011. "An appraisal of the process of protocol review by an ethics review committee in a tertiary institution in Ibadan". *Afr J Med Sci.* 40(2): 163–169.

Familusi, O. O. 2012. "African culture and the status of women: the Yoruba example". *The Journal of Pan African Studies*, 5(1).

Garfield, T and Yudell, M. 2019. "Commentary 2: Participatory Justice and Ethics in Autism Research". *Journal of Empircal research on Human Research Ethics*. Vol. 14(5): 455–457.

Gibson, S., Benson, O. and Brand, S. L. 2012. "Talking about suicide: Confidentiality and anonymity in qualitative research". *Nursing Ethics*, 20(1).

Gyekye, K. 2010. *African Ethics*. Stanford Encyclopedia of Philosophy. Spring Edition.

Howell, Embry and Obado-Joel, Jennifer. 2016. Human Subjects protection in the African context. *African Evaluation Journal*, 4(1).

Idowu, B. E. 1962. *Olodumare: God in Yoruba Belief*, London: Longmans Group Ltd.

Jegede, A. S., Adegoke, O. O. and Ushie, B. A. 2015. "Awareness and Attitude of Social and Behavioural Scientists to Research Ethics in Nigerian Universities". *Journal of West African Bioethics Training Program*, 2(2): 29–40.

Killawi, A., Khidir, A., Elnashar, E., Abdelrahim, H., Hammoud, M., Elliot, H. and Fetters, M. 2014. "Procedures of recruiting, obtaining informed consent, and compensating research participants in Qatar: Findings from a qualitative investigation". *BMC Medical Ethics*, 15(9), 1–13. doi:10.1186/1472-6939-15-9

Lobato, L., Bethony, J. M., Pereira, F. B., Grahek, S. L., Diemert, D. and Gazzinelli, M. F. 2014. Impact of gender on the decision to participate in a clinical trial: a cross-sectional study. *BMC Public Health*. 6;14:1156. doi: 10.1186/1471-2458-14-1156.

Makama, G. A. 2013. "Patriarchy and gender inequality in Nigeria: the way forward". *European Scientific Journal*, 9(17).

Marshall, P. A., Adebamowo, C. A., Adeyemo, A. A., Ogundiran, T. O., Strenski, T., Zhou, J and Rotimi, C. N. 2014. "Voluntary participation and comprehension of informed consent in a genetic epidemiological study of breast cancer in Nigeria". *BMC Med Ethics*. 13:15;38. Doi: 10.1186/1472-6939-15-38.

Mbonera, F. and Chirond, G. 2018. "The relationship between knowledge and perception of patients regarding informed consent in surgical procedures in Rwanda". *International Journal of Research in Medical Science*, 6(2).

Munung, N. S., Marshall, P., Campbell, M., Littler, K., Masiye, F., Ouwe-Missi-Oukem-Boyer, O., Seeley, J., Stein, D. J., Tindana, P and de Vries, J. 2016. "Obtaining informed consent for genomics research in Africa: analysis of H3Africa consent documents". *Journal of Medical Ethics*, 42(2): 132–137.

Mystakidou, K., Panagiotou, I., Katsaragakis, S., Tsilika, E. and Parpa, E. 2009. "Ethical and Practical Challenges In Implementing Informed Consent In HIV/AIDS Clinical Trials In Developing Or Resource-Limited Countries". *SAHARA Journal*, 6(2):46–57.

Nijhawan, L. P., Janodia, M. D., Muddukrishna, B. S., Bhat, K. M., Bairy, K. L., Udupa, N and Musmade, P. B. "Informed Consent: Issues and challenges". *J Adv Pharm Technol Res*, 4(3): 134–40.

Nnebue C.C. 2010. "Informed Consent in Research". *Afrimedic Journal*, 1(1).

Obono, O., Arowojolu, A., Ajuwon, J., Ogundipe, G. A., Yakubu, J. A. and Falusi, A. G. 2006. "Ethics in Research." In Olayinka, A.I., Taiwo, V.O.,Raji-Oyalade, A. & Farai, I.P. (ed.), pp.281–320, Methodology of Basic and Applied Research. Ibadan: Postgraduate School, University of Ibadan.

Olabode, B. O. 2009. *African Gender myth in proverbs and verbal discourses; A case study of the Yoruba of South Western Nigeria*. In Kehinde, A. (ed) Gender and Development: Essential Readings, Ibadan: Hope Publications.

Onuoha C. 2007. Bioethics across borders. An African perspective. Uppsala University, 2007.

Opoku, K. A. 1978. West African Traditional Religion, Jurong, Singapore: FEP International Private Limited.

Osamor, P. E, and Kass, N. 2012. Decision- making and motivation to participate in Biomedical Research in Southwest Nigeria. *Bioethics*, 12(2): 87–95.

Roache, Rebecca. 2014. "Why is informed consent important?" *J Med Ethics*, 40(7).

Sarantakos, S. 2013. *Social Research*. 4th Edition, Palgrave Mac-Millan, New York.

Scott, J and Gordon M. 2005. *A Dictionary of Sociology*. Oxford: Oxford University Press.

Shamoo, A and Resnik, D. 2015. "Responsible conduct of research". 3rd ed. New York: Oxford University Press.

Sumola, A. M., Mayungbo, O. A., Ashefọr, G. A. et al. 2019. "Does relation between women's justification of wife beating and intimate partner violence differ in context of husband's controlling attitudes in Nigeria?" *Journal of Family Issues*, 41(1).

Tai, M. C. 2012. "Deception and informed consent in social, behavioural and educational research". *Tzu Chi Medical Journal*, 24(4): 218–222.

Tomljenovic. L, and Shaw C.A. 2013. "Human papillomavirus (HPV) vaccine policy and evidence-based medicine: are they at odd"s? *AnnMed.*, 45(2): 182–93. doi: 10.3109/07853890.2011.645353. Epub 2011 Dec 22.

University of Ibadan Research Management Office. 2020. www.rmo.ui.edu.ng/node/4

Ushie, M. A., Eneji, C. V. O., Ugal, D. B., Anyaoha, O., Ushie, B. A and Bassey, J. E. 2019. "Violence against women and reproduction health among African women: The case of Bette Women of Obudu in Cross River State, Nigeria." *African Journal of Gender and Women Studies*, 4 (1).

Wassenaar, D. R. and Mamotte, N. 2012. *Ethical issues and ethics reviews in social science research*. In: Leach, M. M. Stevens, M. J., Lindsay, G., Ferrero, A and Korkut, Y, editors. Oxford Handbook of International Psychological Ethics: Oxford University Press.

Yakubu, A. A., Hyder, A. A., Ali, J and Kass, N. 2017. "Research Ethics Committees in Nigeria: A survey of operations, functions and needs". *Ethics and Human Research*, 39(3).

Yip, C., Han, N. R., and Sng, B. L. 2016. "Legal and ethical issues in research." *Indian Journal of Anaesthesia,* 60(9): 684–688.

Yusuff, O. 2019. "Reproductive rights and reproductive choice of Yoruba Women in Southwestern Nigeria." *Advanced Journal of Social Science,* 6(1): 138–151.

Index

3Rs   251, 252
#BringBackOurGirls   290

Abacha   248
Abdulsalami Abubakar   209
Abubakar Shekau   281
Abuja   92, 99, 106, 107, 254, 255
abuse   6, 105, 118, 151, 187, 190, 194, 297–299, 301, 304–306, 310, 332
academic   12, 45, 27, 47, 73, 205, 297–302, 304–306, 309
Academic Abuse   6, 297
accountability   36, 72, 73, 125, 127, 330
activism   1, 23, 27, 134
Adamawa   280, 285
Adam Habib   IX, 125
Adekunle Fajuyi   249, 250
adolescent   6, 309, 310, 313, 316, 317
Adolescent   309
adolescents   300, 304, 308–318
Adolescents   6, 308, 317
Afghanistan   211
Africa   X, IX, 1, 3–5, 11, 24, 31, 32, 34–36, 39, 42, 51, 73–75, 77, 81, 83, 117, 118, 121–124, 126–130, 132, 134, 135, 146, 147, 171, 176, 178, 191, 201–207, 209–214, 217, 219, 220, 224, 243–247, 262–267, 270–273, 275–277, 284, 301, 321, 324, 332, 333, 335
Africa Examination Council   301
African   X, XIII–XVII, 1, 2, 4, 31, 34–36, 40–42, 77, 119, 122, 127, 128, 130, 131, 133, 134, 148, 177, 186, 201, 203, 205–207, 209–213, 217, 222, 232, 254, 262–267, 272, 275, 298, 299, 321, 322, 324, 331–335, 337
African National Congress   122, 128, 148
African philosopher   205, 206, 213, 263, 267
African philosophers   205, 206
African philosophy   XIV, XVII
African Philosophy   XV
Afrikaner   127, 129
Afrocentrism   271
Agbero   99
Agberos   91, 102, 107, 111
Agbor   XV, XVI, XVII, 309, 311, 312

agenda   13, 50, 54, 63, 117, 128, 129, 208
agricultural   46, 47, 51–53, 56, 60, 61, 119, 228
agriculture   52, 55
Aguyi-Ironsi   248
Ahmadu Bello University   248
Alabama   324
albinism   149, 150, 151, 156, 157, 159
alienation   1, 25, 247, 271
America   82, 117, 120, 227
American   119, 120, 210, 211, 227, 266, 268, 324
Americas   11, 206
Amilcar Cabral   35
Anambra   91
ANC   120, 122–125, 127–132, 135
ANCYL   129–132, 134
Andry Nirina Rajoelina   77
Angola   IX, 263, 272
angular kyphosis   149, 151, 156, 157, 159
Anonymity   327
anti-colonialist   50
Arabic   264, 281
area-boys   101
Area-Boys   91, 107
Argentina   120
Aristotelian   267, 268, 273
Aristotelian metaphysics   267
Aristotle   72, 262, 267, 269, 273, 276, 322
Asia   206
Asouzu   263, 267–271, 273, 274, 276, 277
Atlantic   12, 92
Australian   21
authoritarian   1–3, 13, 120, 218
authoritarianism   2, 11, 13, 32, 47

ballot boxes   102
Basic Science   302–304
Bayelsa State   91
beggars   169, 172
begging   169, 170, 172, 173
Belgium   120, 176
beliefs   32, 147, 148, 155, 169, 322, 323
beliefs about disability   147
beliefs and perceptions of disability   147
Belmont Report   324, 331

Bendel State   91
beneficence   323, 324, 328
Beneficence   328, 331
beneficiaries   54, 59, 61, 133
Benin City   150, 151
Benue   243
Biafra   77, 240–243, 250–256, 266
Biafraism   240
Biafrans   241, 242, 249, 251, 252, 254
Bible   128, 284, 333
Bight of Benin   91, 92
biomedical   6, 325, 335
Blaise Compaore   208
Boer   129
Boko Haram   5, 77, 266, 280–285, 287–291
Bolivia   120
Borno   280, 282, 284–288
Bosasa Company   128
Bosco Ntaganda   210
Britain   2, 82, 208, 250
British   74, 101, 210, 243, 255, 268, 271
Broken Windows Theory   94, 96
brotherhood   17
Budiriro   5, 217, 219, 220, 222–233
bureaucratic   127, 218, 224, 232
Bureau of Statistics   73, 91, 92, 75, 187
Burkina Faso   36, 208
Burundi   2, 243, 247
businesses   214, 220, 224, 226, 227, 232

Cairo   217
Calabar   74, 203, 267
Calabar   xiv
Cameroon   208, 209, 243, 283, 288, 289
Cameroun   287
Canadian   77, 149
candidates   75, 76, 80–83, 130
Canovan   117, 118, 121
Cape Town   134, 148
capital   14, 47, 49, 125, 132, 134, 168, 201, 205, 213, 218, 220, 224, 226, 232, 240, 241, 282, 284
capitalisation   227
capitalism   ix, 12, 13, 17, 20, 35, 120, 263
Chad   263, 287–289
Charles Taylor   210
Chicago   301
child   168, 169, 171–174, 179, 266, 285, 298, 299, 302, 305, 306, 309, 333, 334
childhood   171, 298, 299

children   5, 6, 88, 152, 166, 168–171, 174, 179, 198, 220, 251, 252, 282–290, 297–301, 304–306, 324, 331, 333
Children   5, 169, 170, 175, 280, 283, 298, 305
Chinese   264, 266
Christian   17
Christianity   12, 169, 194, 237
Chukwuemeka Odumegwu Ojukwu   250
CIA   211
citizen   72, 74, 127, 132, 212, 257, 265, 334
citizens   19, 24, 25, 50, 70, 72, 74, 118, 154, 160, 168, 203, 212–214, 238, 247, 265, 272, 273, 275, 281, 289
citizenship   50, 132
civic duty   71
Civil War   245, 247, 249, 250, 253
Civil Wars   245
Co7   53–56, 58
cognitive development   298
Cold War   3, 11, 14, 202, 210
College of Education   xv, xvi
colonial   1, 11–13, 15–20, 23, 27, 31, 34, 35, 51, 72, 74, 77, 207–209, 211, 243, 273
colonialism   11, 12, 19, 50, 72, 207–209, 212
Colonialism   11
coloniality   11, 12, 14, 16–21, 25, 27
colonization   11
commercial   2, 46, 47, 92, 191, 197, 227, 228, 331
commodities   220, 227
common good   262–264, 266, 267, 269, 270, 273–277
communal   46–48, 55–61, 64, 53, 158, 281, 332
communalism   35, 322
communities   46, 49, 92, 54, 18, 100–103, 26, 105, 107–109, 126, 129, 148–151, 177, 191, 237, 252, 254, 282, 286, 287, 290
companies   103, 179, 221, 222
complementarity   23, 262, 267–271, 273–277
confidentiality   192, 325, 327, 328, 330
Conflict   6, 106, 109, 112, 308, 312, 314
conflicts   40, 42, 186, 208, 210, 257, 308–310
Congo   208, 209
consent   6, 144, 192, 321, 323, 324, 326, 327, 329–337
conservational   37, 38, 42
Conservatism   1, 3, 11, 15, 31–33, 38, 39
conservatisms   ix, x, 1
conservative   1, 3, 15–17, 27, 36, 39, 42, 78
Conservative   15

INDEX   343

conservative-radicals 1
Conservatives 39, 40
Constitution 74, 75, 124, 172
constitutionalism 73, 124
consumption 57, 165, 220, 225, 227
conversationalism 31, 37, 42
conversational philosophy XIV
Conversational philosophy 36
conversational thinking XIV, 1, 32, 36–41, 202
Conversational Thinking 1, 31, 36
corruption 45, 79, 61, 123, 126, 128, 131, 209, 210, 212–224, 280, 309
cosmopolitanism 11
countries 2, 13, 18–20, 25, 31, 34, 35, 51, 72–74, 80, 118, 164, 167, 168, 171, 174, 176, 180, 186, 187, 201, 203–205, 209–213, 243, 246, 264, 265, 272, 298, 301, 308, 324, 332, 334, 335
coup 2, 77, 78, 249, 250
courts 56, 153
Covid-19 13, 20, 24, 25–27
CPI 312
credit 52, 166, 178, 220, 226, 232, 301
criminal activities 77, 96, 108, 188, 198, 239
criminals 109, 111
CRPD 143–146, 155–159, 172, 179
cultural IX, 13, 18, 27, 35, 36, 46, 56, 70, 79, 83, 148, 165, 166, 169, 180, 206, 207, 218, 232, 237, 238, 241, 271, 322, 331–334, 337
culture IX, 15, 24, 34–36, 56, 82, 83, 90, 91, 96, 98–100, 103–105, 124, 144, 147, 149, 188, 197, 237, 238, 281, 304, 305, 331, 333, 334, 336
customary practices 110, 147, 152, 156
Cyril Ramaphosa 125, 127

Dar es Salaam 217
data 48, 121, 124, 167, 172, 174, 176, 187, 191, 192, 194–196, 219, 221, 226, 282, 286, 301, 302, 314, 325, 327, 330
Dawda Jawara 208
deception 329
Deception 328
Decolonial 1, 11
decoloniality XVII, 12, 14, 22, 23
Delta 2, 6, 88, 89, 91–94, 77, 96, 99–112, 148, 151, 242, 251, 252, 287, 297–299, 301, 304–306, 309, 311
Delta State XV, XVI, XVII, 6, 91–94, 99, 101–108, 151, 297, 299, 301, 304–306, 309, 311

democracies 20, 117, 124, 213
democracy 5, 11, 13, 15, 22, 35, 36, 62, 70–73, 75, 76, 79, 80, 82, 117, 124, 126, 127, 129, 132, 172, 257
democratic 36, 25, 70, 75, 81, 132, 210, 213, 241, 242
Democratic Alliance 128
Democratic Republic of Congo 77, 83, 210
Denmark 74
development 5, 12, 20, 22, 31, 35, 36, 39, 41, 51, 52, 58, 62, 71, 77, 80, 81, 126, 128, 129, 143, 145, 164, 167, 168, 171, 173, 174, 180, 186, 188, 189, 198, 204, 208, 212, 218, 240, 241, 246, 250, 266, 276, 281, 282, 297, 298, 300, 301, 305, 306, 318, 321, 332, 337
dictatorial 5, 209, 210, 211, 213
dictators 203, 209, 210
dictatorship 5, 12, 207, 209–211
dignity 22, 144, 156, 157, 159, 202, 204, 206, 207, 323
dirty-relevance 3, 4, 88, 90, 91, 96, 98–100, 102–108, 110–112
disabilities IX, 4, 143, 144, 146, 147, 149, 150, 152–159, 164, 166–180
Disabilities XV, XVI, 143, 144, 154–160, 180
Disabilities Act 144, 154–160
disability 4, 143, 145–148, 154, 155, 158, 160, 164, 166–171, 173–176, 178, 180, 324, 331
Disability 143, 145–147, 164, 166–168, 171–173, 175
Disability Act 172
disabled 153, 164, 166–168, 170–174, 176, 179–181
disabled people 164, 166, 168, 171, 173, 174, 176
discrimination 19, 143, 144, 147, 150, 152, 154, 157, 159, 169, 172, 174, 176, 180, 245, 266, 272, 326, 333
discriminatory 4, 15, 144, 148, 152, 154, 156–159, 275
dollarisation 222, 232
Dollarisation 222
Dollarising 222
Domboshava 228
Donald Trump 121
drug 4, 105, 157, 186–190, 194–198, 309, 329, 331
drug use 5, 186–190, 196, 198
Dunstan 47, 53, 55, 56, 64
Dutch 119

East 5, 14, 16, 47, 191, 243, 246, 250, 266, 280, 282, 283, 286, 287, 290, 291
Eastern Europe 17
Ebonyi State 152
economic IX, 5, 6, 13, 21, 25, 26, 31, 34–36, 45, 46, 51, 52, 56, 58, 59, 72, 77, 82, 119, 120, 125, 127, 129–131, 135, 144, 147, 149, 164–170, 175, 178–180, 186, 190, 191, 196, 198, 208–210, 213, 214, 217–226, 230–233, 241, 242, 246–248, 262, 263, 266, 271, 273, 280, 281, 283, 285, 291, 334
Economic 3, 4, 52, 76, 117, 120, 125, 128, 144, 165, 219, 221, 223, 246, 290, 309
Economic Freedom Fighters 4, 117, 128
Economic Freedom Front 3
economies 209, 210, 212, 229, 282
economy 16, 25, 26, 32, 35, 42, 52, 59, 73, 119, 120, 125, 130, 135, 186, 188, 189, 209, 212, 219–223, 226–228, 231, 265
Edo State 91, 147, 150, 151, 311
education IX, X, XIV–XVI, 72, 73, 77, 121, 146, 152, 156, 158, 165, 167, 170, 172–174, 177, 178, 188, 194, 202, 205, 206, 218, 229, 253, 280–286, 288–291, 297, 298, 300, 331, 334–336
Education X, 3, 6, 101, 104, 134, 174, 284, 285, 289, 290, 304, 312
EFF 3, 4, 117, 118, 120–124, 127–135
egalitarian 40, 153, 154, 159
elections 6, 54, 64, 70, 73–76, 79–81, 83, 128, 135, 263
elephant in the room 14, 126
elite 1, 3, 4, 35, 45, 52, 57, 60, 63, 117, 118, 120, 121, 123–126, 131, 132, 135, 257
Emmanuel Macron 77
empathic 310, 311, 313, 315–317
Empathic Responding 6, 308, 310, 317
employment 2, 5, 90, 56, 82, 62, 125, 146, 152, 153, 156–159, 167, 170, 173, 174, 176–178, 190, 194, 197, 198, 218, 220–222, 226–228, 230, 232, 300
England 301
English language 301, 302
English Language 302–304
Enlightenment 11
Enugu 255
environment 26, 36, 49, 51, 52, 56, 58, 125, 145, 146, 149, 170, 175, 177, 218, 219, 224, 225, 231, 238, 241, 242, 288, 298, 334, 337
epistemic 11, 12, 18, 19, 31, 37, 38, 40

epistemological 334, 336
equality 13, 82, 117, 144, 153, 273, 321, 337
Eritrea 247
ethical 16, 17, 321–331, 335, 337
ethics 6, 22, 306, 321–327, 329–332, 334, 336
Ethics 321–325, 328, 329, 332
ethnic 5, 20, 23, 27, 34, 50, 72, 122, 208, 237–250, 253, 256, 257, 266, 268, 333
ethnicism 280
ethnicity 70, 237, 238, 240, 244, 246, 247
Ethnicity 237, 244, 257
Ethnic Militias 5, 237, 241
Ethnos 238
ethos 322
Etieyibo IX, 1, 143, 144, 153, 159, 169, 172, 173
Eurocentric 11, 19, 27
Europe 13, 15, 17, 20, 50, 117, 121, 208
European 11, 17, 18, 23, 119, 120, 187, 208
Europeanism 12
Evo Morales 120
exploitation 6, 12, 57, 58, 120, 126, 208, 209, 242, 245, 273, 276
export 47, 228
expropriation 130, 131

Facebook 125, 255
fairness 154, 159, 273, 328
family 61, 62, 77, 83, 133, 148, 149, 151, 169, 177, 189, 190, 196–198, 218, 228–230, 266, 285, 332, 334, 335
farmers 2, 47, 48, 50, 54, 56, 62, 119, 131, 227, 228
farming 46, 48–51, 53–55, 57–64, 168, 170
farms 47, 48, 50, 51, 53, 54, 57–59, 61, 62, 227, 228
fascist 4, 16
fast track land reform programme 45
female 6, 41, 75, 151, 152, 191, 194, 312, 316, 321, 331–335, 337
Female 6, 286, 321
females 100, 284, 311, 316, 334
feminism 334
feminisms XVII
financial 52, 74, 76, 82, 118, 120, 127, 152, 157, 168, 171, 175, 178, 179, 203, 206, 210, 224, 226, 227, 229, 232, 273, 281, 328, 331
First Republic 78, 78, 247
flora and fauna 57, 58
focus group 48, 53, 55, 60, 61, 219, 220, 224, 226, 229

INDEX 345

Fordism   12
foreigners   5, 103, 121, 169, 264– 266, 271–273, 275–277
Fourth Republic   2, 77, 88–90, 93, 94, 96–101, 103–105, 108, 111, 253
France   77, 120, 263
Francis Fukuyama   14
Frantz Fanon   35
freedom   13, 16, 24, 25, 32, 35, 78, 118, 125, 130, 131, 135, 158, 218, 242, 276
Freedom Charter   128, 129, 131
free market   25, 32, 263
French   11, 264, 268
FTLRP   4, 45–47, 49–52, 57–60, 63

Gambia   208
gangsterism   105
gender   12, 72, 82, 166, 170, 187, 239, 316, 317, 321, 331–336
Gender   6, 317, 321, 332, 337
General Assembly   88, 180, 264, 273
German   268, 271
gerontocratic conservatives   3
Ghana   IX, 35, 36, 208, 262, 263, 265, 266, 267, 273
Ghanaian   265, 266
Ghanaians   264, 265, 271, 273
girl   100, 334
global   1, 11–18, 20, 21, 24–26, 80, 117, 118, 135, 143, 144, 174, 201–204, 207–213, 217, 272–275
globalization   IX, 13–15, 18, 21, 26
Global South   XV, XVII
Gnassingbé Eyadéma   209
Goodluck Jonathan   76, 144, 212, 255, 287
goods   14, 165, 220, 221, 228, 229
Gordon   16, 18, 19, 290, 322
Goromonzi   47, 54, 57
government   4, 32, 48, 50, 51, 54, 57, 59, 60, 62, 64, 70–74, 77, 78, 82, 120, 122, 124, 125, 129–131, 134, 135, 152, 154, 168, 170–173, 175, 177–179, 198, 205, 208, 209, 211, 212, 227, 229, 230, 238, 242, 245–252, 254–257, 264, 265, 271, 273–275, 280–282, 285–291, 306, 311, 324
governmental   71, 105, 173, 178, 181, 241, 245, 263, 289, 305, 328
governments   2, 13, 71, 77, 89, 155, 156, 158, 171, 173, 181, 188, 201–207, 209–213, 217, 257, 287

grass root   26
Great Britain   250
Greek   238, 263, 322
groups   2, 5, 15, 17–22, 35, 39, 40, 49, 58, 73–75, 77, 79–81, 118, 124, 207, 237–247, 250, 256, 257, 262, 264, 280, 290, 311, 313, 314, 329, 333
Guinea   35

happiness   21, 203, 262, 322
Harare   5, 47, 217–219, 221, 228–231
harmful practices   144
Hastings Kamuzu Banda   1
Hausa-Fulani   250, 253, 256
health   2, 73, 77, 145, 146, 165, 166, 170–173, 175, 179, 187, 202, 298, 324, 325, 331, 333
Helsinki Declaration   324
herbalist   149, 151
heterogeneity   24, 244
Heterogeneity   244
heterosexism   16, 17
history   IX, 14, 15, 19, 35, 36, 47, 50, 131, 143, 213, 222, 226, 229, 237, 238, 252, 253, 263, 269, 273, 281, 324, 326
HIV/AIDS   157, 206, 264
hooliganism   4, 90, 105
household   57, 62, 165, 168, 171, 179, 218–223, 225–230, 232, 233, 290, 300
households   45, 51, 59, 218, 219, 225–229, 232, 233
House of Assemblies   75, 81
House of Assembly   70, 74, 76, 80, 80
House of Representative   70
House of Representatives   70, 74, 76, 78, 80, 81
Houses of Assembly   93
Hugo Chavéz   121
human   2, 5, 11–13, 15, 18–21, 23, 26, 32, 49, 52, 61, 71–73, 143–145, 148, 149, 153, 154, 157, 159, 165, 168, 174, 186, 190, 202, 204, 209, 211, 232, 237, 251, 252, 257, 262–264, 266–271, 273–276, 277, 282–284, 288, 289, 297, 308, 321, 323–326, 329, 330, 337
human interest   5, 262–264, 266, 267, 269, 271, 273, 274, 276, 277
humanity   18, 19, 159, 211, 251, 252, 272, 275, 330, 331

human rights 2, 15, 20, 52, 73, 143, 144, 153, 154, 159, 202, 209, 211, 251, 252, 276, 288, 289
humans 18, 20, 25, 148, 202, 204, 270, 271, 274, 305, 323
husband 266, 333, 334, 336
Hutus 243, 245, 247
hyperinflation 218, 221, 225
hyperinflationary 225

Ibrahim Babangida 209
ICC 210, 211
idealist 48
identities IX, 12, 15, 17, 18, 50, 127, 239, 243, 244, 266
identity 20, 53, 64, 79, 206, 237–241, 244–247, 250, 264, 271, 275, 321, 327, 337
ideology 17, 18, 33, 35, 36, 50, 74, 118–120, 126, 127, 132, 209, 240, 267, 277, 287
Idi Amin Dada 208
IDP camps 282, 287
IDPS 285, 287, 288
Igbo 77, 207, 240–242, 244, 247, 249, 250, 253, 255, 268, 269
Igbos 78, 245, 247, 248, 251, 252, 254, 256
illicit 4, 186–190, 194–198, 218
illicit drug use 4, 186–190, 195–198
immigration 20, 119, 157, 264, 274
Imo 91
imperialism 2, 12, 50
income 52, 58, 60, 72, 74, 165–167, 171, 175, 179, 186, 188–191, 196–198, 201–203, 217–219, 221, 222, 224–228, 230, 232, 285
independence 2, 49, 51, 73, 77, 78, 78, 126, 177, 208, 209, 243, 249, 250, 252, 253, 255, 256
indigenes 78, 208, 271, 273, 275, 276, 277
Indigenous People of Biafra 5, 242, 255
individuals 18, 20, 25, 39, 40, 49, 62, 71, 73–75, 83, 144, 145, 153, 154, 157, 159, 165, 167, 168, 173–177, 179, 180, 188, 204, 218, 237, 240, 244, 245, 262, 283, 309, 322, 327
industrialisation 208
industrialization 35, 186
industrial revolutions 11
inequalities IX, 17, 186, 198, 242, 272
inequality 22, 24, 124, 130, 135, 188, 189, 197, 233, 246, 257, 321, 332, 333, 336
informal 26, 218, 220, 221, 222, 224–231, 308

informal businesses 226
informal economy 226, 227, 232
Informed Consent 6, 321, 329, 336
infrastructure IX, 46, 51, 53, 54, 73, 155, 166, 173, 201, 203, 208, 213, 217, 219, 232
injustice 6, 202, 242, 248, 280, 333
institutions 14, 31, 32, 34, 40, 48, 50, 52, 54, 57, 71, 72, 78, 83, 118, 152, 166, 177, 178, 201–205, 207–213, 217, 219, 223–227, 283, 290, 297, 309, 323, 325
interest rates 227
International Criminal Court 210, 211
International Institute of Sociology IX, 11, 24
Interpersonal Reactivity Inventory 313
interview 16, 149, 153, 192
interviews 48, 54, 226, 229
Intolerance 3, 5, 237
IPOB 5, 242, 255–257, 266
IRI 312–314
Ironsi 249
Islam 169, 194, 237, 281
Ivory Coast 208, 247

Jacob Zuma 122
job 99, 153, 157, 176, 177, 196, 197, 221, 228, 258
jobs 14, 18, 24, 55, 134, 179, 197, 198, 203, 220, 222, 265
Johannesburg IX, 11, 24, 217
John Rawls 154
Jose Mujica 120
Joseph Kabila 77, 209
Juan Perón 120
Juju 146
Julius Sello Malema 3
justice IX, 1, 144, 153, 154, 156, 159, 188, 206, 211, 251–253, 257, 262, 323, 324, 328
Justin Trudeau 77

Kano 92, 173, 243
Kano State 92, 173
Kenya 243, 324
kidnapping 99, 149, 151
kidnappings 285
killings 148, 149, 150
Kim Jong-un 77
Kinshasa 217
kinship 237, 238

INDEX

knowledge 1, 6, 12, 17, 19, 22, 23, 25, 27, 36, 41, 131, 174, 191, 240, 267, 299, 305, 322, 325, 329, 330, 332, 336
Kosofe Local Government Area 191
Kwame Nkrumah 35, 207, 208

labour 47, 51, 56, 59, 62, 65, 157, 176, 219, 226
Labour 62, 176
Lagos XIV, XVI–XVIII, 2, 4, 74, 78, 88, 89, 91–96, 98–110, 147, 148, 153, 172, 186, 189–191, 198, 217, 265
Lagos State 91–93, 95, 98, 99, 101, 103–106, 108, 109, 112, 147, 153, 172, 190, 191
Laissez-faire 32
land 2, 17, 35, 45–50, 53, 55, 56, 58–61, 63, 64, 120, 121, 130, 131, 148, 166, 222–228, 232, 243, 271, 333
land reform 2, 35, 45, 46, 49, 59, 64, 130, 227, 228, 232
Latin 117, 119, 120, 207, 238
Latin American 119, 120
Laurent Gbagbo 208
Laurent Kabila 209
lawmakers 75
leaders 1, 2, 18, 51, 53, 56, 62, 63, 79, 64, 117, 118, 169, 209, 210, 228, 250, 257
leadership 2, 4, 48, 57, 25, 75, 78, 79, 83, 123, 127, 130, 186, 208, 209, 213, 242, 281
learners 6
leftist 15, 17
legislation 143, 144, 146, 154, 155, 160, 172, 180
Legislative 112
legislatures 132, 133
legitimacy 13, 25, 243, 248
LERP 6, 310, 311, 313–318
Lewis Gordon 16, 19
liberalism 17, 154
liberation 32, 50, 122, 124, 127, 128, 131, 337
Liberia 210
Libya 36
lifestyles 90, 99, 105, 107, 112, 210
livelihood 46, 48, 52, 56, 165, 178, 179, 187, 198, 217, 219, 221–223, 226, 228–230, 232, 233, 266, 272, 273, 275
loans 175, 178, 179, 201, 203, 213, 224, 226, 229
local IX, 1, 12–14, 24, 26, 46, 48, 50, 51, 53, 54, 57, 58, 60, 61, 62, 64, 119, 148, 150, 151, 173, 177, 180, 202, 203, 209, 212, 217, 229, 231, 282, 288–290, 311, 331, 332, 334
Local Governments Councils 93

Lome 254
Luanda 217

Madagascar 77
Magnetic Resonance Imaging 297
Maiduguri 286, 289
Malawi 1, 2
Malema 121–123, 129–133
males 100, 190, 311, 312, 316, 324, 334
marginality 5, 218, 231–233
marginalization IX, X, 77, 79, 165, 238, 239, 242, 244–248, 253, 257, 280, 333
market 57, 58, 120, 157, 176, 186, 219, 227, 242
Marxism 35, 130
Marxist 18
MASSOB 241, 242, 253–255, 266
Mathematics 301–304
Mbeki 122, 123
media IX, 20, 26, 50, 83, 119, 125, 126, 129, 133–135, 151, 207, 213, 214, 254, 255, 322, 324
medical 144–146, 164, 171, 175, 177, 179, 202, 323, 324
medical model 146, 164
medicine 148, 171
mental illness 149–151, 156, 157, 159
metaphysics 48, 267–269, 276
migrants 19, 264, 265, 271, 273, 275, 276
migrations 18
militancy 4, 90, 91, 77, 311
militant 15, 21, 101, 107, 134, 238, 239, 248, 280, 329
military 35, 77, 78, 209, 210, 242, 245, 248, 250, 252, 254, 288, 289, 291
militias 5, 238, 241, 250, 257
Minorities 3, 6
minority 241, 245, 247, 257
mismanagement 119, 186
mismanagements 213
M.K.O Abiola 242
Mmusi Maimane 128, 134
mobilisation 54, 56, 122, 126
Mobutu Sese Seko 208, 209
modern 11, 12, 16–20, 23, 27, 117, 122, 124, 126, 281
modernity 11, 12, 14, 15, 17–22, 25–27
Modernity 12, 14
money 24, 55, 70, 74–76, 81–83, 128, 171, 203, 218, 220, 222, 224, 225, 227, 228
morals 322

MOSOP   241
Movement for the Survival of Ogoni People   241
Mozambique   264
MRI   297, 304
Mugabe   2, 3, 36, 49, 50, 130, 208, 209
Muhammadu Buhari   70, 80, 144, 209, 212
Murtala Mohammed   77
Musemwa   IX, 217, 219
Museveni   208

naira   254, 280, 281
Naira   158, 186
national   90, 92, 50, 51, 77, 79, 82, 117, 127, 129, 133, 135, 180, 187, 189, 201, 202, 209, 212, 219, 221, 223, 227–229, 231, 244, 245, 247, 249, 253, 255–257, 264, 266, 268, 271, 273, 275, 280, 282, 297, 300, 306, 324
National Assembly   75, 132, 133, 134, 164
National Drug Law Enforcement Agency   187, 191
nationalism   11, 13, 18, 34, 35, 50, 127, 240, 242, 253, 262, 266, 271
nationalists   13, 17, 74
nationalization   35, 130
National Social Security Authority   225
nationhood   5, 280
nations   23, 180, 201, 203, 208–210, 212, 245, 262, 266, 272, 273, 275, 277, 331, 334
Nativism   50
nativists   16
Nazi   323
NDLEA   187, 191
Nelson Mandela   123
neocolonial   5
neocolonialism   11
neo-imperial   5, 15
neoliberal   13–15, 17, 21, 24–26
neoliberalism   IX, 15
nepotism   45, 61
New York   96, 143, 301
NGOS   201, 202, 289, 318
Niger   91, 92, 77, 102–104, 106–109, 148, 170, 242, 243, 287, 288, 311
Niger-Delta   91, 92, 102, 109, 242
Nigeria   IX, 2, 4–6, 70, 72–82, 88, 89, 143, 144, 146–151, 153, 154, 156–159, 164, 168–174, 176, 178, 186–191, 194, 196–198, 203, 209, 212, 237, 240–258, 262–267, 270–273, 275–277, 280–291, 297–299, 301, 306, 311, 321, 324, 325, 333–336

Nigeria   XIII–XVII, 4, 70, 76, 78, 81, 143, 148, 151, 153, 154, 156, 168, 176, 178, 188–191, 196–198, 203, 241, 242, 245–247, 249–253, 255–257, 262, 265, 267, 270, 274, 276, 277, 280–284, 287, 290, 299, 321, 333, 335, 336
Nigeria-Biafra War   252
Nigerian   4, 73, 74, 76, 78, 89, 90, 92, 93, 97, 99, 83, 144, 150, 152, 155, 164, 168, 169, 172, 173, 178, 186–188, 196, 198, 212, 238, 242–245, 247, 250, 252–255, 257, 263, 265, 266, 273, 275, 280, 283, 287–291, 308, 318, 335
Nigeria National Democratic Party   78
Nigerian Civil War   245, 253
Nigerian Federation   238
Nnamdi Azikiwe   78
Nnamdi Kanu   255, 256
non-governmental organizations   173, 178, 181, 289
Non Governmental Organizations   318
Non-Maleficence   327
normative   17, 73, 119, 164, 277, 322
North   5, 13, 14, 24, 34, 54, 77, 243, 247–249, 266, 280, 282, 283, 286, 287, 290, 291, 311
north east   280–284, 288
North east   280, 283
Northern Nigeria   92, 150, 173, 250, 285
Northern region   246, 284
North Korea   77
North Sudan   247
Norway,   74
Not too Young to Run   70, 73, 75, 80–83
Not too Young to Run bill   70
Not too Young to Run law   70, 73, 80–82
Not too Young to Run movement   75
NSSA   225
Nuremberg Code   324
NURTW   101, 102, 104, 106, 107, 197

Obafemi Awolowo   78, 249
Odera Oruka   204
Odirin Omiegbe   XVI
Oduduwa Republic   242
Odumegu Ojukwu   249
Ogoni   241
Ogun State   92
Ojukwu   78, 149, 244, 255
Olusegun Obasanjo   77, 209, 254
Omiegbe   4, 144, 147, 150, 151, 164, 169, 172, 173
ontologies   22, 48

INDEX

ontology 19, 21–3
Oodua Peoples Congress 241, 242
OPC 109, 241, 242, 248
opportunities 14, 46, 52, 58, 59, 62, 64, 74, 81, 144, 146, 153, 167, 173, 176, 180, 197, 198, 201–203, 224, 274
Oruka 204
Osun State 151

pan-Africanism 50
pandemic 13, 20, 24, 25, 123
parliament 63, 64, 70, 117, 131–133, 135
Parliament 128, 133
participant 53, 56, 196, 324, 329, 330, 332, 335
participants 4, 6, 14, 53, 58, 59, 64, 80, 195, 219, 310, 312, 323–332, 335, 336
Participants 53, 62, 332
participation 4, 27, 62–65, 70–78, 80–83, 117, 145, 146, 165, 166, 221, 246, 326–330, 336, 337
particularisms 1, 14
parties 4, 72, 76, 79, 117, 120–122, 124, 125, 129, 130, 132, 143, 155, 157, 271, 288
party 2–4, 41, 45, 50, 54, 63, 70, 72, 75, 76, 78, 79, 82, 118–120, 122–124, 127–135, 144, 145, 154, 158, 159, 243, 257
patient 323, 331
Patrice Lumumba 208
Paul Biya 208, 209
people with disabilities 4, 143, 144, 147, 154, 157, 159, 167–169, 174, 176, 177, 178
Perception 6, 308, 310, 317
Persons Living with Disabilities 4, 164, 174
persons with disabilities 143, 144, 146–149, 152, 154–160, 169, 171, 173, 174, 176, 178–181
Persons with Disabilities 4, 143, 144, 147, 149, 152, 154, 172, 179, 180
philosophers 153, 202, 205, 206, 268
philosophical 33, 37, 38, 202, 206, 262, 263, 267, 269, 277, 322
philosophy IX, XIV, XVII, 23, 31, 36, 38, 205, 267, 269, 270, 280, 322, 323
Philosophy IX, XIII–XVI, 267
Pidgin 92, 93
Plato 153, 267, 269
Platonic 270
Pogrom 249

policymakers 189
political IX, 1, 2, 4–6, 11, 14–18, 25–27, 31–36, 38, 40–42, 45, 46, 48–52, 54, 56, 58–60, 62–64, 70–83, 117–122, 124, 126–129, 131, 132, 134, 135, 144, 164–166, 180, 186, 201, 207–210, 213, 214, 217, 218, 227, 228, 231–233, 238, 241–248, 253, 257, 262, 266, 273, 280, 281, 283, 285, 287, 290, 323, 334
political participation 63, 70–72, 75, 78, 82
political parties 3, 54, 56, 58, 62, 63, 70, 72, 75, 76, 78, 79, 81–83, 243
politicians 4, 90, 93, 99, 102, 104–107, 112, 118, 121, 123, 126, 132, 201–203, 205, 210–214
politics IX, X, 3–5, 16, 17, 19, 22, 24–26, 31, 33, 34, 40, 46, 62, 63, 70–813, 85, 117–119, 121, 124–127, 131, 132, 134, 135, 212, 213, 244–247
Politics, X
population 4, 11, 13, 19, 21, 34, 50–52, 70–77, 80, 81, 83, 120, 126, 134, 143, 168, 174, 176, 186–188, 191, 192, 194, 198, 203, 217, 219, 246, 247, 271, 285, 312
populations 20, 63, 119, 217
populism 1, 3, 4, 21, 35, 47, 117–128, 132, 135
Populism 3, 50, 117, 118, 122, 123
populist 2, 3, 13–15, 19, 21, 35, 117–124, 126, 128–133, 135
populist rhetoric 2, 126, 131
populists 13, 14, 121, 123
post-apartheid 12, 122, 126–128, 132, 134
post-cold war 73
post-colonial 1, 31, 40, 209, 210, 253, 263
postsocialism 14
post-truth 15–18, 24, 26
Post-truth World 1, 11
poverty X, IX, 1, 2, 4, 5, 52, 79, 120, 124, 130, 134, 145, 165–169, 173, 174, 176, 177, 179–181, 186, 188–190, 198, 201–207, 209, 211–214, 217–219, 221, 233, 258, 282, 291
Poverty X, 3–5, 164–166, 168, 171, 174, 186, 188, 201, 202, 204, 206, 207, 213
practice 1, 42, 58, 61, 122, 123, 148, 172, 281
practices 4, 15, 70, 129, 143, 144, 147, 148, 152, 154, 155–159, 169, 175, 217, 219, 222, 231–233, 241, 298, 323, 332, 333, 336, 337
pragmatism 48
pre-primary school 298, 299

protectionism 13
protectionist 14
protests 72, 73, 78, 125, 129, 132, 134, 152, 256
public 2, 15, 24–26, 49, 54, 71, 80, 82, 83, 121, 122, 126–128, 150–152, 155, 158, 160, 165, 169, 171, 173, 179, 197, 201, 203, 206, 207, 209, 213, 219, 229, 230, 242, 254, 263, 277, 280, 312
public officials 71
PYTON DANCE 256

questionnaire 48, 191, 192, 312
Quran 128

racial 12, 20, 23, 118, 127, 129
racism 12, 16–19, 245
radical 1, 3, 15–17, 23, 25–27, 33–36, 45, 46, 120, 129, 130, 134, 135
radical-conservatives 1
radicalism IX, 3, 11, 13, 15–17, 31–34, 36, 38–42
Radicalism 1, 3, 11, 17, 31, 32, 38, 40
radicalisms IX, X, 1
Radio Biafra 255, 256
Ralph Uwazuruike 242, 254
Ramaphosa 127, 133
Rational Choice Theory 94
Rawls 154
realist 48
reason 16, 18, 32, 39, 48, 54, 121, 126, 128, 132, 134, 170, 175, 203, 220, 268, 270, 271, 290
Reconciliation 124, 251, 252
Reconstruction 251, 252
redistribution 59, 60, 61, 127, 130, 202, 227
refugee 14, 20
refugees 19, 331
regime 2, 17, 35, 62, 63, 65, 119, 120, 123, 130, 208–210, 213, 247, 248
regimes 13, 20, 35, 209, 210, 211, 242, 248, 273
rehabilitation 108, 110, 146, 175, 177, 178, 180, 247
Rehabilitation 172, 177, 251, 252
Reintegration 251, 252
relationality 17, 19, 23
relationship 37, 38, 40, 41, 54, 126, 144, 166, 188, 189, 190, 195, 196, 232, 237, 241, 254, 266–270, 275, 277, 283, 301, 302, 311, 222, 226

religious, 14, 23, 27, 34, 169, 262, 280, 334
representative 26, 55, 248, 264
Republic of Benin 92, 254
research 6, 23, 48, 134, 152, 168, 189, 190, 192, 194, 205, 206, 211, 219, 227, 239, 285, 300, 302, 304, 311, 313, 314, 321–332, 334–336
Research 6, 88, 89, 99, 112, 187, 190, 192, 297, 302, 311, 314–316, 321, 323–325, 327, 331, 332, 335
respondent 53, 57, 194, 219, 221, 222, 227, 231, 286, 287, 327, 328, 330
respondents 48, 54, 57, 61–64, 170, 191, 192, 194, 195, 196, 220, 221, 224, 225, 229, 265, 323, 325–329
revenues 168, 228, 246
revolution 17, 35, 119
revolutionary 31, 34, 35, 40, 78
rightist 17
rights 1, 14, 19, 45, 50, 24, 63, 132, 143, 144, 152–159, 167, 172, 173, 175, 176, 180, 206, 211, 231, 241, 252, 263, 271, 273, 275, 287, 289, 325, 330, 332, 334
right-wing 4, 13, 14, 19, 33, 121, 129
rightwing 3
rituals 148–151, 158, 159, 333
Rivers 91
Robert Gabriel Mugabe 2
Roman 263
rural 4, 46, 49, 51, 52, 59, 62–64, 126, 148, 170, 171, 175, 221, 228, 230, 237, 290, 308
Russia 21, 119, 120, 263, 301
Russian 119, 120
Russian socialists 119
Rwanda 247
Rwandan 245

Sambisa Forest 289
Sani Abacha 209
SAPS 186
school 2, 6, 71, 168, 170, 174, 175, 195, 198, 220, 231, 253, 282–288, 290, 297–306, 309, 310, 313, 318
sciences 11, 119, 297, 322, 325
SDGS 201, 214, 290
secession 242, 248–250
secessionist 77, 247, 250, 253, 266
secondary school 6, 198, 298, 299, 301, 302,

INDEX

security   5, 15, 16, 50, 54, 76, 156, 157, 172, 176, 178, 191, 224–228, 230, 257, 263, 272, 280, 284, 285, 288, 290
sexual   12, 122, 151, 157
Shehu Shagari   78, 150, 265, 266
Shomolu LGA   192
slave trade   11
social   IX, 1–5, 15, 17, 21, 22, 24–27, 31–36, 40, 46, 47, 49, 51, 54, 58, 64, 74, 79, 82, 119, 125, 135, 143–147, 150, 153, 154, 159, 164–166, 169, 170, 172, 173, 177–181, 187–190, 196, 198, 202, 207, 217, 218, 225, 228, 231, 232, 237–242, 244, 245, 248, 250, 253, 254, 255, 257, 266, 280–283, 285, 287, 291, 297–300, 308, 309, 321–332, 334–336
Social Action Theory   332
Social identity theory   239, 240
Social Identity Theory   239
socialism   12, 14, 35, 127
socialist   14, 20, 35
Socialist   14, 21, 130
social justice   IX, 144, 153, 154, 159, 188
Social Justice   3, 4, 143, 153
social models   26, 145
societies   25, 49, 73, 80, 82, 90, 96, 143, 282, 321–333, 335
society   2, 3, 13, 17, 24, 27, 34, 36, 39–42, 49, 58, 63, 71–73, 75, 80, 81, 83, 118, 132, 144, 145, 153, 154, 156, 159, 165, 166, 169, 177, 180, 186, 188, 196, 205, 206, 207, 212, 237–240, 244–246, 257, 262, 269, 282, 283, 290, 297, 305, 306, 310, 318, 321–323, 327, 328, 331, 332, 334, 337
socioeconomic   5, 82, 124, 126, 130, 186, 188, 190, 198, 309
sociological   33, 55, 62, 64, 242, 244
Sociology   IX, XIII–XVII, 66, 188
Socratic Method   37
Somalia,   264
South   IX, 3–5, 11, 14, 24, 117–124, 126–135, 150, 175, 176, 178, 208, 220, 222, 224, 240–243, 247, 249, 250, 262–267, 270–273, 275–277, 311, 312, 324
South Africa   XIV, XVI, 124, 127, 135, 178, 220, 244, 247, 263, 264, 271, 274, 275, 277

351

Soviet Union   3
SSA   217
stakeholders   75, 187, 189, 198, 213, 257, 270, 271, 273, 275, 323, 325
state   2, 13, 14, 17, 20–22, 24, 25, 27, 31–33, 35, 40, 42, 45, 47, 50, 54, 57, 58, 70, 72–75, 81, 82, 117, 120, 121, 124, 125, 131, 134, 135, 143–145, 147, 153–155, 157, 158, 168, 170, 172, 173, 191, 196, 208, 218, 219, 224–227, 230–233, 238, 242–246, 248–253, 255–257, 262–264, 266, 270, 272, 277, 281, 283–288, 298, 309, 327
State of Capture   124
States   2, 68, 88, 89, 91, 93, 94, 96, 100–112, 117, 144, 167, 170, 263, 324
Street begging   172
Structural Adjustment Programmes   186
student   134, 152, 175, 312
Students   6, 297, 308, 312
subjectivities   12
sub-Saharan   3, 5, 36, 38, 39, 41, 42, 201–205, 207, 209, 210, 212–214, 219, 232
Sub-Saharan   1, 5, 31, 32, 34, 35, 40, 42, 201, 217
sub-Saharan Africa   5, 36, 201, 202, 204, 205, 207, 210
Sudan   247
Sudanese   247
superstitious   169
survey   48, 82, 168, 170, 174, 190–192, 219, 226, 264, 265, 284, 300
Sustainable Development Goals   285, 290
Swiss   120, 210
Swiss Peoples Party   120

tax clearance   224
taxes   179
teachers   282, 284, 285, 288, 290, 299, 305, 308, 313
technology   25, 166, 226
teleologists   203
terrorism   280–283, 290
Terrorism   3, 5, 280, 281, 287, 290
terrorist   257, 280, 281, 283, 284, 286
tertiary school   298
Thabo Mbeki   122

townships   5
traditional   12, 31, 32, 34, 39, 48, 51, 53, 56, 165, 168, 237, 310, 321
traditional rulers   110
transnational   13, 14, 17, 23, 290
transport   102, 146, 197, 221, 226, 229, 230, 288
tribal   92, 127, 237, 243, 246
Truth and Reconciliation Commission   124
Tunisia   83
Tuskegee   323, 324
Tuskegee Syphilis Study   323
Tutsi   245, 247
Tutsis   123, 243

Uganda   IX, 208
UN   143, 152, 164, 176, 180, 188, 217, 263, 273, 289
unemployment   52, 59, 77, 88, 98, 124, 134, 135, 174, 176, 178, 186, 189, 190, 195, 196, 198, 225, 264, 291
UNESCO   174, 285
UNICEF   174, 285, 287–289
unions   13, 15, 17, 178
United Kingdom   74, 167, 176, 248, 290
United Nations   66, 80, 143, 144, 146, 154, 157, 164, 165, 171, 174, 176, 180, 181, 187, 263, 275, 276, 285
University of Ibadan   XIII, XVI, XVII, 152, 325
University of Lagos   XV, XVI, XVII
University of the Witwatersrand   XIII, XIV, 11, 24, 134, 324
University of Zimbabwe   XIII, XVII
urban   5, 47, 57, 58, 126, 148, 170, 175, 190, 217–219, 228–233, 237, 308, 335
urbanisation   5, 93, 217, 233
Urbanisation   217
urbanism   12
Uruguay   120
U.S   186, 211
US   23, 26, 62, 119, 151, 158, 168, 211, 228
USA   IX, 17, 263, 264
USAID   284, 285, 286, 288
utilitarian   203
utopias   15, 21
Uwazuruike   254, 255

violence   1, 4, 6, 35, 40, 50, 51, 58, 63, 79, 81, 129, 157, 170, 188, 189, 197, 237–239, 253, 255–257, 265, 272, 274, 276, 280–282, 284, 285, 290, 298–301, 304–306, 308, 310
Violence   6, 89, 11, 97, 101, 104, 297
Vladimir Putin   21
voluntary   54, 71, 221, 327, 330, 336
voters   64, 72, 74, 75, 122, 128
voting   64, 72, 74, 77

Wacquant   218, 232, 233
WAEC   299, 301
wellbeing   54, 58, 148, 150, 168, 300
West   2, 5, 13, 16, 24, 50, 74, 146, 191, 208, 243, 246, 247, 256, 299, 301, 311
western   1, 92, 190, 201, 205, 206, 208–213, 219, 250, 280, 281, 284, 331, 334
Western   1, 2, 14, 18, 23, 24, 78, 119, 132, 180, 209, 249, 281, 331
white   2, 16, 17, 50, 120, 123, 129, 131, 134, 150, 227, 243, 253, 271
whites   50, 122, 129
WHO   143, 171, 188, 189, 209
women   6, 75, 149, 151, 156, 159, 166, 174, 187, 251, 252, 321, 331–337
World Bank   167, 174, 188, 204, 205, 209
World Health Organisation   143, 145, 146
World Health Organization   145, 174, 309
World War II   120, 323

xenophobia   119, 264, 266, 276
Xenophobia   5, 262
xenophobic   5, 262, 264, 265, 267, 270–273, 275, 277
Xenophobic   271
Xhosas   244

Yakubu Gowon   77, 209, 249, 251, 252
Yobe   280, 285, 288
Yoruba   93, 241, 242, 244, 250, 253, 333, 334
young people   46, 48, 51–57, 59–62, 64, 80, 188, 189, 190, 194, 197, 198, 301
youth   IX, 1, 2, 4, 46, 47, 50–56, 58–65, 70–73, 77–81, 83, 125, 131, 186, 189, 190, 195, 196,

INDEX

Youths 2, 4, 70, 75, 77, 80, 88, 94, 96, 100, 172, 186, 190

Zambia, 272
ZANU (PF) 45, 49, 50, 54, 63, 64
Zaria 248
Zikist movement 78
Zikist Movement 78
Zimbabwe IX, XIII, XIV, XVI, 36, 45, 46, 49–52, 59, 62, 64, 66, 130, 208, 209, 217–220, 222, 224–226, 228, 230, 231, 264, 272, 324
Zulus 244
Zuma 122–124, 129, 133, 134